THE FAITH OF THE
MITHNAGDIM

JOHNS HOPKINS JEWISH STUDIES

Sander Gilman and Steven T. Katz
Series Editors

THE FAITH OF THE MITHNAGDIM

Rabbinic Responses to Hasidic Rapture

Allan Nadler

THE JOHNS HOPKINS
UNIVERSITY PRESS
Baltimore and London

This book has been brought to publication with the generous assistance of
Mr. Moses Deitcher and the Bloomfield family, of Montreal,
through the Eldee Foundation.

The Johns Hopkins University Press
2715 North Charles Street
Baltimore, Maryland 21218-4319
The Johns Hopkins Press Ltd., London

Library of Congress Cataloging-in-Publication Data
will be found at the end of this book.
A catalog record for this book is available from the British Library.

ISBN 0-8018-5560-8

To the memory of my beloved *Zayde*
Harry Herschel Nadler
Yehezkel Zevi ben Aaron
1888–1972

CONTENTS

PREFACE

The remarkable revitalization of ultra-Orthodox Jewry following its devastation during the Holocaust has generated widespread contemporary fascination with the Hasidim. Aside from the flourishing serious scholarship on Hasidism, which is evaluated in the introduction to this study, a wide array of popular books about the Hasidim have been published in recent years, including such evocative titles as *Holy Days: The World of a Hasidic Family, Piety and Power: The World of Jewish Fundamentalism, Defenders of the Faith: Inside Ultra-Orthodox Jewry, Hasidic People: A Place in the New Work,* and *Boychiks in the Hood: Travels in the Hasidic Underground.*[1] Although these and numerous other books about the ultra-Orthodox Jews—or Haredim, as they are known in Hebrew[2]—help to illuminate many aspects of the rather secretive Hasidic society and the often recondite system of Hasidic beliefs, they all share in a principal failing: they ignore the other, rather less exotic but equally important sector of ultra-Orthodox Jewry, the Mithnagdim, the traditional opponents of Hasidism. This failing is mirrored in the state of scholarly research on eighteenth- and nineteenth-century eastern European Judaism, in which enormous attention has been paid to the study of Hasidism but virtually nothing has been written about Mithnagdism.

Approximately one-half of today's ultra-Orthodox Jews are in fact not Hasidim at all but rather Mithnagdim, the spiritual heirs of the rabbinic movement that, beginning in the third quarter of the eighteenth century, waged fierce battle with Hasidism, denouncing it as a heretical deviation from traditional Judaism. Not only has the nature of the particular faith of the Mithnagdim, and how it differs sharply from Hasidism, been ignored in the burgeoning scholarly and popular literature on Jewish ultra-Orthodoxy but the differences between these very distinct components of the world of the Haredim have been further blurred by the tendency to treat today's Hasidim and Mithnagdim together as an orthodox religious monolith. All too often ultra-Orthodox Judaism is understood to be synonymous with Hasidism.

Although to the untrained observer the Mithnagdim in their black dress, their austere way of life, and their strict social segregation from both gentiles and non-Orthodox Jews often appear to be indistinguishable from the Hasidim, they are in fact the bearers of a very different set of beliefs and traditions within Orthodox Judaism. To this day the spiritual discord between Hasidim and Mithnagdim often manifests itself in extreme belligerence, such as the current fierce contention between the followers of Rabbi Menachem Shach in Bnai Berak and the Lubavitcher Hasidim of Brooklyn. And although there is a large and growing literature about the Lubavitchers, almost nothing has been written about the theology of Rabbi Shach, whose teachings influence hundreds of thousands of Orthodox Jews.

Although the present book is not concerned with the contemporary Mithnagdim, it will serve to dispel the widespread confusion of Hasidim and Mithnagdim by addressing the lacunae in Hasidic scholarship through the investigation of the religious underpinnings of the original Mithnagdic rejection of Hasidism. This study aims to introduce and elucidate the fundamental precepts of classic Mithnagdic Judaism as they emerge from hitherto unstudied rabbinic texts of the late eighteenth and early nineteenth centuries.

My training in the critical study of rabbinic texts began at Harvard University under the exacting tutelage of Professor Isadore Twersky, to whom I remain ever grateful for his rigorous training and continual academic guidance. During my early years at Harvard I also had the good fortune to study with Professor Yosef Hayyim Yerushalmi, whose courses in Jewish history and historiography sparked my interest in the modern period, though not necessarily in its most modern subjects.

My initial academic interest in the Mithnagdim was the result of a remarkable Yiddish seminar, "Khsidim un Misnagdim," given at Harvard in 1978 by the late Yiddish writer Chaim Grade. Grade was one of several scions of the prewar Mithnagdic civilization of Lithuanian Jewry who inspired me to investigate the origins of non-Hasidic Orthodoxy. Foremost among them is my rabbi and teacher, Leib Baron of Montreal, a master of Lithuanian Talmudic scholarship with whom I was privileged to study for many years.

I completed the first version of this book while serving as rabbi of the Shaar Hashomayim Synagogue in Montreal, a truly remarkable congregation. I remain grateful to the members of the Shaar's board of directors for their enlightened interest in my scholarly work and for always allowing me the time and freedom necessary to pursue my studies. I am particularly appreciative of the support for my work of the Shaar members Moses Deit-cher and Harry Bloomfield.

The YIVO Institute for Jewish Research, my intellectual and cultural home for the past five years, is an ideal place in which to write about the Orthodox "Litvaks" while consorting with their secular "landslayt." YIVO's chairman, Bruce Slovin, is not only a remarkably committed supporter of YIVO's and my work but an unusually loyal friend.

I have been fortunate to enjoy the close personal friendship and intellectual fellowship of David Fishman, Leon Wieseltier, Reuven Poupko, Lawrence Kaplan, Leslie Barrett, Karen Kennerly, David Woolfson, Neil Mathews, and Jack Jedwab, each of whom contributed, at different stages and in his or her own way, to the completion of this book. I have been especially blessed with the devotion and constant support of my parents, Joseph and Doris Nadler. This book is dedicated to the memory of my dear grandfather "Zayde" Harry. It was from him that I first learned to cherish the humanity and abundance of eastern European Jewish civilization.

THE FAITH OF THE
MITHNAGDIM

INTRODUCTION

The Forsaken Mithnagdim

The Hasidim were long reviled by the early scholars of Jewish historical *Wissenschaft* as the dark and primitive practitioners of the most backward and superstitious aspects of Kabbalah. They were, in the eyes of the great historian Heinrich Graetz, "an order of wonder-seeking confederates . . . a daughter of darkness, born in gloom which even to-day proceeds stealthily on its mysterious path . . . the adherents of which announced the grossest superstition to be the fundamental principle of Judaism."[1] Today, however, the history and theology of Hasidism are fields of significant scholarly attention as well as popular fascination. The past three decades especially have witnessed a profound interest in Hasidism within the fields of Jewish history and philosophy, resulting in a veritable flood of scholarship in the critical examination of this major Jewish religious movement. Since the pioneering scholarly contributions of Shimon Dubnow to Hasidic history and Gershom Scholem to Hasidic mystical theory a half century ago,[2] scores of monographs and hundreds of academic articles have been published in the field of Hasidiana.

Primarily concerned with the origins, growth, and development of the Hasidic movement, as well as the nature of Hasidic mysticism, only a tiny part of this recent scholarship deals specifically with the antagonism to Hasidism on the part of its established rabbinic opponents, the Mithnagdim, and the resulting split of traditional eastern European Judaism into two bitterly opposed religious camps. Although Shimon Dubnow, the true maverick of Hasidic historiography, did consider the struggles of the early Hasidim with their rabbinic opponents of the late eighteenth and early nineteenth centuries and was the first to publish some of the most important primary sources for the history of that religious conflict,[3] most subsequent scholars have focused almost exclusively on historical and theoretical developments within Hasidism. When scholars of Hasidism do consider the Mithnagdim, it is almost always from the purely negative perspective of their hostility to the Hasidic movement and the resulting bans and polemics they issued against its adherents. Thus, with the notable exception of a few fine essays on the two towering leaders of the Mithnagdim—R. Elijah ben Solomon, the Gaon of Vilna, and R. Hayyim of Volozhin—the focus of any analysis of the non-Hasidic rabbinic culture of this period has invariably been negative and limited to the communal and political struggles of the rabbinic establishment against the Hasidic movement. Aside from some brief, introductory essays preceding the documents published in Mordechai Wilensky's massive anthology of the primary sources of the Hasidic-Mithnagdic controversy,[4] there exists no single, thorough scholarly analysis of the non-Hasidic rabbinic thought of this period. Certainly, there has been no attempt at a comprehensive, constructive portrait of the fundamental, positive religious doctrines of the Mithnagdim. Whereas many important contributions have been made to the study of the history and theology of Hasidism, as well as of the specific doctrines of individual Hasidic schools of thought,[5] precious little academic attention has been devoted to the constructive religious doctrines of the enduring opponents of Hasidism, the Mithnagdim.[6]

Confounding matters further is the impression, fostered by some of the finest recent scholarship on Jewish mysticism, that Hasidism is far less original or radical a deviation from earlier Jewish thought than historians once assumed. In his recent revisionist studies of Kabbalah and Hasidism, Moshe Idel has called attention to the hitherto underappreciated prominence of consistent and pronounced ecstatic and magical traditions throughout the history of the Kabbalah, with which Hasidism is largely harmonious. Although Idel does acknowledge original elements in Hasidism's reinterpretation, integration, and social application of various doctrines of the earlier mystical schools, he tends to emphasize the extensive and profound influence of the teachings of earlier Kabbalists, Abraham Abulafia and Moses Cordovero in particular, on Hasidic thought.[7]

Mendel Piekarz has gone even further than Idel in his "discovery" of many of Hasidism's most radical doctrines in the earlier traditions of seventeenth- and eighteenth-century eastern European rabbinical literature.[8] Not content with denying Hasidism's theological originality and ideological daring, Piekarz has gone so far as to question whether Hasidism is a mystical school at all and to contend that even its apparently most radical mystical doctrines, such as acosmism, the sensual service of God and the descent of the zaddik, are no more than the conventional "heritage of [Jewish] men of faith in every generation." In fact, the only novelty Piekarz concedes to Hasidism is the manner of its widespread transmission of these allegedly classical rabbinic doctrines in the new social context of the Hasidic community, centered around the court of the zaddik.[9]

Zeev Gries, in his detailed study of the literature of Jewish ritual manuals and Halakhic handbooks *(sifruth ha-hanhagoth),* argues that works of this genre by Hasidic authors are generally indicative of the essentially conservative and Halakhically normative nature of Hasidism. Gries contends that since the bulk of material contained in the conservative ritual handbooks of Hasidic origin emanates primarily from the school of the Maggid of Mezeritch, one of early Hasidism's greatest and most original mystics, these works provide compelling testimony to the essential conformity of Hasidic practice, even on the part of its most radical masters, to existing rabbinic norms. Gries concludes that it was the social separatism of Hasidism and its threat to the existing communal structures and institutions of rabbinic authority, not any substantive theological deviation, that most exercised the opposition of the Mithnagdim.[10] Jacob Hisdai has argued that there are no clearly delineated theological differences that consistently divide Hasidic and Mithnagdic theoretical and ethical writings and that the principal Mithnagdic hostility to Hasidism emanated from the *perushim,* the elite pre-Hasidic circles of rabbinic ascetics and mystics.[11]

The most recent attempt to downplay the originality of the Hasidic religious revolution is also the most outlandish. Moshe Rosman in his otherwise refreshingly original biography of the BESHT (Baal Shem Tov) attempts to demonstrate that, contrary to the established stereotypes of Jewish historiography, the founder of Hasidism shared much with the father of Mithnagdism, the Gaon of Vilna. In a chapter suggestively entitled "Hasidism before Hasidism" Rosman points to a number of presumed affinities—most of no real significance—between the Gaon and the BESHT (such as their mutual interest in music and practical Kabbalah, that neither held an official community post, and that both were deeply venerated by their respective followers) and concludes that like the Baal Shem Tov, the Gaon was a Hasid, albeit of a different stripe. The Baal Shem Tov did not innovate Hasidism, which existed long before his emergence, Rosman argues; he merely shifted the emphasis in Hasidism away from asceticism.[12] Rosman's conclusion about the context of the emergence of Hasidism exemplifies the misdirection of much of the most recent scholarship on the movement: "Hasidism, then, was an outgrowth of an already existing religious orientation and not, as many have suggested, a radically new phenomenon that came as history's response to a crisis of Judaism or of Jewish Society."[13]

All of these recent studies of Hasidism combine to create the not entirely inaccurate, but exaggerated and distorted, impression that Hasidism, firmly rooted in the earlier Jewish mystical and rabbinic traditions, was not the radical departure from previous Jewish spirituality that early scholarly chroniclers depicted. According to the logic of these scholars, the fierce hostility that the emergence of Hasidism provoked in the rabbinic establishment and the ensuing bitter and prolonged battles against Hasidism on the part of the Mithnagdim must be understood primarily in social, rather than theological, terms. Since very little in the religious and mystical teachings of Hasidism is new, the only possible explanation for the virulence and endurance of the rabbinic response to it must lie in the realm of politics, not in the realm of religion. What this approach cannot explain, of course, are the deep religious and theological divisions between Hasidim and Mithnagdim, which this book documents.

It is doubtless true that both a substantial part of Hasidic doctrine and the ritual-mystical practices of the great Hasidic masters had deep roots in a variety of preexisting rabbinic and Kabbalistic traditions. Nonetheless, the significance of a normative, consistent, well-defined rabbinic religious philosophy radically different from the emerging Hasidic spiritually has long been ignored by scholars. In light of the emphasis in the most recent scholarship on the deep Kabbalistic and rabbinic roots of Hasidism, there is, moreover, a tendency to downplay both the importance and the distinctiveness of the well-developed, non-Hasidic, positive system of belief maintained by the rabbis who became known as Mithnagdim, which, as we shall demonstrate, underlies and explains their strong resistance to Hasidic spirituality.

Two Mithnagdic Masters

Not only are there no serious general examinations of the distinctive religious thought of the rabbinic opponents of Hasidism but the few isolated studies of Mithnagdic figures that do exist focus their attention on the two dominant personalities of the Mithnagdic camp: the Gaon of Vilna, Rabbi Elijah ben Solomon (hereafter to be referred to by the Hebrew acrostic of his name, GRA), and, to an even greater extent, his most distinguished disciple, R. Hayyim of Volozhin.[14] Indeed, in some studies the term *mithnagduth* is simply understood as being synonymous with the thought of the GRA and R. Hayyim.[15] Most other Mithnagdic rabbis, teachers, and writers are simply ignored or at best referred to very sporadically in the footnotes to these studies.

There is no question that the GRA and R. Hayyim of Volozhin were the most original and striking non-Hasidic rabbinic thinkers of their day. Moreover, their theological writings and personal religious example have proven to be the most influential in the subsequent rabbinic literature and the most enduring in later Mithnagdic thought. Although he never formally gathered or instructed a well-defined group of students, the GRA did inspire a rather important circle of disciples, who spread his basic religious ideas in their own preaching and writings. In the years following his death these disciples published a wealth of material either written or directly inspired by him.[16] As for R. Hayyim, an important coterie of his students in the Volozhin yeshiva, many of whom themselves became eminent rabbis and founded major Lithuanian yeshivot, were highly influenced by his religious doctrines and later propagated his ideas. R. Hayyim's masterpiece, *Nefesh ha-Hayyim,* endures as an influential theological work in learned rabbinic circles to this day.[17] Consequently, the intellectual and doctrinal legacy of the GRA and R. Hayyim has largely become the inspirational cornerstone of contemporary Mithnagdic life and thought, centering as it does on the network of yeshivot spawned by the Volozhin school founded by R. Hayyim in 1803.

The enduring fame and posthumous influence of these two men notwithstanding, in attempting to paint a historically accurate portrait of the principal teachings of classic Mithnagdism (i.e., non-Hasidic rabbinic thought in late-eighteenth- and early-nineteenth-century eastern Europe) the tendency to refer exclusively to the writings of these two legendary figures is problematic from the perspectives of both social and intellectual history. As the aforementioned studies on them make abundantly clear, both the GRA and R. Hayyim were elite, unique, highly independent, and original thinkers. Thus, although it is true that they were in a certain sense the patriarchs of subsequent non-Hasidic eastern European rabbinic Judaism, neither of them can be considered as a representative popular thinker of his own day or a typical Mithnagdic theoretician. The GRA was notorious for his reclusive, idiosyncratic personality, his distinctive, bold, and highly personal approach to Jewish learning, and his independent Talmudic methodology. Although these characteristics affected neither his significant influence on a small circle of disciples nor his expanding legacy over the course of later generations, they severely limited the scope of his influence on the Jewish masses of his own day. Nor can his writings be considered emblematic of any wider tendencies in the rabbinic thought of that period. Aside from his famous letter of excommunication against the Hasidim,[18] the GRA rarely addressed the general Jewish public, and he wrote only very technical, highly cryptic notations to classic texts, as well as intricate exegetical studies, from which it is difficult to garner any general sense of the religious ideas he might have prescribed for his followers or for the Jewish masses. Indeed, for these very reasons the GRA's attitude toward the larger Jewish community has been critically described by early historians of Hasidism as one of total disregard, bordering on utter contempt.[19]

The same is largely true of R. Hayyim of Volozhin. He was an unusually original theologian whose writings, although ultimately quite influential in certain elite scholarly Lithuanian Jewish circles, reflect the purely personal response of a remarkable thinker to the theological challenges of his day, in particular those posed by Ḥabad Hasidism. Furthermore, scholars are deeply divided over the question whether R. Hayyim can be considered a true Mithnagged at all. In his monograph on R. Hayyim, Norman Lamm argued that he was not actively involved in the Mithnagdic battles and that his attitude toward Hasidism and its adherents was moderate and concessionary, in fact almost neutral.[20] While Immanuel Etkes and Isaiah Tishby have questioned Lamm's characterization of R. Hayyim's posture toward Hasidism as mild,[21] Mendel Piekarz has argued that many of R. Hayyim's ideas are strikingly similar to those contained in the works of his Hasidic contemporaries.[22] Most recently, Shaul Stampfer, in his study of the origins of the Lithuanian yeshivot, pointed out that R. Hayyim did not play an active role in the communal struggle against Hasidism and that he was silent in the anti-Hasidic polemics that raged in his lifetime.[23] These very ambiguities regarding R. Hayyim's part in the Hasidic-Mithnagdic controversy render his writings a less than ideal paradigm of Mithnagdic religious thought.

The unrivaled stature of these two men and the singular nature of their thought is tangibly reflected in their respective communal activities and careers, both professional and literary. Although both in their writings and especially through their widespread, activist popular preaching the early Hasidic masters clearly were directing their novel theological doctrines at the untutored Jewish masses in eastern Europe, neither the GRA nor R. Hayyim of Volozhin maintained any significant relationship with the common folk. As noted above, the GRA was renowned for his hermetic existence, and R. Hayyim of Volozhin's main communal concern was the establishment of a yeshiva in his own city in order to develop a prime cadre of Talmudic students and scholars. Both of these men, then, were elitists who surrounded themselves with select, learned individuals and never intended their teachings for mass consumption.

Probably for this reason neither the GRA nor R. Hayyim published popular, homiletical works directed at a broad Jewish audience. The GRA apparently was not concerned with the wider propagation of his ideas and published nothing. And even the best-known and most widely reissued of R. Hayyim's few writings, *Nefesh ha-Hayyim,* was not published until after his death and clearly was not intended as a popular book, based as it is on difficult and complex interpretations of the *Zohar* and other Kabbalistic texts. Nor is *Nefesh ha-Hayyim* an openly polemical handbook of Mithnagdism urgently directed at the Jewish masses of the period, who were coming under the influence of Hasidic ideology.

Thus, neither the GRA nor R. Hayyim elucidated in his writings a popular philosophy of Judaism constituting a clearly formulated, positive spirituality intended as an antidote to Hasidism for consumption by the Jewish masses of eastern Europe. Consequently, the originality and enduring influence of their religious doctrines notwithstanding, the exclusive attention paid by scholars to the writings of two such exceptional, creative, and elitist thinkers cannot possibly result in a sufficient or balanced picture of the general currents of Mithnagdic religious thought during the period of Hasidism's rapid spread across eastern Europe.

Ideally such a broad portrait would include analysis of the works of more popular and representative Mithnagdic religious thinkers, men who were clearly interested in actively combating the rapidly expanding influence of Hasidism upon the masses of European Jewry and who, for that very reason, formulated and widely propagated a popular religious alternative to Hasidism to the very same Jewish audience among which the teachings of the Hasidic masters were spreading so rapidly. In other words, a representative portrait of Mithnagdism demands the examination and analysis of the thought of Mithnagdic thinkers who were more popular and more prolific than either the GRA or R. Hayyim of Volozhin.

Phinehas of Polotsk: A Paradigm of Mithnagdic Religion

This study has as its goal precisely such an extensive description of the most salient features of the religion of the early Mithnagdim as reflected in the writings of its most popular and prolific advocates, with a particular focus on the writings of one prototypical Mithnagdic preacher, the outspoken disciple of the GRA, R. Phinehas ben Judah, Maggid of Polotsk.

My goal here is not, strictly speaking, an intellectual biography of R. Phinehas of Polotsk, although such a biography will emerge from this study. My task is far more ambitious, namely, to delineate the fundamental aspects of the religion of the Mithnagdim primarily as reflected in the writings of R. Phinehas of Polotsk but also as clearly corroborated in the teachings of his mentor, the GRA, and in the thought of a wide spectrum of his contemporaries, including R. Hayyim of Volozhin. I shall attempt to arrive at a balanced appreciation of the religion of the Mithnagdim through the prism of both Phinehas's works and the ideas contained in the writings of his great mentor, the GRA, and many of his peers. The more prominent Mithnagdic rabbis whose writings will be referred to in the course of this book are R. Hayyim of Volozhin, R. Abraham ben ha-GRA, R. Abraham Danzig, R. Ezekiel Faivel of Dretzhyn, R. Hillel of Kovno, R. Benjamin Rivlin of Shklov, R. Menahem Mendel of Shklov, R. Jacob Kranz, Maggid of Dubno, and R. Meir ben Elijah of Vilna.[24] The theological doctrines and spiritual posture reflected in Phinehas's works will be analyzed in the broader context of the religious ideas of these and other representatives of Mithnagdic Judaism. R. Phinehas remains, however, the central prism through which I shall attempt to reflect upon the major features of Mithnagdic theology.

The choice of Phinehas's writings as the central focus for this book is a consequence of my conviction that he represents an almost perfect paragon of the classic Mithnagged. There coincide in him a remarkable amalgam of biographical and intellectual components that render him an ideal subject of a case study.

1. Chronology and geography. R. Phinehas lived at the right time and in the right place. His literary career (1788–1820) was concurrent with the period of the most rapid and extensive spread of Hasidic writings and ideas throughout eastern Europe. Furthermore, he spent the early years of his career as the maggid, or preacher, of the town of Polotsk, living therefore at the epicenter of the Hasidic-Mithnagdic controversy. At the end of the eighteenth century Polotsk was a veritable hotbed of early Hasidic activism. One of the leading early figures of Belorussian Hasidism was the preeminent disciple of the Great Maggid, Dov Ber of Mezeritch, R. Israel of Polotsk,[25] who had established a solid base for Hasidism in his city before emigrating to Israel in 1777, along with R. Menahem Mendel of Vitebsk and R. Abraham of Kalisk. Generally speaking, during this period the Polotsk and Vitebsk regions of Belorussia were vibrant centers of Hasidism where the Mithnagdim often felt overwhelmed by the social and political prominence of the Hasidic leaders.[26] As other scholars have already noted, Phinehas's writings reflect a sense of alarm at the rapid and widespread growth of Hasidism that is unmistakably that of an eyewitness to this development.[27] Phinehas spent the latter part of his life both in Vilna, the epicenter of Mithnagdic activism, and traveling throughout Lithuania and Belorussia preaching to Jewish communities and agitating against both Hasidism and the Haskalah. Clearly, Phinehas was acutely aware of the spread of both these new trends in his region, and he addressed himself directly and urgently to their perceived dangers.

2. Professional life. Although he spent the last three years of his life as the rabbi of the Vilna suburb Shnipishuk, Phinehas was above all else, and for most of his years, a maggid, first in Polotsk and later in towns throughout

Belorussia and Lithuania. He desired the widest possible dissemination of his ideas to the Jewish communities of these regions. As the lists of many subscribers to at least two of his works testify, he traveled to numerous cities and towns and succeeded in inspiring many of their inhabitants. He was therefore in a very real sense an anti-Hasidic propagandist and activist who took the Mithnagdic campaign on the road.

3. Literary corpus. Unlike many other rabbinic figures of this period, most pointedly the GRA and R. Hayyim, R. Phinehas was a prolific author.[28] Furthermore, many of his writings are infused with a pressing sense of historical mission. Unlike much of the rabbinic elite, which devoted itself to the publication of abstract, casuistic Talmudic pilpul and *hillukim,* or purely Halakhic writings, R. Phinehas was a popular author whose target audience was the untutored masses of eastern European Jewry. He not only wrote many exegetical works but also published books that lend themselves to intellectual-historical analysis, most notably a polemical tract against both Hasidism and the Haskalah and an anti-Hasidic and anti-Haskalah ethical will. Phinehas's published sermons and his carefully selected abbreviation of the medieval classic by Kalonymous ben Kalonymous, *Even Bohan,* reiterate some of the basic themes of his anti-Hasidic polemic.

4. Intellectual consistency. One of the great advantages for scholarly analysis of Phinehas's literary corpus is that it reflects a religious posture that remained unchanged over the long years of his career. Unlike many other rabbinic figures, Phinehas seems not to have undergone dramatic or sudden changes in his ideological development. This is readily apparent when one compares the central ideas of his first and last published works, the pious polemic *Kether Torah* (1788) and the ethical will *Rosh ha-Giveah* (1820). As we shall have many occasions to observe, these two books reflect a remarkable coherence in spiritual outlook over a period of thirty-two years.

5. A devoted student of the GRA. No person who did not receive direct religious inspiration from the Gaon of Vilna can be considered a proper prototype of the "model Mithnagged." It is, however, often very difficult to document and clarify the exact nature of the relationship, if any, that supposed "disciples" of the GRA actually enjoyed with the Mithnagdic master. Phinehas, however, was demonstrably one of the select few who benefited from an unusually close association with the GRA.[29] There can be no doubt that he was deeply influenced by the GRA's personal spiritual example and by his religious teachings. R. Phinehas is, moreover, the most prolific among the very circumscribed number of clearly identifiable members of the GRA's inner circle. That the GRA himself reviewed Phinehas's writings and personally advised him on the ideal approach to the study of rabbinic texts indicates that the GRA's influence pervaded R. Phinehas's life and thought. Conversely, that the GRA personally selected him to be the private Torah tutor for his grandchildren reflects the high esteem in which he held Phinehas.

6. *An unexceptional figure.* Finally, Phinehas can be considered a fine prototype of the dominant currents of Mithnagdic thought precisely because he was not an exceptionally original or innovative thinker. In Phinehas's writings we have the rather prosaic reflections of an ordinary rabbi and popular preacher of the day. That is not to say that Phinehas was an unimpressive or unimportant scholar; this study provides ample evidence of both his intellectual seriousness and his literary sophistication. Yet the ideas Phinehas advanced so forcefully, effectively, and consistently throughout his lifetime were for the most part conventional and reflective of the mainstream of rabbinic religious doctrine of his time. This is precisely why they are valuable to the intellectual historian. Through a close, contextual study of his writings one can discern, not the unusual and daring creations of an original genius, but rather the fundamental, salient features of the religious posture he shared with his peers, the Mithnagdim.

In the larger context of other Mithnagdic writings, the religious philosophy found in R. Phinehas's works testifies not only to a distinctive non-Hasidic rabbinic theology but also to the radical originality and distinctiveness of early Hasidic thought, both of which many contemporary historians of Hasidism have tended to minimize.

Chapter 1

THE IMMANENCE OF GOD IN
MITHNAGDIC THOUGHT

Hasidim and Mithnagdim on Divine Immanence:
The Traditional View

The vast literature of Mithnagdic polemics against Hasidism contains surprisingly little material of a genuinely theological nature. While there is an
abundance of the usual Mithnagdic social and Halakhic criticism of Hasidic
behavior, allegations of notorious antinomian tendencies, as well as repeated
denunciations of the Hasidim as heretics *(minim)* and Sabbateans, there is
almost no reference to specific Hasidic religious doctrines. An exceptional
instance of such theological criticism, albeit brief and oblique, is to be found
in the famous letter of the GRA issued to the rabbinic leadership of several
Belorussian and Podolian communities (including the town of Polotsk) in
the fall of 1796.[1] After the traditional introductory salutations, the epistle
assaults the perceived central religious doctrine of Hasidism, the belief in the
pervasive immanence of God in the created, physical universe:

> Into your ears I cry: Woe unto he who says to his father, "What have you
> begotten?" and to his mother "What have you brought to birth?" a generation
> whose children curse their fathers and do not bless their mothers; who have
> sinned greatly against them by turning their backs to them. Their stubborn
> hearts insist on rejecting good and choosing evil, transgressing the Torah and
> changing its laws. . . . In the Torah of Moses they have established a new
> covenant, working out their evil schemes with the masses in the House of the
> Lord . . . interpreting the Torah falsely while claiming that their way is precious
> in the eyes of God. . . . They call themselves Hasidim—that is an abomination!
> How they have deceived this generation, uttering these words on high: "These
> are thy gods, O Israel: every stick and stone." They interpret the Torah incor-
> rectly regarding the verse "Blessed be the name of the glory of God from His
> dwelling place" (Ezekiel 3:12) and also regarding the verse: " . . . and You give life
> to everything" (Nehemiah 9:6).[2]

This epistle against the Hasidim, while repeating the stock, familiar complaints of the Mithnagdim regarding the filial irreverence, moral deviance, and antinomian tendency of the new "sect," introduces a rare but important theological critique. Put simply, the GRA accuses the Hasidic masters of preaching panentheistic heresies. He protests that in misinterpreting certain key biblical verses that refer to the nature of God's transcendence and providence the Hasidim are in fact guilty of identifying God with nature. Indeed, as some scholars have argued, it would appear from this text that the main theological foundation of the GRA's hostility toward Hasidism was his belief that it was a genuinely heretical, panentheistic school of mystical thought.[3]

The pronounced tendency of the early Hasidic masters to preach popularly the notion that God is immanent in the created world and available to man through it is recorded in numerous Hasidic texts and has been amply documented by scholars. Although they were only rarely extended to the point of actually equating God with nature, the spirit and possible consequences of the early, radical Hasidic teachings regarding divine immanence are concisely captured in the advice attributed to R. Israel Baal Shem Tov in the pseudoepigraphic *Tsava'ath ha-Rivash:* "One must always think that the Creator fills the earth with His glory and that His providence is always with him. . . . And one should consider that when he looks at physical things, it is as if he is beholding the *Shekhinah,* which is within him."[4]

The popularization of the belief that the presence of God thoroughly pervades the created universe and, more pointedly, Hasidism's emphasis on the religious importance for all Jews—not only Kabbalistic initiates—of focusing upon the immanence of the divine in the earthly realm apparently had reached the ears and provoked the ire of the GRA. Although it is not clear whether the Gaon of Vilna was simply reacting to oral traditions and hearsay regarding the doctrines of the Hasidim or whether he had certain particular Hasidic texts in mind, his specific citation of the panentheistic interpretation of scriptural verses from Ezekiel 3:12 and Nehemiah 9:6 calls to mind the uses of precisely those same verses by R. Shneur Zalman of Lyadi, the founder of Habad Hasidism, in the section "Shaar ha-Yihud veha-Emuna" of his classic *Likutei Amarim: Tanya* to support his radically immanentist conception of God:

> With this in mind, the statement in the *Zohar* that the verse "Hear O Israel" (Deuteronomy 6:4) teaches the higher unity of God, while the verse "Blessed be the name" (Ezekiel 3:12) teaches the lower-level unity can be understood. . . . Now this is lower-level unity . . . namely, that His very essence and being, may He be blessed, which is called by the name *Eyn Sof,* completely fills the earth

both in space and in time; for in the heavens above and on earth below, and in all four directions, everything is filled with the light of the Eyn Sof, may He be blessed ... and all ... are completely nullified in the light of the Eyn Sof.[5]

This work, published just a few months after the circulation of the GRA's 1796 letter of excommunication, was destined to become the clearest, most important, most enduring, and most popular formulation of Hasidic panentheism. Indeed, Ḥabad Hasidism eventually emerged as the most radically immanentist—according to some, acosmic—major school of Hasidism. Furthermore, not only did R. Shneur Zalman of Lyadi and the Ḥabad leaders who followed him teach theoretically of the reality of divine immanence but they considered a heightened awareness of the immediate, overwhelming presence of God throughout the world to be an essential cornerstone of the faith of each and every Jew. They therefore encouraged all of their followers, regardless of their intellectual or religious background, to contemplate and try to master the understanding of this sublime yet central aspect of faith.[6]

Ḥabad acosmism was rooted in a figurative understanding of the Lurianic theory of zimzum, or divine contraction prior to Creation. While in its original interpretation zimzum served as the basis for a God-cosmos dualism and a deep sense of man's—and his world's—distance and alienation from the Creator, certain later mystics tended to interpret it figuratively in order to soften the dualism and gross anthropomorphism that could result from a literal understanding of the notion that God had somehow to withdraw spatially from the created universe.[7] R. Shneur Zalman's own, less literal interpretation of zimzum, according to which the divine contraction Luria described was a deliberate act of self-eclipse or concealment from human consciousness rather than an actual delimitation or contraction of the Divine essence and spirit per se, suggests more about the world's inability fully to sustain God's glory and about the human incapacity fully to perceive the Eyn Sof than about the actual ontology of God's relationship with the created world.[8]

R. Shneur Zalman's theory of divine immanence went far beyond various earlier Kabbalists' allegorizations of the Lurianic theory. For it was motivated by much more than the philosophical fear of anthropomorphism. The founder of the Ḥabad mystical doctrine was virtually possessed by a radically monistic belief in the immediate presence of God in all of creation. Moreover, and again in contrast to all earlier Kabbalists, who treated such esoteric matters discretely, he believed that this mystical faith must be propagated to the widest possible audience, indeed to each and every Jew. At the same time, he was, of course, religiously committed by tradition to the sanctity of Lurianic Kabbalah. By redefining and limiting *zimzum* to a merely apparent contraction of God from the world, namely, the obscuring of his actual pervasiveness in creation from human perception, R. Shneur Zalman was able to formulate a monistic cosmology that was decidedly at odds with Lurianic dualism while still formally employing the rhetoric of Lurianic doctrine. When he felt challenged by the Mithnagdim regarding this obvious departure from the original, literal sense of R. Isaac Luria's dualistic doctrine of *zimzum*, R. Shneur Zalman took the ideological offensive, arguing that it was the GRA and his disciples, not he, who had a literal, primitive, and incorrect understanding of Lurianic Kabbalah and were not faithful to its true meaning. Moreover, R. Shneur Zalman provocatively questioned whether the GRA himself actually considered the Lurianic system to be a sacred, inspired one, and he intimated that he neither comprehended nor fully believed in the mysteries of *zimzum*. In a letter addressed to his Hasidim in Vilna regarding the ideological conflict with the GRA, R. Shneur Zalman focused especially upon divine immanence and the Mithnagdic allegations of Hasidic panentheistic heresies:

> [It is] especially regarding matters of faith that the Gaon's critique of the book *Likutei Amarim,* and others like it, is directed; for therein the meaning of the religious maxims "He fills all worlds" and "There is no space void of Him" are explained literally. In his [i.e., the GRA's] opinion, it is total heresy to suggest that God is actually present in any base or lowly, earthly things; and according to their own epistle, this was the reason for the burning of the known book [R. Jacob Joseph of Polnoe's *Toledoth Jacob Joseph*].
>
> As for their interpretation of these scriptures, they have obscure and fanciful methods [according to which] "The earth is filled with His glory" refers to divine providence [as opposed to the divine essence]. . . . It is furthermore known to us with absolute clarity that the GRA does not believe that the total system of Lurianic Kabbalah was inspired by the prophet Elijah. Rather, he accepts that only a very small part is from Elijah and the rest is the product of his [i.e., R. Isaac Luria's] personal wisdom, and that there is therefore no obligation to accept it.[9]

Besides calling into question the degree of the GRA's faith in, and acceptance of, the sanctity of Lurianic Kabbalah, this letter suggests that the real basis for his opposition to Hasidism was its new and deviant understanding of the nature of God's presence on earth. Later Ḥabad traditions, consistent with this view of the movement's founder, assert that the GRA's incorrect, literal understanding of *zimzum* and, by extension, of the very nature of God's relationship to the world was the major cause for his strenuous opposition to Hasidism. Ḥabad historian H. M. Heilman, in his biography of R. Shneur Zalman, describes the reception of the latter's magnum opus, *Tanya,* thus:

> In the year 5556 (1796) our master [R. Shneur Zalman] submitted his work *Likutei Amarim,* also known as *Tanya,* for publication. It is based upon the holiest of holies, the writings of the Ari [R. Isaac Luria], of blessed memory, as well as upon the traditions of his own teachers. In the winter of 5557 (1797) the printing of this work was completed and it appeared publicly; it was also seen by the GRA, of blessed memory, and he found certain incorrect doctrines in this book, e.g., the figurative interpretation of the doctrine of *zimzum,* the belief in the uplifting of foreign thoughts, the raising of sparks, etc. He considered these theories to be words of heresy and skepticism, God forbid, and he therefore slandered this holy work.[10]

Another Ḥabad historian, M. Teitelbaum, argued that the GRA understood *zimzum* literally as a "physical" withdrawal of God into himself in order materially to "make room" and allow for the possibility of the creation of a realm of corporeal existence.[11] The net result of such a literal understanding of the Lurianic doctrine *zimzum ki-pheshuto* was a dualistic world-view according to which God per se is not immanent; rather, only his will, providence, and actions—but not his transcendent essence—are at times manifest in the created world. According to Teitelbaum, the ideological split between the GRA and R. Shneur Zalman centered upon their respective literal and figurative understandings of the meaning and nature of *zimzum.* The GRA was a dualist for whom God was distant and inaccessible to man and the world, whereas R. Shneur Zalman was a monist for whom God was immanent and close to the man of spirit who proved able to achieve mystical union with him.

Following in this Hasidic historiographical tradition, Samuel Dresner argued that not only was the question of immanence versus transcendence the basis for the GRA's opposition to Hasidism[12] but this cosmological question lies at the very center of the entire Mithnagdic polemic: "The opponents of Hasidism, the mithnagdim, locked horns with them on this very issue. They found this doctrine heretical and made it the source of controversy."[13] Finally, in his recent study of the GRA's confrontation with Hasidism, Elijah Schochet endorses uncritically the Hasidic analysis of the theological basis for the contention between Hasidim and Mithnagdim, taking at face value the Hasidic insistence that it hinged on a fundamental dispute regarding the question of divine immanence and asserting that "the GRA found a clear and present danger in the hasidic interpretation of immanence."[14]

However, as a closer examination of the Mithnagdic sources reveals, there was virtually no substantive theological difference between Hasidim and Mithnagdim in their respective theoretical understandings of the nature of divine immanence. Where they did differ was on the place and application of this belief in religious life and the propriety of propagating it to the Jewish masses.

The GRA on Divine Immanence

While the GRA's epistle of 1796 certainly suggests that the Hasidic masters' preaching and popularizing to a mass audience their radically mystical belief in divine immanence was a source of some deep concern to the Mithnagdim, the tendency of Hasidic historians to make this belief, and the resulting Hasidic panentheism, the cornerstone of the enduring Hasidic-Mithnagdic controversy is highly problematic. Neither the bulk of the polemical literature nor the significant body of Mithnagdic theological and religioethical writings suggests any clear or substantive theological differences regarding cosmogony between the Hasidim and their rabbinic adversaries. In fact, the only sources for such a view of the theological or cosmogonical roots of the Mithnagdic polemic are of Hasidic origin. For aside from the above-quoted passage from the GRA's 1796 epistle, there does not, to my knowledge, exist a single theoretical critique of Hasidic cosmogony or cosmology anywhere else in the entire Mithnagdic literature. As already noted, the thrust of the critique of Hasidism found in Mithnagdic writings and in the polemical writs of condemnation and excommunication is overwhelmingly directed against Hasidic social behavior and Halakhic practice, not against Hasidic mystical theology. Furthermore, nowhere in the GRA's writings or those of his disciples is a strictly literal understanding of *zimzum* or a strictly transcendent cosmology elucidated. The closest the GRA ever comes to such a position is in his interpretation of Isaiah 6:3:

> "The earth is filled with his glory": The meaning here is akin to "and the earth was enlightened by His glory," for the manifestation of the Divine here on earth cannot possibly be equal to that in the heavenly sphere; for the [earthly sphere] does not endure eternally, and they [i.e., those who dwell on the earth] are governed by free choice, and the evil impulse often rules them. Rather, it is God's dominion that rules over every domain, and He is the Lord over all of them. Therefore the name *Ado-nai* [i.e., Sovereign] applies to the earth, whereas *Je-hova* [the unknowable God] applies in the heavens above.[15]

Although the GRA did not interpret the verse in question as the foundation for a panentheistic conception of the created universe to be distilled to the Jewish masses as a basic postulate of faith, as did R. Shneur Zalman and other Hasidic masters, he also did not elucidate a strict God-cosmos dualism based on a literal understanding of *zimzum*. Rather, the GRA implied that it was because of the inherent limitations and imperfections of God's physical creations, specifically those of man, and not any limiting attribute of the Divinity per se, that the full reality of the *Eyn Sof* cannot be perceived by his mortal and imperfect creatures to infuse the earth. Consequently, only those aspects of the divine that are in fact perceptible to the human senses—the creative power, providence, and supreme sovereignty of God—are claimed by the prophet to fill the world.

In the supplementary notes to his commentary to the *Safra de-Zeniutha* the GRA defines *zimzum* figuratively as a screening of the divine essence from human perception rather than as an activity affecting or limiting the nature of God's omnipresence per se:

> You must know that it is forbidden to contemplate the *Eyn Sof* at all or to attribute anything to Him, even existence. For even the first *sefirah* is called nought, whereas the second is called something; for all we know about it [the second *sefirah*] is that it exists, as opposed to the first *sefirah*. Certainly, then, the *Eyn Sof*, blessed be He, is unknowable, and we may not contemplate Him at all, nor are we even allowed to call Him *Eyn Sof*. We can only talk of the will and the providence of the *Eyn Sof* and the sefiroth, which can only be known via His deeds. This is a basic principle for the entire Kabbalah. Now it is known that just as He is infinite, so is His will infinite. This is [the meaning of] the term *Eyn Sof*, i.e., his simple will; and it is forbidden to contemplate even this [divine will]. Just this is known: that the worlds are of a limited nature and a finite number; therefore He contracted His will in the process of creating the worlds, and that is [the meaning of] *zimzum*.[16]

It is clear that the context for the GRA's explication of *zimzum* is epistemological, founded on man's inability to comprehend the *Eyn Sof*, and not cosmological. As far as man, with his imperfect senses, can comprehend, the finite world is unable to contain and manifest the fullness of God's infinite glory. Earthly man has consequently been shielded from the full reality and force of God's presence in the created universe by a gracious primordial act of self-containment exercised by God's will upon his divine essence, which would otherwise have overwhelmed the finite human physical and sensory capacities and obliterated man's limited corporeal universe from cognition. As a result of this merciful and disciplined act of divine self-screening from human perception, it is only God's *kavod*, or his glory and providence as reflected in the daily operations of the created natural universe, that are apparent to the human senses.

Although the GRA does not assert that the divine contraction is only apparent from the perspective of man, it is the inherent human cognitive limitations that form the background for understanding the very need and initial reason for divine self-concealment. The GRA speaks of the constriction of the full divine will owing to the necessity of its concealment from the finite and imperfect world of human sensory perception, and not of the contraction of the *Eyn Sof* per se. Nowhere in his writings is the GRA's explanation of the concept *zimzum* a simple, unambiguously literal one. The process of divine self-eclipse is thus precipitated not by any need inherent in God in order to allow him to create but by the spiritual and cognitive limitations of man. That this is the GRA's principal orientation in considering the nature of the divine presence on earth is clear in his commentary to the *Zohar*:

> This is a major principle: i.e., that it is forbidden to contemplate God's essence, but rather it is only His powers and His deeds that we can readily perceive, as it is written (Isaiah 40:26), "Lift up your eyes to heaven and behold Him that has created all of these." In other words, God infuses His creatures with life, and thus it is written, "Lift up your eyes," in order that you might see His wonders. For to each [of His creations] He has allocated a very limited part of His vitality and energy, and thus each of His powers is appropriately named. For example, it is written [of God], "The Lion has roared," etc. Scripture here merely compares God [to a Lion]. For if we were to say generally that God is more mighty than any created entity in the universe, what would we really understand about His might? For the only things that we can know are His specific [i.e., manifested] wonders; but in truth He is without any limitations. We can, however, see that He has created the Lion, which is braver than all other creatures in the world. Thus, we call God by this name, for this is something that we can apprehend with our own eyes, and that which we cannot apprehend with our senses we are not allowed even to mention, for God is without any limitation, so that *in referring to Him we ourselves set a boundary.*
>
> Nonetheless, that we refer to God only in accordance with the limitations of what we are able to perceive in no way implies that there is any restriction of the glory of God per se. *For we set boundaries [when referring to God] only in accordance with what we can see.* It is as if we were saying, "Our intellects are simply unable to comprehend any more of His infinitude."
>
> That is what is meant [when God is referred to] in Scripture [as] "He who dwells in the heavens." Is God limited to the heavens only? Rather, it is only because we can see no further than the heavens that we only refer to God as dwelling in the sky. . . .
>
> We do not refer to anything other than the heavens simply because we do not know how to speak of Him, for He is really without any restriction or limitation.

> Therefore it does not, God forbid, imply any deficiency in His glory when we establish such limits and boundaries [of human reference]. This is what is meant by "that which is beyond you." That is to say, we are not allowed to investigate beyond the heavens, and we are forbidden to investigate anything that we are unable to see and grasp. For any such investigation might, God forbid, imply a deficiency or a limitation in Him.
>
> That is why in our blessings we refer both to the evident and to the hidden. The evident corresponds to the fruit [being blessed], in which we can readily see the wonders of God; but beyond that is the hidden glory of God, which is without any limitation, and because it is infinite no man can perceive it.[17]

Although the GRA insists that God himself is in no way limited or constricted, he is most concerned that man respect his own epistemological limitations. Therefore, it is from the perspective of its necessarily limited manifestations to the human senses only that God's glory is said to be withdrawn or circumscribed. This is not an ontological judgment about the real extent to which the divine presence infuses all earthly things but rather an insistence that man acknowledge and defer to the limits of his own ability to discern the immanent presence of the Divine.

This firm resolution that man not try to arrive at a full comprehension of the infinitude and pervasive presence of God stands in diametrical opposition to the Hasidic insistence, most pronounced in the Ḥabad doctrine of *hithbonenuth,* or the intense intellectual scrutiny of the saturation of the world with the Divine—that every Jew, regardless of his level of knowledge or spiritual sophistication, must strive to overcome the limitations of his natural senses, which veil the fullness of the divine presence from him. For the very nucleus of Ḥabad doctrine was, from the inception of the movement, the conviction that man must endeavor constantly to surmount his natural condition, in which religious knowledge is determined solely by the inherently limited human sense perceptions and powers of reason. The spiritual ideal for which every Jew must struggle is, according to R. Shneur Zalman, *bitul ha-yeshuth,* or release from the common sensation of the mundane as having inherent reality "outside of God," in order to arrive at the highest awareness that "all is in God" and thus "all are as nought before him."[18] In clear contrast to this mystical activism and popularism, the GRA—as well as his disciples, as we shall presently see—considered this to be not only an infeasible ideal but also a pretentious and perilous religious objective that was wholly inappropriate for the untutored masses of contemporary Jewry to whom Hasidism was addressing its mystical teachings.

The GRA's most celebrated student, R. Hayyim of Volozhin, articulated an immanentist view that, as has been widely noted, is strikingly similar to the radical acosmism of R. Shneur Zalman of Lyadi. The differences between the two men's formulations are so subtle that scholars are almost hopelessly divided regarding precisely where they differ.[19] In fact, this rather intricate theological closeness has been explained by some experts as a symptom of the decline of the Hasidic-Mithnagdic controversy during R. Hayyim of Volozhin's generation.[20] They argue that R. Hayyim, not being directly involved in the Hasidic-Mithnagdic polemic, was, unlike the GRA and other "true" Mithnagdim, in a position to accept a monistic position closer to that of the Ḥabad school. This conclusion is based on the assumption that the controversy was mired in theoretical mystical issues of cosmogony and cosmology. However, the Mithnagdic sources do not support such a conclusion; quite the contrary. According to them, it is precisely because the dispute between Hasidism and Mithnagdism was *not* rooted in the issue of divine immanence or the meaning of *zimzum,* but rather in radically differing assessments of human spiritual capacities, that R. Hayyim was able to take a monistic position in his anti-Hasidic work *Nefesh ha-Hayyim* without feeling that his agreement with Hasidic cosmogony *eo ipso* identified him with Hasidism.

R. Phinehas of Polotsk on Divine Immanence

The central Hasidic doctrine of divine immanence is not on R. Phinehas of Polotsk's long list of grievances against the Hasidim in his polemic *Kether Torah.* R. Phinehas could hardly have been unaware of that view, since the most radical Hasidic acosmists were successfully spreading their doctrine, especially in R. Phinehas's own backyard, the Hasidic-dominated Vitebsk region of Belorussia.[21] Still, the fact that the Hasidim believed that there is literally "nothing but God" was apparently not, in R. Phinehas's view, a significant part of their otherwise very extensive perfidy. Quite the contrary, R. Phinehas himself indicated in that same work that the ultimate awareness of the consummate nature of God's unity and his pervasive immanence on earth is the highest manifestation of religious belief: "The highest level is to understand fully the unity of God: that He constitutes the truest oneness; that there is no unity like His unity; that there is no limit to His perfect unity; that His glory fills the earth; that He surrounds and defines and fills all places; and that there is nothing outside of Him and nothing except Him in the world."[22]

This definition of a correct conception of the very nature of God and his relationship to the world, could, of course, convincingly be attributed to a disciple of the Great Maggid or even to R. Shneur Zalman of Lyadi himself. It is as clear a theoretical statement of panentheism as can be found anywhere in the Hasidic literature. And the theological agreement between R. Phinehas and R. Shneur Zalman does not end here; it extends to their very choice of metaphors in describing the nature of divine immanence. In an attempt graphically to convey the overpowering immanence of God both R. Phinehas and R. Shneur Zalman employ the analogy of the creative powers of God manifested on earth to the rays of the sun. In his commentary to the liturgy, *Maggid Zedek*, R. Phinehas writes, "Behold how the sun illustrates the nature of the glory of God, that He, may He be blessed, fills the entire earth; and from it [i.e., the sun] one can also derive proof that it is impossible to fathom God's true essence."[23] But the practical warning to his readers that immediately follows R. Phinehas's proclamation of divine immanence suggests an important difference between him and his Hasidic counterparts on this issue: "You must know that in order to attain this highest level of knowledge and understanding of God's unity in His world—namely, that there is nothing outside of Him or other than Him in the entire cosmos, but only Him—you must first master the entire wisdom of the true Kabbalah."[24]

Of course, such mastery of Kabbalah was, as R. Phinehas forcefully and repeatedly asserted throughout his writings, unavailable to all but a very small religious elite who had first mastered the entire oral Torah and attained the highest degree of religious and ethical perfection.[25] For the vast majority of Jews in a generation that R. Phinehas perceived to be spiritually depleted, simple fear of God, not a genuine understanding of the elusive and finally unknowable divine presence, was the only realistic religious expectation:

> The meaning of "fear" of God is shame before Him, may He be blessed, shame that is due to the vast chasm between His greatness and the lowliness of man.
> Man must first of all recognize the greatness of God and His transcendence in all the higher worlds and angelic spheres and that all are as nought before Him. Then will he recognize the lowliness of man, that he is base and dim in comparison with all lower creatures and certainly compared with the higher creatures and, *a fortiori*, compared with Him, may He be blessed.
> Automatically there will fall upon him a spirit of modesty and shame from raising his head against the Lord, blessed be He, or even from inquiring regarding His glorious presence, which is exalted beyond human comprehension.[26]

It is precisely the theoretical knowledge that the entire cosmos is "as nought" before the glory of the Lord that leads to the position of pious resignation regarding theosophical understanding that R. Phinehas prescribes. Unlike the Hasidic acosmists, who thirsted fully to understand, and ultimately to become one with, God, R. Phinehas is convinced that it is precisely because of God's overwhelming majesty and the world's nothingness that any attempt at such knowledge is both arrogant and futile and reflects an insufficient fear of God.

Practically, then, for reasons of inherent human inadequacies, human comprehension of the unquestioned cosmological reality of God's immanence is simply not possible. How different this is from the entire spirit of R. Shneur Zalman's teachings and those of his disciples, as well as those of many other early Hasidic masters, who consistently and vigorously encouraged all Jews to contemplate the divine immanence.[27]

The panentheistic conviction that "God is all," alongside a pessimistic belief in contemporary man's inability to know God or to understand the extent of his unity and his immanence in the world, is a theme to which R. Phinehas returns in much greater detail in his later works, particularly in his commentary to the liturgy, *Maggid Zedek*. There, as in *Kether Torah*, R. Phinehas argues that the absolute immanence of God is an inescapable consequence of the traditional belief in his total and perfect unity. Commenting on the verse in the liturgical ballad "Yigdal," which reads, "He is one, and there is no unity like unto His unity; concealed is He, and there is no limit to His oneness," R. Phinehas argues that God is, as a consequence of his absolute unity, immanent in the created universe, and yet his essence and true presence must, on account of man's cognitive limitations, remain unintelligible:

> Ultimately, despite all the postulates regarding His unity, the truth is this: When we are no longer able to divide Him nor add to Him, that is to say, when He is [understood to be] filling every space such that there is no place void of Him so that we might be able to divide Him or separate one of His parts from the rest, or add something extraneous to Him, or apply metaphors or analogies to Him, the result being that when I say, "the true unity" [regarding God], it is like one who says, "the endless one" [Heb., *Eyn Sof*]. This is what is meant when it is written that "there is no end to His unity." Now behold how wondrous it is that He fills the entire earth and there is no place void of Him, and that He fills all places; nonetheless, we are not given to see or understand anything at all regarding His essence. . . . This is how [the liturgist] magnifies and praises God wondrously, saying, "He is hidden, yet there is no end to His unity," i.e., even though there is no end to His unity and He invariably fills all spaces, nevertheless, He and the essence of His true glory are hidden from the eyes of all [creatures].[28]

In other words, an essential distinction must be drawn between cosmological and theosophical realities and the human capacity to comprehend them. God is indeed immanent, but it is futile, indeed proscribed, for man to focus upon that fact; moreover, it is both presumptuous and dangerous for him to try to base his religious life upon the knowledge of God's immediate presence. For God's closeness or immanence can never be fully or properly understood.

The notion that God is immanent in creation yet at the same time transcendent and thus beyond human perception enables R. Phinehas to explain the repeated descriptions in the sacred literature of God as holy. Divine holiness is understood in the classical rabbinic tradition as indicating God's distance and separateness from the created world. Such distance might seem, prima facie, to contradict the notion that God is immanent in creation. R. Phinehas resolves the tension between the simultaneous insistence upon God's transcendence and upon his immanence by distinguishing between the realms of ontological reality and human perception:

> But if He fills the entire earth, how is it appropriate to apply the notion of transcendence to Him or to say that He is removed [from the world]? For were it ever to enter our minds, God forbid, that the Holy One, Blessed Be He, is removed from a given thing, that thing would cease altogether to exist. For the Holy One, Blessed Be He, infuses everything with life and with energy, and there is no space empty or removed from Him, God forbid; and the entire earth shines from His glory, as it is written, "When You hide your face, they are terrified; when you take away their breath, they return to dust" (Psalms 104:29).
>
> The truth, however, is that God is not at all removed in essence but is only remote from our wisdom and comprehension, and from the perception of all emanated and created beings in the world, as it is written, "For it is not a vain thing for you . . ." (Deuteronomy 32:47). So He is only removed beyond our understanding, but He is not [transcendent] in essence.[29]

By thus distinguishing between the ontological reality of God's pervasive presence in the world, and the religious experience available to man R. Phinehas is able to resolve the tension between the simultaneous affirmations, in the classical tradition, of God's immanence and his transcendence. For R. Phinehas, as for the GRA before him, the only aspect of God that is readily intelligible to man is his providence and glory reflected in the daily divine governance of the affairs of the world. Through God's actions in the physical world man is reminded of the ultimate, unfathomable reality of God's immanence:

> It is remarkable how utterly hidden God is insofar as the apprehension of the truth and essence of His glory is concerned and yet, at the same time, how utterly revealed He is insofar as His wondrous actions and deeds are concerned.

For they [i.e., God's actions on earth] reflect His glory as if to say, "Behold this our God" who sustains us and infuses us with His energy and does with us as He pleases.[30]

R. Phinehas of Polotsk's approach to this entire matter was far from unique. His assertion that God's immanence can only be known by man via the physical manifestations of divine providence can also be found in the GRA's posthumously published commentaries.[31] And his tendency to distinguish sharply between what he accepts as ontologically correct and what he believes is intelligible to man constitutes a major theme of R. Hayyim of Volozhin's *Nefesh ha-Hayyim*. In fact, the entire third section of that work consists of an elaborate argument for precisely such a distinction. R. Hayyim expresses this differentiation in terms of the contrast between man's epistemological "perspective" and that of God. God is, from his own "perspective" (i.e., in ontological reality) truly immanent. From his "perspective" there is, therefore, no reality outside of God's own divinity. However, practically speaking, this acosmic mystical reality is completely unintelligible to man, for whom the material world must remain real. Thus, although from his own perspective God is immanent and the world is illusory, from man's "perspective" God is transcendent and the world is very real indeed.[32]

This approach to fundamental questions of cosmogony and cosmology, which maintains that God's transcendence is only apparent to man but not real, was shared by R. Hayyim's Hasidic contemporaries in Belorussia. Besides the very similar viewpoint of R. Shneur Zalman noted above, R. Hayyim's most eminent disciple, the radical Hasidic monist R. Aaron of Starosselje, endeavored to harmonize his theology with the apparent existence of a physical world independent of God by drawing the same distinction between man's perspective and God's as that proposed by R. Hayyim. Only the terminology was different. R. Hayyim's *mitzido* ("from His perspective") is referred to by R. Aaron in Aramaic as *legabei didei,* and R. Hayyim's *mitzideynu* becomes *legabei didan.* The concepts are strikingly similar.[33] But R. Hayyim, like the GRA and R. Phinehas, was intent on preserving the distinction between the human and divine perspectives on the nature of the cosmos, in sharp contrast to their Hasidic contemporaries, whose goal was the obliteration of that distinction. While the Hasidic masters made it their central spiritual goal to overcome the flawed human perception of an apparently (but not really) transcendent God, R. Hayyim and the Mithnagdim persisted in discouraging such mystical heroics and preserving the distinction between ontology and epistemology. R. Hayyim vigorously and repeatedly warned his readers not to endeavor transcending the limitations imposed by the human senses and the human condition. His entire presentation of acosmism is rife with warnings against both the popularization of the doctrine of immanence and any attempt by man to gain the "perspective" of God whereby all reality is nullified. In fact, R. Hayyim claimed that the only reason he entered into any discussion of this dangerous, esoteric subject was to stem the popularization and potential antinomian abuses of this doctrine by the Hasidim:

> In truth, I would have abstained from discussing this matter at all, just as the earlier sages, of blessed memory, hid this matter. . . . But I came to see that such [discretion] was appropriate for them and their generation; but now there have been many days without a guide, and it is the way of every self-righteous man to follow the inclination of his intellect; and he is filled with the desire only to soar in his thoughts to wherever his mind can take him. And most of all, this has become the doctrine of all common men, and it has even become a parable in the mouths of fools to proclaim, "Behold, in every place and every thing there is total divinity." Their eyes and hearts contemplate this deeply all their days to the point that even the hearts of youngsters are inclined to base all of their deeds and actions upon this awareness [of God's immanence].[34]

R. Hayyim was troubled by Hasidism's popularization of a belief that carried with it antinomian possibilities, specifically the blurring of concrete moral distinctions. Thus, his opposition to Hasidic acosmism was directed not at the theosophic theory or belief per se but rather at the enthusiastic and reckless popularization of that belief and the encouragement given by the Hasidic masters to their followers to focus upon divine immanence and make it the cornerstone of their faith. This fear of the practical and popular application of sublime religious truths also underlies the condemnation of Hasidic acosmism in the "Herem Vilna."[35]

The GRA, R. Hayyim, and R. Phinehas all accepted in theory the ultimate truth that God was immanent in the created world. Their formulations of that truth hardly differ from those of their Hasidic contemporaries. But very much unlike the Hasidic masters, they strongly discouraged their readers and followers from contemplating divine immanence. They were especially concerned that such contemplation not interfere with the everyday religious life and Halakhic obedience of man. They insisted that the distinction between God's knowledge and man's limited perceptions be respected and maintained. The Hasidim, on the other hand, encouraged man to transcend the barrier between human understanding and ultimate cosmological reality, and to try to gain God's "perspective," by overcoming the ordinary limitations of the human senses.

This difference between the Hasidim's and the Mithnagdim's approaches to the universally recognized truth that in reality God is immanent persisted in subsequent generations. The Hasidim, especially those of the Ḥabad school, continued to encourage practical mystical experiences rooted in a heightened understanding and perception of the immediate presence of God in all of creation.[36] The Mithnagdim, on the other hand, although consistently admitting that in some ultimate but unfathomable sense God does indeed permeate the physical universe, continued to discourage extensive contemplation of this reality. Thus, for example, a disciple of R. Hayyim of Volozhin, Asher Ha-Kohen Tiktin, acknowledged that God's immanence ultimately nullifies all worldly, physical reality. Yet in the same breath he warned that this realization must never be allowed to form the basis of man's practical service to the Creator:

> All things that He created, emanated, and made in this world cannot interfere with His simple, unified essence, which fills all things, as if they do not exist at all. Yet in these matters it is for the glory of God that we must hide such truths; and heaven forbid that we serve God on the basis of this. . . . Rather, our entire worship of God must be from the perspective of the contraction [*tzimtzum*] of His essence in order to create the finite world.[37]

An even more striking Mithnagdic affirmation of the immanence of God, alongside a simultaneous warning to man not to contemplate that reality, is to be found in the unpublished mid-nineteenth-century polemic against Hasidism *Milhamoth Ado-nai*, by the GRA's grand-nephew Meir ben Elijah:[38]

> Of course it is true and right that God did create the entire world and all the fullness thereof with His simple power, and He permeates all of the creations, infusing each and every thing and place and creature, all in accordance with its needs for existence and viability and survival; and He, may He be blessed, saturates and is hidden in all of them in order to maintain them in life. That is the meaning of His having condensed [*tzimtzem*], as it were, His glory and power into each and every thing, all in accordance with its value—the large creatures received much, and the small, little.
>
> Nevertheless, the contemplation and examination of the essence of this matter—i.e., how everything was created and . . . how God's glory is hidden in all places, both good and evil—all this has been forbidden to us, for we may not study and contemplate this matter, as it is written, "Do not examine that which is beyond you." For there is no man in the world who is able to comprehend the needs of all created things . . . nor should any man try to be so smart as to understand the way in which God infuses and is hidden in all, for all of this is simply beyond the human capacity. . . . Rather, only God Himself can know these things, for "the secret things belong to the Lord, while the revealed things are ours." . . . for our main task is simply to perform (the commandments).[39]

Like the earlier Mithnagdim, R. Meir, although implying that *zimzum* is to be understood not quite literally as the *Eyn Sof*'s withdrawal into itself but rather as the appropriate and proportional concentration of God's glory in every aspect of the finite creation and although thus accepting that God's glory does in fact completely saturate the created universe, still insists that this final truth should not be made the subject of human examination or form a foundation for the religious life. Rather, he argues that these ultimate cosmogonic truths are both inaccessible to man and irrelevant, even potentially damaging, to the practice of Judaism, which need involve no more than the God-fearing observance of the divine law.

Conclusion

Decades ago Martin Buber described Hasidism as "kabbalism turned ethos." Gershom Scholem went further in arguing that Hasidism had innovated little in the realm of Kabbalistic theory. The real originality of Hasidism, Scholem insisted, lay in its popularization and personalization of once abstract, highly esoteric mystical doctrines. As Scholem put it, Hasidism's distinctiveness "is to be found in the fact that the secrets of the divine realm are presented in the guise of mystical psychology."[40] While there was very little that was new in Hasidic theosophical theory, the popular and practical orientation of the early Hasidic masters was, according to Scholem, a highly significant novelty: "In the Hasidic movement, Kabbalism appears no longer in a theosophical guise. . . . What has really become important is the direction, the mysticism of the personal life. Hasidism is practical mysticism at its highest."[41]

The evidence from anti-Hasidic sources on the question of God's immanence supports Scholem's view of the essence of the Hasidic religious revolution. And of course the sociopsychological nature of the Hasidic masters' innovations was not lost on their opponents. The Mithnagdic critique of Hasidic acosmism relates not to theosophical or cosmological theory but to its propagation and practical application. What the Mithnagdim apparently feared most was the psychoreligious consequences of the popularization and personalization of the theory of divine immanence.

The crucial difference between the Hasidim and the Mithnagdim on this issue, then, was less one of theosophy than one of religious anthropology. All agreed that in theory the *Eyn Sof* fills all worlds and all spaces. However, for the Hasidim, who maintained a supremely optimistic view of man's spiritual and psychoreligious capacities, this truth must not remain a matter of esoteric theory but must become the object of extensive human contemplation, enriching the religious life of all Jews and ultimately allowing them to achieve mystical union with God in and through the created world. For the Mithnagdim, on the other hand, who harbored a deeply pessimistic view of man's spiritual capabilities, the truth of God's immanence must remain in the realm of mystical speculation, reserved for an small, select and well-guarded spiritual elite. The average Jew, they insisted, must conduct his life in this world as if estranged from a distant, transcendent, unknowable God.

These differences between the Hasidim and the Mithnagdim on divine immanence do not represent substantially opposing conceptions of God. Then again, they should not be reduced to mere matters of social theory, pedagogic tactics, or communal politics, as many historians have done. For although Hasidic and Mithnagdic authorities did not disagree on the basic question of God's presence in the world, their dispute reflects two vastly differing religious world-views with broad theological implications, as we shall see. As the controversy regarding divine immanence suggests, Hasidim and Mithnagdim maintained radically different approaches to the very nature of religious experience and, underlying these, fundamentally different assessments of the capacities of the human spirit.

Chapter 2

THE MITHNAGDIM AND
THE KABBALAH

The Polemics against Hasidic Kabbalism

In the introduction to *Merkeveth ha-Mishna,* published in 1751, Rabbi Solomon ben Moses of Chelm offers a highly critical description of three "sects" of Torah students.[1] The first of these sects is made up of those who spend too little time on the in-depth study of the Talmud and rabbinic codes in order to spend time on other, more spiritual but less intellectual disciplines. Among the religious interests that were distracting his contemporaries from rabbinic scholarship was, according to R. Solomon, the study of the Kabbalah:

> There are those who try to make themselves holy and pure by studying the works of R. Isaac Luria and the *Zohar.* Despite the fact that they are not yet competent in the exoteric disciplines, they are already involved in esoteric study. . . . How dare they try to ascend the ladder whose head reaches to the heavens, up to the world of souls, and attempt to unravel mysteries whilst they are yet void of ideas and their imaginations are filled with crudeness. . . . Now, the author of responsa *Havoth Yair* has already commented on this, roaring like a lion.[2]

While it is not entirely clear against whom this initial critique was directed, it is followed immediately by an attack on behavior that is clearly identifiable with that of the leaders of early Beshtian Hasidism (zaddikim).[3]

> There is among them one who is small and impoverished and who is completely empty of any knowledge, who has attempted to study neither mysticism nor Talmud; he acts deceitfully, raising his voice, skipping upon the mountains with music and loud songs. . . . Although he has not learned, he is called a sage and "Rebbe." The more he engages in movements and gesticulations, the more he is praised in the mouths of women and children. . . . The dim-witted and simple-minded offer up some of his praises, saying: "What a Hasid; what a righteous man; how wondrous are his deeds; he is of the disciples of our forefather Abraham; in both exoteric and esoteric disciplines, he is one of the truly exalted."[4]

Although the former students of Kabbalah and the latter practitioners of mysticism (i.e., the Hasidic zaddikim) are described by him as two distinct types, the fact that R. Solomon groups them together as members of the same *kath* (sect), an attribution employed widely in the anti-Sabbatean literature to identify the followers of Shabtai Zevi and later used repeatedly in the Mithnagdic polemics to refer to the Hasidim, is highly significant. The Hasidic zaddik is here accused of religious pretentiousness and arrogance, rendered all the worse by his being untutored in rabbinic learning. Like the student of the Kabbalah, he stands indicted for reaching beyond his spiritual and intellectual means. While the Kabbalistic pseudoscholar aspires, without proper academic preparation, to master cognitively the secrets of the Torah and the mysteries of the cosmos and the latter mystical enthusiast does not engage in any intellectual study at all, they share, in the view of R. Solomon of Chelm, two key traits: an ignorance of classical rabbinic studies, which renders them unfit for grasping the wisdom of the Kabbalah or attaining any legitimate mystical experience, and presumptuousness. It is highly plausible that the two types cited in this text represent two distinct schools of early Hasidism: those deeply interested in Kabbalistic study and contemplation and those involved in ecstatic mystical practice. R. Solomon's critique might then constitute an early, twofold assault on the Hasidic involvement with the Kabbalah, for he attacks both the illegitimate claims to Kabbalistic scholarship and the pretension of mystical experience on the part of the Hasidim.

In the subsequent polemical literature provoked by the rapid spread of Hasidism the accusation that the Hasidim pay too much attention to Kabbalistic study and indulge in illicit mystical practices at the expense of normative rabbinic learning and ritual observance recurs regularly. The editor of *Zemir Arizim* complained in 1772 that the Hasidim shunned classical rabbinic scholarship in favor of Kabbalistic study, for which they were neither intellectually nor spiritually prepared:

> They [i.e., Hasidim] violate the words of the Sages, for they are irritated by the oral Torah and so choose not to study from the Law of God those revealed rules, statutes, and ordinances which are ours and our children's. Instead they try to anoint themselves with the fine wine and choice produce of the esoteric, exalted, and hidden light [of mysticism], to which they have no proper claim and which is reserved for a small elite—one or two in each generation who are studded with the precious metals and decorated with the gold of erudition in all aspects of the revealed Torah. Only then did they begin to call in God's name in the study of the secrets of the Kabbalah. For not anybody who desires to attain such distinction is free to do so.[5]

Rumors that the new Hasidic sect was popularizing and abusing the hitherto carefully guarded, esoteric wisdom of Kabbalah spread quickly and widely in rabbinic circles, well beyond the geographic region where Hasidism emerged. In 1773 the German rabbi Joseph Steinhardt, in the introduction to his responsa *Zikhron Yosef*, provided a depiction of the Hasidim that suggests much about their popular image among the rabbis:

> They are completely void of any Torah scholarship, and they distract others, both young and old, from it; they wander in the PaRDeS day and night, constantly studying the books of the Kabbalah, which is their downfall. They boast that they have a true and ultimate mastery of mysticism, whereas in fact they have no real grasp of its wisdom. They probably teach heresy and may cause many evils, for they are completely ignorant of the hidden mysteries of [the *sefiroth*]. . . . They furthermore reveal secrets that are of cosmic importance and were deliberately concealed by the Ancient One from the ignorant and boorish masses and from minors and ignorant lads. They even reveal the basis of esoteric doctrines to children.[6]

R. Joseph here extends the critique of the Hasidic preoccupation with Kabbalah. Far from attacking the sanctity of the Kabbalah per se, he accuses the Hasidim of misunderstanding the true meaning of the Kabbalistic sources and distorting their message to those who could not possibly know better. This criticism reflects a concern for the integrity of Kabbalistic learning and a pronounced anxiety regarding its correct and limited transmission. R. Joseph here echoes the fear, which was to become so common in Mithnagdic thinking, that the untutored Hasidic interest in mysticism and the obsession to preach its doctrines recklessly and far too widely might not only cause great damage to its unprepared students but also do irreparable harm to the state of esoteric knowledge itself.

R. Joseph's alarm at the Hasidic misappropriation and perversion of Kabbalistic wisdom was echoed some years later by the polemicist R. David of Makow in his massive anti-Hasidic compendium *Shever Poshim* (redacted between 1787 and 1797). He accused the Hasidic zaddikim of distorting basic Kabbalistic doctrines and perverting the meaning of "all the internal secrets that have been transmitted to us orally from our holy ancestors, beginning from Moses at Sinai, and all of the sacred books that have reached us, such as the *Zohar, Tikkunim, Bahir,* etc., and especially the precious writings of the ARI [R. Isaac Luria]."[7]

R. David specifically targeted the Belorussian zaddik R. Hayyim Haikel of Amdur, accusing him of opposing the proper method of Kabbalistic study and of cursing and demeaning the true scholars of Kabbalah. R. David argued that it was because the Hasidim did not study Kabbalah "as we study rabbinics" that they had not produced a single notable scholar of Lurianism.[8] In other words, because they do not approach the study of mystical texts with the same intellectual rigor and high scholarly standards and academic prerequisites that are essential for all sacred Jewish study, the Hasidim are destined to remain hopelessly untutored in the Kabbalah as well as in rabbinics.

During this period of the rapid rise of Beshtian Hasidism the Polish rabbi Eliezer ben Aryeh Leib of Pilz (1758–1837) similarly complained, in a letter written in 1799 to the famed Mithnagdic rabbi of Pressburg, Meshulam Igra, of the misguided ways of the Hasidim: "The parchment is too short to list thereon all of their errors and deviations; yet anyone who observes them and their behavior will see how perverse their ways are in the study of the Kabbalah."[9] Following this general critique of Hasidism's interest in mystical study, R. Eliezer endeavors specifically to document the precedents for his own anti-Kabbalistic posture by referring to a wide array of earlier authorities who were, in one form or another, opponents of the popular, undisciplined study of the Kabbalah and the illicit practice of mystical ecstasy.[10] The sources range chronologically from the Talmud to eighteenth-century rabbinic texts, and all of them warn against the dangers of indulgence on the part of the untutored and uninitiated in mystical study and practice. Most of these authorities proposed ways to limit both the theoretical study of the Kabbalah and initiation into ecstatic mystical experiences. Implicit in this comprehensive list of anti-Kabbalistic sources is that it was not simply the fact of popularized mystical study that exercised the Mithnagdim. It was also—perhaps primarily —the fear, rooted in a deep respect for Kabbalah, that being poorly prepared for such study, the Hasidim were not true Kabbalistic scholars and were therefore bound to err in both their interpretation of the Kabbalistic sources and, consequently, in their aspirations for genuine mystical experience.

Criticisms of the ignorance of the Hasidim in matters mystical became commonplace in the subsequent Mithnagdic polemics. It is important to note, however, that the tenor of the Mithnagdic animadversions betrays acceptance of and reverence for the sanctity of the Kabbalah on the part of their Mithnagdic authors. In fact, it was precisely this reverence, and not any intrinsic animosity toward the Kabbalah per se, that caused the greatest alarm among the Mithnagdim at the sight of the perceived Hasidic popularization, theoretical distortions, and practical abuses of a precious, esoteric doctrine. This is especially evident in the harsh criticism of the Hasidim by the Mithnagdic Kabbalist R. Eliezer Fishel of Stychov. In the introduction to his seminal mystical work, *Olam Gadol: Midrash la-Perushim*, he suggested that the most severe sin of the Jewish nation in his day, which was in fact obstructing the messianic redemption, was the premature and fallacious study of the Kabbalah in which the Hasidim were engaged. R. Eliezer complained not only that the Hasidim were insufficiently learned to delve into the mysteries of mystical texts but that they dabbled in Kabbalah chiefly in order to impress the ignorant Jewish masses. What was really needed but sadly lacking, he said, was a small circle of authentic and learned students of the "secrets of the Torah."[11]

The general picture that emerges from the rabbinic and polemical literature is that the Hasidim were popularizing mystical concepts that hitherto had zealously been kept concealed by the rabbis. They were thus perceived as encouraging the study of highly esoteric and dangerously potent texts on the part of those who were neither intellectually nor spiritually prepared for its consequences. The Mithnagdim, like so many conservative rabbinic thinkers from earlier periods of Jewish history, contended that such popular study by incompetents would inevitably lead to misinterpretations, distortions, and abuses of a sacred discipline.

The Hasidic Reality

As was generally the case with the anti-Hasidic polemics, the Mithnagdim's fears of Hasidic abuses of Kabbalah were somewhat exaggerated. Nonetheless, there was already in the early history of Hasidism a strong interest in the simplification and popularization of Kabbalistic doctrine. This occurred on two levels. Gershom Scholem long ago noted that many Hasidic theoreticians deliberately ignored the complexities of Lurianic doctrine in order to expound a simpler, more personal and mystical, and less intellectually rigorous form of Kabbalah.[12] Moshe Idel's recent work on the history of the Kabbalah has shown that such personal, ecstatic mysticism was not new in Hasidism and that there is a pronounced tendency in Hasidic writings to favor the Cordoveran school of ecstatic mystical enthusiasm over the more theoretical and complex theurgy of Lurianic Kabbalah.[13] As we shall see, some Hasidic masters did indeed, as R. David of Makow claimed, deliberately emphasize personal mystical experiences over the mastery of the very demanding textual study of the intricate Lurianic system.

Nonetheless, despite the greater general interest among many Hasidic rabbis in the mystical way of R. Moshe Cordovero, others tried to simplify and clarify (or reconstruct) Lurianic theory for the benefit of the unsophisticated Jewish masses and to reinterpret some of its myths to make them consistent with Hasidism's monistic doctrine. The best known of these popularizers and reinterpreters of Lurianism were the early masters of the Ḥabad school.[14] Yet, long before the popular mystical writings of Ḥabad's founder, R. Shneur Zalman of Lyadi, first appeared, there were important Hasidic teachers who tried to distill and simplify the Lurianic Kabbalah for the Jewish masses. From 1761 to 1765 R. Barukh of Kossov authored a monumental, two-part explication of Zoharic and Lurianic Kabbalah.[15] The explicit purpose of these works, stated openly on their title pages, was to render the esoteric teachings of Jewish mysticism easily available to even the simplest reader. R. Barukh begins his introduction to these works by affirming the "great obligation upon man to study the true wisdom, which is the knowledge of the Kabbalah and the secrets of the Torah."[16] He then states clearly and boldly his objective to clarify difficult concepts by means of extensive elaborations and the use of similes and metaphors so that the mysteries of Kabbalah might be comprehensible to "the simple scholars," who far outnumber "the great scholars." All this effort is being expended, he claims, in order to spread the wisdom of Kabbalah as widely as possible and thereby "bring merit to the masses."[17]

Determined to spread Kabbalistic wisdom throughout the ranks of Israel, R. Barukh of Kossov was first obliged to dispel the many fears of those who objected to such popular instruction. He identifies what he perceives to be the three most common apprehensions that exercised the opposition to widespread Kabbalistic study. The first and most significant was rooted in the fear that had been generated by the catastrophic consequences of the earlier Sabbatean misuses of Kabbalah.[18] And in the course of his writings R. Barukh engages in a thorough critique of the Sabbatean and Frankist interpretations of Lurianic Kabbalah. More pertinent to our current investigation, however, is R. Barukh's critique of the strong rabbinic opposition to Kabbalistic study that prevailed in his day. R. Barukh's analysis of the anxieties underlying the Mithnagdim's condemnation of the Hasidic study of the Kabbalah and experimentation with mystical experience is highly accurate. He suggests that the Mithnagdic polemic against Hasidic interest in the Kabbalah must be understood in the context of the fear of mystical heresy that had been generated by Sabbateanism.

The Impact of Sabbateanism

The Mithnagdic bans on popular Kabbalistic study and mystical praxis were not new. Extreme caution toward esoteric study and mystical enthusiasm dates back to early rabbinic times. And less than a half-century before the anti-Hasidic outbursts of the early Mithnagdim a meeting of the Council of Four Lands in the Galician town of Brody, responding to the threat of Sabbatean and Frankist antinomian practices rooted in a particular interpretation of Lurianic Kabbalah,[19] pronounced a ban on the study of "the *Zohar* and all other Kabbalistic texts before the age of thirty years; and even after forty years not every person who aspires to such distinction [i.e., the mastery of Kabbalistic wisdom] is permitted to do so; for such study is only permitted to one who has filled his belly with the Talmud and codes."[20]

Just sixteen years after this ban on Kabbalistic study was pronounced in Brody in response to the Sabbatean heresy, the rabbis of the same town condemned the Hasidim, who they believed had turned their backs on Talmudic study as a result of their preoccupation with mysticism: "They [i.e., the Hasidim] despise the oral Torah completely and are interested only in the study of the Kabbalah."[21]

As is evident from the introduction to responsa *Zikhron Yosef,* the early Mithnagdim perceived a dangerous continuity between the Sabbatean mystical heresy and the Hasidic revival of interest in the Kabbalah.[22] Although there was some basis for the Mithnagdim's perception that the Hasidim were encouraging widespread interest in Kabbalistic notions, the intensity of their fear of popularized Kabbalistic study must be understood at least partially as a somewhat exaggerated consequence of the tragic rabbinic encounter with Sabbateanism and Frankism.[23]

The established rabbinate's consternation at the specter of a new sect of mystical enthusiasts eerily reminiscent of the Sabbateans also began, in the earlier generations, to manifest itself as a deep though respectful reticence toward Kabbalah, rooted in the unhappy recent experience with its potent antinomian capabilities. Ultimately, however, this initial circumspection was to evolve into an almost complete indifference to and ignorance of Jewish mysticism among the later Mithnagdim. For example, Jewish mysticism was at no time part of the curriculum of the yeshiva founded by Rabbi Hayyim of Volozhin or the many Lithuanian yeshivot it engendered. And the writings of many of Lithuania's greatest rabbinic scholars in the nineteenth century reflect a complete lack of interest in Kabbalah. Moreover, some important Mithnagdic intellectuals did not hesitate explicitly to proclaim their own ignorance of Jewish mysticism.[24] Still, the gradual elimination of Kabbalistic study and mystical interests from Lithuanian Jewish culture was a slow and almost imperceptible process. Indeed, in the earlier generations many of the leading Mithnagdic scholars continued to study the Kabbalah at least to the same degree that others may have feared it.

The Nature of the Mithnagdic Interest in Kabbalah

Fearful though they might be of the Hasidic popularization and "perversion" of the Kabbalah, the early Mithnagdim were in fact among its leading scholars. The GRA was arguably the greatest Kabbalist of his day, having authored many significant commentaries to the classical mystical texts and having personally undergone remarkable mystical experiences that included the creation of a golem and nightly visitations from a maggid. His students could not praise his mastery of the *Zohar* and other Kabbalistic works enough.[25] And a recent book on the GRA observed, with only slight exaggeration, that "the GRA wrote more extensively on the Kabbalah than all of his hasidic contemporaries combined. He was, in fact, the premier scholar of kabbalistic thought in his generation."[26]

Among the GRA's closest disciples was the important Mithnagdic Kabbalist R. Menahem Mendel of Shklov, who claimed to have studied Kabbalah under his direct tutelage.[27] R. Menahem Mendel in turn trained his students in the GRA's tradition of Kabbalistic interpretation. In Jerusalem, where he immigrated in 1808, he seems to have established a small circle of Lithuanian Mithnagdic Kabbalists who perpetuated the GRA's approach to mystical study. His most notable student in eastern Europe was the remarkable champion of Kabbalistic study and prolific author, R. Yitzhaq Isaac Haber. Haber was not only a great mystical scholar in the tradition of the GRA but also an outspoken champion of the authenticity of the Kabbalah, particularly the Lurianic version, and an advocate of the study of its sacred texts. His *Magen ve-Zina* is a passionate defense of the veracity of the Kabbalah, written primarily as a latter-day reaction to Aryeh Loeb de Modena's anti-Kabbalistic renaissance classic, *Ari Nohem.* In the introduction to his work, Haber declares that he will refute de Modena's polemic "by means of argumentation and thereby establish the foundations of the Kabbalah in accordance with that which I have been taught by my great teacher, R. Menahem Mendel of Shklov."[28] Even more pertinent to the present discussion is Haber's attempt to explicate and simplify the mystical doctrines of the GRA in his Kabbalistic primer, *Pithkhei She'arim.* According to the author's preface, the book is intended to "open the gates of wisdom and enlighten the eyes of those who crave to enter into the palace of truth and to visit in all of the corridors of the teachings of the ARI in order to satiate their souls and spirits with the fruit of the tree of life, which bestows eternal life upon all who taste of it. (The book) will also explicate all hidden and concealed mysteries which are to be found in the writings of the GRA."[29]

The GRA's most famous disciple, R. Hayyim of Volozhin, was also a serious scholar of the *Zohar* and the Lurianic Kabbalah, as his writings, most notably *Nefesh ha-Hayyim,* indicate. R. Hayyim's entire polemic with Hasidism was in fact rooted in his own, alternate understanding of mystical texts. In his introduction to the GRA's commentary to *Safra de-Zeniutha,* R. Hayyim affirms the GRA's total mastery and acceptance of the sanctity of Lurianic Kabbalah against the accusations of R. Shneur Zalman of Lyadi to the contrary.[30] He also provides a remarkable spiritual portrait of the GRA as a rigorously intellectualistic scholar of Kabbalah and a man of significant and unusual mystical experiences.[31] R. Hayyim, in turn, encouraged his disciples to engage daily in some form of Kabbalistic study, which he regarded as the highest of the meta-rabbinic disciplines: "Our Rabbi instructed that it is good to study the *Zohar* and *Shaarei Ora* in order to understand the intention of the *Zohar,*" he told them. "He also taught that Kabbalah begins where philosophy leaves off, and the Kabbalah of the ARI begins where the Kabbalah of Cordovero ends."[32]

R. Hayyim's deep erudition in Kabbalistic literature, as well as his approval of the publication of certain Kabbalistic classics, is evident from an approbation he wrote in 1804 for the publication of R. Hayyim Vital's *Arba Meoth Shekel Kessef.*[33] Some of R. Hayyim's select disciples retained a deep interest in Kabbalistic scholarship and wrote important mystical works and commentaries. There exists a significant manuscript of the early Kabbalistic work *Sefer ha-Bahir* with a commentary by R. Zadok Bloch, a leading student of R. Hayyim's in the yeshiva at Volozhin, and a warm approbation of the work by R. Hayyim himself.[34] R. Hayyim not only gave his approbation to some mystical writings but was actively involved in the publication of the Kabbalistic commentaries of the GRA.[35]

Among the most important disciples of R. Hayyim of Volozhin was the enigmatic ascetic R. Samuel of Dahlinov. At the end of his religious manual, *Minhath Shmuel,* he writes of the tremendous contemporary importance of belief in Kabbalah for a generation in which rationalism (i.e., the Haskalah) has been spreading. Although he is cautious in encouraging the study of the Kabbalah, R. Samuel insists upon an axiomatic acceptance of the postulate that the authority of the entire Torah and the reason for all its commandments are to be discovered in the texts of the Jewish mystical tradition.[36] Finally, in the subsequent generations of Mithnagdic history there emerged several important non-Hasidic Kabbalists, most notably the remarkably prolific Mithnagged R. Solomon Eliashiv, who authored the multivolume Kabbalistic treatise *Leshem Shevo ve-Ahlema* (Pietrekow, 1912), a work largely concerned with the elucidation of the GRA's mystical commentaries.

Nevertheless, although they were far from disinterested in the wisdom of

Kabbalah, from the beginning the Mithnagdim were extremely wary of what they perceived to be its reckless popularization at the hands of the Hasidic zaddikim. This Mithnagdic concern regarding the rapid spread of mysticism among those who were neither worthy of nor prepared for its study is typified in the warnings of the Kabbalistic enthusiast R. Samuel ben Eliezer of Kalvira, whose *Darkhei Noam* (1764) was one of only two published books ever to receive the written approbation of the GRA. Like the Hasidic R. Barukh of Kossov, R. Eliezer begins his book by affirming the tremendous importance of Kabbalistic study.[37] And like R. Barukh, he goes on to identify and refute the arguments of those "sects" that opposed the study of the Kabbalah. Nonetheless, for all of his enthusiasm concerning Jewish mysticism, as well as the sanctity of the Kabbalah and importance of its study for the redemption of the Jewish nation, R. Samuel is markedly more cautious than the Hasidim regarding the scope and appropriate method of its public instruction. He advocates Kabbalistic scholarship only for those few who are intellectually and religiously prepared for such study. Consequently, he is as adamant in warning against the potential abuses of mystical study as he is enthusiastic about its importance and sanctity. Specifically, R. Samuel condemns scholars who encourage Kabbalistic study on the part of those who are still deficient in classic rabbinic learning:

> There is an obligation for every Talmudic scholar to struggle with and to master the wisdom of the Kabbalah so that his service of God will be whole and his prayers complete. . . .
>
> But it seems to me that this only applies to one who has toiled and struggled and studied and learned under the tutelage of the great scholars in this field and to whom the secrets have been passed on orally from the mouth of an expert rabbi. . . . But, not like those who can be found in our own generation who, as soon as they are able to recite the names of the ten *sefiroth* by heart, and subsequent to their first, and very superficial, perusal of the books of the Kabbalah, immediately proclaim publicly that they have a great mastery of the Kabbalah. And then they are considered to be great mystics by the simple masses. Finally, each one of them prepares for himself a *siddur* with the *kavanoth* of the ARI, although they have not yet seen the light, neither in the holy books, nor through oral instruction.[38]

The reference at the end of this censure of the superficial popularizers of Kabbalah to the adoption of private prayer books based on the Lurianic rite clearly indicates that R. Samuel's critique is directed at the Hasidim of his day.[39]

Even R. Hayyim of Volozhin, a Kabbalist who, as already noted, approved of and personally sponsored the publication of many mystical writings, often simultaneously expressed serious caution regarding the contemporary popularization of Kabbalah, most specifically through the publication and careless distribution of mystical works. In his introduction to the GRA's *Perush al Kama Aggadoth* R. Hayyim wonders aloud about the propriety of publishing esoteric works: "A fractional testimony to the greatness of his [i.e., the GRA's] method in Torah is furnished by his very many holy works in the revealed Torah . . . and also in the hidden Torah, regarding which we do not really know if the hour for their publication has arrived, or if the time is right."[40]

Finally, the GRA himself, although personally deeply steeped in the Kabbalah and convinced that the messianic redemption was contingent upon its mastery by the Jews, warned against its premature study,[41] and he considered the practice of *kabbalah ma'asith* (practical Kabbalah) by anyone other than the most highly accomplished scholar to be very dangerous.[42]

R. Phinehas of Polotsk on Kabbalah and Its Study

A similar ambivalence toward Kabbalah, namely, an acceptance of its intrinsic holiness and superiority over other Judaic disciplines along with a reticence regarding its public dissemination, can be found throughout the writings of R. Phinehas of Polotsk. At the very beginning of his commentary to the Psalms, *Midrash Hakhamim*, Phinehas argues that although the Kabbalah is the highest form of Jewish knowledge, its mastery by man is not possible in this world:

> It is written, "Only in the Torah of God is his desire, and in *his* Torah he labors . . ." regarding the two parts of the Torah: the hidden part, which is referred to as the "Torah of God" and which man should desire; and "his [i.e., man's] Torah," which is the revealed part in which man should meditate day and night. . . . "He is like a tree planted between two streams of water"; the "two streams" refers to the two parts of the Torah, which are compared to water. He shall merit both parts, as the Sages have taught: "He who studies Torah in this world, merits to study Torah in the world to come," for there shall he attain it and benefit from its goodness . . . this is the meaning of "which yields its fruit in its due season," that is, in the world to come.[43]

There are, in other words, two Torahs—the Torah of God (the esoteric disciplines, including the Kabbalah) and the Torah of man (the exoteric disciplines, most notably, rabbinics).[44] While mastery of the former is man's ultimate goal, the latter must be his total preoccupation in his this-worldly existence. The reward for such preoccupation is knowledge of the esoteric Kabbalah, which is reserved for the world to come. Throughout his works R.

Phinehas of Polotsk warns of the dangers of mystical study by the uninitiated. He views the Hasidic emphasis upon Kabbalistic learning and mystical practice as direct threats to the preeminence of classical rabbinic scholarship and normative Halakhic observance. The temptation to turn directly to Kabbalah without sufficient grounding in conventional rabbinics is one of the lures of the evil instinct associated with Hasidism, against which Phinehas polemicizes extensively in *Kether Torah:*

> When the evil instinct tires of seducing you in this manner, it will try to tempt you differently, saying to you that there is no greater good in this world than the study of the wisdom of the Kabbalah, for it is the only true wisdom that will bring man close to mystical communion with God. . . . Be very careful that [the evil instinct] does not prepare a wine for you before its time, God forbid, or feed you unripe fruits, which will set your teeth on edge. Remember this central principle: there is nothing that destroys evil as well as the in-depth study of Talmud and nothing that brings one as close to mystical communion as the study of the Kabbalah.
>
> Therefore, a man must first destroy evil by toiling very diligently and with all his might, first in the study of the oral Torah for many years. He must also despise completely all worldly pleasures. Only then can he approach the altar of God and partake of the fruit of the tree of life with a humbled heart, and eat, and live eternally. But if he does not follow this procedure, he is the master of falsehood.[45]

R. Phinehas argues that there are two absolute prerequisites for entry into the realm of Kabbalistic wisdom: total erudition in and mastery of the exoteric disciplines of Judaism (i.e., rabbinic literature) and personal ethical perfection. Clearly alluding to the Hasidim, R. Phinehas argues that any attempts by a person who has not achieved an unusual degree of both scholarly and ethical perfection to master the texts of Kabbalah or to achieve *devekuth* (mystical attachment to God) are completely illegitimate, even dangerous.

Although he cautions against the premature study of the Kabbalah, nowhere does R. Phinehas question its inherent authority or intrinsic worth. On the contrary, he concedes that mystical knowledge is helpful, if not absolutely necessary, for the attainment of true *devekuth*. Throughout his commentaries he also affirms many of the fundamental Lurianic notions about the cosmic effects of Halakhic observance. However, he insists that while the fulfillment of every *mitzvah* automatically achieves great results in the supernal spheres, the specific roles and intentions (i.e., the *kavanoth*) of these *mitzvoth* remain hidden from the average man and are readily known only to

God. Therefore, one should content himself with the meticulous observance of the law, confident that the cosmic effects will follow automatically. For as Phinehas says, "God is in the heavens, but you are only here on earth, such that only he knows the heavenly root and purpose of each of these things; but you are here on earth and can only know the practical aspect. Therefore, let your words be few and do not question the divine roots and reasons."[46]

Similar to his attitude on the specific question of God's immanence, then, R. Phinehas considers Jewish esoterica generally to be a sacred discipline whose total mastery is not humanly possible and whose partial mastery is possible for only a very small religious and intellectual elite. By simultaneously accepting the advantages of Kabbalistic study for the attainment of the highest religious experience and yet denying the possibility of an even partially correct understanding to all but the most exceptional members of his generation, R. Phinehas is engaging, as did R. Solomon of Chelm before him, in a double-edged polemic against both Hasidic study of the Kabbalah and mystical experience.

This respectful reticence toward the Kabbalah is evident throughout R. Phinehas's writings. While Phinehas often refers obliquely to Kabbalistic notions, his sources are usually the secondary, popular writings of the later mystics, most commonly the biblical commentaries of R. Moses Alshikh. Only rarely does he cite primary Kabbalistic classics directly, and even when he does, it is often only to warn against a preoccupation with mysticism.[47] On one occasion he refers to a passage from the *Zohar* that he "saw," and he follows that "citation" with the following remarkable admission: "Look it up! For I did not have in my possession a copy of the *Zohar* at the time of this writing."[48]

Whereas a nonbeliever in Kabbalah would never cite the *Zohar* as an authority, by the same token a true devotee of mystical study would not so readily admit that his library lacked so basic a text. Not only is R. Phinehas unashamed to confess to the absence of the mystical classics from the shelves of his library but at times he openly confesses his own ignorance of fundamental esoteric concepts. He routinely defers the very possibility for the attainment of such knowledge to the posthumous life of the next world. Thus, for example, in explaining his reluctance to explicate some obscure, messianic verses in the book of Job, Phinehas pleads ignorance:

These are hints at great secrets and wonderful mysteries that are hidden and concealed from our eyes . . . all written in esoteric language; therefore, I have chosen to withdraw my hand from attempting to comment in any detail on these verses. For regarding this it is written: "Seek not what is too difficult for you." I have not yet eaten of the leviathan, nor have I ascertained its taste, nor perceived the secrets hidden therein. The Lord will enlighten us in the messianic feast that he shall host for the righteous in the future; then will the gates of knowledge be opened to us.[49]

Occasionally R. Phinehas's reticence toward the popularization of the esoteric takes a distinctly polemical, anti-Hasidic tone. He reinterprets the general admonitions in Proverbs against materialistic cravings in order to warn against the dangers of the Hasidic popularization of mystical concepts. Phinehas specifically attacks the zaddikim who deceive their listeners into accepting their distortions of Kabbalah:

"Put a knife to your throat," that is, to yourself! And do not enter into the greatest of dangers. For even if the rabbi explains the words of the Kabbalah with rationales and explications through the use of allegories, as they do in our day, for they disguise the Kabbalah before the ignorant masses with the clothing of the widow, which is as black as the raven, and they pervert the meaning of the Torah and subvert the words of the living God. . . .

"Use your wisdom to show restraint": that is, restrain yourself from that which lies beyond your wisdom for, "Seek not what is too difficult for you." But so long as you stand before that rabbi, his words will retain the illusion of authenticity.[50]

Phinehas was especially worried about the careless teaching of Kabbalah and advised those who were in the possession of its secrets to exercise maximum discretion.[51]

Many of his contemporaries shared R. Phinehas's ambivalence toward Kabbalah. R. Hayyim of Volozhin's younger brother, Zalman, was reputed to have been a remarkable Kabbalist. His biographer, the Belorussian maggid Ezekiel Faivel of Dretzhyn, enthusiastically praised his unusual mastery of the mystical literature. Nonetheless, these praises are significantly tempered by extensive cautions against premature study and a polemic against those who neglect the Talmud in order to turn immediately to Kabbalah: "Those who have abandoned the fountain of life, the Babylonian and Jerusalem Talmuds, to dig other wells and who arrogantly presume that they have seen the wisdom of the *Zohar* and that the gates of the Kabbalah have been opened to them; I have much to say about this matter, but just as it is a *mitzvah* to say that which will be heeded, so too is it a *mitzvah* not to say that which will be ignored."[52]

The same author cites extensively from R. Jacob Emden's critical textual glosses to the *Zohar* in order to illustrate the complexities and pitfalls of

Kabbalistic study by all but the most eminently prepared, such rare figures as the GRA and R. Zalman of Volozhin. All others are warned not even to attempt any form of esoteric learning before "first studying with the Sages all of the sections of the revealed Torah . . . and filling one's belly with meat and wine." Even then, however, one should not approach the Kabbalah "before he has reached the middle years of his life and has proven to be victorious in the battle against the evil instinct and has become purified through the years."[53]

This same respectful but highly reticent posture toward the study of Jewish mysticism was shared by still more of R. Phinehas's contemporaries. In his ethical will, *Beth Avraham*, R. Abraham Danzig warns his own children to abstain from engaging in any mystical study before they are religiously and academically prepared for it. He alludes to certain "evildoers"—presumably the Hasidim—who despise rabbinic scholarship and turn instead directly and prematurely to the Kabbalah:

> I decree upon you, by the authority of the heavenly angels, that you should not push yourselves to study Kabbalah before you have filled yourselves with Talmud and codes and before you know the way of God, how to perform all of his commandments, and before you have become true God-fearers who occupy themselves only with the Torah. Only then is the one who merits this [i.e., Kabbalah] considered to be fortunate. But be not like the evildoers who despise the study of our holy Gemara, which is our very lifeline; for it was upon the basis of the content of the Gemara that God established a covenant with us and gave us the Torah. Cursed are the evildoers who say that there is no benefit from the study of the Gemara. Quite the contrary, it is the gate of the Lord, for it is impossible for any person to enter into the service of God without the study of the Talmud and codes. Still, fortunate is the one who merits both of these [i.e., Talmudics and Kabbalah].[54]

This attitude toward the premature study of the Kabbalah was universalized and legislated normatively in Danzig's code, *Hayyei Adam*: "A person should not study the wisdom of the Kabbalah before he has filled his belly with Talmud and codes, and even then, only if he is a true God-fearer and a great scholar who spends all of his time studying the Torah. Otherwise, it is forbidden."[55]

For the purpose of protecting the Kabbalah from popular abuse, the traditional rabbinic division of the Torah into its esoteric *(nistar)* and exoteric *(nigleh)* disciplines was vigilantly maintained by all of the Mithnagdim. The Mithnagdim maintained, with a unified voice, that one cannot even begin to ponder the *nistar* before having thoroughly mastered the *nigleh*.

The Causes for Mithnagdic Fears of Premature Kabbalism

A striking contrast to the legislation by R. Abraham Danzig of the widespread Mithnagdic caution regarding the study of the mysteries of the Kabbalah can be found in the equivalent legislative section of the contemporary rabbinic code of the Ḥabad Hasidim, the *Shulhan Arukh* of R. Shneur Zalman of Lyadi. Commenting on the Talmud's pedagogic counsel to divide one's study schedule evenly into three broad areas of interest—the Bible, the Mishna, and the Talmud—R. Shneur Zalman liberally expands each of these, thereby including the study of mysticism in the category of Talmud: "The homiletical interpretation of the Bible and the Aggada are included under the category of 'Mishna,' and the wisdom of the Kabbalah is reckoned as part of the third category, which is dedicated to Talmud."[56]

By dividing the disciplines of the Torah thus, R. Shneur Zalman eliminates the critical distinction between *nigleh* and *nistar* in order to legitimize and encourage the study of the Kabbalah together with the pursuit of other, rabbinic disciplines. The in-depth, analytical pursuit of Talmudic scholarship, which will become the exclusive concern of the advanced student of the Torah, should include, according to R. Shneur Zalman, "the wisdom of the Kabbalah and the knowledge of God." The advanced study of the Aggadoth, moreover, will allow man to " know God and to cling to his ways."[57] In fact, according to a recent study of the early development of the Ḥabad school, the intellectualization of the Hasidic approach to Kabbalah, coupled with a concerted and systematic effort to "translate" its doctrines in order to facilitate and spread its study by rabbinic scholars and the simple folk alike, was R. Shneur Zalman's distinguishing achievement as a Hasidic leader.[58]

A significant part of R. Shneur Zalman's classic mystical work *Likutei Amarim: Tanya* was intended for a wider readership than the elite circle of mystics who had held a virtual monopoly on Kabbalistic learning in the period prior to the emergence of Hasidism. The appropriately named section of the *Tanya*, "Sefer Beynonim" (The book of the intermediates), was directed at those who, while not having reached the stature of the zaddik, had managed to achieve a conventional level of righteousness (defined as freedom from a state of sinfulness) and was composed as a manual in Kabbalah for the uninitiated but pious Jew. In the introduction to the *Tanya* the author addresses himself to the "entirety of the people of Israel . . . from elders to young children" and, in much the same spirit as his predecessor R. Barukh of Kossov, rebukes those who attempt deliberately to keep the "knowledge of God" away from the Jewish masses.[59] The very idea of dedicating a Kabbalistic work such as the *Tanya*, which deals with mystical, cosmogonic, and theogonic issues in addition to more conventional ethical issues, to all of the common folk was, of course, absolute anathema to the Mithnagdim.

The conviction that the widespread popular study of the Kabbalah was imperative in order that all Jews attain "knowledge of God" became even more pronounced and impassioned in the writings of R. Shneur Zalman's most important disciple, R. Aaron Ha-Levi of Starosselje,[60] and his son, Dov Ber of Lubavitch. In the lengthy introduction to R. Aaron Ha-Levi's most important and systematic mystical work, *Shaarei ha-Yihud veha-Emuna,* published in Shklov in 1820 as an extensive commentary to the third section of R. Shneur Zalman's *Tanya,* the classic rabbinic notion that the continual historical decline of the generations mandates increasing circumspection regarding the dissemination of esoterica is completely and radically reversed.[61] R. Aaron of Starosselje argues that the very opposite is the case: that the ongoing spiritual decline in each new generation, which has become so painfully manifest in his own day, demands a single most effective antidote, the increased instruction of the Kabbalah to the masses of Israel.[62] Extending a notion that was originally found in R. Moses Cordovero's famous panegyric to Kabbalistic study, *Or Naarav,*[63] R. Aaron pleads at length that the only possible route to the salvation of his "orphaned generation" is via the widest possible proliferation of mystical study and knowledge.[64] In his brief intellectual genealogy of the then nascent Hasidic movement, R. Aaron suggests that the primary goal of its leaders, from the BESHT down to his own teacher, R. Shneur Zalman of Lyadi, was always to simplify and spread the wisdom of the Kabbalah to the widest possible Jewish audience. This view of the crucial role of Hasidism in the popularization of Jewish mysticism was, of course, agreed (and frowned) upon by the leading Mithnagdim. R. Aaron's great enthusiasm for the spread of mystical understanding, as well as his stated commitment to continue the work begun by the BESHT in simplifying and popularizing the mystical, monistic teachings of his own mentor, R. Shneur Zalman,[65] stand in sharp contrast to the extreme caution manifested by R. Phinehas of Polotsk and his Mithnagdic contemporaries. They also provide the context for the expressed Mithnagdic opposition to mystical study and go a long way toward explaining their fears of the current Hasidic propagation of Kabbalah.[66]

The extensive efforts of R. Dov Ber, the second rabbi of the Ḥabad movement, in furthering the Hasidic task of spreading Kabbalistic knowledge to ever wider echelons of Jewish society are reflected especially in his various mystical manuals, each addressed to a different sector of the community. As Naftali Loewenthal has illustrated in his detailed study of the writings of Dov Ber, his pervasive goal was the "translation" and transmission of the once esoteric body of Jewish mystical knowledge and practice to all Jews.[67] Both R.

Shneur Zalman and R. Dov Ber seemed to believe that their work of spreading Kabbalah as widely as possible was no more than the continuation of the original goal of the founder of the Hasidic movement, R. Israel Baal Shem Tov. That perception was based on the famous letter of the BESHT to his brother-in-law, Gershon of Kutov, in which the messiah is depicted as proclaiming to the BESHT that he will arrive only after "your teachings are publicized and revealed in the world."[68] In the Ḥabad tradition, the enterprise of rendering Kabbalah accessible to the masses of Israel is perceived as the fulfillment of the original and quintessential goal of Hasidism.

Of course, as with virtually all matters, there was no monolithic consensus in the Hasidic camp regarding the need for, or even the propriety of, spreading Kabbalistic study. Significant notes of caution were sounded by certain Hasidic rabbis from time to time, and some even opposed outright the study of specific mystical works. In the case of Ḥabad, R. Shneur Zalman's efforts to broaden the circle of students of Kabbalah were largely the cause of his famous dispute with his colleague and fellow disciple of Dov Ber of Mezeritch, the Belorussian Hasidic master R. Abraham of Kalisk.[69] R. Abraham's opposition to Ḥabad's intellectual approach to mysticism and his emphasis on mystical piety and simple faith were perpetuated in subsequent generations by the Lithuanian masters of the Lechovitch and Slonim dynasties.[70] Another important advocate of circumspection in this matter was Abraham Joshua Heschel of Opatow, who is said to have opposed the publication of even the most elementary Kabbalistic works, such as the *Zohar*.[71]

There was also a tendency in early Hasidic writings to distinguish between the theurgic Kabbalah of the ARI and the attainment of a mystical state by following the mystical teachings of R. Moshe Cordovero and his school. As a result, one often finds notes of caution specifically regarding the study of Lurianic Kabbalah by Hasidic mystical enthusiasts, who nonetheless favored the widespread practice of mystical ecstasy.[72] Nevertheless, the overall consensus of the leading Hasidic masters of the first three generations was to advocate at least elementary Kabbalistic study and to encourage as much mystical experience as one could reasonably attain.

I have argued that the basic disagreement between the Hasidim and Mithnagdim regarding the Kabbalah and its study was most clearly reflected in their divergent attitudes toward the relative status of the revealed and esoteric parts of the Torah. In order to protect the *nistar* from vulgarization and popular abuse, the Mithnagdim stressed the importance of maintaining this division of the Torah. A remarkably bold obfuscation of the sharp lines drawn by the rabbis to divide *nigleh* and *nistar* is found in the collection of Hasidic teachings by Meshulam Faivush of Zaborocz, *Yosher Divrei Emeth*:

I have heard from the holy mouth of R. Menahem Mendel [of Premyszlan], of blessed memory, that *nistar* is anything that a man is unable to communicate to his neighbor, such as the taste of a given food, which one cannot possibly relate to another who has never tasted of it. . . . So, too, the love and fear of the Creator, blessed be his name, cannot be communicated from one to the other—this, then, is called *nistar.*

As for those who refer to the wisdom of the Kabbalah as *nistar,* what kind of *nistar* is that supposed to be? For is it not true that anyone who wishes to study the Kabbalah has the books ready before him. And if he is unable to understand the books, he is simply an ignoramus, and for such a person, the Gemara and the Tosafoth are also called *nistar.* Rather, the concept of *nistar* as referred to in the *Zohar* and the writings of the ARI is the ability to achieve *devekuth.*[73]

The strict rabbinic division of the disciplines of the Torah into the esoteric and exoteric realms is here severely undermined. With this original, bold, and highly subjective definition of the distinction between *nigleh* and *nistar* as corresponding to the difference between intellectual comprehension via study, on the one hand, and mystical experience, on the other, the very foundation for the prohibition against certain forbidden areas of study disappears. In other words, if no entire discipline can objectively be classified as *nistar,* then the very idea of a forbidden, or esoteric, field within the Torah is rendered nonsensical.

Conclusion

There were two approaches to the mastery of the Kabbalah in the Hasidic camp. On the one hand, there were the intellectualists, most notably R. Shneur Zalman and his disciples, who strongly urged the study of Kabbalistic texts and the comprehension of theosophic concepts by the masses of Israel. On the other hand, there were those who encouraged, not Kabbalistic study, but rather the pursuit of mystical experience, most importantly *devekuth.* Both approaches were entirely unacceptable to the Mithnagdim, who warned bitterly against the dangers of widespread Kabbalistic study as well as ecstatic mystical activity. These warnings were not, however, motivated by any disbelief on the part of the Mithnagdim in the theoretical wisdom or intrinsic truth of the Kabbalah; rather, they were motivated by a profound conviction that its comprehension was beyond the capacity of the vast majority of contemporary Jews. This judgment was rooted in the Mithnagdim's pessimistic assessment of the spiritual capacities of man. They believed that whereas in the earlier generations of Jewish history the secrets of the cosmos and the mysteries of the Godhead may have been accessible to many, as a

result of the enduring exile and ensuing decline of the generations, the un-
alterable condition of the contemporary Jew was one of severe religious and
cognitive limitations. Given his circumscribed capacities for theosophical
insight, it was not only pretentious but also harmful for man to try to exceed
his natural, limited condition.

The discord between the Hasidim and the Mithnagdim on the availability
of Kabbalistic knowledge to the Jews of their day may be vividly illustrated by
contrasting the views of R. Phinehas of Polotsk and R. Shneur Zalman of
Lyadi regarding the nature of the wisdom contained in the classic rabbinic
homiletical literature, the Talmudic Aggadoth. Both R. Phinehas and R.
Shneur Zalman agreed that the Aggadoth of both the Talmud and the Midrash included much esoteric wisdom. The conclusions they drew from this
shared assumption could, however, hardly be more diametrically opposed. R.
Shneur Zalman believed that it was obligatory to study the Aggadic literature
in great depth precisely in order to uncover its Kabbalistic secrets. In his
Shulhan Arukh he says that the mature student of the Torah should devote
most of his time to the high-level analysis of the Talmud, including its Aggadic portions, in order to be able to master "the wisdom of the Kabbalah
and the knowledge of God," which is often couched in the esoteric language
of the rabbis.[74]

R. Phinehas of Polotsk takes the opposite stand. According to him, the
inherent mystical wisdom of the Midrash has deliberately been couched in
esoteric language in order to ensure that the average man would not be able
to discover its secrets. Moreover, the attempt to uncover those mysteries that
have deliberately been hidden is not only futile in most cases; it is also
impious and potentially destructive of true faith:

> You must know that the Sages intended to hide the Kabbalistic matters that are
> contained in the words of the Sages in the Aggadoth. They therefore spoke in
> parables and metaphors and with the use of allusions, for "It is for the glory of
> God that one conceals this matter" (Proverbs 25:2). This was most definitely
> their true intention, without any doubt whatsoever. I am confounded by the
> man who desires to explicate the closed words of the Sages for didactic, moraliz-
> ing purposes. . . . For he must certainly allow that there is in the words of the
> Aggadoth a certain esoteric element that only the few erudite persons may
> know, and only the enlightened ones are able to decipher its message.[75]

R. Shneur Zalman and R. Phinehas differed here neither on the nature,
sanctity, and status of the Kabbalah nor on its literary sources within the
Jewish tradition. What divided them was not different levels of reverence for

Jewish mysticism but rather their respective, clearly opposing attitudes toward man. It was not the case that the Hasid was a mystic and the Mithnagged was a skeptic, or a rationalist who rejected the mystical lore outright; nor was it that the Mithnagdim were Lurianists who focused on Kabbalistic theurgy, whereas the Hasidim were Cordoverans whose interest was directed at ecstatic mystical experience. It was, quite plainly, that the Hasidic masters were deliberately and insistently optimistic about the potential man possesses to attain, in this life, significant knowledge of the divine mysteries, whereas the Mithnagdim remained thoroughly pessimistic and skeptical regarding any such spiritual or cognitive possibilities. The early Hasidim ceaselessly tried to break the barriers and obfuscate the divisions that had placed the Kabbalah outside the realm of widespread Jewish learning and ordinary human endeavor. At the same time, the Mithnagdim struggled valiantly to retain and, in reaction to Hasidism, reinforce those very obstructions. The Hasidim encouraged the masses, via the simplification and wide dissemination of Kabbalistic doctrine, to aspire to the intimate "knowledge of God" and to experience union with him. For the Mithnagdim however, man's goal in this life must be far more modest. They believed that the way to attain piety was assiduously to study conventional rabbinic texts and faithfully to obey the commandments of the Torah; in other words, to heed the basic requirements of the faith, without any heroic attempts at acquiring a profound knowledge of God or understanding the mysteries of creation. As far as the Mithnagdim were concerned, the attainment of Kabbalistic erudition or mystical union with God was possible, if at all, only in the world to come.[76]

Chapter 3

MITHNAGDIC
PRAYER

One of the most distinctive features of the early Hasidic movement was the innovative form of mystical prayer it prescribed for its followers. In the eyes of the contemporary established rabbinate the Hasidim's emphasis on prayer and their strangely ecstatic behavior during it were the most obvious and offensive deviations of the new "sect" from normative practice. In fact, no issues feature more prominently in the polemical literature than that of the Hasidic inversion of the traditional place of prayer within the hierarchy of religious values and the perversion of both the liturgical text and the manner of its recitation.

The Mithnagdic critique of Hasidic prayer was expressed on three distinct levels: social, legal, and theological.

1. The social critique of Hasidic prayer was engendered by the threat to the traditional Jewish social order inherent in Hasidism's establishment of separate houses of worship and the publication and use of their own *siddur*, or prayer book, based on the mystical traditions of R. Isaac Luria.[1]

2. The legal critique of Hasidic prayer centered around the widespread neglect of the prescribed times for the three daily services.[2] In addition, the execution of bizarre bodily movements and enthusiastic gestures, as well as the Hasidim's uneven and often clangorous recitation of the prayers, were seen as violations of the law requiring sober, silent devotion and a respectful composure during worship.[3]

3. From a broader theological perspective, the Mithnagdim found fault with the Hasidic inversion of the traditional religious hierarchy of values within Judaism, namely, the favoring of prayer over study. In addition, they condemned what they perceived as Hasidism's neglect of the literal meaning of the liturgy and its attempt to engage in a highly enthusiastic form of mystical worship.

Of course, the social and Halakhic critiques of Hasidic prayer addressed only the external manifestations of Hasidism's deeper, revolutionary approach to Jewish worship. At the root of these symptoms lay a belief in ecstatic worship as a potent vehicle for the attainment of a mystical state as well as the channeling of magical powers. It was precisely the novel Hasidic understanding of the fundamental nature and main objectives of divine worship that necessitated separate houses of worship and a distinct *siddur*. It also underlay the seemingly bizarre external forms that Hasidic prayer often took. Two basic ideological issues therefore form the basis for the Hasidic transformation of prayer that so antagonized the contemporary rabbinic authorities: (1) the status of prayer in Hasidism's altered hierarchy of religious values, particularly vis-à-vis Torah scholarship; and (2) the nature and goals of properly intended prayer (i.e., the definition of *kavana* and its effects).

The Hasidic Inversion of the Hierarchy of Prayer and Study

A Talmudic story illustrates the respective places of prayer and Torah study in the conventional rabbinic hierarchy of values:

> Raba observed Rabbi Hamnuna prolonging his prayers. Said he: "They forsake eternal life [i.e., Torah study] and occupy themselves instead with temporal life [i.e., petitional prayer]." He held that the times for prayer and for study are defined and (to be kept) distinct from each other. Rabbi Jeremiah was sitting before Rabbi Zera engaged in study. As it was growing late for the service, R. Jeremiah was making haste to adjourn. Thereupon R. Zera applied to him the verse (Prov. 28:9), "He that turneth his ear away from hearing the law, even his prayers are an abomination."[4]

In the classic rabbinic system of values, then, prayer is second in importance to Torah study. Although prayer consists in man's petitioning God for temporal sustenance, only Torah scholarship secures him eternal life. This preference given to study over prayer is one specific manifestation of the older, general rabbinic appraisal of study as being superior in value to all of the *mitzvoth ma'asiyoth,* or practical religious obligations.[5] As early as Tannaitic times rabbis assembled at Lydda had decided that "study is greater than [religious] action, for study leads to deed."[6] Although there were some significant dissenting views both in the classical and the early medieval period,[7] the general consensus remained in normative rabbinic thought in the five centuries following the redaction of the Talmud, up to the end of the millennium.

With the rise of various forms of mystical Judaism, beginning in the late twelfth century calls were heard for the replacement of the primacy of scholarship with an elevated form of mystical prayer. By the sixteenth century the voices of the mystics had become quite bold. One such voice was that of R. Moses ibn Makhir. In daring contradiction to the Talmudic tradition, Ibn Makhir writes in his mystical-liturgical work *Seder ha-Yom,* a book that was to enjoy great popularity among the Hasidim: "When the time for the afternoon prayer arrives, one must break off immediately from one's work or Torah study. . . . Do not say: 'He who is engaged in [the performance of] one *mitzvah* is exempt from another *mitzvah.* Behold, I am learning; why should I interrupt my study?' This is no argument. . . . For in this exile, God has nothing but the four cubits of *prayer.*"[8] Not only does Ibn Makhir's advice contradict that of the above-quoted Talmudic sages but it is in striking and apparently deliberate contrast to the very well known Talmudic epigram, "Since the destruction of the Temple, God has in His world nothing but the four cubits of *Halakhah.*"[9]

The reason for the Kabbalists' elevation of the status of prayer within the religious hierarchy of values lies in its changed nature and status in the Jewish mystical tradition. In contrast to earlier, rabbinic prayer, which was essentially petitionary and centered upon the temporal needs of the individual, in the Kabbalistic tradition prayer was accorded far greater importance. Whereas a small number of Jewish mystics viewed prayer as a vehicle for the attainment of an exalted spiritual state, leading to mystical union with God, most Kabbalists, particularly those of the Lurianic school, believed that the text of the liturgy was endowed with cosmic significance, that the power of its words and formulas contributed to the goal of universal *tikkun,* or the rectification of heavenly imperfections originating in the cosmogonic catastrophe, by achieving the reunification of the shattered divine name.[10]

By according it cosmic, theurgic powers the Kabbalists raised prayer to the very center of religious life. Prayer, for the Jewish mystics, was much more than an expression of thanksgiving or petitions to God for earthly material blessings. For them the liturgy had hidden, exalted intentions and powers far beyond those suggested by its literal meaning. The prayers, as understood by the Kabbalists, were concerned more with the rectification of the Divine, the unity of God's name, and the correction of flaws in the supernal world of the *sefiroth* than with the petty emotions and mundane desires of man. The words and letters of prayer were consequently extended far beyond their literal signification and endowed by the Kabbalists with remarkable, supernatural powers. Interestingly, this resulted not only in a greater general attention to and interest in prayer but also in an increased vigilance regarding its detailed laws and regulations. Endowed as it now was with mystical and theurgic powers, the exact text of the liturgy was accorded canonical sanctity, and the precise times for the various services were vigilantly observed. Hence Ibn Makhir's reversal of Talmudic priorities regarding study and prayer. For, given prayer's new significance, any deviation, however slight, from any of the regulations regarding the text or times of worship represented a possible frustration of its potentially cosmic effects.

The new importance accorded to prayer notwithstanding, the indispensability of *Talmud Torah* as a supreme personal religious obligation generally remained unchallenged. While prayer may have been perceived as having greater cosmic influence than study, the two were not usually seen as direct competitors, for each retained a distinct purpose. Whereas the liturgy, uttered with the proper intentions, might help one achieve cosmic perfection, Torah study remained the most important subjective personal religious obligation and, as such, demanded most of the faithful Jew's time. Continuous study was still considered a key to personal spiritual perfection, and Torah scholarship the ultimate mark of individual achievement. Furthermore, in a paradoxical way, the mystics' obsessive concern with the exact formulation and limited time frame of the prayers prevented them from taking up time that might otherwise be devoted to study.

It was only in Hasidic thought that the mystical elevation of the status of prayer began to come into serious, direct conflict with that of Torah study. For the early Hasidic masters were more concerned with the personal, mystical potentialities of prayer than with its cosmic powers. As several scholars have already noted, Hasidism shifted the emphasis in Kabbalistic prayer away from the cosmic and theurgic and toward the personal and mystical.[11] For the early Hasidic masters, then, prayer, and not Torah study, became the central vehicle for the attainment of knowledge of God and, ultimately, mystical communion.

It is reported of the founder of Hasidism that "the upper world was revealed to him [i.e., the BESHT], not because he had studied much Talmud and commentaries, but because of the prayers he had always uttered with the greatest intensity."[12] In contrast, the Mithnagdim affirmed that it was precisely the study of "Talmud and commentaries" that remained man's most exalted personal religious pursuit, and the sole means for attaining knowledge of the divine will.[13] According to them, if the "upper worlds" were to be at all revealed to any man, it would be only on account of his exceptional devotion to rabbinic scholarship.

The BESHT's precedent of placing prayer at the very center of personal spiritual achievement was continued and intensified by virtually all of his students.[14] But the elevation of prayer to the pinnacle of religious life was most pronounced in the school of the Great Maggid, Dov Ber of Mezeritch.[15] In the thought of R. Dov Ber the traditional nature and goals of prayer became radically transformed. In contrast with rabbinic prayer, which was essentially petitionary in nature, and unlike earlier Kabbalistic prayer, in which the text of the liturgy was directed primarily toward cosmic *tikkun,* Hasidic prayer, particularly in the school of the Maggid, had very different, almost opposite, goals, namely, the annihilation of the individual ego and its needs and personal mystical union with the Shekhinah, or the divine presence. Thus, not only did the literal meaning of the text of the liturgy become unimportant but the exact formulas and prescribed times for *tefilla* came to be largely ignored. The words and letters of the liturgy were isolated (or "atomized") by the Hasidic masters and focused upon, not for their inherent literal meaning or their technical theurgic intentions and powers, but rather as vehicles for ecstatic religious experience. Through spiritual concentration on both the forms and the oral sounds of the words of prayer the Hasidim sought mystical union with the divine.[16]

The Hasidic approach to worship therefore inherently rejected the primacy of both the literal rabbinic view of prayer as man's thanksgiving or personal petition to God and the Lurianic view of the text of prayer as a theurgic blueprint for cosmic *tikkun.*[17] In Hasidism, contemplative, mystical prayer became man's most important personal religious obligation, upon which no limitations, temporal or literal, might reasonably be set. There was in early Hasidic literature, as a consequence of this subjective, mystical approach to prayer, a clear tendency to favor and give priority to the act of worship over all other religious duties, including the formerly supreme obligation of Torah study.[18]

The Great Maggid's disciple R. Shneur Zalman of Lyadi, although accurately renowned in the context of the Hasidic intellectual history as a champion of both rabbinic and "sober" mystical scholarship who criticized the Hasidic followers of his contemporary R. Abraham of Kalisk for their unruly displays of ecstasy during prayer, also rose to the defense of the Hasidic emphasis upon prolonged and enthusiastic prayer. In his letter to R. Alexander of Shklov he encouraged him to withstand the criticisms and pressures of the Mithnagdim, who, he claimed, "mock and ridicule anyone who desires to serve God in truth with the service of the heart, that is prayer, for they champion only Torah study and charity . . . and they have declared war on prayer, insisting that we should pray only like them—quickly and without any bodily movement or raising of the voice."[19] Against this alleged Mithnagdic sacrifice of enthusiastic prayer upon the altar of sober scholarship, R. Shneur

Zalman prompted his disciples to be vigilant in maintaining the supreme status of prayer, which, he argued, was the only effective means to attain closeness with God.

The Mithnagdic Response

The Mithnagdim were not slow to react to this Hasidic spiritualization of prayer and the attendant reversal of the traditional rabbinic order of religious values. They viewed the Hasidic approach to prayer as both a rebellion against the supremacy of *Talmud Torah* and a transformation of the status, essential nature, and very purpose of prayer. In the polemical literature the most common complaint against the Hasidim relates, in one form or another, to the peculiar style and nature of their worship. The Mithnagdim were particularly troubled by the general Hasidic emphasis upon the centrality of prayer and the resulting subversion of the religious supremacy of scholarship.

In the 1782 letter of excommunication from Vilna the Hasidim are accused of proclaiming that one must not, "God forbid, waste one's time in the study of Torah, but rather [focus] on the divine service, i.e., prayer."[20]

Even the elite circle of non-Hasidic Kabbalists in Vilna who engaged regularly in mystical prayer could not tolerate the Hasidic form of worship and blamed the protracted nature and the enthusiastic mannerisms of their prayers with "distracting the people from the study of the Torah."[21] Most disturbing to the Mithnagdim was the sheer amount of time the Hasidim spent in prayer, at the expense of study: "They prolong their prayers until the sun is already in the middle of the heavens [i.e., noon], and they thus destroy the very [time] balance of Torah study and prayer that has been established by our holy ancestors, for they try to reach the heavens."[22]

Beginning with the Gaon of Vilna, all of the important Mithnagdic authorities asserted emphatically that *Talmud Torah* was of greater religious weight than *tefilla*. The GRA, employing the exact terminology of the Talmud, maintained that unlike prayer, which is concerned only with man's temporal needs, Torah study is the sole guarantor of eternal life. The GRA not only reaffirmed the classical rabbinic attitude regarding the primacy of scholarship; he boldly contrasted the limited nature of (petitionary) prayer with the unbounded powers of study:

Our rabbis have interpreted this verse as referring to deep devotion in prayer. They said, "What is its cure [i.e., for unanswered prayers]? The study of Torah."

This is because prayer is only concerned with matters of this world, and is therefore temporary. But Torah study is the path to eternal life and the world to come. It can happen that God will not provide man with his requests in this world, even if he prays intensely, such that he only has heartache. Thus they advised that its cure is the study of the Torah, which bestows eternal life; and through Torah study, man will most certainly attain his requests and desires. For this reason they call the Torah "A tree of life."[23]

As already noted by the late Hayyim Hillel ben Sasson, his alarm at the Hasidic reversal of the order of religious priorities and his interest in maintaining the primacy of *Talmud Torah* over all other *mitzvoth*, especially *tefilla*, lay at the very center of the GRA's dispute with Hasidism.[24] This defense of the centrality of study (typical also of the later Mithnagdim, as we shall soon see) was rooted in a literal, rabbinic understanding of the purpose, goals, and context within Judaism of prayer.[25]

In the tradition of his great mentor, R. Hayyim of Volozhin, although himself also an advocate and practitioner of mystical prayer,[26] clearly assigned pride of place to *Talmud Torah*.[27] The very structure of his *Nefesh ha-Hayyim* illustrates the degree to which he viewed study as every Jew's supreme religious priority. He explicitly rejected the arguments of those who accorded preeminence to prayer.[28] Convinced that the Jews of his generation lacked the depth of knowledge to comprehend the Lurianic system, R. Hayyim was careful to remind his readers of the futility of trying to master the *kavanoth* of the liturgy.[29] More to the point, R. Hayyim, himself a Kabbalist who devoted a large section of his opus to a discussion of mystical prayer, was nonetheless vigilant—as were many earlier Kabbalists—in preserving the carefully limited schedule for the prayer services, which he perceived to be threatened by Hasidism's overemphasis upon mystical *kavana* and its attendant, excessive spiritual preparations for worship. In the course of defending the integrity of the liturgy, as well as the Halakhic regulations for the precise times of prayer, against the Hasidic subversion of these values, R. Hayyim waxed unusually polemical. He referred to the Hasidic tendency to ignore the legal conventions and restrictions regarding all of the *mitzvoth ma'asiyoth*, including prayer, as the temptations of the evil instinct and as "a fire that consumes everything and destroys many of the foundations of the Torah and the teachings of the Sages." The study of the Torah, even without deep spiritual intentionality, was more valuable than the most spiritualized fulfillment of any of the other *mitzvoth* in the Torah, prayer included.[30] Referring unmistakably to the Hasidim, R. Hayyim bitingly complained that the overemphasis on Kabbalistic prayer, specifically the extensive preparations intended to attain a mystical state before worship, had finally led to a complete distortion of religious priorities:

> Now I have indicated to you the ways in which the evil instinct tries to deceive . . . and pretends as if it is not at all enticing man to evil; on the contrary, it tries to show man that all of the Torah that he has learned and the commandments that he has observed have not yet yielded any good. . . . With my own eyes have I seen many *who seek the closeness of God* who have failed in these matters. . . . With my own eyes have I seen some people in a certain place who have become trained in this matter for so long that they have almost entirely forgotten the correct time for the afternoon prayer established by the Sages . . . to the point where if one of them says to his friend, "Let us offer the afternoon service," the other responds, "Let us first ascertain that the stars have already appeared." May God forgive them.[31]

Vigilant concern for the recitation of the prayers at the correct times is expressed in virtually all Mithnagdic writing. R. Abraham Danzig was especially emphatic, in his ethical will, to remind his children to be punctilious in the observance of "zemanei tefilla," or the precisely prescribed times for each of the daily prayer services.[32] In the next generation, Meir ben Elijah repeatedly castigated the Hasidim for neglecting the correct times of prayer, attributing this neglect to their obsession with the supreme mystical importance of the act of worship.[33]

R. Phinehas of Polotsk on the Status of Prayer

Many years before the appearance of *Nefesh ha-Hayyim*, R. Phinehas of Polotsk complained repeatedly of the Hasidim's neglect of the limited, proper times assigned to prayer and their preoccupation with ecstatic worship to the detriment of *Talmud Torah*. Like his mentor, the GRA, R. Phinehas affirmed both the practical priority and the religious superiority of study over prayer. In his commentary to the proverb "He that turneth his ear away from hearing the law, even his prayers are an abomination," he recalls the Talmudic dictum: "This verse can be explained by the fact that Torah is eternal life, while prayer is only concerned with temporal life."[34]

In his ethical will, *Rosh ha-Giveah*, R. Phinehas warned against the excessive Hasidic preoccupation with prayer to the exclusion of all other religious duties.[35] And in *Kether Torah* he reflected the typically alarmed reaction of the Mithnagdim to the Hasidic elevation of prayer above Torah study. Expressing his concern in terminology almost identical to that voiced by R. Hayyim of Volozhin years later, and referring unmistakably to the Hasidim,

Phinehas paraphrases the deceptions of the evil inclination to direct man away from Torah scholarship:

> The sole purpose [of the *yezer ha-ra*] is to escape from the Torah, for it [Torah] is like a fire burning in its bones . . . and it will tell you: "Did the Sages not teach that the world rests upon three things—Torah, worship, and charity? Take note that divine service is the middle pillar upon which the world stands, and the divine service is none other than prayer. . . . Now, why should you die in the tents of Torah? . . . Rather, rise up and take hold of the middle pillar upon which the house is secured and cling to the worship of God, and serve Him with all your heart and soul.[36]

R. Phinehas responded vigorously and expansively to this malefic challenge, rebuffing the Hasidic elevation of prayer over study on three distinct levels—philosophical, legal, and historical. His first line of defense against the Hasidic assault upon the primacy of Torah study was to reaffirm the classical rabbinic appraisals of Torah and prayer as guarantors of eternal and material life, respectively, as the GRA had done before him. R. Phinehas warned against the evil instinct's tactic to lure Jews away from Torah, which is the only guarantor of eternal life *(hayyei olam)*, using prayer, which only secures temporal, material sustenance, as bait. Succumbing to these temptations would, he warned certainly lead to spiritual death. Second, from a purely Halakhic perspective, the study of Torah, a biblical imperative, takes legal precedence over the merely rabbinic imperative regarding the institution of fixed prayer.[37] Finally, from a historical perspective, since the destruction of the Jerusalem Temple and the abolition of its ancient rituals and their replacement with verbal prayer, the central pillar, religion, had been transferred by the Sages from the sacrificial rites of divine worship *(avodah)* to the study of Torah.[38] As if addressing himself directly to the mystics' claim—as evidenced by the citation from Moses ibn Makhir above—that since the destruction of the temple God has desired nothing more than the prayers of Israel that have replaced the sacrificial order, Phinehas warns: "Do not say that since the day of the destruction of the temple, and now that there is no priest at the service nor Levite at the platform, God desires nothing more in this world than prayer. . . . that is not what the Sages have taught . . . for R. Hiyyah b. Ami instructed that since the destruction of the Temple, God has nothing in his world but the four cubits of Halakhah; note that it does not say four cubits of prayer."[39]

In a bold reinterpretation of the Tannaitic counsel against allowing prayer to become routinized *(keva)*, R. Phinehas startlingly argues that prayer, unlike

Torah study, should be carefully limited so as not to occupy too much of one's daily agenda.

"When you worship, do not regard your prayer as a fixed, mechanical task; rather as an appeal for mercy and grace before the Omnipresent"; Behold the greatness of the Torah, regarding which the Tanna insists, "Make your Torah study fixed," whereas regarding prayer he says, "Do not make your prayer fixed, but rather an appeal for mercy and grace," because [prayer] is only temporary life, and since it is written that God is merciful and compassionate, it is not necessary to cry out to Him all day.[40]

In a very similar vein, Meir ben Elijah tried some years later to downplay the significance of this same Mishnaic passage by asserting that the advice against routinized prayer was not directed at the masses of Israel: "That which is taught, 'Do not make your prayer a fixed task' (that is, do not intend only to fulfill your legal obligation), is really advice intended only for the saintly. But for people like ourselves, it is perfectly sufficient to intend only routinely to fulfill the *mitzvah* correctly."[41]

In the system of R. Phinehas, as in classical rabbinic thought, prayer is again classified together with other active Halakhic obligations (*mitzvoth ma'asiyoth*), all of which share a status subordinate to that of Torah study.[42] The explicit preference for study over all other religious obligations, including prayer, was common among the leading Mithnagdic thinkers in Phinehas's day and for generations to come. At the conclusion of his panegyric to Torah study, *Maaloth ha-Torah*, R. Abraham ben Solomon, the GRA's brother, reinterpreted the commandment to love the Lord with all of one's heart as referring not to devotional prayer, as it is most commonly understood in the rabbinic tradition, but rather to sober study. He argues that it is in fact through study, not prayer, that spiritual excellence, and ultimately *devekuth*, can be achieved.[43]

In the same spirit, R. Abraham Danzig emphatically reaffirmed, on the basis of his more general conviction regarding the inherent spiritual superiority of study to prayer, the Talmudic ruling that the study hall has more sanctity than the synagogue:

The most holy place in the diaspora is the study hall, in which learning takes place all day, as it is written, "The Lord loves the gates of Zion more that all the dwelling places of Jacob." The "gates of Zion" refers to the gates that excel in Halakhah [i.e., the study hall], whereas the "dwelling places" refers to the synagogue. .. The place in which the Torah is studied is more precious to God, for "the Lord has nothing in this world but the four cubits of Halakhah."[44]

In his ethical will, Danzig more explicitly states his personal conviction that Torah study is of far greater importance than prayer. Thus, for example, he pleads with his children to devote more time after his death to studying Torah in his memory than to reciting memorial prayers and the *Kaddish,* for, as he says, the prayers "are not the most important thing. Rather, what is essential is the daily study of the Torah."[45] Virtually all of the significant Mithnagdic thinkers of subsequent generations continued consistently to uphold this hierarchy. Notable among them were R. Isaac Haber, the great Mithnagdic mystic and the most important disciple of R. Menahem Mendel of Shklov;[46] R. Asher Ha-Kohen, an important disciple of R. Hayyim of Volozhin;[47] and R. Meir ben Elijah, the grandson of R. Abraham ben Solomon of Vilna,[48] all of whom repeatedly and vigorously asserted the supremacy of *Talmud Torah* over any other religious values, including prayer.

This dispute between the Hasidim and the Mithnagdim over the status of prayer and study in Judaism is in turn rooted in their differing evaluations of the nature and the extent of the powers of prayer itself. At the very center of these opposing evaluations lies a fundamental difference regarding the definition of the rabbinic requirement for *kavana,* or proper intent and inwardness during prayer. The supremacy of *Talmud Torah* over all other obligations and its specific dominance over prayer as the ultimate act of personal religious perfection must, of course, also be understood as a consequence of the unique spiritual powers accorded to scholarship by the Mithnagdim.[49] For now, a comparative examination of the respective interpretations of *kavana* by the Hasidim and their opponents will shed much light on their sharp disagreement regarding the place of prayer in the hierarchy of Jewish values.

Kavana in Classical Rabbinic and Medieval Thought

The practice of the "ancient Hasidim" to try to attain a mental state conducive to proper *kavana* is documented in the Mishna.[50] The Talmud, citing favorably the exemplary behavior of the ancient "Hasidim," rules that "the worshiper must direct his heart to the heavens."[51] Elsewhere, the Talmud says that "the worshiper must consider himself as if in the direct presence of the Shekhinah, as it is written: 'I imagine the Lord before me always.'"[52] While the exact meaning of such direction of heart remains vague, the common understanding of *kavana* in the subsequent rabbinic literature was a heightened awareness of God during prayer, as well as attention to and comprehension of the words of the liturgy. Maimonides, culling from various Talmudic discussions of the requirements for proper prayer, understood the rabbinic notion of *kavana* to be essentially a mental and intellectual preparedness to pray. *Kavana* requires a complete absence of external distractions in order to allow for a state of mind conducive to proper concentration and focusing upon the object of prayer. Proper *kavana* is achieved only when the worshiper is not conscious of anything standing between himself and God. Adopting the strictest interpretation of the Talmudic requirement for *kavana*, Maimonides ruled that prayer without it was legally invalid and required repetition.[53] In later rabbinic sources *kavana* increasingly assumed a dual definition. Many authorities actually understood *kavana* to comprise two distinct and very different matters: on the simple level, attention to the literal meaning of the words of the liturgical text; on the more sublime level, an inner spiritual state appropriate for communion with God. R. Jacob ben Asher thus defined *kavana* in his Halakhic code, the *Tur,* as follows:

> What should one's mental state be [during prayer]? As it is written, "The worshiper must direct his heart. . . ," that is, he should focus on the meaning of the words that leave his lips. Also, he should consider the divine presence to be before him . . . and he should rid himself of all distracting thoughts until his mind and intention in prayer are pure. . . . Such was the practice of the [early] Hasidim and men of merit, who would isolate themselves and concentrate on their prayers until they arrived at a state of transcending their own corporeality through the total ascendancy of their intellectual faculty, to the point where they nearly reached the level of prophecy.[54]

R. Jacob here presents two very different definitions of *kavana* not made explicitly distinct in the Talmud and earlier rabbinic texts. The first is objective and literal; it relates to focusing intellectually on the text and words of prayer and their intended literal meaning. The second is highly spiritual and subjective, relating to the ideal mental state and religious mood of the man engaged in divine worship.[55]

Kabbalistic *Kavana*

While Jacob ben Asher, later in the same code, pointed out (in disagreement with the ruling of Maimonides) that the second type of *kavana*, exemplary as it might be, was not legally required in order for one to fulfill the Halakhic obligation of prayer, the medieval Kabbalists focused almost exclusively upon, and significantly deepened, the mystical definition of *kavana*. For they saw in the act of prayer the best opportunity for a direct encounter with, and an opportunity to affect, the heavenly spheres. Mystical prayer thus took on entirely new and original intentions, not at all related to the literal meaning of the text of the liturgy and unanticipated by the earlier rabbinic authorities.

Whereas in many schools of medieval Jewish mysticism *kavana* connoted the exalted state of the worshiper's soul, in the Lurianic system the notion assumed an entirely new significance. Rather than referring to the state of mind and soul of the worshiper, *kavana,* or more precisely the *kavanoth,* were understood as the designated cosmic functions of properly directed words of prayer, the keys to an elaborate map for universal correction, or *tikkun.* Prayer with *kavana* was now considered a bold theurgic exercise, directed at transforming heaven and earth. In light of the cosmic powers attributed by Luria to the very letters and words of the Hebrew prayers, their simple meaning was largely ignored or, as they might claim, transcended by many Kabbalists of the Lurianic school.

In the period prior to the rise of Hasidism, however, many leading rabbis, while not questioning the bold Kabbalistic claims for both the mystical significance and cosmic power of prayer, began to doubt the contemporary Jews' ability to engage in the second, spiritual type of *kavana* referred to in the classical codes, particularly as it had been redefined by the mystics. These authorities were particularly skeptical about the highly specialized form of theurgic prayer that employed the esoteric Lurianic *kavanoth,* doubting aloud whether the Jews of their generation had the necessary religious knowledge and spiritual stature to gain access to such cosmic powers. They thus advocated a limited definition of *kavana* and strongly suggested that the worshiper limit himself to attending to the literal meaning of the words of prayer. In that spirit, the leading Halakhic commentator to the *Shulhan Arukh,* R. Abraham Gombiner, quoting the *Zohar,* warned the average Jew to restrict his *kavana* to the literal meaning of the text:

> It is written in the *Zohar* that "any man who attempts the unification of the Holy Name but does not have the proper, fearful and burning intent to bring blessing to the upper and lower realms, such a man's prayers are considered alien and all of his words are transformed for evil, and God proclaims of him: 'When you come to seek my Presence, who asked this of you?'" [Isaiah 1:2]
>
> Therefore, it seems to me that anyone who himself is unable to have the proper *kavana* for this, should not intend such *kavana* regarding the names and unifications [of the divine name] at all. Rather, he should pray with simplicity in order only to understand the words with the intent of his heart.[56]

There is here no denial of the potential power of the text of prayer to achieve its cosmic goals and no rejection of the truth of Lurianic doctrine in theory. Rather, because of the contemporary, exiled Jews' limited intellectual and spiritual capabilities, there is a distinct pessimism about their ability to engage consciously in such exalted spiritual techniques. This betrays the fear that any attempt by the spiritual incompetent to engage in Lurianic *kavanoth* not only might fail but also is sure to distract him from the legally mandated "simple" *kavana* of attention to the meaning of words.

This simultaneous acceptance in theory of the validity and powers of the Lurianic *kavanoth,* along with a pragmatic rejection of their widespread contemporary use, became one of the central themes of the seminal and highly influential eighteenth-century Lithuanian spiritual work, *Yesod ve-Shoresh ha-Avodah.* According to its author, R. Alexander Zisskind of Grodno, there are two kinds of *kavana: kavanoth pashtiyoth,* or concentration upon the simple meaning of the words, and *kavanoth ha-Ari,* or the mystical/theurgic *kavanoth* based on Lurianic doctrine. The average Jew, being neither intellectually nor spiritually capable of mastering the latter, should, he advises, focus exclusively on the former. As for the noble goal of liturgical *tikkun,* he assures his readers that as long as they recite the words and letters of prayer accurately and carefully, the words and letters will of themselves automatically achieve the appropriate *tikkunim,* even without the express knowledge of the worshiper.

The notion that the exact pronouncement of the letters and words of the *siddur,* even by a Jew lacking all comprehension of their theurgic powers, would be sufficient to allow the prayers autonomously to play out their cosmic restorative role runs like a thread through *Yesod ve-Shoresh ha-Avodah.* What R. Alexander Zisskind insists upon, however, is a deep and personalized understanding of the literal intention of each of the words and phrases of the service and a total, intense sincerity when reciting those words and phrases. In a typical paragraph, R. Zisskind advises:

> Now I intend to reveal to the ears of men such as myself that the entire order of all of the prayers is based upon the hierarchical order of the *sefiroth* and the pattern of the worlds. The holy men of the Great Assembly clothed these mysteries in the words of prayer in such a way that they retain at the same time a literal meaning that is intelligible to the vast majority of our people. So that when a man prays with intense [literal] *kavana,* even though he is unable to comprehend and direct his words to the esoteric level, nonetheless, the Angels in charge of the elevation of prayer . . . to the King of Kings, the Holy One, redirect this man's limited, literal and well-intended prayer to the mystical level and raise it from *kavana* to *kavana* and from exoteric to esoteric.[57]

As long as prayer is recited with verbal exactitude and literal, simple *kavana,* the deeper, cosmic *kavanoth* will be automatically fulfilled. Man's role in all of this becomes limited to that of a conduit, an almost mechanically faithful reciter of the liturgical text. All that is asked of him is simple, literal comprehension of the prayers and sincere intention during the act of worship. Most significantly, the two types of *kavana* are not regarded as being mutually exclusive. On the contrary, they coexist as two complementary levels of divine service. For the worshiper needs only to focus on the literal sense of the liturgy, and the mystical *kavanoth* will automatically be fulfilled.[58]

The Hasidic Redefinition of *Kavana*

The early followers of the BESHT also despaired of the contemporary Jews' competence in the Lurianic form of theurgic prayer. Nevertheless, rather than advocating intense literal prayer, as R. Alexander Zisskind did, they tended instead to prescribe a new variation on the second, subjective type of *kavana* referred to by R. Jacob ben Asher, namely, the attainment of an exalted state of mind and soul on the part of the worshiper, to the point of *hithpashtuth ha-gashmiyouth* (spiritual transformation). But instead of seeing this as a prerequisite mood to be achieved before prayer, they argued that the act of prayer and the words of the liturgy might themselves be used to advantage as apparatuses for achieving this ideal spiritual state. And although they employed the terminology of the traditional Halakhists, such as that found in the regulations concerning prayer in Jacob ben Asher's *Tur*, they transformed the nature of the prescribed mental state of prayer, from a heightened cognitive awareness of the presence of God to a sublime state of mystical ecstasy.

Removing the barriers that separate man from God was, in classical Hasidism, no longer a preparation for prayer; rather, it was its final objective. As a result of their extreme spiritualization of the act of prayer itself, the literal meaning and obvious original intention of the prayers became even less relevant in Hasidism than they had been in the earlier Lurianic mysticism.[59] For Hasidism replaced the very difficult and esoteric theurgic *kavanoth* of R. Isaac Luria with a technique for highly emotional and enthusiastic prayer. This technique, referred to by scholars of Hasidism as "the atomization of letters," was, as mentioned above, popularized by the Great Maggid of Mezeritch and his disciples. The soul of the worshiper was to be attached to the letters of the liturgical text, and the forms and sounds of these letters were to transport him to a higher spiritual state. While all of the details of Hasidic *kavana* need not concern us here, its net effect on the traditional imperative to direct one's heart during prayer must be appreciated. Not only did the literal meaning of the words of prayer become irrelevant to the Hasidic worshiper but he saw it as alien and disruptive of his ultimate goals in prayer. Thus, we find Hasidic theoreticians not content merely with ignoring the simple, literal *kavana* but actually counseling against having it in mind. R. Hayyim of Tchernowitz boldly protested against literal, petitionary prayer: "When a man prays and intends the plain sense [*peshat*] for his own sake, that is, to attain healing or to be blessed with rain and dew, it is certain that such worship is not valued before God, for he is only serving himself, and he is asking only for his own good and welfare, not that of God."[60]

In a similar vein, the great synthesizer of Hasidic thought, R. Kalonymous Kalman of Cracow, warned: "Heaven forfend that one should corrupt any of the words or letters of the prayers by thinking that they signify the simple meaning of the words, God forbid. Rather, he must consider . . . that thousands upon thousands of worlds derive their vitality from the holiness of the words and depend upon every word and letter, even every vowel."[61] This reference to the cosmic significance of the liturgical text should not, however, be understood to suggest that R. Kalonymous Kalman was advocating a return to Lurianic prayer with its attendant theurgic *kavanoth*. Quite the contrary; just as he advised his followers against intending the *kavanoth pashtiyoth,* so, too, he excluded the theurgic *kavanoth ha-Ari* for his generation:

In our generation it is improper for a man to have in mind the *kavanoth* of prayer handed down to us in the prayerbook of the ARI, of blessed memory, whether from the written text or whether he has learnt them and has them in mind by heart. So did I hear it from my master and teacher, the holy Rabbi . . . Elimelekh. . . . He said that a man should not have in mind thoughts or reflections on the *kavanoth* of the divine names. Instead, he should bind both his external and his inner self, that is, his vital force, his spirit and soul, to *Eyn Sof,* blessed be He. As a result, he binds all the revealed worlds and all the inner aspects of the world to Him. Man's thought should be so attached to the pleasantness of the Lord that he has no time, even for a moment, to have the *kavanoth* in mind. When a man's prayers are of this order, the *kavanoth* are effected automatically.[62]

This Hasidic variation on the notion (already advanced by R. Alexander Zisskind) that as long as one prays with great enthusiasm and spiritual attachment, without having to pay any attention to the Lurianic cosmic mapping of the liturgical text, the theurgic effects of the *kavanoth* will automatically follow, can be traced back to the teachings of the Great Maggid, Dov Ber of Mezeritch, who insisted that "when one says each word with great attachment, all the *kavanoth* are by that very fact included."[63] Both literal *kavana* and the theurgic Lurianic *kavanoth* were thus replaced by the early

Hasidic masters, with intense personal concentration aimed at achieving a state of heightened spiritual attachment.

The Lurianic *kavanoth* had traditionally been perceived by the rabbis as embodying a higher level of meaning that could coexist with the "simple *kavanoth.*" They did not have to distract the mind of the worshiper completely from the original plain sense of the liturgy. Not so Hasidic *kavana,* however, which by virtue of its psychologically intense and enthusiastic nature precluded the possibility for a sober, literal approach to prayer and also prevented any cognitive focus on the theurgic Lurianic *kavanoth.* Of course, Hasidism's concession that the average Jew was incapable of theurgic Lurianic prayer did not lead to a limitation of prayer to its simple, literal meaning, nor did it result in a return to the Talmudic evaluation of the power and status of prayer. Quite the contrary, by maintaining a mystical role for prayer the Hasidic approach resulted finally in a much greater neglect of the classical rabbinic equation of *kavana* with attention to the simple meaning of the prayers.[64] This, in turn, opened the door to changes in the text of the *siddur,* which, when added to the Hasidic neglect of the mandated times for the daily prayer services, outraged the Mithnagdim.

In the wake of the radical changes that Hasidism introduced to prayer, the Mithnagdim rose to uphold not only the primacy of scholarship but also the original sense, sanctity, and inviolability of the Jewish liturgical canon. The Mithnagdim complained that the Hasidim not only disregarded the *peshat,* or the original literal intent of the liturgical text, but went so far as to accuse those who focused on its plain meaning of idolatry.[65]

Mithnagdic *Kavana*

The Mithnagdim, while not entirely rejecting the importance of attaining an appropriate level of spiritual concentration in prayer, tended to emphasize the statutory, Halakhic need for simple, literal *kavana,* that is, attention to the plain sense of the words of the liturgy. Consistent with their general pessimism regarding man's inherent spiritual capacities, they despaired that he might ever, in their days at least, comprehend the Lurianic cosmic *kavanoth* or rise to the level of that mystical divestment from corporeality being advocated by the Hasidim. Accordingly, the Mithnagdim, like the earlier Halakhic authorities, tended to restrict their understanding of statutory *kavana* to the first half of the *Tur*'s binary definition: attention to the literal meaning of the text of the liturgy. This was true even of the GRA and R. Hayyim of Volozhin, who were exceptional in the Mithnagdic camp by virtue of their deep interest in contemplative, mystical prayer.

The Gaon of Vilna, though himself a master of mystical prayer, legislated that the universal Halakhic requirement of *kavana* did not extend beyond a general religious sincerity in prayer and an appropriate focus upon the meaning of the words:

> "One must direct one's heart to heaven": This means that one should be thinking of heavenly matters and not extraneous thoughts. "One's heart" refers to the intention of the heart, which corresponds to the meaning of the words. So that the *Tannah* has taught two things with this statement: (1) that the worshiper should be thinking of God; (2) that he should focus on the meaning of the words.[66]

In the posthumous collection of the GRA'S daily religious practices the requirement for *kavana* is accordingly defined in the following limited fashion:

> One must pray with intention, [that is,] recite each word distinctly and keep in mind the meaning of the words. If a distracting thought should appear to him in the middle of prayer, he must simply wait for that thought to disappear. It is not necessary to focus upon each of the Divine names, but only generally to have the Master of All in mind.[67]

Even R. Hayyim of Volozhin, a strong advocate of mystical *kavanoth* in prayer, prefaced the section of *Nefesh ha-Hayyim* that deals with prayer with an important caveat and practical concession. Repeating the rabbinic binary definition of *kavana*, he allows that the latter form, involving a heightened awareness of God before prayer, while very commendable, is not necessary for the sake of fulfilling one's legal obligations in prayer:

> When it is written that prayer must be intended "with all of thy heart," it is clear and obvious that two matters are intended: (i) To empty one's heart of all distracting thoughts in order to focus complete attention upon the words of the liturgy . . . (ii) To uproot from the heart during worship all of the pleasures and vanities of this world . . . to the point where all the energy of the heart is extended upwards . . . as they taught in *Shemoth Raba;* "Man has to purify his heart before prayer." Granted, however, that the essence of this matter of purification of the heart is only for the sake of added merit [*mitzvah*] and is not an absolute legal requisite . . . for the essential matter with regard to all of the commandments is actual performance.[68]

Later in the same work, while polemicizing against the Hasidic spiritualization of the laws of prayer and the resultant neglect of its details and time regulations, R. Hayyim emphasizes this point repeatedly. Given the choice

between precise mouthing of the words of prayer without any mystical intent, on the one hand, and engaging in deep, subjective Kabbalistic *kavana*
while neglecting the legal requirements of timely, literally intended prayer, on
the other hand, R. Hayyim clearly prefers the former:

> If one contemplated the words of prayer without actually pronouncing them, he
> would not in any way have fulfilled his obligation to pray . . . and if he prayed in
> thought only, he would have achieved nothing at all with his prayer. However, if
> one simply pronounced the words precisely, without adding any thoughts or
> *kavanoth* of the heart to it, although such prayer is certainly not on an appropri-
> ately high level . . . at least he will have fulfilled his obligation and it is not a total
> waste.[69]

It is possible that R. Hayyim was reacting here to the teaching of early
Hasidism that the most sublime form of personal prayer is silent meditation,
in which no words are uttered. It is well known that R. Jacob Joseph of Polnoe
struggled with the idea that according to Jewish law the prayers must be
pronounced verbally. His resolution of this problematic notion involved a
compromise—an affirmation that both silent devotion and verbal prayer are
needed and that each has its respective place. Still, R. Jacob Joseph insisted
that the former was more elevated:

> This is how I perceive the universally posed question as to why speech is at all
> necessary during prayer, when God, after all, knows our inner thoughts: The
> answer I heard is that the purpose of speech is to construct a vessel that can be
> used to bring the divine influence down to earth from the heavens. . . . Truthfully,
> however, he whose goal in prayer is to merit the attachment of his thoughts to
> God does not really need this bringing down of divine abundance. It can be said
> that for prayer of this nature, thought [without words] is sufficient.
>
> This is what is meant by the verse: "At that very time I pleaded with the Lord,
> saying . . ." The meaning of this verse is that it was only in that specific time [i.e.,
> when Moses was engaged in a high level of personal prayer] that I could "say"
> my prayer with thought and without the use of any words. For this is the kind of
> prayer that does not require any vessels with which to bring down the divine
> abundance, as we shall explain later on.
>
> Still, at other times, it is correct to order one's prayer [verbally].[70]

The other disciples of the GRA continued to limit the concept of *kavana* to
the literal sense of the prayer text. R. Phinehas of Polotsk, although not
uninterested in Kabbalistic interpretations of the *siddur,* clearly regarded
them as beyond the comprehension, let alone the mastery, of his contempo-

raries. In his introduction to *Siddur Shaar ha-Rahamim* he thus justified his abstention from citing Lurianic *kavanoth* in his own commentary:

> Regarding the explication of the liturgy on the basis of the Kabbalah and the *kavanoth* . . . it is of no benefit to most men. For I have seen only very few, rarely exalted men who actually engage in this precious wisdom, which is to know and comprehend all of the Sages' mysteries and secrets regarding all of the worthy *kavanoth*. . . . Not every mind can tolerate this, that is, to focus his psyche, to arise and master his soul, and properly to empty his thoughts of all external distractions during prayer.
>
> As for us, then, would that we only benefit ourselves by knowing and intending [Heb., *k'v'n'*] the meaning of the words during prayer, as is proper.[71]

In even bolder terms, R. Abraham Danzig, although often emphasizing the fact that prayer without *kavana* is entirely futile, rigidly limits the type of *kavana* that is binding in his generation:

> Know that wherever it is written that a person must pray with intention, it means that he must focus upon the meaning of the words; but he should not try to focus upon the [mystical] *kavanoth* and *sheymoth*, for due to the multitude of our transgressions, we have become filthy with sin, and there is no doubt that he who intends the mystical *kavanoth* engages in heresy. Even those who study the writings of R. Isaac Luria understand nothing beyond the meaning of words, and not the [deeper] essence. There cannot be found even one in a thousand who is learned in this.[72]

All this must be seen in sharp contrast to Hasidism's repeated insistence that focusing on the plain sense of the words of prayer is not true worship but rather the service of the human ego and is therefore unacceptable.

Although both Hasidim and Mithnagdim, then, despaired of man's ability to employ the Lurianic *kavanoth* and went back to definitions of *kavana* found in the earlier sources, each exclusively emphasized only one-half of the classic binary rabbinic definition and downplayed the significance and urgency of the other component. The Mithnagdim were primarily concerned with *kavana* as simple verbal comprehension, whereas the Hasidim completely sacrificed the literal meaning of the liturgy on the altar of mystical experience.

In limiting the stature of prayer generally and the practical definition of *kavana* specifically and insisting that prayer be, as its text literally suggests, no more than man's entreaties to God for sustenance (i.e., *hayyei sha'a*), the Mithnagdim were, of course, rejecting all attempts to engage in any form of spiritually enthusiastic prayer, theurgic or mystical. Thus, although they tactically shared the Hasidic masters' abandonment of the Lurianic *kavanoth,* they were absolutely appalled at Hasidism's bold replacement of their theurgic role, not with simple literal *kavana,* but with radically new forms of enthusiastic and ecstatic prayer aimed at *unio mystica.* Still, at the very root of the Mithnagdic protestations there does not lie a theoretical dispute with Hasidism about the sanctity and mystical potencies embedded in the liturgical text, but rather a sharp disagreement about the capacity of the contemporary Jew at prayer to unleash and employ those powers in his daily worship.

The Mithnagdim on the Limits of Mystical Worship

The primacy of *Talmud Torah* and the proper definition of *kavana* were not the only casualties of the new Hasidic understanding of prayer, according to the Mithnagdim. The very institution of prayer itself as understood in both the rabbinic and earlier Kabbalistic systems was threatened by the Hasidim's radically enthusiastic approach to divine worship. For although Kabbalistic prayer may have attributed new meanings and powers to the liturgy that had been completely unanticipated by its rabbinic authors, in practical terms that only served to strengthen the status of prayer by attributing cosmic significance to each of its details and attendant Halakhoth. Not so the Hasidic transformation of prayer into a purely contemplative exercise and the *siddur* into a handbook for mystical meditation.

As noted above, this new Hasidic departure in divine worship undermined certain of the prayer laws, and it directly challenged the classical rabbinic order of religious values, which clearly subordinated prayer to rabbinic learning. It also placed in jeopardy the minimally required plain-sense understanding of the service. Even more seriously, the transformation and popularization of a form of mystical (or at least nonliteral) prayer that had always been respected but zealously concealed from the Jewish masses threatened the continued elite status and integrity of genuinely esoteric Kabbalistic worship itself.

Aside from the obvious social factors, as well as the fear of separationist challenges to communal religious institutions and rabbinic authority, Mithnagdic opposition to Hasidic prayer practices was therefore motivated by a variety of religious concerns. Not least among the fears of the Mithnagdim was Hasidism's perceived corruption of genuine Kabbalistic prayer. There is no indication in the extensive polemical and homiletical writings of the Mithnagdim that their outrage at Hasidic worship was in any way rooted in a general opposition to mysticism or in any skepticism regarding the theoretical truth of Kabbalistic doctrine. Quite the contrary, it was the very Mithnagdic reverence for the exalted status of that wisdom that motivated them vigilantly to safeguard its sanctity against the corruptions of popular abuse. Of course, that same reverence produced a deliberate distancing from all Kabbalistic or mystical enterprise that was to become pervasive in Mithnagdic circles.

As with their concern over Hasidism's popularized instruction of Kabbalistic doctrines generally, the Mithnagdim largely were motivated pragmatically to limit prayer to its literal, petitionary understanding *(hayyei sha'ah)* by their pessimistic assessment of man. The restriction of *kavana* to the *peshat* and the resultant general limitation of the status of prayer and its place in the hierarchy of religious values were, as we shall presently see, rooted largely in the Mithnagdic evaluation of the very circumscribed spiritual capacities of the contemporary Jew. While it is not at all clear how much the Mithnagdim really understood about the details and techniques of Hasidic worship, they perceived quite correctly that Hasidism was attempting to popularize some form of ecstatic, enthusiastic mystical worship, which had hitherto been the exclusive prerogative of small elitist Kabbalistic circles, such as the Brodie *kloyz.* Aside from the threat to the integrity of the Kabbalah itself of such popularization, this behavior was viewed as a typical reflection of the arrogance and spiritual presumptuousness of the Hasidim. Consequently, a very large part of the Mithnagdic polemic is expressed in purely behavioral, rather than theological, terms.

R. Phinehas of Polotsk reflects precisely such an attitude toward Hasidic prayer in his own writings. His strongest objections are directed at Hasidic behavior, not mystical doctrine. He never condemns any form of Kabbalistic prayer per se, only the arrogance and vanity of spirit of its modern-day popularizers and practitioners. In his ethical will he warns his son not to be impressed by the false and vain showiness of the Hasidim at prayer:

> My son, be not one of those tainted sectarians who act out publicly even with regard to the most private of religious duties and who try to demonstrate to all the purity of their heart and inner intentions: and they reveal very strange gesticulations and loud moans in their prayers, and they gesture with their hands and with their fingers so that all will know of the purity of their hearts. Behold that theirs is a false deception. So, escape from their path, and understand from this that all of their worship is insincere and idolatrous.[73]

Phinehas rejects the public enthusiasm of Hasidic prayer, yet he never questions the inherent spiritual powers of properly offered mystical worship. In fact, nowhere in his literary corpus is there to be found any denial of the cosmic significance and theurgic potentialities of the liturgy; there is, rather, a strong sense that the pragmatic application of these powers lay beyond the grasp of the Jewish masses, among whom Hasidism was endeavoring to spread the practice of mystical worship.

This attitude, characteristic also of the other Mithnagdim, is especially evident in the structure of Phinehas's own edition of the *siddur* and in the content of his commentary to the liturgy, *Maggid Zedek. Siddur Shaar ha-Rahamim* includes a wide variety of mystical texts and interpretations. Surprisingly, and despite the well-known objection of other contemporary rabbis (most notably R. Ezekiel Landau) to their inclusion in the *siddur,* the major ceremonial aspects of worship (e.g., the donning of talit and tefillin, the taking of lulav and ethrog, the ceremony of *kaparoth,* and the sounding of the shofar) are all prefaced in this *siddur* with references to the appropriate Lurianic *kavanoth* to be recited by the worshiper, calling attention to the potential powers of prayer and its attendant rituals to achieve cosmic unification. In addition, the physical actions associated with prayer (e.g., bending of the knees at specific times during the *Amidah,* the symbolic banging of the heart during confession, and the prostration of the body during the *tahanun* service) are all furnished with Kabbalistic interpretations rooted in the Lurianic tradition.[74] Furthermore, entire sections of the service and prayers of great individual significance (e.g., the *Amidah* and the *Kaddish*) are furnished with general introductions which elaborate on their mystical or Kabbalistic implications and powers.[75]

Yet, in the same *siddur* that includes such significant Kabbalistic material Phinehas often warns against the dangers of not being highly circumspect with regard to Kabbalah. He speaks often of the absolute inaccessibility of mystical doctrine to the very limited minds of contemporary men and warns against the dangers of popularization. Like Alexander Zisskind of Grodno, he advises the worshiper to restrict his thoughts during prayer to the plain sense of the liturgy and simply to maintain a general, subliminal intention that the prayers might automatically effect their cosmic mission. Phinehas's introduction to the High Holiday liturgy in *Maggid Zedek* clearly illustrates this attitude:

> Insofar as the *kavanoth* of the prayers for this day and the *kavana* of the sounding of the shofar and all the other things that are done at this time of year are very profound and esoteric, and not every mind can tolerate it, and there are precious few men of stature; therefore I will copy for you from the text of a certain devotion transcribed from the ancient "Hasidim" in order that you recite it *before* beginning the prayers on this day. Intend to incorporate within it

all of the prayers that you will be reciting on these days and to attach your own prayers to the worship of the men of true knowledge who were capable of genuine *kavana*.[76]

Phinehas called the attention of the worshiper to the secret powers of mystical prayer and then discouraged him from attempting to access those very powers himself. He accordingly limited the Kabbalistic content of his own *siddur* to general introductory statements or to explications of the physical acts and symbolic rituals associated with prayer. For these do not actually distract the worshiper from the *peshat,* or simple meaning, of the *siddur* during the actual recitation of the words of prayer. But Phinehas diligently avoided explicating mystically the actual text of the recited part of the liturgy for fear of encouraging the very popularization and abuse of Kabbalistic worship of which he accused the Hasidim.

The limited use of Kabbalah in Phinehas's *siddur* can serve as a paradigm for the mitigated nature of Mithnagdic objections to Hasidism's spread of enthusiastic prayer among the Jewish masses. Rather than emanating from a negative assessment of the wisdom of the Kabbalah per se, this attitude is informed primarily by the limited Mithnagdic assessment of man. It is also to be understood, as we shall see below, as the result of a rather gloomy perspective on Jewish history and the spiritual attrition that is the inevitable consequence of exile.

A careful examination of Phinehas's edition of the *siddur* reveals the religious foundations for his clear delineation of the acceptable and the illicit in the realm of mystical prayer. Phinehas often uses his introductions and commentary to the text of the liturgy to affirm contemporary man's inability to master the full, hidden intentions of the prayer book. The descriptive paragraph on the title page of *Siddur Maggid Zedek* already reflects the deliberately circumscribed spiritual agenda of the author. Phinehas, we are informed, has based his commentary on the Aggadic traditions of the Talmud, as well as on three important liturgical commentators: R. Abudarham, R. Herz, and R. Jacob Emden. In culling from these sources, however, Phinehas was careful to concern himself only with their exoteric commentaries *(perush nigleh)*. He claims deliberately to have avoided any discussion of the mystical and esoteric content of his sources: "In turning to these three [sources], he [Phinehas] did not approach their hidden treasures, neither to add nor to subtract, neither to reveal nor to comment upon their mysteries or their secrets. Rather, in keeping with his task, he appended all form of good and blessing only to their simple and revealed words."[77]

True to this description, the commentary, *Maggid Zedek,* which is faced on each page of the *siddur* with the full text of R. Abudarham's work, approaches the liturgy in much the same way that Phinehas's exegetical works approach biblical texts. *Maggid Zedek* takes the form of a classical rabbinic commentary to the text of the *siddur*, relying almost exclusively upon traditional methods of midrashic exegesis and referring heavily to Talmudic sources in order to expound homiletically upon the text of the liturgy.[78] Rather than viewing the prayer book as a blueprint for cosmic restoration or a manual for mystical union, Phinehas, the commentator, treats the liturgy as he would any other sacred Jewish text—homiletically and philologically.

Phinehas occasionally reminds his readers of the folly of delving too deeply into the mysteries that lie beneath the surface of the words of prayer. His comments on the classic petitionary prayer from the High Holiday liturgy, "Hear our voice, Oh Lord our God, pity and have mercy upon us, and accept our prayer with compassion and favor," clearly reflect this posture: "'Hear our voices. . .,' that means, even though we do not know the true intention of all the prayers, nor their mysteries and secrets, nonetheless 'hear,' the superficial sounds of our prayers when we cry out to You. . . . Thus [the appeal to God to accept the prayers] with 'compassion' and 'favor,' using two distinct terms: 'compassion' regarding our impoverished needs and 'favor' regarding the impoverished nature of our understanding of the prayers."[79]

True understanding of the deepest meanings and hidden secrets of the liturgy is unavailable to contemporary man. The attainment of such knowledge is reserved for the world to come. Many of the prayers referring to the messianic redemption are explicated by Phinehas in precisely this spirit. For example, in explaining the use of the future tense in prayers referring to the unification by man of God's name, Phinehas reminds the worshiper that the contemporary exiled Jew is unable to achieve mastery or unification of the holy name of God:

> Only [in the messianic era] when the dead will be revived will we [be able to] sanctify thy name just as the angels sanctify it in the high heavens; that is when we will be able to mention the full name of God. But in our days, due to the multitude of our sins, the name of God is, as it were, incomplete, as it is written, "For a hand is against the throne of Yah [the Lord]. God will be at war with Amalek from generation to generation" (*Exodus* 17:16). That is, God has sworn that neither His name nor His throne will be complete until the memory of the Amalekites will be eradicated. Thus, we are only able to bless and sanctify the abridged name of God [i.e., Yah], that is half of His name. . . . But know that there will come a time when God will reign and the monarchy shall return to its rightful possessor, and then the full name of God shall be magnified and sancti-

fied. But today, and from generation unto generation, we shall praise Yah. That is to say, that until God fulfills His promise to wage war with the Amalekites we are allowed to bless only the [half] name Yah.[80]

In this fashion Phinehas manages to conjure up a deeply pessimistic mood during prayer. In contrast to the Hasidic masters' sustained attempts to invoke an optimistic spirit of ecstasy in prayer, the Mithnagdic maggid reminds the Jewish worshipers not of their boundless capabilities but, quite the contrary, of the severe limitations to which history and exile have destined them. Where the Hasidim speak boldly of unification with God and unifying and uniting with the holy letters of his name, Phinehas notifies his readers that in the present era of deep spiritual alienation the effective invocation of the divine name is not only forbidden but spiritually impossible.

Similarly, commenting on the use in the Sabbath morning service of the future expression, "From generation to generation will Your name be praised," Phinehas remarks:

"Among the assembled throngs of your people . . . Your name will be praised in song." This refers to the future when the masses of the House of Israel will assemble. Then will your name be praised in song, for then will the name [of God] be complete. Thus is it written: "When God restores the exiles of Zion . . . then will our mouths be filled with laughter and joyous song will be on our tongues" [Psalm 126]. *Then, but not now!* For, due to the multitude of our sins, when we today say, "May God's great name be blessed," the Holy One Blessed be He laments and shakes His head . . . and we too are in great sorrow, as it is written, "I will remember God and weep."[81]

Far from serving as an occasion for mystical daring, man's spiritual inadequacies are brought into focus during the act of prayer. Simultaneously recalling fondly a glorious past in which the Jew could truly commune with God by invoking the divine name and longing for the messianic era, in which that will once again become possible, has the final effect of turning the act of prayer into a mournful and humbling experience. Rather than employing enthusiastic prayer as a means to rise spiritually with the ultimate goal of *devekuth*, contemporary man is reminded by the frustrating limits upon him in his merely pathetic attempts at genuine communion with God in prayer of his spiritual lowliness and the great abyss that separates him from the Creator. Phinehas insists that the necessary psychological preparations for prayer involve primarily recalling man's lowliness, spiritual inadequacy and distance from his Creator:

The rabbis instituted the recitation of the verse "Open my mouth, O Lord, and allow my lips to proclaim Your praise," for a man must clothe himself with trepidation before coming unto the great and awesome King, to the point where he is unable even to open his mouth for great fear to speak. . . .

This is on account of the great distance [between man and God], the inadequacies of human cognition, and the [inaccessible] depth of the object [of prayer, i.e., God].[82]

Interestingly, the phrase "Open my mouth, O Lord" was most commonly understood by Hasidic theoreticians as a mandate for automatic speech in prayer—an act of total mystical passivity, which is one of the symptoms of the attainment of true union with God.[83] Yet, for Phinehas, these words underscore the very opposite, namely, the awesome transcendence of God and the inadequacies of man in trying to approach God in prayer.

Phinehas was not alone in his rather pessimistic and self-limiting view of prayer. R. Jacob Kranz, the famed Maggid of Dubno, introduced the section regarding prayer of his ethical work, *Sefer ha-Middoth,* with an almost identical thought:

The essence of prayer is the product of the honest self-appraisal of the man whose heart knows all too well its own corruption, lowly status, weak stature, and numerous inadequacies. As a result of these [the rabbis] obligated the worshiper to stand submissively and with a broken spirit; to straighten his feet and close his eyes and not raise his hands or feet nor even bat an eyelash. Rather, he must submit himself under the shadow of the highest Influence; and he must be aware of his lowly and poor status, and be aware that he has no intrinsic power even to open his mouth in prayer. Rather, he is totally dependent upon the heavenly mercies, and thus he says: "Open my mouth O Lord, and allow my lips to proclaim your praise."[84]

In the same spirit, their contemporary Hillel of Kovno contrasts the biblical period, in which man had direct access to God through worship, with his own, religiously degenerate generation:

During the time of the temple, no man dwelled in permanent sin, for the sacrificial offerings would atone . . . and nothing stood in the way and prevented our prayers from rising to our Father in heaven. Today, however, that is not the case. For due to the multitude of our sins, and the many accusers against us, on account of our flaws and impurities, there is an iron wall that separates us [from God] and stops [our prayers]. And there is no direct route for the ascent of our prayers . . . and our worship is like a barren woman, for it does not give birth and it yields no fruit, for the gates of prayer have been locked.[85]

Conclusion

The Mithnagdic approach to prayer is thus rooted in a deep sense of historical decline, religious alienation, and personal spiritual inadequacy. The prescribed mood of prayer is that of extreme humility, a heightened and profound awareness of human inadequacy, and fearful awe before a transcendent, hopelessly distant Creator. The contrast with the Hasidic approach to prayer is striking. In Hasidism, prayer is a joyful experience entered into with an almost strident confidence and optimism about man's ability not only to communicate directly with God but ultimately, with the help of mystical *kavana*, to become completely lost in and united with him. Far from a painful reminder of man's spiritual alienation and unbreachable distance from, and inferiority to, his Creator, prayer, for the Hasidim, occasions the highest human confidence for ecstatic closeness to God.

A letter from the activist Mithnagdic rabbi Avigdor of Pinsk to the Russian czar complaining of Hasidic arrogance captures the very essence of the rabbinic rejection of Hasidic prayer. After documenting the Hasidic conviction that in prayer man mingles with the Shekhinah herself, R. Avigdor proclaims:

> As for their claim that during prayer the divine and the human become completely intermingled, this is a false delusion. . . . The very opposite is true, as we find in the case of Moses, who said: "I then appealed to God"; and God answered him: "Enough! Do not continue to speak to me of this matter." It is clear from this that they did not become one with God in their prayers. Prayer is similar to the case of a very simple man who speaks to an honoured nobleman; can he really imagine that he becomes completely united with him?[86]

At the very root of the differences between the Hasidim and the Mithnagdim regarding the status and proper form of prayer and the definition of *kavana* there once again lies a fundamentally different appraisal of the spiritual mettle of the contemporary Jew. It is the Mithnagdic pessimism regarding the diminished soul of man, and not any general antimystical bias, that results in the rabbis' restriction of prayer to its limited, literal sense and that consequently firmly relegates prayer to a status subordinate to that of Torah study. And it is that same historical pessimism that does not allow for any *kavana* beyond a literal focus upon the meaning of the text of the liturgy.

Prayer is, according to the classical rabbinic definition, "the service of the heart." Hasidim and Mithnagdim differed most dramatically not in their understanding of the ultimate truths embedded in the text of the divine service itself but rather in their respective appraisals of the depth of the human heart and its spiritual capacity to reach those truths.

Chapter 4

MITHNAGDIC
ASCETICISM

It has often and accurately been observed that asceticism was at no time among the dominant spiritual impulses of Judaism. Throughout the classical rabbinic period the dubious religious stature of the ascetic, or Nazirite, was the subject of vigorous Talmudic debate. And although there is textual evidence of the existence of various Jewish ascetic sects in Tannaitic times, the Pharisees tended to restrict the abstemious impulse, and self-mortification always remained a very minor part of the subsequent normative, rabbinic Judaism.[1]

In medieval Jewish thought, however, there were some significant manifestations of ascetic piety.[2] In fact, among the chief characteristics of medieval Jewish *hasiduth*, or pietism, was its pronounced asceticism. The notion that a life of deliberate self-deprivation was the surest path to personal religious fulfillment was, however, only partially based upon the classical rabbinic sources. It was also heavily influenced by notions of saintliness in other religious traditions. The two most significant instances of medieval Jewish asceticism—Bahya ibn Pakuda's *Hovoth ha-Levavoth* and the twelfth-century Franco-German pietists, known as Hasidei Ashkenaz—developed their ascetic beliefs at least partly under external influences.[3] Bahya was largely influenced by Sufi mysticism and Neoplatonic dualism, and the Hasidei Ashkenaz, at least according to some scholars, by Christian monasticism.[4] Although ascetic behavior never became prevalent even in medieval Jewish culture, and although it is true that Hasiduth Ashkenaz remained a peripheral religious phenomenon within Judaism, Bahya's *Hovoth ha-Levavoth* did become one of the most influential ethical works in medieval Judaism, especially in the period preceding the rise of Hasidism.[5] Bahya, under the influence of Neoplatonic anthropological dualism and Sufi mysticism, strongly advocated a life of pious self-deprivation. Through the popularity and very wide dissemination of *Hovoth ha-Levavoth*, the spiritual importance of *perishuth*, or voluntary separation from the material world, became quite widely accepted in late medieval Jewish thought and society.

A third, very significant school of Jewish asceticism developed among the mystics of sixteenth-century Safed.[6] Partly under the influence of the earlier anthropological dualism of Bahya and very possibly also as a consequence of the cosmic dualism inherent in Lurianic cosmogony (specifically the myth of *zimzum,* whereby God and the physical world became separated during the drama of creation),[7] the pietists of Safed advocated and engaged in various forms of radical material abstention and penitential self-mortification in order to transcend the created universe and thereby reach a mystical state. The asceticism of the Safed mystics was especially pronounced in the works of R. Isaac Luria's key disciple, R. Hayyim Vital,[8] as well as in the *hanhagoth,* or rules of religious behavior, which they recorded.[9]

The concept of *perishuth* (asceticism) as a pathway to personal holiness remained a common theme in many pietistic and ethical Hebrew writings during the seventeenth and eighteenth centuries.[10] On the eve of the rise of the Hasidic movement in eastern Europe a large number of rabbis and mag-gidim continued to preach the great religious value of self-denial and physical suffering. Hayyim Hayka ben Aaron of Zamocz, for example, instructed repeatedly and graphically that the body and soul of man were in a state of perpetual conflict and that the only way to refine the human soul was through deliberate abstinence from all physical gratification.[11] In a similar spirit, Rabbi Mordechai ben Shmuel of Vielkocz, in his famous and highly influential pietistic work, *Shaar ha-Melekh,* prescribed a life of material sim-plicity, abstinence, and physical suffering.[12]

Of course, in this same period there were those who strongly opposed the pious asceticism of these preachers and reaffirmed the classic, more moder-ate rabbinic approach to the relationship of body to soul and the religious uses of material gratification. They maintained, as had the vast majority of earlier rabbinic thinkers, that the felicity of the soul is contingent upon the strength and health of the body and thus moderate bodily nourishment and comfort are the essential ingredients that enable one to pursue a life of dedication to Torah. Take, for example, the comments of R. Abraham Abosh of Zamocz, who, very much unlike his above-quoted *landsman,* rejected the extremes of both materialism and asceticism:

Sometimes the evil instinct beholds a man over whom it cannot prevail through physical excesses. It therefore devises a sinister method whereby this man will inherit two *gehenna*—one in this world and one in the world to come. For [the evil instinct convinces this man that] it is good and proper for him to punish himself through all kinds of tortures—with fasting beyond his strength and various types of mortifications. And it dupes him into believing that in this way he will become an acceptable and proper servant of the Lord.

The truth, however, is that this is not the chosen path. For just as God despises the man who pursues the other extreme, that is, the path of material excess, so too does God despise the extreme of self-deprivation. Instead, a man should always follow the middle path of moderation.[13]

This reaffirmation of what might generally be regarded as the normative, moderate rabbinic and Jewish philosophical notion of the golden mean is, given its polemical tone, further testimony to the persistence into eighteenth-century Jewish thought of not only the pietistic ascetic ideal but also the advocacy of active self-mortification on the part of a significant minority of Jewish spiritualists. It seems clear from many of the sources from this period that both the dualistic asceticism of Bahya and the mystical self-mortifications of Safed retained a significant number of adherents on the eve of the rise of the Hasidic movement.

Hasidism's Monistic Materialism

The most common term employed to describe the ascetic individual in the medieval literature was, as noted above, *hasid*. The Hasid's saintly behavior, classically described as *hasiduth*, or piety, was generally synonymous with the ideal of *perishuth*, or saintly abstemiousness. Despite the common nomenclature, however, the eighteenth-century Hasidic movement in eastern Europe did not share this particular approach to *hasiduth*. Although Beshtian Hasidism did, in a certain sense, share the final goal of the earlier mystics, namely, to transcend the physical universe in an attempt to attain mystical union with the Shekhinah, its method for achieving that exalted state was radically different from that of the Lurianic ascetics.

Beshtian Hasidism was primarily a monistic doctrine that conceived of God as being immanent in the physical world even if not always readily manifest to the human senses. Achieving proximity to him could therefore be done without forsaking, repressing, or punishing the material dimension of human existence. Quite the contrary, the BESHT and his disciples taught that by managing to perceive the divinity inherent within nature, one might succeed in transforming his ostensibly physical activities into genuinely spiritual exercises. For Hasidism, then, the physical world was to be transcended precisely through partaking of it with the correct spiritual insight. The Lurianic notion that sparks of divinity were entrapped in the physical realm and had to be liberated through man's spiritual efforts was adapted, transformed, and popularized by Hasidism. In the Hasidic version, however, man is instructed to perceive, through heightened spiritual awareness, the divinity that is inherent but concealed in all matter, regardless of how coarse it might appear. He is then able to serve God through material gratification as well. This technique, termed *avodah be-gashmiyouth* in later Hasidic sources, was informed by the conviction not only that man might, through heightened spiritual awareness, engage in material pursuits without being distracted from divine contemplation but also that such cognizance of the divinity inherent in all matter would enable man to transform even his most mundane physical activities into profound mystical experiences.[14]

This doctrine reflected a thorough, two-tiered monism—anthropological and cosmological. For it advanced a harmonious, holistic view of man whereby body and soul need not be in a state of continuous conflict or tension but might cooperate to serve God and harmoniously to attain holiness. This anthropological monism was in turn rooted in the larger monistic cosmogony of Hasidism, according to which man must make himself aware that there is no real rift separating God from the created universe. The physical reality that it is man's task to transcend in approaching God is, according to this view, nothing more than an illusion of the human senses. And the mind of man, when properly directed, can overcome the purely illusory sense of divine distance and transcendence, thereby liberating the corporeal universe from its coarse exterior, revealing its innate sanctity and directing all worldly realities back to their divine roots. The Hasidim consequently took quite literally the notion that God was to be served with both human dimensions, physical and spiritual, and with both natural inclinations, good and evil.[15]

Based on this comprehensive monism, many of the Hasidic masters taught that the material universe was in fact a vehicle for, rather than an obstacle to, the achievement of the most sublime mystical states. Legends and traditions abound regarding the Baal Shem Tov's forceful and consistent rejection of material self-denial as a religious value and his disapproval of asceticism as a method for achieving proximity to God.[16] The BESHT's emphasis on joyfully serving God with one's physical senses and his insistence that an immanent God completely pervades the created physical universe combined forcefully to eliminate any place for ascetic piety in early Hasidism.

The Hasidic master Zeev Wolf of Zhitomir (d. 1800), in a typology of the two predominant religious outlooks of his day, distinguished sharply between the earlier Kabbalistic-ascetic and Beshtian-Hasidic approaches to divine service:

Behold, there are two ways in which the people of Israel serve their Creator. Every single Jew, in the way in which he prays or studies the Torah, falls into one of these two categories. Those of the first sect are aroused to serve God with all of their hearts and souls as a result of the intensity of their awareness and the heightened nature of their realization of the immanence and providence of God even in the smallest details of this world and the extent to which He examines everyone's heart and conscience. Now, this is the superior and chosen way. The second sect, as a consequence of its limited perception and understanding of the greatness of the Creator, is only aroused to the Torah and to the service of God by means of afflictions, and the like.

. . . for our eyes have seen that there is a [type of]) man who engages in all kinds of self-mortifications and ritual immersions for the sole purpose of attaining the holy spirit or for receiving a revelation from Elijah.

I have heard that in the days of the BESHT there was such a person who engaged in self-mortifications and went to the ritual bath in order to acquire the Holy Spirit. And the BESHT said that in the world of recompense [i.e., the world to come] they are laughing at him. For the truth is that all of this is not necessary, particularly when one's heart is lacking in the essential worship, namely, *devekuth*.[17]

Thus, the classic Hasidic theory of *devekuth*, in direct opposition to the earlier Kabbalah's ascetic piety, was rooted in a heightened realization that God thoroughly pervades the material creation and a conviction that abstinence from the material dimension of life is to be regarded as not only unnecessary but even sinful. For since God is immanent in the world, *devekuth* cannot possibly be achieved by renouncing it. Therefore the BESHT consistently opposed the ascetic practices of those with whom he came into contact. Legend has it that he firmly rebuked his disciple R. Jacob Joseph of Polnoe on account of the latter's continual fasting, arguing that "this is the way of melancholy and sadness, and the Shekhina does not inspire man through sadness but only through the joy of performing *mitzvoth*."[18]

According to a well-known Hasidic tale, R. Jacob Joseph ultimately heeded his mentor's critique and renounced his extreme, dualistic asceticism. In conformity with the optimistic, monistic doctrine of the BESHT, R. Jacob eventually came to preach the service of God through physical pleasure and material gratification: "In each individual man there is a binding of body and soul. The body serves as the external garment of the soul. Thus it is that only the happiness of the body will cause the soul to rejoice in its clinging [*devekuth*] to God."[19] Thus, spiritual excellence is achieved not through the suppression of man's material needs but rather by means of their gratification and satisfaction in order to transform them back to their holy origins:

"The essence of each man consists of both form and matter. The form is called day, and the matter is called night. The ultimate goal is to transform the matter into form."[20]

Of course, as with the other main doctrines of Hasidism, there was no monolithic, clear consensus on this issue. Not all of the Hasidic theoreticians championed material celebration as an appropriate spiritual method. Some leading masters advocated the older, mystical approach of ascetic sanctification. A distinctly puritanical, often ascetic tone is to be found in some of the classic writings of early Hasidism. In fact, the Great Maggid's son, Abraham ben Dov Ber, was known in Hasidic lore as "the Angel" because of his strict asceticism.[21] Many Hasidic masters, such as R. Elimelekh of Lizensk, warned repeatedly against the materialist excesses of their contemporaries and advocated a life of utter simplicity.[22] Others, like R. Hayyim Haikel of Amdur, the Lithuanian Hasidic master and mystic who was the target of some of the most violent Mithnagdic attacks, and the enigmatic R. Nahman of Brazlav were themselves ascetic spiritualists.[23] Hayyim Haikel, reacting to what was likely the manifestation among the masses of a vulgar understanding of the doctrine of *avodah be-gashmiyouth*, complained constantly in his writings of the gross materialism of his own disciples, particularly their overindulgences in food and drink. Significantly, his critique was formulated in remarkably dualistic terms:

> I have observed many among our own people who have broken down the barriers by turning their stomachs into their gods. . . .
> I am extremely surprised by these people who eat meat like the hungry bear and have become fat just like a bear . . . until their hearts too have become corpulent and they have been blinded to the truth that when the one rises, the other will fall. That is, when the body rises, the soul will descend.[24]

Yet these minority ascetic voices were overpowered by the celebratory, monistic-materialist majority in the Hasidic camp. Moreover, it must be remembered that many Hasidic texts that seem, *prima facie*, to be advocating asceticism through their insistence on negating material existence belong in truth to the materialist school as well. For, practically speaking, what they often really are advising is that the Jew indulge his senses with deliberate indifference to the physical dimension of their pleasure in order to discover the inherent Godliness of the material universe. The transcendence, abrogation, or annulment of material reality *(bitul ha-yesh)*, which these Hasidic sources often prescribe, is merely a psychic exercise that is practically fulfilled through bodily indulgence.[25]

More to the point, whatever the actual internal complexities of the various Hasidic ideological approaches to asceticism, the overwhelming Mithnagdic view held that Hasidism was indeed a grossly materialistic, even hedonistic, movement, a perception to which we shall return. In the late eighteenth century, in addition, of course, to the conventional moderate rabbinic perspective, there were, then, two diametrically opposed approaches to the practice of *hasiduth:* the dualistic, ascetic legacy of medieval Hasidism, Bahya's dualism, and Safed spirituality on the one hand and the monistic materialism of Beshtian Hasidism on the other.

Hasidim and Mithnagdim on the Religious Role of Physical Pleasure

The major Mithnagdic thinkers at the end of the century were clearly scandalized by the Hasidic doctrine of *avodah be-gashmiyouth.* They reacted with horror to the Hasidic indulgence in what the Mithnagdim considered to be "the vanities of this world." A recurrent theme of the Mithnagdic polemical literature is that the Hasidim, as a result of their sacramental indulgences in food, drink, and merriment, "transformed all of their days into festivities."[26] The Mithnagdic polemicist R. David of Makow was especially outraged by the attitude to physical gratification he discovered in the writings of R. Jacob Joseph of Polnoe. As mentioned above, R. Jacob Joseph, although once a dualist and ascetic, had become, largely under the influence of the BESHT, an anthropological monist who advocated the satisfaction of the body as an inherent religious value. Thus, for example, he taught that one should not be content with the traditional utilitarian view of eating and drinking as merely providing the bodily strength necessary to engage in divine service. Rather, the consumption of food should in itself be viewed as an act of worship:

> It is a general principle that when one does any act for the sake of heaven, that act itself should be transformed into a form of worship. So, for example, when one eats for the sake of [serving] God, the intention should not merely be to gain sufficient strength from the food in order to be able to serve God. Although this too is a legitimate purpose, the highest perfection requires that the very act of eating—by means of raising the holy sparks [in the food]—should itself constitute worship. . . . And so one should intend in all of one's endeavors.[27]

In his anti-Hasidic writings R. David of Makow reacted angrily to this perceived subversion of Jewish values and reaffirmed at great length that asceticism was the true way of Torah:

All of his [i.e., the BESHT's] words are directed toward a single conclusion, namely, his claim that the only true good for man is to sit upon the fleshpots and to build lacquered houses and that there is no greater benefit for him than to spend days of vanity just eating, drinking, and celebrating. . . . For according to his view, man's only advantage over the beasts consists in eating flesh and drinking wine. . . .

Now, we have all heard and seen how the Hasidim became soft and fat and grew a double belly through eating like the locust and transforming all of their days into festivities with meat, quails, and fish. They said: "What is the divine service of the heart? It is none other than eating and praying." Thus has the holy Torah become neglected.

Now, anyone who has eyes in his head can see that all of this is antithetical to the way of Torah and is contrary to common sense and completely alien to both. For in the Torah that Moses commanded to us, all excesses were forbidden to us, and deprivation was prescribed for us, as it is written: "When Jeshurun grew fat, he rebelled." Furthermore, they [i.e., the rabbis] instituted certain protective ordinances and legal restrictions [to the effect that] all physical pleasures should be considered negatively and all cravings abominable; and all who partake thereof are culpable, and all who touch them are unclean.[28]

It was in all likelihood largely as a result of their reaction to the celebratory and monistic-materialist nature of Hasidic worship that almost all of the Mithnagdim strictly adhered to a dualistic view of man and an ascetic ethic. For although they may have shared the theoretical Hasidic belief that God is immanent in the created universe, they discouraged the popularization of such theosophical wisdom and suppressed any behavioral tendencies, such as material indulgence, that were rooted in such a cosmological monism.

The extent to which the Hasidim differed from their opponents in this matter was especially evident in their respective views of the religious significance of eating and drinking. As Louis Jacobs has noted, the early Hasidic masters viewed food and drink as constituting, at the very least, a necessary and therefore sacred prerequisite to proper prayer and Torah study. Moreover, they believed that when engaged in with the proper intentions and appropriate mystical "unifications," eating ideally became much more than a necessary preparation for divine service: it attained an intrinsic sanctity and was thereby transformed into an autonomous religious activity. Not only did the BESHT inform his disciples regarding the utilitarian importance of food (i.e., simply in order to have the necessary strength to serve God properly and out of joy rather than out of the pain of privation) but he indicated that the very act of eating might be transformed into a mystical experience: "When a man eats, he should consider that the taste and the sweetness of that which he is eating derives from the power of the divine vitality and sweetness which infuses the food with life."[29] In that same tradition, R. Levi Isaac of Berditchev taught that "all that a person eats is in order to have the energy to serve God. In this way, he can raise the divine sparks that are contained within the food. If, God forbid, he fails to raise the divine spark in the food that he is eating, then that divine spark must undergo transmigration until somebody eats it with the proper intention of raising it. . . . Thus is the act of eating in itself a form of worship."[30]

In chapter 2 I argued that while the GRA and his disciples may have accepted in theory the abstract concept of divine immanence on every level of existence in the created world, for practical purposes they opposed the popularization of this notion. What they feared was precisely the practical conclusions and behavioral consequences that early Hasidism derived from its monistic cosmology. Whereas the Hasidim were engaging in the sanctification of eating and drinking, the Mithnagdic rabbis were counseling their followers to pay as little attention as possible to the food they ate, focusing instead on their spiritual and intellectual goals. Thus the GRA advised his family to read the Yiddish translations of the classical medieval ethical works while eating, in order not to allow the partaking in food to lead to frivolous behavior, such as engaging in idle gossip.[31] According to his student Benjamin Rivlin, the GRA even discouraged excessive eating on the Sabbath, when such consumption constitutes a *mitzvah*. The master insisted that one was better off focusing on Torah study instead:

> When I spoke of this matter before my teacher, the Gaon, of blessed memory, he told me that he had a general principle that even though it is a *mitzvah* to eat and drink on the Sabbath, it is also a *mitzvah* to study Torah on the Sabbath. It is then much better to increase one's study than to increase one's eating and drinking. For increasing study will help develop study habits, and study is a *mitzvah* at all other times as well. On the other hand, eating on the Sabbath will lead to a greater appetite on weekdays as well.[32]

Similarly, the pietist R. Alexander Zisskind of Grodno complained at length in his ethical will of the frivolity he observed among Jews during mealtime, and he urged study of *musar* works at the dinner table as an appropriate antidote.[33] R. Alexander thus argued that only such study would be effective in distracting man from the materialistic indulgences in which he was engaged and would truly serve to "sanctify" the dinner table.

Whereas eating in itself was regarded by the Hasidism as a potentially sacred activity endowed with mystical potential when entered into with the proper *kavana*, the Mithnagdim insisted that external, religious distractions were necessary in order to elevate man beyond his material indulgences, which they regarded as inherently and irredeemably profane. The Mithnagdim clearly believed that there could be no inherent spiritual value in the physical act of consumption. They thus endorsed the medieval rabbinic-philosophical view that the only real importance of food and drink was utilitarian; that is, its true value was merely to provide man with the minimum strength necessary to pursue his religious agenda of Torah study and the observance of *mitzvoth*. Benjamin Rivlin characterized his master's attitude toward participation in a meal as follows: "When someone invites his friend to join him for a meal, the latter should respond: "'You should rather feed your heart,' that is to say, intend [in your meal] only to have energy for sustaining your good instinct, with which to engage in Torah study and observance of the commandments."[34]

Eating and drinking without this higher end in mind was of absolutely no value. In fact, the GRA viewed all physical indulgences, including eating, as being inherently rather repulsive: "The things of this world, such as eating, in which one takes food and turns it into feces and excrement, or the sexual act, are intrinsically loathsome. It is only what may result from them that might be for good, such as if the only purpose of the eating is to be able to turn again to Torah study."[35] His student R. Hayyim of Volozhin seems to have shared this sensibility, as the following, rather ascetic statement indicates: "The truth is that this whole business of eating, whereby man's very existence is dependent upon putting a material thing into his bowels, is a great disgrace to the dignity of a human being. Now surely his soul, the spiritual part [of man], must scorn all of this with utter contempt."[36] R. Hayyim accordingly advised that one should consume only the amount of food that is absolutely necessary for physical endurance.

These very different perspectives on eating and drinking are not a reflection of divergent culinary sensibilities. They are but one specific manifestation of fundamentally antithetical views on the relationship between the physical and spiritual dimensions of human existence and endeavor. In sharp contrast to Hasidism's advocacy of religious practice that reflected their heightened awareness of the cosmic unity between God and the creation, and the resulting anthropological monism, the leading Mithnagdic theoreticians instructed that matter and spirit must be viewed as conflicting forces in the cosmos as well as within man. Following the dualism of the Neoplatonic philosophical tradition, they believed that the greatest obstacles to spiritual growth were man's physical needs and material pursuits. Only the suppression of, or at the very least distraction from, the innate instincts and desires of the body would allow the soul of man to prosper.

The Ascetic Piety of the GRA

The Gaon of Vilna was renowned for his personal asceticism. Legends abound regarding his strict neglect of his own bodily needs and comforts. R. Hayyim of Volozhin seems to have considered the GRA's ascetic piety to be as distinctive an attribute as his learning: "Even if a man were to live for one thousand years, he could never manage to record all of his [i.e., the GRA's] wisdom, which was revealed to him like a veritable flowing fountain. And no mouth could properly recount the very many ways of his piety [*hasiduth*] and asceticism [*perishuth me-olam ha-zeh*] and the extent of his holiness and many good deeds."[37] Consistent with this characterization of the twofold greatness of the GRA, he remained known in subsequent generations by the binary title "ha-Gaon he-Hasid mi-Vilna" (the prodigy and saint of Vilna), testifying to both his renowned scholarship and his personal ascetic attributes.[38]

The GRA's son R. Abraham testified to his father's extreme neglect of elementary bodily needs: "All the many days of his life, we learned from him how he spurned all of the many pleasures of this world—food, drink, and sleep—and only then found good fortune in the land of the living."[39] The GRA's asceticism derived in part from his very strong conviction that the body is the mortal enemy of the soul. He neglected his own body, therefore, so that his soul would be elevated. The extent to which the GRA's lifestyle was in harmony with this radical anthropological dualism was, once again, testified to by his own son: "Who can properly express his wonderful ethical traits, how like a heavenly angel he nullified his saintly body, lest his corporeality [*geshem*] obstruct his [spiritual] path."[40] Benjamin Rivlin also spoke at length of the GRA's ascetic spirit, which resulted in a general antimaterialism:

> I have heard from my teacher, the Gaon, that it is well known that "the Torah does not endure except in someone who regurgitates his mother's milk for its sake," namely, someone who is ready to destroy all of his desires. And my teacher, the Gaon, further instructed that there exists a type of person who does destroy all of his desires, yet he continues to covet money. Such a person is equally unable to attain the crown of Torah. For this person who has broken all of his desires yet still craves money is comparable to a child who has been weaned from his mother, yet every time she brings him close to her he approaches her breasts, for he still remembers fondly the great enjoyment which he had from them. . . . It is similar with this man. Even though the whole point of craving money is that wealth enables one to satisfy his other desires, and even though this man has overcome those desires, nevertheless, he still craves the money because he recalls how happy the money made him in the days when other desires ruled over him.[41]

This rabbi who, legend has it, denied himself the elementary physical pleasure even of sleep and who studied Torah all of his days and nights in a darkened, windowless study hermetically sealed from the outside world, with his feet immersed in ice water, expected no less from his students and disciples.[42] Thus he continuously reminded his disciples and children that "all of the material of this world is vanity and all of its pleasures are worthless."[43] And he accordingly insisted that they rigorously deny themselves all forms of material or physical gratification. Yet in the very same breath the GRA warned against practicing active mortification or engaging in self-afflicting forms of physical torture. An advocate of rigorous discipline in all of one's affairs, he rejected the extremes of both hedonism and asceticism: "This is the essence of man: he must not give in to his desires, and he must tightly curb and buffer himself from gratifications. Until his dying day must a man suffer. But not through fasts and self-flagellation, but only through the tight control of his mouth and his appetites."[44]

The GRA seems here to have distinguished between abstemious asceticism and active self-mortification. In other words, he advocated passive asceticism through the rigorous control of the natural human instincts and appetites but disapproved of active asceticism via self-torture and flagellation. The reason for this distinction lies in the context and limited purpose of the GRA's asceticism. For him, the deprivation of the sensual appetites was neither an appropriate mystical technique nor a method for attaining *devekuth*. He viewed it, rather, as merely a disciplinary action intended to curb the human appetites for the limited period of man's this-worldly existence. Such worldly abstention is sensible only in the larger perspective of the GRA's conception of the very circumscribed significance of man's earthly existence. For the GRA, physical indulgence was wrong primarily because it tended to attribute permanence and importance to this life, thereby distracting man from his soul's ultimate purpose and true destiny: the spiritual life of the posthumous world to come. The GRA vividly compared the human soul's existence in the physical world to a sailor lost in the stormy seas, whose ultimate goal is not to enjoy the treacherous voyage but to survive it in order to arrive safely on land. So, too, man must be aware that the soul's existence within the physical universe is turbulent and unnatural and that all of life's material pleasures are but temporary vanities, reduced to insignificance in the light of the eternity to be enjoyed by the soul in its next life.[45] Only physical and material austerity can create the framework for such other-worldly awareness. The GRA's asceticism must then be understood not only in the context of his anthropological dualism but also in the larger context of this fundamental cosmological dualism. Just as the value of food and drink is purely utilitarian, the significance of ascetic practice too is limited as a consequence of its purely utilitarian role. By rejecting material pursuits, man does not attain immediate holiness but is simply reminded of his physical mortality and is thereby better prepared for his true spiritual destiny.

The GRA was thus a rigorous dualist who insisted that a perpetual battle must be waged, literally to the death, against the world's corporeal forces and man's material desires. He insisted that "the evil instinct will only emerge out of eating and celebration" and, conversely, that "the Holy spirit will only appear to a broken body."[46] In sharp opposition to Hasidism's monistic doctrine of *avodah be-gashmiyouth*, he contended that the path toward eternity was via the disciplined deprivation of the physical senses. However, this approach mandates only strict abstention and self-deprivation, not active mortification. The GRA accordingly endorsed a passive, conservative form of asceticism, rejecting the extremes of both Hasidic materialism and penitential or punitory self-mortification. Only Torah study, which was of course nurtured by extreme material simplicity, would enhance the religious life and ultimately assure the eternity of the human soul.

Mithnagdic Asceticism

There were many Lithuanian rabbis and preachers in the generation following the GRA who reflected an almost identical body-soul dualism and asceticism. Perhaps the most severe and consistent of them was the maggid Hillel ben Zev Wolf of Kovno. His homiletical work *Heilel Ben Shahar* is primarily an extensive and thorough condemnation of all forms of materialism, personal/physical as well as economic. Reminding his reader constantly of the very temporary nature of earthly existence and all its material trappings, R. Hillel railed repeatedly against the pitfalls of greed and physical desire. He warned that indulgence in the pleasures of the material world has a devastating effect on the human soul. Like his two spiritual models, the GRA and Alexander Zisskind (both of whose eulogies are appended to the text of *Heilel Ben Shahar*), R. Hillel viewed the need to eat as a particular challenge to human spiritual excellence. Having established that eating and drinking were prime occasions for the ascendancy of the evil inclination, R. Hillel counseled the maximum abstention possible: "A man should be humiliated and ashamed to engage in eating before he has sated himself with the study of the Torah and its *mitzvoth*."[47] Practically, R. Hillel counseled that in order to alleviate the snares of food consumption, one ought to mourn for the Temple and lament the spiritual degeneracy of the times while "feasting" on no more than "a thin piece of herring."[48]

Typical of the Mithnagdic maggidim of his day, R. Hillel constantly mourned the moral and spiritual decline of his generation. He attributed this largely to the physical indulgences of contemporary Jews. In a rather romantic reference to a more pious Jewish past, he suggested that it was its materialism that set his generation apart in its spiritual coarseness:

> It is fitting that we break all of our bones and cast away all of our limbs and organs because of our many sins and because of the limitations of our deeds. For we are wandering like lost sheep, intoxicated with wine and drunken with the vanities of this world. We do not subject ourselves to the scalding waters, for our hearts desire nothing other than the fulfillment of our bodily cravings. . . .
>
> We no longer spend all of our days and hours only in the study of Torah and Halakhah, as did the previous generations. For they consumed their time only in Torah study. . . . They were materially satisfied with the bare minimum, that is, with very little sleep, very little commerce, and very little of this earth's indulgences.[49]

On several occasions R. Hillel cited the GRA as the chief inspiration for his asceticism. Yet he went even further than the GRA in attributing not only individual religious decline but all of the Jewish social and national ills of his time to the contemporary preoccupation with material acquisition. Accordingly, much of his work is devoted to a stinging castigation of the upper classes of Jewish society. Condemning the rich for their material excesses and the poor for daring to envy the former's wealth, R. Hillel asserted repeatedly that only a life of poverty and deprivation could secure spiritual well-being for both the individual Jew and the nation of Israel.[50] Like that of the GRA before him, R. Hillel's consistent asceticism was rooted in a clearly articulated anthropological dualism.

R. Abraham Danzig shared this same perspective on the inversely proportional relationship between worldly pleasures and spiritual attainments. In his ethical will he firmly counseled his children against overindulgence in food and drink and urged extreme sexual restraint.[51] Reminding his reader rhetorically that "the soul is not at all joined with the [destiny of the] body, for what could they possibly share in common?" he warned that a man should never become too preoccupied with material success, thereby losing sight of his ultimate spiritual aspirations.[52] In a remarkable homiletical interpretation of the laws pertaining to the paschal lamb, Danzig elaborated on the importance of closely controlling the bodily instincts:

> In the middle years of his life, man ought to conduct himself as he does on the intermediate days of the festivals—that is, *hol ha-mo'ed,* when we are only

allowed to engage in labours whose neglect might result in serious economic loss. In other words, man ought only to engage in that which is absolutely necessary for the mere survival of the body, and all superfluous material pursuits are forbidden. . . .

Nonetheless, since in our days it has become impossible to abrogate the evil instinct entirely . . . thus there is a hint that we must slaughter an unblemished lamb, which refers to our evil instinct at its very height. For the lamb is a symbol of *Samael*, the chief officer [of the demonic forces], which at its height, that is, in the middle of the month [of Nissan], must be slaughtered. So must man slaughter his evil inclination. . . .

Now the *mitzvah* is to consume the paschal lamb broiled and not [slowly] cooked; this is a hint that every pleasure with which man indulges his evil inclination should be enjoyed only very quickly and not deliberately—like the broiling, which is very fast—in order that that the evil inclination not [be given the opportunity to] dominate man.

And we may not break the bones thereof [i.e., of the paschal lamb]. For it is the nature of man that when he derives great pleasure from food, he tends even to gnaw at and suck the bones. Thus we are taught not to derive too much pleasure from the food we eat, only that which is absolutely necessary for the sake of performing the mitzvah, and no more.

It [the paschal lamb] is eaten only at night; this indicates that the physical appetites only apply to the night, which is our this-worldly existence. . . .

And the stranger may not partake thereof; this teaches that someone who has become estranged from God because his evil appetites dominate him must minimize his indulgences and abstain even from those things that are legally permitted to him.[53]

Rabbi Ezekiel Faivel, the maggid of Dretzhyn, echoed similarly dualistic and ascetic sentiments in his writings. In the opening chapter of his biography of R. Zalman of Volozhin (brother of R. Hayyim) he emphasized the strict temporality of this-worldly existence and the ephemeral and very uncomfortable nature of the coexistence of the "divine soul of man in his filthy, earthly body." According to R. Ezekiel, the proof of the eternity of the soul subsequent to the demise of the body is to be discovered in the fact that there exists an inversely proportional relationship between the respective welfares of body and soul. It is for this reason that as man ages and his body becomes weaker, his soul progressively strengthens itself. And with the complete demise of the body, the soul gathers ultimate strength and is liberated to join with God. R. Ezekiel then contended that the true sage and pious man has no use for, nor any interest in, the pleasurable vanities of the material world.[54] In another context, R. Ezekiel Faivel cited with approval the positive rabbinic disposition toward material abstention:

Our true Sages have instructed us to derogate from all matters concerning eating and drinking in order that we may plunder and despoil our bodily territory and level off the material dimension of our lives with exalted moral attributes. For this [abstention] allows for the attainment of wisdom. . . .

It is for this very reason that the wise men say that it is only in his declining years that man is able truly to discern good from bad, for only then does his physical matter, with all its attendant evil forces, become progressively weaker.[55]

Many other Mithnagdic sources reflect this same perspective. In fact, the Mithnagdim speak with one voice regarding man's inherently divided constitution and the resultant need to suppress the material dimension of human nature in order to allow for spiritual felicity. This perspective is certainly reflected throughout the writings of R. Phinehas of Polotsk.

The Dualist Asceticism of R. Phinehas of Polotsk

The attitude of R. Phinehas of Polotsk toward the relative merits of physical gratification and materialism on the one hand and ascetic self-denial on the other was, as we shall see, compatible with the dualistic asceticism of both the GRA and his own Mithnagdic contemporaries. As pointed out earlier, R. Phinehas's most important work, *Kether Torah,* was largely modeled after Bahya's *Hovoth ha-Levavoth.* More generally, Bahya was one of the most important general sources of inspiration for the religious philosophy of R. Phinehas. His *Hovoth ha-Levavoth* is quoted throughout R. Phinehas's writings more than any other single work, and it clearly exercised a profound influence upon R. Phinehas. Given this influence, as well as the pronounced asceticism of his teacher, the GRA, it is not surprising that R. Phinehas's writings are saturated with a rather extreme anthropological dualism, and, most significantly, a pronounced asceticism.

Clearly paraphrasing the ninth section of *Hovoth ha-Levavoth* ("The Gate of Abstinence"), R. Phinehas warns that the indulgence of the human appetites is the most dangerous temptation of the evil inclination. He accordingly advises that indulgence in eating merely for pleasure's sake, even of Halakhically permitted foods, is reprehensible: "This [eating] should be considered like consuming a mouse or a pig, which one should by nature abhor and which your soul must surely hate."[56] He says that the same attitude should apply to excessive sexual gratification and, more generally, to all of man's material or financial acquisitions.[57] R. Phinehas is convinced that as a rule man ought to avoid any physical pleasures or material pursuits that are not absolutely necessary for his health and physical sustenance: "Do not seek after anything in this world of yours beyond that [which is absolutely essential] to remove hunger or cover nakedness."[58]

Like both Bahya and his own personal mentor, the GRA (and his disciples), R. Phinehas conceives of man as constituting a moral battleground between two constantly opposing forces, those of the body and those of the soul. The primary animating forces of the body are the material appetites and desires, whereas the soul derives its strength solely from the study of Torah. Yet, the *yezer ha-ra* (the evil inclination) operates, in R. Phinehas's view, in complex, multifaceted ways. Beyond simply deploying the innate physical drives of man in order to distract him from Torah study, the evil inclination employs more subtle and insidious techniques as well. Among these more covert distractions are some ostensibly spiritual pursuits, which, when engaged in obsessively, have the unwitting effect of alienating man from his most important religious vocation, that is, the study of Torah.

Although R. Phinehas consistently espoused anthropological dualism and asceticism, he remained somewhat suspicious of any manifestations of excessive ascetic piety. In fact, R. Phinehas included the inordinate commitment of any individual to self-mortification on his long list of the ostensibly pious, subtle distractions of the *yezer ha-ra* from a life of Torah. Most specifically, he rejected the notion that such radical ascetic practices—clearly identifiable with the concept *teshuvath ha-mishkal*, or commensurate repentance, which originated in the medieval German pietist movement, or Hasiduth Ashkenaz —are essential prerequisites to the study of Torah.[59]

> The evil instinct will try to seduce you by telling you that there is no point in clinging to the divine Torah so long as you are filthy from sin and transgressions . . . and that you are much better off clinging to the attribute of penitence and purifications from your sins. Consequently [the evil instinct] proposes for you all kinds and variant forms of atonement . . . such as rolling in the snow and immersing in icy waters, or wearing sackcloth and fasting constantly. All these are contrary to human reason. For the entire purpose [of the evil instinct] is none other than to exempt itself in this way from the Torah and break its bonds from off of its neck, and to weaken you and drain you of all your strength. It does not care if, as a result of these many self-mortifications, you may become sick or mentally confused and deranged, or even if you die; so long as it can alienate you from the Light of Life [i.e., the Torah] through these, its perverse ways.[60]

In opposition to the fraudulent piousness of extreme asceticism, R. Phinehas argues that divine forgiveness is most effectively attained through the study of Torah, and not through acts of self-flagellation. Elsewhere in his writings R. Phinehas roundly condemns a religious preoccupation with self-mortification. In the course of a protracted assault upon various forms of religious pretentiousness R. Phinehas targets the arrogant excesses of the ascetic Hasidim:

> Hearken, my son, to the lesson of your father! Should you desire to accept upon yourself any type of ascetic behavior, make sure that you do not go to the extreme of harming yourself. Therefore, be not like the madmen and the fools who waste away their lives in self-flagellation, in fasts, and in immersions in icy waters. These things freeze the mind and the heart; and the people who engage in such acts die even before their days are half over, and they will have to answer for their sins. . . . As for us, in this declined generation of ours, we have no reason to torture our souls.[61]

While R. Phinehas does continue to advocate moderate abstention from obvious evils such as alcohol, he warns that extreme abstinence is always dangerous and contrary to the true and moderate way of Torah. Of course, these condemnations of asceticism read very much like statements by earlier rabbinic maggidim as well as the teachings of the BESHT and his disciples on this subject. But R. Phinehas's concerns seem more narrowly defined. He voices two very specific warnings about the hazards of extreme asceticism: first, that self-flagellatory practices should not become a dominant or central expression of spirituality, for any such prevalence accorded to ascetic behavior might derogate from the absolute religious supremacy of *Talmud Torah;* and second, that abstemious behavior should not be taken to such extremes as to pose a threat to human bodily or mental health. Unlike the Hasidic masters, R. Phinehas does not follow his critique of asceticism with an affirmation of the need to worship God out of joy and material plenitude. Quite the contrary, despite his reservations about ascetic extremism, he rigorously adheres to the moderately ascetic anthropological dualism of the medieval philosophical and Neoplatonic traditions and advocates, often to the point of idealization, a life of material deprivation and passive suffering—though not active self-flagellation—as being most conducive to the pursuit of piety via Torah study.[62]

That the body and the soul of man are in a state of constant competition is a theme that runs through all of R. Phinehas's works, most notably *Kether Torah.* The extent to which R. Phinehas adhered to this view of a perpetually turbulent human psyche torn between matter and form, body and soul, is also vividly illustrated in his abridged reformulation of the classic medieval ethical tract *Even Bohan,* by Kalonymous ben Kalonymous. Besides reproducing completely the most graphically dualistic portions of that work, most notably the very colorful debate between the body and the soul,[63] R. Phinehas furnished commentary and editorial embellishments of his own, which indicate the extent of his adherence to Kalonymous's anthropological dualism, his cynicism about material pursuits, and his fundamental asceticism. The editor of a posthumous edition of *Kizzur Even Bohan* captures the essence of Phinehas's message:

> This [chapter] explains that the very source for all the evil deeds of man is the body. As for the soul, it is pure, and no sin is to be found therein. Verily it is that the body is cunning like the snake. It will seduce the soul and prevail over it. And the soul, in following after the body and heeding its deceptions, will be found guilty. Therefore, one must subject all matters of the body to the control of the human heart, which is the king of the limbs; and one must rebuke and refute [the body's] actions and words.[64]

Consistent with the Neoplatonic view adopted by so many of the medieval rabbis and, later, by the GRA, R. Phinehas viewed the body not only as the soul's competitor but as its captor. Miserable in its corporeal incarceration, the soul "struggles at every single moment [of this life] to escape the [body of] man." The body is content with the vanities and ephemeral pleasures of this world and does not share in the soul's thirst for union with God. This is because the body and the soul are governed by entirely different forces. Whereas the soul of man is of divine origin and hence under God's constant providence, "the body, regardless of whether it is that of the righteous or of the evil man, is under no form of divine providence whatsoever."[65]

As a consequence of this thoroughly dualistic conception of the human constitution, R. Phinehas advocated a spiritual program of rigorous self-abstention and strict domination over the material impulses as a requirement for the attainment of piety. His championship of material simplicity and advocation of a life of deliberate abstention from pleasure, evident in all of his works, are presented most dramatically in R. Phinehas's exegetical work *Giveath Phinehas*, his very novel reading of the book of Job.[66]

R. Phinehas construes the torment of Job as being a justified, albeit harsh, punishment for the sin of material overindulgence. Although it is certainly true that Job is introduced in the biblical narrative as a simple, God-fearing man, R. Phinehas suspects that he was lacking in piety and that this is why Job is never referred to in the biblical text as a *hasid*, for he failed to instruct his children in the ways of true righteousness:

> Note that Job is never referred to by God as a *zaddik* or as a *hasid* who is truly concerned about the glory of his Creator. The proof of this is that his own sons

were eating and drinking constantly and transforming all of their days into festivities, and Job did nothing to rebuke them. On the contrary, he offered sacrifices on behalf of each of his sons. . . . Now this [failure] was the basis for the [heavenly] prosecution against him on the day of judgment.[67]

Although Job was an otherwise good and believing man, his wealth and materialism stood in the way of true *hasiduth,* or spiritual refinement. It was only through the terrible afflictions and suffering that were visited upon him that the soul of Job could become properly refined and that he was then able to serve as a paradigm of piety for others. Until he had gone through his mortifying ordeal and been stripped of all his material acquisitions, Job, despite all of his righteous innocence, remained alienated from God on account of his wealth and comfort. Through poverty and suffering, however, Job was able to ascend to great spiritual heights. R. Phinehas suggests that this is the rule not only in the case of Job but in the case of all men, for most men live in a state of alienation from God mainly on account of their material interests and physical indulgences:

> So long as he does not perfect himself in this manner [i.e., through suffering, like Job] . . . man has not completed the very purpose of this creation and he remains estranged from God and spiritually incomplete.
>
> Now, the entire cause of all such estrangement is the filthy body that is known as the flesh of man and that became contaminated through the sin of Adam. Behold that the body is, then, the curtain that separates the form of man [i.e., the soul] from its Creator. The extent to which man is drawn after the body and its matter in all of his activities is precisely the extent to which he will be similarly alienated from God. Consequently, it is the body that separates the human soul from God.
>
> Therefore, a man must purify his matter and cleanse his human flesh so that it will not interfere between him and God. The extent of the purifications and afflictions of the body exists in direct proportion to the extent of the divine spirit emanated to man. The more a man purifies and afflicts his material being, the more will God be near to that person in order that he will cling [Heb., *d'v'k'*] to Him. And such a person will behold God in the fullness of the glorious divine speculum.[68]

Two religious values emerge from this interpretation of Job: first, a distinct antimaterialism is implicit in the view that Job, simply because of his wealth, was alienated from Divine favor; second, the conviction that physical pain and affliction have inherent spiritual value springs from the suggestion that Job's excruciating torments were, in the final analysis, a religiously beneficial experience.

The Value of Poverty

The belief that Job's misguided materialism and inordinate wealth somehow justified his punishing ordeal reflects Phinehas's general hostility to material wealth and its possessors, the upper classes. Like R. Hillel of Kovno before him, R. Phinehas repeatedly castigated the wealthy for the inherent corruption of their lives and their lack of spirituality.[69] Whereas wealth is a religious curse and will obstruct the pathway to holiness, poverty is the ultimate blessing in disguise. In his ethical will, R. Phinehas implores his son not to rebel against or mourn his impoverished state but rather to accept it happily as a great gift from God intended to enhance the spiritual quality of his life.[70] It is in this spirit that R. Phinehas interprets the proverb, "He who ignores rebuke [*musar*] will come to poverty." He claims that only the suffering and personal deprivation inherent in a life of poverty can take the place of moral instruction in the event that the latter goes unheeded: "So that one who rejects *musar* and mocks it, and who therefore can have no salvation via moral suasion, as it is written, 'do not bother to rebuke the mocker,' his only possible hope is through poverty and suffering. Thus the rabbis have said that whosoever mocks will become poorer; for it is only through this poverty and suffering that his shame will be exposed and his wild heart will be tamed."[71]

Of course, R. Phinehas does not view poverty as an intrinsic value; rather he sees it as being of purely utilitarian importance. Being poor is of religious significance only in the context of a life dedicated to the Torah, whose study and observance are the true guarantors of religious fulfillment. This partnership of poverty and allegiance to the Torah is vividly advocated by R. Phinehas in his exegesis of yet another verse from Proverbs.

> "The commandments are a candle and the Torah is a light. . . ." The point is that there are two methods whereby God tames the tumultuous spirit of the children of Israel in order to deliver them into the life of the world to come: The first method is via poverty, as the Sages have instructed: "Poverty is for Israel like the red reigns of a white horse."
>
> The second method is that [God] subdues them via the Torah and its *mitzvoth*.
>
> Thus have I interpreted the verse: "The Lord has chastened me again and again, but He has not given me over unto death." For there are two types of chastening to which God has subjected me: the first is the Torah, which is called the *musar* [i.e., chastening] of God, for it is acquired through suffering; the second is the chastening effect of poverty.[72]

There thus exists a natural, mutually supportive relationship between Torah scholarship and the impoverished life. Not only is poverty valuable in taming the impulses of the human body and promoting the welfare of the spirit but it is positively conducive to a life of dedication to *Talmud Torah*. For, as R. Phinehas writes, "it is poverty that promotes the study of the Torah."[73] Therefore, in his view, one of the key and constant characteristics of the true sage of the Torah (i.e., the *talmid hacham*), aside from the obvious quality of scholarship, is his financial indigence and generally impoverished condition.[74]

Physical Affliction As Salvation

R. Phinehas goes beyond advocating a life of economic self-denial and material simplicity. On a number of occasions he suggests that actual physical pain and torment are often a valuable form of spiritual healing. His conviction that the punishment of the body is at times required for the felicity of the human soul emerges from his interesting elaboration upon a rather famous passage in Maimonides' *Mishneh Torah*. In attempting to illustrate the truth of Proverbs 23:13, which reads, "Do not withhold discipline from the child; if you punish him with the rod, he will not perish. Rather punish him with the rod and save his soul from death," R. Phinehas cites Maimonides' rationalization for the legal institution of the coerced writ of divorce:

> Do not say that whatever a man does under duress will not last, arguing that as soon as the external cause of duress has been eliminated, he will revert to his previous behavior. Rather, take note of the remarkable statement of Maimonides in this context. He has explicated the law that a coerced writ of divorce is valid and that [the court] may physically beat a man until he states that he desires to [grant the divorce], and that this is so because, in truth, the Jewish soul desires to do that which is good in accordance with Jewish law. However, his physical matter overcomes man's soul. Therefore, as a result of the beatings, which weaken the body, the true inner desires of the human soul are enabled to emerge and, consequently, the divorce is granted with spiritual volition.[75]

This remarkable paraphrase of Maimonides' legal interpretation places it in the broader philosophical context of ascetic body/soul dualism. In fact, he reinterprets and expands upon Maimonides' original statement to argue *against* the Maimonidean notion that the welfare of the soul is contingent upon the welfare of the body.[76] R. Phinehas claims that as a rule the weakening and punishment of the human body actually enhances the welfare of the soul.

Physical affliction is, moreover, not merely something to be applied by the courts of Israel under extenuating legal circumstances. R. Phinehas prescribes active self-affliction on a very personal, individualized level. In the course of reminding his own son of the importance, for the purposes of *kashruth*, of salting animal flesh before it is consumed, R. Phinehas draws a remarkable analogy between the animal and human souls in their relationships to their respective bodies:

> My son, be very diligent in the matter of salting meat so that absolutely no blood will remain and so that, through salting, all the blood will depart and not even the "doubtful blood" will endure. Furthermore, be extra careful to salt out all blood, so that none of the *dam* [blood] of man will remain therein either. For *dam* has a double meaning, as is well known. See to it, then, that you do "not consume the soul together with the flesh" [Deuteronomy 12:23]. Also, be sure to salt the meat so that it does not become rotten and go to waste. . . .
>
> Likewise, be sure to "salt" your own body so that it too will not go to waste. Now, with what can one "salt" the body? With afflictions and self-flagellation. For the word *brith* is used in connection with both salt [i.e., *brith milah*] and physical affliction [i.e., circumcision]. For just as salt renders the meat edible, so do physical afflictions cleanse man of sin.[77]

Just as the Torah requires the salting of meat in order to free the soul of the animal, which is contained in the blood, so will the mortification of the body liberate the soul from its corporeal captivity and allow it to reach great spiritual heights. The contrast between these sentiments regarding the role of Halakhic ritual in removing all spirit from an animal in order to prepare it for human consumption and the Hasidic approach to eating as a form of communion with the divine sparks inherent in the meat is, of course, striking.

Beyond advocating a life of poverty and abstinence from physical indulgences, then, R. Phinehas goes so far as to prescribe occasional active exercises of self-mortification. Interpreting rather oddly the Deuteronomic verse that presents life and death as two distinct options contingent upon man's moral choices, R. Phinehas observes: "'Behold I set before you on this day, life and death': That is to say, a life of death (i.e., mortification), as the Sages have instructed: 'What must a man do in order to live? Mortify himself in this world in order to live in the world to come.'"[78] R. Phinehas's reservations regarding extreme or obsessive mystical self-mortification must thus be balanced with his general advocacy of asceticism, which is often expressed in such forceful terms.

Conclusion

The spiritual pessimism and conservatism that motivated almost all of the Mithnagdim to reject Hasidism's divine service of an immanent God through nature and physical indulgence also aroused suspicion of very different but equally intense pietistic forms of spiritual expression. Although, practically speaking, they were antithetical to the methods of *avodah be-gashmiyouth*, these other, mystically based expressions of extreme asceticism shared its final goal, namely, *devekuth*. The dualistic ascetics of the Lurianic tradition and the monistic religious materialists of the Hasidic tradition did in fact strive to attain the same spiritual heights, albeit through antithetical means.

For R. Phinehas and many other Mithnagdim the ambitious goal of mystical union via extraordinary pietistic behavior, regardless of whether such behavior manifested itself materialistically or ascetically, lay well beyond the grasp of contemporary man. Although they were deeply offended by Hasidism's spiritualization of the material earthly realm, they rejected with equal fervor obsessive self-mortification as an effective route to *devekuth* for his "declined generation." Instead, the Mithnagdim advocated the moderate and conservative path of subduing the material passions through a disciplined life characterized by material modesty in order to be able to focus exclusively on the one safe and guaranteed route to religious fulfillment—*Talmud Torah*.

The belief that man's this-worldly existence is not to be celebrated and that its sensual pleasures cannot be channeled into paths for spiritual salvation derived not only from Mithnagdism's anthropological dualism but also from a larger temporal-existential dualism, namely, the rigorous separation of this-worldly time and existence from the life of the world to come. This latter dualism, in its emphasis upon the ephemeral nature and final insignificance of this-worldly vitality, had the practical effect of placing the ultimate religious goal of union with God in abeyance. According to this view, self-mortification is important only as vehicle for subduing man's passions, limiting his worldly aspirations and reminding him that his present life is illusory and of no lasting religious significance beyond preparing him for life in the next world. The human body must be repressed insofar as it is both the center and symbol of physical, earthly reality. Since there can never be true salvation in this world, all of its various temptations and fleshly pleasures must be limited, tamed, and channeled to serve the preoccupation with Torah study. For it is Torah alone that will prepare the human soul for man's truly significant next-worldly existence. As R. Phinehas insists: " 'Wisdom will not be attained in the land of the living': that is to say, it will not be attained by those who consider this life to represent real living and who seriously pursue this life. Wisdom only comes to he who mortifies himself in this life and tosses his corporeal existence by the wayside."[79] The deferral of salvation to the next life stands in clear contrast to both the Hasidic sanctification of this life through *avodah be-gashmiyouth* and the conviction of the ascetic Lurianic mystics that by means of their own forms of pious self-denial the mystical experience of God's presence can be enjoyed in the context of man's this-worldly existence.

Thus it is Mithnagdism's religious conservatism and general pessimism about life that underlie the Mithnagdim's mitigated form of dualistic asceticism and rejection of both extreme mystical self-mortification and Hasidic materialism. For, unlike the asceticism of the Kabbalists, their dualistic perspective is purely disciplinary, the result of a total negation of the inherent spiritual significance of the life of *olam ha-zeh,* the temporal world. And it is that very pessimism and negation of temporal life that underlies Mithnagdism's trenchant critique of the spiritualized materialism propagated by the early Hasidic masters. For the Mithnagdim, man can never achieve spiritual greatness in this life. Neither extreme asceticism nor *avodah be-gashmiyouth* can offer man any such deliverance. Ultimately, it is only through death that genuine salvation might come.

Chapter 5

THE SPIRITUAL BLISS
OF DEATH

In biblical Judaism life was defined, simply and consistently, as being good, and death as evil. Eternal life was Adam's destiny until he sinned; death, originating in human transgression, remained man's irrevocable punishment, the legacy of his primordial failing. And though the prospect of eternal life ended with Adam's initial transgression, the extension and enrichment of human life remained the biblical promise of reward for moral behavior, while physical suffering and immediate death represented expressions of divine vengeance for sin.

This was the case for Israel nationally as well as on the individual level. The covenantal God of Israel, although transcendent, was portrayed in biblical literature as acting in the world and being intimately involved with the affairs of human destiny and history. Consistent with the notion of a historical, providential deity, the biblical and prophetic assurances of reward and salvation were invariably expressed in temporal and physical terms. In the Pentateuch, Israel is promised immediate national prosperity, agricultural plenitude, and political and geographical security as a reward for faithfulness to the divine covenant. Moses presents Israel's options quite simply and unequivocally: life, with its maximum physical and temporal blessings, is the final good; death is the absolute evil: "Today I offer you a choice: life and good, or death and evil."[1]

In the books of the later prophets the promises to Israel of divine recompense differed largely in relationship to changing national circumstances. Ezekiel has visions of a future world in which the dead will be resurrected, yet the promise of resurrection is expressed in temporal and physical terms.[2] And the prophetic assurances, though by now largely messianic, remained mostly concerned with the national restoration of Israel to its former worldly, political glory at the end of days. The forum for the realization of human excellence and spiritual fulfillment remained the life of physical, earthly existence, though not necessarily identical with this temporal world nor necessarily a continuation of historical time.

The simple biblical view of life as the true blessing and death as the final curse began seriously to disintegrate in the wisdom literature, as a consequence of more developed philosophical thinking and a more sophisticated theodicy as well as a greater emphasis upon the spiritual endurance of the soul after death. Job cursed the day of his birth, while Koheleth both praised death over life and suggested that subsequent to physical death the "soul will return unto God who gave it."[3] In the very early history of Jewish theology, then, there began to develop two distinct understandings of the nature of religious deliverance; the Pentateuchal-prophetic notion of material, earthly reward and historical salvation, on the one hand, and the later hagiographic belief that divine grace is deferred to an afterlife, or future world, on the other.

With the endurance of the Jewish exile, the exclusive identification of salvation with prolonged life or with immediate physical and agricultural blessings faded. Already in early postbiblical Jewish thought there were two competing approaches to the attainment of divine favor: the notion of earthly blessing and the postponement of such salvation to the future life. E. P. Sanders has argued compellingly that these contrasting soteriologies constitute the most important distinction between Palestinian and Hellenistic Judaism in the New Testament period: "The significant distinction is between *realized* eternal life and *post mortem* eternal life. It is not said that one who eats the bread and drinks the cup and is annointed with the ointment . . . *will gain life,* but rather that such a person *has life.* In Philo, one who see the *logos* escapes death and *has* eternal life. This is a motif which is missing, as far as I see, in Palestinian Judaism."[4]

In later rabbinic Judaism, largely as a response to Jewish suffering and Israel's enduring exile, the literal acceptance of biblical promises became increasingly problematic, and thus the theories of human salvation became far more complex. The rabbis came unanimously to adopt the dualistic myth of *olam ha-ba,* a future world in which the individual Jew's true and final reward for faithfulness to the covenant would be realized. The denial of any final spiritual prominence to the temporal, historical experience of this world in favor of the ultimate significance of *olam ha-ba* was clearly designed to alleviate the evident failure of covenantal, biblical promises. The rabbis compared this world to a vestibule leading to the living room of the future world, in which true eternal life would be enjoyed.[5] The theological problem posed by the suffering of the righteous was accordingly downplayed by some rabbis as a mere preparation for the bliss stored up for them in the afterlife.[6]

Rabbinic thought never entirely abandoned the notion of life as supremely good and death as man's final misfortune and punishment for his sins, but there was important resistance to it. An early midrash quotes Rabbi Meir as suggesting that it is human death that is being referred to in the biblical claim that God perceived his creation as being very good.[7] R. Ami's suggestion that "there is no death without sin, no suffering without transgression" was, in the course of the Talmudic deliberations, firmly rejected by the rabbis.[8] On the other hand, Beth Shammai's pessimistic sense that man would have been better off had he never been created at all is supported by a consensus of authorities over Beth Hillel's contrary assertion.[9]

With the persistence and intensification of Jewish suffering, death, far from being perceived as man's ultimate surrender to evil, increasingly was perceived as a blessing or a sign of human virtue, particularly the death of a martyr. Something of a martyrdom complex, or what Salo Baron famously called the "lachrymose view of Jewish history," became a prominent feature of medieval Ashkenazic Jewish thought. Consistent with this morbid view of human worldly existence, medieval Kabbalistic Judaism developed a gnosticlike cosmogony of catastrophe. The Kabbalistic theories of *zimzum,* according to which God distanced himself from the created, physical cosmos during the creation drama, and *shevirah,* according to which the vessels containing the divine emanations shattered, became part of the theoretical basis for the pronounced otherworldliness and asceticism of many Jewish mystics. The notion of a primeval divine contraction and alienation from the created universe helped to confirm and heighten the dualism already inherent in the earlier rabbinic belief in two distinct worlds—*olam ha-zeh* and *olam ha-ba.* This radical dualism naturally resulted in a general, pious aversion to the corporeal dimension of human existence and fostered certain ascetic forms of religious expression in later medieval rabbinic and Jewish mystical thought.

The Hasidic View of Life, Eternal Life, and Death

On the eve of the rise of the Hasidic movement such asceticism was, as pointed out in chapter 4, a major expression of Jewish piety in eastern Europe. Shimon Dubnow described at some length the emphasis on the role of physical privation, suffering, and death as the major avenues to holiness in popular rabbinic *musar* literature prior to the rise of Hasidism.[10] Dubnow suggested that the remarkable early popularity of Hasidic doctrine can best be understood if one appreciates it largely as an optimistic revolution against the gloomy, restrictive rabbinic view of life.

There is much truth in that speculation. For the dualistic asceticism of the early Mithnagdim, a direct heir to this theological tradition, was rooted in the hopeless sense of God's vast distance from the created world of human sense perceptions and in the resultant pious contempt for its material pleasures. For the rabbis, the only way to avoid becoming entrapped in the Godless realm of the created universe was to suppress the material appetites and to carefully control all physical indulgences by waging a constant war upon the human body and its desires. This ascetic campaign against the physical senses was the best man could do temporarily to contain the evil, or material, instincts. Ultimately, however, only the full and final liberation from the created cosmos offered man complete salvation from a physical world so far removed from God and so saturated with the evil desire. As we shall see, for many of the Mithnagdim only physical death allowed man to attain that proximity to the Lord that is his final good. Consequently, the Mithnagdim tended regularly to emphasize the positive religious signification of man's passing from this life. Their perspective on death was optimistic in direct proportion to their pessimism regarding the spiritual opportunities available to man in this life.

Hasidism's popularized rejection of a literal understanding of *zimzum* and its accompanying affirmation of the belief in a radically immanent God whose closeness is ultimately discernible to man in this corporeal life underlay its rejection of rabbinic Judaism's otherworldly asceticism. Although Hasidic theoreticians shared the general consensus that the physical world might prove to be an obstacle in the way of perfect divine service and the attainment of proximity to God, they did not view such corporeal barriers as being insurmountable during man's this-worldly sojourn. Much of early Hasidic doctrine, in fact, comprised spiritual strategies for overcoming the earthly barriers between man and God. Consequently, unlike the Mithnagdim, the Hasidim did not defer the attainment of final spiritual felicity to a future existence awaiting man after his passing from this life. Many Hasidic masters harbored the optimistic belief that man is able, while still in the physical world, to overcome its material apparitions and sensual obstacles through the cognizance that the distance and alienation of God from the created universe is more apparent than real. In its most radical form—the doctrine of acosmism, which was circulating widely among the Hasidim of Belorussia at the beginning of the nineteenth century—Hasidism instructed that man can, indeed must, through intense mystical contemplation cognitively eliminate the physical obstacle and achieve *devekuth* with God while his soul is still incorporated within the human body and attain divine union in the confines of the created, corporeal universe. Hasidism therefore instructed man to deny the material world mystically within the context of corporeal, worldly existence.

The Mithnagdim were far less optimistic about that possibility in *olam ha-zeh,* the earthly here and now. Their antimaterialist posture was founded upon a generally dismal view of the spiritual potentialities of man. As we have already noted, one of the fundamental features of early Mithnagdic thought was its consistent pessimism regarding the limited possibilities in this life for human spiritual attainment, contemplation of the divine, and mystical union with God. Unlike the Hasidim, the Mithnagdim generally regarded the physical limitations of worldly existence as being insurmountable. This resignation to the severe spiritual limitations of corporeal life, so dramatically different from Hasidism's mystical enthusiasm, resulted in a dismal, pessimistic appraisal of this-worldly human existence and an almost equally "optimistic" conception of physical death, which for the Mithnagdim marked the true beginning of spiritual life.

This is not to say that the Hasidim consistently viewed death as the great human tragedy. For most of the classical Hasidic thinkers also viewed death as an ascent, most often the *final* elevation, of the human soul. Many tales describe the great joy experienced by the Hasidic masters upon their release from this world and their final ascent to God through physical death. Although the most mystically radical Hasidic masters did not tend to dwell too much on the religious significance of death, R. Nahman of Brazlav was obsessed with the inevitability and great spiritual importance of his own death and interpreted it as both an opportunity for final personal perfection and a key contribution to cosmic *tikkun.*[11] The Hasidic celebration of the anniversary of the zaddik's death, the *yohrzeit tisch,* must be understood as a manifestation of a belief in the great spiritual and cosmic effect of the elevation of the soul of the zaddik.[12]

Yet, in contrast to the Mithnagdic distinction between the absolute misery of this life and the postmortem glory awaiting the righteous, the Hasidim appreciated death more harmoniously as the culmination of the religious works already partially attained in this world and as life's final, crowning spiritual achievement. They also insisted, again in contrast to the strict dualism of the Mithnagdim, that the souls of the deceased righteous men continue to interplay with and bless the living. Thus R. Israel Baal Shem Tov is said to have described his impending passing simply as "leaving one door and entering into another door,"[13] thereby likening the significance of the lives of the two worlds, linking them and intimating that the future life was less a radical liberation of the soul from its abject condition as the body's prisoner than it was a progression to yet a higher state. Elsewhere in the hagiographic Hasidic literature the BESHT is depicted as taking this complementary view of life, death, and the afterlife somewhat further: "Once the spirit of the Baal Shem was so oppressed that it seemed to him that he would have no part in the coming world. Then he said to himself: 'If I love God, what need have I of a future world?' "[14]

Perhaps the most significant and dramatic illustration that the BESHT attributed greater value to the life of this world than he did to that of the world to come is to be found in his celebrated letter to his brother-in-law, Gershon of Kutow. In the course of describing the joy he discerned upon visiting with the inhabitants of heaven during one of his more spectacular "ascents of soul," the BESHT wrote: "I thought that this joy was, heaven forbid, because of my departure from this world. But they notified me afterwards that I had not yet departed, but that they derive pleasure up above when I perform contemplative unification below by means of the holy Torah."[15] In other words, man can attain through the mystical love and service of God in this world below all (and often even more) of the blessing usually associated with the world to come. Even for R. Nahman of Brazlav, death was necessary largely in order to progress yet "one rung higher" in his life's spiritual journey.[16]

The Lithuanian Hasidic master Menahem Mendel of Vitebsk very clearly stated his conviction that the spiritual attainments of man while still in this world are necessary preparations for the life of the world to come. Consequently, it is imperative for him to engage in mystical union with the Shekhinah while his soul still dwells within the body in order to pave the way for the blessings of eternal life:

> The general principle is this: The [observance of the] entire Torah and its commandments are entirely useless to man unless they are accompanied by the aforementioned *devekuth* as well as every possible effort on his part to cognize [God] while clinging to physical matters. Now, there are all kinds of men, and everyone must act according to his maximum capacities. Man is obligated to engage in this *devekuth* in the service of God. . . .
>
> Therefore, while he is still Adam [i.e., while alive in this worldly existence], he must devote all of his capacities to the Creator so that after he dies and is separated from his body he will *continue* to retain the name of Adam and continue to use all of his capacities and thus serve God triumphantly and with pleasure.
>
> On the other hand, if he does not accordingly regulate his capacities and his pleasures while still alive, but rather pays attention only to the corroding and dissipating physical dimension of life, then after his separation from corporeal

existence [i.e., death], his body will simply decay and evaporate, and what blessing will he leave behind? How can he expect then [i.e., after death] to begin his spiritual pleasures and utilize his innate powers if he has not previously learned the way of the living and eternal God while still alive?[17]

Thus, according to R. Menahem Mendel, the bliss stored up for the righteous in the world to come must be earned by the spiritual groundwork of mystical achievement in this world. Hasidism presents a harmonious continuum between man's present/earthly and future/heavenly lives. Postmortem existence is simply a succession to the spiritual state of the virtuous man while still alive. The same essential spiritual pleasures and proximity to God that man attains while still alive are merely extended and intensified after death. So although they too were able to discover elements of salvation in death, for the Hasidim this was simply the final step of a spiritual process of approaching God that had begun during the corporeal life.

There is a strong affirmation of life and a definite sense of the harmony and continuity that exists between this life and the future world in the abundant Hasidic lore about the deaths of the great masters.[18] The living zaddikim are depicted as experiencing the religious-mystical encounter with spiritual death, moving between this life and the future life, between coarse earthly existence and the sublime divine realms, while they were still physically alive. Parallel to this, the deceased zaddikim are depicted as visiting the living and acting continuously on their behalf. The difference between the life of *olam ha-zeh* and that of the future world is for them relative, not absolute; the latter is a progression beyond the former but not a fundamentally altered or radically new or resolutely separate existence. And the border separating physical life from posthumous spiritual existence was regularly crossed by the zaddikim in a dialectic mystical process most often referred to as *retzo va-shov*, or spiritual coming and going.[19] Precisely because the Hasidim instructed that *bitul ha-yesh*, or the transformation of man into mystical nothingness through union with the divine realms, can be realized in the material world, the change that occurs at the point of real physical death was viewed as an entirely relative matter. It is precisely in that spirit that the following posthumous remark was attributed to the BESHT's disciple Yehiel Michel of Zlotchov: "The world which yesterday was spread over my head as heaven, is today the earth under my feet, and the heaven of today is the earth of tomorrow."[20]

Finally, the Hasidim's nearly obsessive concern with recording the last moments of the lives of the zaddikim is a reflection of the supreme preciousness they attached to every single last hour and minute of life in this world.

The final deeds and statements of the masters were recorded with the greatest care and seriousness precisely because they were the legacy and the wisdom whereby the living could sanctify their own ongoing lives. As we shall see, the Mithnagdic literature reflects a sharply different posture regarding the significance of man's last moments on, and his final departure from, earth.

The GRA's Otherworldliness

The GRA's asceticism, described in chapter 4, was the practical consequence of his thoroughly dualistic view of the relationship between the human body and the divine soul. The body, in his view, was an alien, temporary, oppressively unhappy physical home to the soul in its this-worldly sojourn. The rigidly ascetic discipline and suppression of bodily appetites the GRA both advocated and practiced were viewed as nothing more than temporary holding measures for man while he is compelled to endure the trials and temptations of *olam ha-zeh* existence. The ultimate felicity of the soul is, however, only possible subsequent to its final departure from the physical world and its liberation from the human body. In other words, only *physical death* provides the soul with the opportunity for true spiritual fulfillment. The GRA makes this clear in a number of pronouncements, especially those regarding death.

The most dangerous kind of heresy, in the GRA's view, derives from the notion that one can attain spiritual felicity and closeness with God while still in the confines of the body and the temporal, physical world. The GRA strongly condemned those who attributed any type of sanctity, realized or even potential, to the material elements of the created universe. He insisted that man's final confrontation with the sacred is impossible in the context of this-worldly existence and must wait until after death and the soul's separation from the body and entry into *olam ha-ba:* "This world is but a corridor before the world to come; one must prepare himself in the corridor in order to enter the reception room. But the evildoers focus [all of their attention], all of their days on the corridor."[21] In a clear reference to Hasidism's sanctification of the material world, the GRA warns: "For the evil instinct beguiles man into believing that this world exists for the sake of ultimate repentance, which reaches right up to the divine throne of glory. It [i.e., the *yezer ha-ra*] thus advises man that all of the elements of this world are [potentially] heavenly, holy matters."[22] While it is not clear whether the GRA had any specific "evildoers" in mind when he criticized their opinion that the created world could be the stage for ultimate spiritual bliss, it is evident from his firm rejection of such optimism that he would have reacted strongly against the Habad Hasidic teachings in this regard.

Rabbi Shneur Zalman of Lyadi was one Hasidic master who repeatedly and strenuously affirmed that human life in this world does indeed exist for the sake of ultimate sanctification and repentance, which can reach the highest heavenly realms. A fundamental doctrine of the early Ḥabad school, and the centerpiece of the spiritual life of its adherents, was that through intense *hithbonenuth,* or mystical contemplation, man could transcend the apparitions of the material world while still living within it, thereby ascending to the divine throne. The attainment of this exalted state of mystical transcendence was the very goal of creation and represented the perfection of human existence. Far from being an irreparable condition of exile from divine grace that could be corrected only subsequent to death, as the Mithnagdim believed, the spiritual potential of the corporeal life of this world was, for R. Shneur Zalman, even greater than that of the ethereal soul both before its descent into the body and subsequent to its departure from it. In clear discord with the GRA's pessimism regarding the insurmountable restrictions placed on the spirit by its bodily abode and the material world in which it dwells, R. Shneur Zalman insisted that the mystical transcendence of the physical limitations of *olam ha-zeh* was the basic challenge of human existence and the very purpose of creation. Whereas the Mithnagdim surrendered to the realities and constraints of corporeal existence, R. Shneur Zalman demanded that man set as his goal the spiritual conquest of these limitations:

> "Mighty waters are unable to quench love, and rivers will not drown it" [Song of Songs 8:7]. Behold that "mighty waters" refers to the preoccupation with material sustenance and the contemplation of this-worldly concerns. Regardless of these, nothing is able to quench the love that is the hidden passion naturally inherent in the heart of every single Israelite, deriving from his Godly soul, whose nature it is to rise and to be consumed in the heavenly flame. . . . For this Godly soul used to benefit from the luminescence of the divine presence, and was once unified in a perfect unity with the *Eyn Sof.* Still, even after its materialization in the physical body in order to engage in material pursuits—referred to as "mighty waters"—nonetheless, these pursuits cannot deter it from its deep love and profound desire to ascend and be subsumed on high. Quite the contrary, by virtue of its very materialization in these mighty waters, the soul is able to reach a far more exalted level than that which it attained before it descended into the *olam ha-zeh,* as we shall see.[23]

R. Shneur Zalman not only refused to resign himself to the corporeal restrictions of this life but boldly suggested that the soul could reach higher spiritual heights while in the human body than it could in its prebirth ethereal state:

Therefore, it is only by virtue of the descent and materialization of the divine soul in the animal soul in order to struggle with life's destitution and to be preoccupied with material concerns and monetary matters, referred to as "mighty waters," only then can [the soul] attain the level of loving God with all of one's might. This love of God is without limit and thus is the soul on a more exalted plane than it was before its descent into the body.

That is what the Sages intended when they proclaimed, "One hour of repentance and good deeds in this world is more precious than the entire existence of the future world."[24]

The GRA, as previously observed, assumed a diametrically opposed position regarding the relationship of body and soul, namely, that the descent of the soul into the body is its worst torment and that, far from allowing for even greater perception of the godly realms, corporeal existence hopelessly obscures the divine domain from the human senses. According to the GRA, there was absolutely no basis for R. Shneur Zalman's enthusiastic appraisal of the unparalleled spiritual potentialities of life in the material world.

The GRA's conviction that no genuine or total spiritual bliss is possible in man's bodily, worldly existence is expressed most dramatically in his interpretation of the biblical book of Jonah. Jonah's escape from his divine mission, described in the opening verses of the book, is interpreted allegorically as referring to man's birth, his initial departure from before God into the created world. For the duration of his life in this world man is comparable to one lost in a storm at sea. The goal of physical life can entail nothing more than the successful employment of the survival tools of diligent Torah study and Halakhic obedience until man is able to reach the true land of the living, *olam ha-ba*. Like R. Shneur Zalman, then, the GRA used the metaphor of the mighty waters of the sea in order to connote the life of the material world. But in striking contrast with R. Shneur Zalman's belief that man can ultimately tame those stormy, treacherous waters and spiritually transcend the physical constraints of this life, the GRA suggested that the best one can hope for is disciplined, righteous living, and mere spiritual survival until "land," or physical death, is finally reached. Commenting on the verse, "And the Lord let loose a storm, and the sea ran so high in the hurricane that the ship threatened to break up" (Jonah 1:4), the GRA wrote:

"The sea" refers to this world, which is compared to a sea, while the future world is compared to the land. Thus did Alexander the Great ask the sages of the Negev: "Would you rather live on land or at sea?" And they answered him, "on land." For all those who go out to sea never find peace until they return to land. The significance of this tale is that (even Alexander the Great), who had attained all of the aspirations of this world and ruled over it, . . . sensed that the future world was superior, for it is impossible for the physical senses to attain the good of the world to come. That is why scripture never details its [i.e., the future world's] blessings.

From this story we learn that the days of the life of this world, even if thoroughly enriched, are nothing but pain; the more wealth, the more worry. Now the ethical works have already dealt at length with this subject; that is, that there is no true fulfillment for man in this world, neither in wealth, nor in children, nor in any of its goodness; for no man dies with even half of his desires and lusts satisfied; for the more he attains, the more he desires. All this stands in contrast to the future world, where man finally finds security, contentment, and true peace of mind. Thus it is said: "In the world to come there is no jealousy and no hatred." And therefore, with regard to the death of the righteous it is said that "their soul has rested." And for the same reason the Sages taught that "a single hour in the future world is more precious than the entire life of this world."[25]

What is especially noteworthy about this contrast between the daring mystical optimism of R. Shneur Zalman and the pessimistic religious conservatism of the GRA is that both relied upon precisely the same rabbinic text for support from the classical sources. But each chose to cite only one-half of that complex, paradoxical aphorism, the half he found theologically acceptable. In the tractate *Aboth* of the Mishna, R. Jacob declares that "an hour of good deeds and repentance in this world is more precious than the entire life of the world to come"; then immediately, and paradoxically, he adds the apparently contrary notion that a "single hour of bliss in the world to come is more precious than the entire life of this world."[26] Clearly, this paradoxical statement invites precisely the kind of selective ideological interpretations evidenced in its partial citation in the writings of R. Shneur Zalman and the GRA, who, for obvious reasons, quoted only the first or the second part.[27]

Jonah's subsequent tribulations were understood by the GRA as metaphors for the soul's reincarnation *(gilgul)* into other human bodies. The climax of the story is reached when an exhausted Jonah proclaims, "And now, Lord, take my Life! For I am better off dead than alive!" (4:3). The GRA viewed this statement as a philosophical affirmation, consistent with rabbinic sources, that human life is a baffling, unfortunate, and inferior form of existence that the human soul must bitterly endure:

"For I am better dead than alive"; as it is written, "I praise the dead, who have already passed away, above the living, who still have life. . . ." The redundant words in this verse come to instruct that those who, having died, did not have to return in a new incarnation are more fortunate than those who are now reincarnated. Thus can we resolve the Talmudic consensus that it would have been better for man had he not been born. . . . How can such a thing be said, for if that is the case, why was man created at all? Rather, this discussion refers to the reincarnation of man.[28]

The GRA here suggests that once man has been blessed with death, it is a great curse for him to be born again into this world. It comes as little surprise that the GRA generally awarded great prominence to the Kabbalistic idea of the reincarnation of souls. Reincarnation theories generally tend to blend well with dualistic, pessimistic theologies. The idea of the tormented, exiled soul unable to find its final resting place is a recurrent one in theologies of exile and alienation.[29] For the GRA, *gilgul neshamoth* (transmigration of souls) is the tragic destiny of those who do not in their first life sufficiently deflect the corruption of bodily existence by means of the study and observance of the Torah; they are therefore required to endure this-worldly existence recurrently until they succeed in maintaining the purity of their souls in the context of *olam ha-zeh.*

The ultimate lesson to be derived from Jonah's tribulations is stated simply and succinctly by the GRA toward the end of the book, where God causes the gourd that been protecting Jonah from the sun to wither. The gourd is symbolic of this world, and with its withering, "God removes all of Jonah's material possessions in order to proclaim that all of the good of this world is absolutely negligible."[30] No genuine spiritual ecstasy is conceivable in this world. The final attainment of divine knowledge occurs only subsequent to man's passing away into the future life. It was in the same spirit that the GRA interpreted the story of another, even less fortunate biblical character, Job. After suffering the initial round of mysterious tragedies that were to befall him, Job responds by "cursing his day" and proclaiming his preference for death over a life of intolerable affliction. Commenting on Job's curse and his protest that those mortals who would desire death are unfairly compelled to retain life, the GRA shifted the focus away from the text's original antitheodicy to suggest that man quests for death because of the afterlife's increased spiritual capacities:

The essential pleasure of the future life is the constantly and endlessly increasing knowledge of God and of the depths of His Torah. At every moment we add to our cognizance of Him, and there is a parallel increment in the soul's thirst to cling to Him. This quest for God swells and expands at every moment. This is what the Sages have referred to as the "feast of the Leviathan"—"Leviathan" signifying *devekuth.* . . . This intense knowledge [of God] is impossible while still in the confines of the lowly body and its corrupt matter. . . .

This, then, is the sense of this verse—"those who rejoice with gladness"; that is, they will rejoice when they fulfill unto me the gladness, which is death. . . . It says that they will rejoice from the moment of death on. . . . Thus it says that they will celebrate upon finding their grave. . . .[31]

In a remarkable exegesis of the opening verse of the book of Deuteronomy, which introduces Moses's final admonition to Israel before crossing the Jordan River to enter the Promised Land, the GRA—once again using water as a metaphor for material pursuits—suggested that the river represents the life of this world. Moses is portrayed as advising the Israelites regarding the type of human behavior that will assure their crossing the Jordan in order safely to enter the future life. Once again, asceticism and a heightened awareness of, and preparedness for, physical death are strongly prescribed:

"These are the words which Moses spoke to all Israel on the desert east of the Jordan [ever ha-Yarden], the Arava, opposite Suph. . . ."

This world [olam ha-zeh] is called the Jordan; the words "ever ha-Yarden" indicate that man is a mere transient sojourner in this life. Now, just as the Jordan borders the land of Israel below, so too, in the heavens, one cannot arrive in Paradise before passing through the River Dinur. Only then is the soul raised as a sacrifice. So that "ever ha-Yarden" is a general statement, followed by specific teachings. "On the desert" instructs that it is the correct thing for man to ignore all of the passions of this world, such as food, and he should render himself as a desert, only to study Torah. . . . "Opposite Suph" teaches that man should always contemplate the day of his death and have his termination ("soph") before his eyes at all times.[32]

Perhaps the most remarkable expression of the GRA's pessimism regarding the spiritual potential of man's earthly, material existence is to be found in his unusual appreciation of the consequence of Adam's first sin: the consumption of the forbidden fruit, which resulted in human mortality. Far from seeing the advent of physical death as a catastrophe or a great primordial tragedy, as is so common in the Jewish exegetical tradition, the GRA suggested that man is better off as a mortal being than he would be had he continued to enjoy eternal life after Adam's sin: "It was decreed upon man for his own welfare that he should not live eternally, for there is nothing better for man than the decomposition of his physical matter; thus the Sages have instructed [re: God's comment upon having created man that all was] " 'Very good'—this refers to death."[33]

The GRA's optimism about death and the spiritual bliss awaiting man only in his posthumous life did not, however, lead to a despairing or cynical attitude toward the religious goals and obligations of man in this world. For all his pessimism about the limited spiritual potentialities of the physical life of this world, the GRA deeply cherished the opportunities for the unique religious achievements that this world afforded man, that is, the study of the Torah and the observance of its commandments.[34] Needless to say, he was as passionate and enthusiastic about the pursuit of these circumscribed religious obligations of corporeal life as he was insistent about their inherent limitations. Rabbi David Luria attributed a remarkably moving deathbed statement to the GRA:

> Seconds before his soul departed, he [i.e., the GRA] took hold of his *zizith* and tearfully proclaimed: "It is so difficult to depart from this world of deeds in which, by virtue of a single *mitzvah* such as *zizith,* the righteous man will [ultimately] behold the divine presence. Even if man were to expend all of his energies towards this, nowhere in the world of the souls could we find a similar accomplishment."[35]

The Mithnagdim on Death As Salvation

The sentiment that man's death is the true and exclusive remedy for the incurable spiritual handicaps imposed by the soul's entrapment in the body was shared by many of the GRA's contemporaries and students. In his introduction to the highly influential ethical work *Shevet mi-Yisrael,* R. Israel Jacob of Kremenetz insisted that the unique perfection that raises man above the animals is neither his intellectual prowess nor his power of articulation, as is most commonly suggested, but rather man's awareness of his own mortality. As long as it is trapped in the physical body, the human soul is crippled and cannot achieve any glorious spiritual state; nonetheless, an active cognizance of the inevitable day of his death is the one thing that can remind man of the ultimately sublime destiny of his soul, the postmortem eternal union with God.[36]

The renowned Belorussian preacher R. Eliezer Segal of Pinsk understood the biblical account of the sin of the first man in much the same uncommon way as did the GRA. Far from being a curse, the "punishment of mortality for man subsequent to primordial Adam's consumption of the tree of knowledge, was—given his now corrupt physical nature—the greatest religious blessing." In the course of his eulogy for R. Aaron Ha-Levi of Cracow, R. Eliezer elaborated on the true blessing that death constitutes:

> It is well known that the essential purpose of the Lord in having created man is in order for him to attain true and clear knowledge of his Creator, may He be

blessed, and thereby to acquire eternity for his soul. But when the first man, Adam, sinned, his body became more coarse, and he became corrupted by the filth of the serpent, such that his matter became a screen preventing him from attaining immortality. Man could thus only attain this blessed state subsequent to the departure of his soul from his body; only then could he achieve his religious perfection. Thus it is written: " For man can not see me and live!" ...

Thus did R. Eliezer Ashkenazi nicely interpret the verse, "For on the day that you shall eat of it [i.e., the tree of knowledge] you shall certainly die," that death is not, God forbid, intended as a punishment, but on the contrary, that it is an act of compassion and mercy. For now that Adam has eaten of the tree, man must die in order to attain his true purpose. Thus did God explain to Moses that no man can behold Him and live; in other words, as long as man is composed of body and soul united, it is impossible for him to attain the knowledge of God, for this is possible only after death.[37]

Since the sin of Adam, then, man is a hopeless spiritual invalid. Given his incurable existential state of inherent sinfulness, the best man can do is bide his time and endure the torments, trials, and spiritual tests of this-worldly existence, observe the legal requirements of Torah, and piously anticipate the spiritual bliss he will enjoy only subsequent to the day of his death. The constant contemplation of man's death day that was, as we shall see, a central moral concern of the Mithnagdim was strongly underscored by R. Eliezer:

Man must forever remember that he is here today and in the grave tomorrow. Thus did King David exclaim: "I am a stranger with you." That is, just as a stranger must always be ready to move on, so must man always be in a state of readiness to move on. That is what is meant when it is written, "The day of death is more precious than the day of birth." That is, man must begin to contemplate the day of his death beginning from the day of his birth. ...

Now, since man is compared to a stranger, he must always be ready to prepare his sustenance and his traveling provisions for the long road ahead. For he must know that he has no real standing in this world, which is darkness.[38]

In rather startling antithesis to the biblical promises that life will be prolonged in direct proportion to human merit, the Mithnagged Rabbi Zevi Hirsch Katzenellenbogen suggested that only the good die young, for death is the righteous man's greatest possible reward:

Whosoever follows in the way of God, fears the Lord, and eschews evil will not last for many days on this earth. For "the death of the righteous is precious in the eyes of God" [Psalms 116:15], in order to distance them from this corrupt land. For thus they might go on to witness the pleasantness of the Lord. This, then, is the sole purpose of our very birth in the first place, that is, that we might quickly, in the minimum number of days, merit the future life. Why bother with a needless delay here? Its only result will be the deviation from the right path and descent into the ways of sin.[39]

Two themes consistent with this prevalent rabbinic perception of the spiritually limiting nature of earthly human existence since the sin of Adam continuously recur in the later writings of the disciples of the GRA: (1) that man cannot attain his ultimate religious perfection—true knowledge of God —until after death; and (2) that it is important that he be acutely aware of this constraint and thus focus constantly on his mortal limitations and, specifically, that he consciously anticipate and intensely contemplate the day of his own death. The tremendous importance that the Mithnagdim attached to death itself and to man's heightened cognizance of his own mortality is vividly reflected in the opening paragraphs of the mystical commentary to the *Idrah Zuta* by the GRA's disciple Menahem Mendel of Shklov:

> The point is that the day of his death is the very purpose and fulfillment of man's existence, and this fact represents the highest, unique level of human understanding. . . . For upon dying, man instantly attains more knowledge than he cumulatively could ever achieve all of the days of his life. In other words, at that moment man has wisdom that is simply impossible to acquire so long as he remains in *olam ha-zeh*, as it is written, "For no man can see me and live." But as the Sages have said, at the moment of death he can see, and that instant of death is equal to all the days of his life. This is the true meaning [of the verse] that "the day of death is more precious than the day of man's birth."[40]

Elsewhere in the same work R. Menahem Mendel maintains that it is not only direct communion with and knowledge of God that may not be revealed to the soul until after the demise of the body. Even the true meaning of the Torah and the secret signification of the *mitzvoth* will only be disclosed to man on the day of his death.[41]

We have already observed that the GRA's son Abraham was an ascetic dualist who greatly admired and emulated his father's abstemious philosophy and way of life. Like the GRA, Abraham portrayed death as man's final fulfillment. Only the wicked materialists, who foolishly cherish the vanities of *olam ha-zeh* existence, consider death to be a tragic occurrence. The righteous, on the other hand, have absolutely no fear of their final, physical demise. Quite the contrary, they actually anticipate dying in order to experience the blessings of the hereafter: "Thus the one who is evil is afraid of dying, lest after his passing he will be visited by great torments in Gehinnom; but the righteous man is not the least bit fearful of eternal sleep, for he knows that if he goes to his rest, he will find the final slumber most pleasurable."[42] The righteous are cognizant, R. Abraham continues, that death and the subsequent "entry into the world of the souls" is the very purpose of man's existence.[43]

The attitude of Hillel of Kovno, whose dualistic asceticism and deep pessimism were discussed in chapter 4, to the physical life of this world was one of unrelenting hopelessness and skepticism. His rigidly ascetic prescriptions were the consequence of both an untractable pessimism about the spirit of man and a strong sense of the relentlessness of historical decline. The logical extension of this despondent world-view is expressed in Hillel's conviction that it is only through death that man can be redeemed.

> These days, as a consequence of our many transgressions, at a time when we have neither altar nor sacrifice nor Torah nor true worship, how shall we approach and worship [God], and with what shall we reconcile ourselves with the Lord, our King?
>
> Only with the departure of our souls, as if to say: "Take my spirit, which belongs to You." This is the worship appropriate for God-fearers and those who honor His name. For when a person realizes that he is barren in Torah and worship and incurably iniquitous, he will return to a forgiving God and proclaim: "Please take my soul, because death is better for me than life. For thus [i.e., in dying], will I put an end to the wasted and barren days and years of my life. For God forbid that I should continue to squander my remaining days in this manner."[44]

Phinehas of Polotsk on the Vanities of Life

The two themes emanating from the pronouncements of the Mithnagdim on the "life and death" question, that is, that the perfection of human life is found only in death and that the contemplation of human mortality is an essential tool for righteous living, were fully developed in the writings of Phinehas of Polotsk. Like the GRA and his disciples, Phinehas saw very little hope that man would have any final spiritual felicity in this life. He too compared earthly existence to a ship in stormy seas.[45] The key to arriving at the final landing goal of the future life lies in adamantly refusing to attach any significance to the life of this world. While the Hasidic masters were preaching that the physical boundaries of *olam ha-zeh* were illusory and meant to be overcome and transcended by man in his quest for *devekuth*, Phinehas remained unfailingly respectful of the formidable limitations imposed by man's position in the created universe. In sharp contrast to the Hasidic teaching that the spiritual ambitions of man in this world should respect no physical or sensual constraints and can all be surmounted mystically, Phinehas regularly referred to *olam ha-zeh* as the absolute "universe of borders." These borders are the commanding and insurmountable limitations of the physical world of the senses, which no man can transcend until his soul departs from the corporeal confines of the body.

I argued in an earlier chapter that the essential difference between the Hasidic and contemporary rabbinic convictions regarding the nature and extent of the divine presence in the physical universe was their opposing appraisals of the limits of the spiritual insight available to the human senses. This same divergence is at the very root of the Hasidim's and the Mithnagdim's divergent evaluations of the basic worth of physical life itself and of the corresponding significance of its passing.

Phinehas repeatedly maintained that death is to be preferred to life precisely on account of the inherent, onerous epistemological and spiritual limitations of physical existence. Where, for example, the Psalmist triumphantly declares that he will behold the face of God in the "land of the *living*," Phinehas insists that in reality he is speaking only of the life of the future world:

> When he says, "I, by my righteousness will perceive Your face," he means that this will occur after death and the departure from this world. Still, he declares that until that parting from this world occurs he will be content with being blessed by the likeness of God. Regarding this matter, God has written, "For no man can see me and live." That is, man is not shown anything more than a detached likeness of God. . . . Therefore, with regard to this [true vision of God] which is the reward of the world to come, it has been written [Isaiah 64:3], "No eye has seen any God other than you," for it is impossible to see God as long as one is alive; rather, one is only rewarded by seeing the distant image.[46]

It is subsequent to death, and never before, that man will attain spiritual greatness. His resignation to the epistemological limitations of earthly life lead Phinehas to a pronounced disdain for physical vitality. That attitude could only have been reinforced by the harsh and depressing socioeconomic realities of Jewish life in late-eighteenth-century Belorussia.

Not surprisingly, then, Phinehas's otherworldly dualism was expressed most often in the context of his discussions of theodicy. In struggling with the injustices of a cruel world, a world particularly cruel to the Jews of eastern Europe, Phinehas repeated and extended with great passion the standard rabbinic view that the justice of this world exists in inverse proportion to the final judgment of *olam ha-ba.* For in this world the wicked are given limited rewards for their few good deeds, but the righteous are punished fully and finally for their sparse record of sins. True punishment for the wicked and definitive bliss for the righteous will be realized only after death and entry into the future world.[47]

> Our Lord has created two distinct worlds: The *olam ha-zeh* is the world of boundaries, whose purpose is circumscribed and whose reward and punishment are strictly limited. It is for precisely this reason that the wicked, who have embraced the *olam ha-zeh* and who have put all of their efforts and hopes in its temporal rewards, are indeed rewarded [by God] in this world. . . . But the righteous, who loathe the life of this meaningless and transient world and whose only purpose and goal is to cling to God and come closer to His will and to benefit from the radiance of the Divine presence—they will be rewarded with all this in the life of the world to come, which no living eye can perceive.[48]

For this very reason, Phinehas consistently maintained that the raison d'être of this life is nothing more than "to lead man into the life of the world to come."[49] Like his master, the GRA, Phinehas clearly expressed his pious contempt for the corporeal life in his empathetic comments on the despairing words of Job. Phinehas not only interpreted positively Job's bitter cynicism regarding the negligible value of human life but he universalized the personal anguish of this suffering servant of God. Phinehas suggests that Job's comparing his days to those of a "slave longing for the rest of evening" (7:2) reflects an exemplary attitude. Man should detest his life and constantly anticipate his own physical demise. In diametrical opposition to the biblical notion that length of days is God's greatest reward to man, Phinehas suggests that every day by which human life is shortened is a magnificent blessing:

> There is no point or divine purpose in living the days of this meaningless life, be they many or few, other than man's perfecting himself and then dying and leaving this world. In this way, man is, in this world, like a slave who longs for the shady rest of evening . . . and who anticipates his sunset, even if it involves the abbreviation of his days. For all that man cares about is attaining the personal perfection that he is able to acquire. The duration of his life should be of no importance whatsoever to him, for all the days of this life are totally futile. The true servant of God, whose heart does not stray after the vanities of life, desires only to condense and expend all of his time into a single hour in which he will attain his maximum excellence and then to die. It is with regard to this that Rabbi Judah lamented, declaring: "There are some who are able to achieve the purpose of this life and arrive at their true perfection in a single moment," but sadly there are others who must endure length of days and years of toil in order to merit this.[50]

Rather than the blessing they constitute for the Psalmist, "length of days and years" on this earth are, for Phinehas, a source of bitter lament; for him, an abbreviated life or premature death are the true portents of blessedness and good fortune.

At the very root of his devaluation of earthly life is, of course, Phinehas's consistent pessimism regarding not only man's aforementioned epistemological limitations but also the spiritual restrictions inherent to the human condition. So long as his soul is trapped in the body and besieged by its corporeal appetites, man's salvation is not assured. As a result of this incurable state of severe spiritual handicap, "It is impossible for man to trust himself to avoid sin until the day of his death."[51]

One of the principal moral themes of Phinehas of Polotsk's ethical will, *Rosh ha-Giveah*, is the condemnation of two major sources for the complacency, arrogance, and pretentiousness that he felt were spreading like wildfire among the Jews of Belorussia in his day. The first type of arrogance is the materialist egotism of the wealthy, assimilating classes, a phenomenon decried in virtually all of the moralist works of this period and throughout Phinehas's literary corpus. The second is the excessive spiritual haughtiness and sense of pious self-importance of the Jewish pietists of his day, an unmistakable reference to the Hasidim. Phinehas is especially harsh in his criticism of the latter, religious manifestations of these unsavory characteristics. In many long passages of his ethical will he decries what he perceived to be the cardinal sin of these falsely pious ones, namely, spiritual arrogance and religious showiness. Referring extensively to classic, Talmudic critiques of the sanctimonious showoff (or *yuhara*), Phinehas focuses in particular upon the pretensions of the Hasidim, who in their very public and bizarre demonstrations of various forms of mystical piety violate countless rabbinic prohibitions against vanity and conceit on the part of the God-fearing public. Phinehas also repeatedly expresses his outrage at the specter of the cold snobbishness and the vain sense of superiority and power exhibited by the affluent members of the Jewish community of his day.

The most effective weapon Phinehas can find to wield against each of these disparate manifestations of the same unsavory natural instinct—human arrogance and egotistical impudence—is to underscore the fundamentally frail, insecure, and ephemeral nature of human existence itself and, above all, the insignificance of earthly life. And Phinehas can find no more effective means of dramatizing this most elementary of existential uncertainties than by focusing upon human mortality and calling upon his readers to concentrate upon their inevitable day of death and final reckoning with their Creator. For

Phinehas, the arrogance of the wealthy, on the one hand, and the spiritual conceit of the Hasidim, on the other, are only possible for those who forget how frail, uncertain, and transient life itself is. By highlighting life's many infirmities to both the wealthy and the exceedingly pious, he will jolt them into recognizing the ultimate vanity of their material or religious stature and accomplishments. In other words, meditation upon death is, for Phinehas, the most effective moralizing device possible. The true sign of the wicked is their deliberate ignoring of the inevitably looming day of doom. I have repeatedly noted that the Mithnagdim were most cautious and circumspect regarding the ability of man to attain any knowledge in the world of the physical senses. This pessimism regarding the limits of human knowledge was largely the basis for Phinehas's general derision of the very value of earthly life. Interestingly, the one single type of sure knowledge that Phinehas insisted that man attain in this world was the certain awareness of death:

My son, our Sages have instructed that a person should always set his good instinct against his evil instinct. If the good instinct emerges victorious, fine! If the good instinct fails to win, let man meditate upon the day of his death. This is a basic principle: that the remembrance of the day of one's death should always be before one's eyes—for it shall most certainly arrive. It is in this spirit that I have interpreted the verse: "For the living know that they shall die, whilst the dead know nothing" [Ecclesiastes 9:5]; that is, that there is no certain knowledge that a man can possibly have regarding his life—not regarding his health or illness, his wealth or poverty, his sustenance and riches, his children's welfare, or anything else at all, for everything is solely dependent upon the will of God. There is, however, one matter regarding which man can have certain and true knowledge, that is, that he will certainly die. That is a sure thing that will not disappoint. Now, this certain awareness [of death] is only possessed by the righteous men, who are referred to as "living"; but the wicked are the evildoers, who are referred to as the [living] dead. These latter know nothing at all, and even this certain consciousness is hidden and unfamiliar to them . . . they are indifferent to the day of death and complacent with life, and perhaps their own obvious demise is to them the greatest mystery.[52]

Conclusion

It was Voltaire who suggested that the most significant critical insight distinguishing man from the animals is that "the human species is the only one which knows that it will die." For Phinehas, this awareness separates not man from the animals but the righteous from the wicked. This consciousness and heightened awareness of inevitable human mortality is so critical for Phine-has's religious anthropology that without it man can never advance spir-itually. For death is the only sure and perpetual reminder of the falseness, temporality, and insignificance of life's material and temporal attainments, and the constant remembrance of death is the key to attaining divine favor in the world to come.

Nowhere are Phinehas's obsession with the utter futility of life in *olam ha-zeh* and his sense of the blessing and magnificence of passing away from this world into *olam ha-ba* more manifest than in his abbreviated paraphrase of Kalonymous ben Kalonymous's medieval tract *Even Bohan*. Phinehas here culls the most radically dualistic, world-denying sections of the original work in order to negate any significance to the life of this world. In section after section of the *Kizzur Even Bohan* the same theme is sounded, namely, that the life of this world is made up of pure misery and religious alienation and that the best that man can do is to survive with a minimum of sins in order posthumously to attain the grace of God in the future world. Once again, as in his aforementioned sermons, Phinehas compares the world to a stormy sea; he mocks those who take the world and their accomplishments in the material universe with any degree of seriousness. At the root of their spiritual blindness and deception is, once again, their failure to remain ever cognizant of human mortality and their own impending day of death:

> Listen well, you foolish ones, you who together with your friends sit compla-cently upon your false sense of security. . . . How can you possibly be so interested in amassing your fortune in silver and gold . . . when you must surely know that inevitably you and they—your souls and all of your wealth—will all perish. . . . For the death of all flesh comes before the Lord, including all of the great fortunes. . . . So that even if you attain great things in this world, at the conclusion of seventy years—behold how they have all become dead cadavers. . . . For it is the command of the Lord that all flesh will expire; to this rule there are no exceptions.[53]

The point that Phinehas is here once again driving home is that in light of the inevitability of death, man ought radically to alter his life's priorities. Faced with the realization of his unavoidable demise, he should feel compelled to deny any true importance to the pursuits, whether religious or profane, of *olam ha-zeh*.

The final result of Phinehas's obsession with the supreme importance of pondering death at all times is a very pronounced skepticism about all di-mensions of corporeal human existence itself. This attitude results in a remarkable cynicism about the termination of life as well, and it is this sentiment that underlies one of the most remarkable documents in Phinehas's literary corpus, his stunning ode to death. At the end of his most important work, *Kether Torah*, Phinehas presents a poem about the day of death that he claims to have written in his youth.[54] It begins with his oft-repeated assertion of the great spiritual importance of recalling one's day of death at all times. What follows is a vivid and often gruesomely graphic description of the social commotion and personal trauma that surround the death of everyman.

The genre of death poetry has a long history, and such verse was an especially popular part of eighteenth-century Western European literature.[55] But the poetry that follows Phinehas's initial assertion is truly exceptional; indeed, I have not found its equivalent elsewhere. Phinehas's poem is absolutely startling in its intense skepticism, and riveting in its powerful depiction of the inherent depravity of the human condition and in its callous and almost mockingly cruel insensibility regarding the pain, suffering, and sadness that death imposes upon all men, both the dying and their loved ones.

The central purpose of Phinehas's vividly grim and frightful death poem is graphically to illustrate the utter futility and overwhelming misery of physical human existence on earth and especially to underscore the inherently decrepit nature of the human body. Man is born in shame and dies in depravity. In birth he is a "lowly product of a repugnant drop who twice must pass through the urinary shaft submerged in blood." Throughout his life he is beset by "nothing more than misery, pain, and affliction." And when he is finally blessed with death, "his corpse remains filled with humiliation and shame—what with his face turning green and his limbs deteriorating, his mouth wide open and his stomach bloated." Ultimately the "flesh will succumb to vermin and insects, snakes and scorpions," which will "penetrate into your guts and cultivate thorns inside your entrails." The point of these extended, horrifying descriptions of death—which Phinehas offers with apparently abundant pleasure—is, of course, to remind man of his limitations and to warn him against both material and spiritual hubris:

> How filled was your home with specially selected gold and silver; and now, how you have fallen from heaven, bright morning star [*heilel ben shahar*]; how you have been felled to earth. You thought in your heart that you would rise to the heavens and establish your seat among the great Sages; but in fact you will be brought down into the inner pits of Sheol. How, then, could you ever have gloated in the material world, and bragged of your wealth, wisdom, and bravery. You should have known all along that you were destined to rejoice, together with us, only after your burial.

In the course of this deeply bitter portrayal of the last days of life, Phinehas targets the vain conceit of two specific offenders: the overly pious and the wealthy classes. Apparently annoyed by both of these groups' pretensions to meaningful and lasting achievements in life, Phinehas uses the morbidly colorful reminders of the day of death as the stick with which to beat down any optimism or enthusiasm about man's temporal, material, and even religious possibilities. Phinehas's is a *Weltanschauung* entirely obsessed with the idea of human putrefaction and death. Not only is life to be led with no intrinsic hopes and with only dying as its final purpose but the perennial consciousness of death is man's central moral guide to righteous living.

The Mithnagdic elevation of death to man's final blessing and highest ideal is not, of course, unique in the phenomenology of religion. The pious spiritual contempt for the life of this world and the attendant religious fascination with, and anticipation of, death were among the central components of medieval European Christian spirituality. Innocent III's classic, *De Contemptus Mundi* (revealingly subtitled *Liber de Miseria Humanae Conditionis*), was frequently reproduced and translated across Europe throughout the late Middle Ages and was in fact the basic textbook of a veritable Christian tradition of extreme otherworldliness, or *contemptus mundi*. And at the very same time that the Mithnagdim of Belorussia were preaching their disdain for life and the centrality of death as the fullest expression of religious deliverance, the Puritans of New England were "constantly urging themselves to direct their lives toward that moment when their earthly pilgrimage would end."[56] According to David Stannard, in eighteenth-century Puritan thought "it was becoming the norm, the accepted norm, for the Godly to die in 'raptures of Holy Joy': they wish, and even long for death, for the sake of that happy state it will carry them into."[57]

In the light of its consistently otherworldly, death-oriented religious posture, Mithnagdism emerges as a classic manifestation of what M. Westphal has categorized as "exilic religion," in which creation is the consequence of a primordial catastrophe, life is a ceaseless misery, and the escape from the world of matter through death is man's only option for true salvation. Hasidism, by contrast, reveals itself to be a form of "mimetic religion," in which creation is celebrated, God is served through the sanctification of the elements of the created physical universe, and salvation is attained in the context of this life.[58]

Chapter 6

THE MITHNAGDIM
AND THE HASKALAH:
A REAPPRAISAL

The scholarly consensus is that the Gaon of Vilna was the most accomplished Talmudic scholar in European Jewish history. He is also widely considered to be the founding father of the rabbinic movement of opposition to Hasidism. But in addition to these accurate ascriptions, the GRA is often credited with yet another, far more problematic legacy: that of being the most important rabbinic forerunner of the eastern European Jewish enlightenment.

Both the early proponents of the Haskalah and many later nineteenth-century *Wissenschaft* historians were fond of viewing the GRA and his select circle of disciples—the Mithnagdim—as precursors of enlightenment. Of course, viewing the GRA as a forerunner of the eastern Haskalah lended authoritative rabbinic precedent to their own departures from strictly traditional rabbinic Judaism. The GRA was therefore quite deliberately cast by the early Maskilim and their sympathetic chroniclers of the Wissenschaft des Judentums school as "the originator of the movement" of Jewish enlightenment in the East.[1] The GRA's uncommon interest in many scientific disciplines and his publications in the areas of geometry, astronomy, and geography have often been cited as indications of his anticipation of the Haskalah's eventual development in eastern Europe and as proof that he nurtured many of the academic pursuits that ultimately became synonymous with enlightenment Judaism.[2] Furthermore, the GRA's "lower critical" approach to the sacred texts of Judaism, his passionate rejection of the rabbinic casuistry known as pilpul, and his advocacy of Jewish curricular reform have all been appreciated as affinities between him and the early Maskilim.[3]

In his remarkable article "Ha-Hasidut ve-ha-Haskalla," the Hebrew essayist and champion of rationalism Shai Ish Hurwitz offered the following, rather typical Maskilic appreciation of the Gaon of Vilna as a precursor of Jewish enlightenment:

It was the GRA who first created an opening, like the eye of a needle, for the critical textual study of the Talmud, which finally resulted in today's critical, literary scholarship. It was the GRA, long before Zunz and Graetz came along, who allowed himself to amend rabbinic texts critically. And certainly the GRA's critical textual insights were far more authoritative than those of the founders of Wissenschaft des Judentums.

The GRA was a trailblazer in the field of Jewish education; he eliminated rabbinic casuistry (pilpul) and was the first to establish a logical pedagogic order of study whereby Jewish children would begin with Bible and Hebrew grammar, followed by Mishna, and only then begin the study of Talmud—a program that was later championed by all of the Maskilim, in particular by Isaac Baer Levinsohn.

Who knows if all of the latter's [i.e., the Maskilim's] efforts for the improvement of Jewish education would have taken root had it not been for the pioneering work of the GRA?

Moreover, the GRA was a scientific scholar the likes of whom had not been seen in Israel since the days of the great Gaonim of Babylonia and North Africa. At his behest, Joshua Zeitlin established his center for Jewish scientific scholarship . . . and at his command did Barukh of Shklov decide to translate Euclid into Hebrew. . . . And in all of this he was a shining example for his many disciples. The GRA's students came into close contact with the biblical scholars and pioneers of the enlightenment, who were assembled in those days in Berlin under the direction of Moses Mendelsohn in a joint effort to find ways to improve the spiritual condition and education of the Jewish people.[4]

Although such a skewed appreciation of the GRA has been partially discredited by later scholars, and although a few contemporary studies have questioned the precision of classifying him as a genuine precursor of the eastern European Jewish enlightenment, his image as a remarkably broad, diversified scholar, and unusually enlightened Lithuanian rabbi for his day has endured.[5] Even Immanuel Etkes, whose essay on this question effectively challenged early *Wissenschaft* claims about the extent of the GRA's modernity and who correctly insisted that one cannot really speak of proper Maskilim in Russia before the third decade of the nineteenth century, conceded that if the GRA was not an immediate precursor, he must at least be viewed as a distant harbinger of the Haskalah.[6]

This portrait of the GRA as a proto-Maskil has been extended to many of his students and disciples and more generally to the rabbinic opponents of Hasidism, the Mithnagdim. And the evidence of alleged enlightenment tendencies in their ranks has served, in turn, to reinforce this image of their mentor. Thus, for example, it is commonly pointed out that the scientist and rabbi Barukh Shick of Shklov, who claimed that the GRA enthusiastically endorsed his campaign of translating scientific classics into Hebrew for the advancement of wisdom among the Jews, was also a passionate Mithnagged, as were his benefactor, the patron of liberal arts Joshua Zeitlin, the scientifically inclined Benjamin Rivlin, and the enlightened Rabbi Judah Leib Margolioth.[7] Many other Vilna associates or admirers of the GRA are added to this list of alleged enlightened Mithnagdim, such as the biographer Ezekiel Faivel of Dretzhyn, whose proposals for Jewish curricular reform have been interpreted as reflecting the influence of the West,[8] and, later on, the highly enigmatic Menashe of Ilya, whose eclectic writings reflected broad worldly knowledge as well as strong convictions about the moral significance and importance for Jewish social advancement of secular studies.[9] That the first eastern center of Jewish enlightenment, the city of Shklov, was also the place where the very first shots in the rabbinic war against Hasidism were fired is seen as more than mere coincidence.[10]

Finally, in addition to their Renaissance-like interests in meta-rabbinic and scientific studies, the very intellectualism of the Mithnagdic elite of this period has been perceived as effectively constituting a bridge between the traditional rabbis and the Maskilim. As Immanuel Etkes has observed, the fact that the earliest manifestations of the Haskalah in Russia were invariably expressed in terms of scholastic, academic interests "is simply consistent with the tradition of intellectual intensity which was so prevalent in Rabbinic circles."[11] In this sense, the academic interests of the early Maskilim are said to have been an almost natural outcome of the classical rabbinic emphasis upon scholastic excellence as the highest measure of human achievement.

As a consequence of these perceived associations there has emerged in the intellectual historiography of the present century the general notion that in the complex religious and ideological discord of late-eighteenth- and early-nineteenth-century Jewish eastern Europe the Hasidic movement faced two similarly hostile, though not entirely allied, groups: the Mithnagdim and the Maskilim. Thus, citing their meta-rabbinic academic interests as well as their critique of the pedagogic deficiencies of the Hasidim, the historian Michael Stanislawski has simply concluded that a large number of Lithuanian Jews associated with the GRA were "perched on the borders of traditional society" and that as a result "it is often quite impossible to differentiate between a traditionalist of the Lithuanian school and a maskil."[12]

In addition to their common interests in meta-rabbinic and "scientific" learning, historians point out that the Mithnagdim and the early eastern European Maskilim shared a common literary enterprise, the anti-Hasidic polemic. That the Maskilim followed the classic Mithnagdim in the publication of satirical anti-Hasidic tracts has served further to foster the impression of their intellectual and religious affinities. Thus, for example, in the *Encyclopedia Judaica* biography of the greatest of the Mithnagdic polemicists, R. David of Makow, one finds the following: "David of Makow is the most noted polemicist against Hasidism. . . . Echoes of his criticism of Hasidism are to be found in Haskalah literature as in the writings of Joseph Perl and Peter Beer."[13] The implication is clear: there is both a similarity and a continuity between the Mithnagdic and Haskalah polemics against Hasidism. Of course, a substantive comparative reading of the Mithnagdic polemical tracts and the satires of the Maskilim would reveal just how different their respective arguments against Hasidism really were. Yet the very coincidence that both parties were engaged in a religious conflict against the same group serves to create the impression that the Mithnagdim and the Maskilim were partners in a kind of tradition and helps strengthen the argument for their religious and intellectual affinities.

There is no questioning the associations and similar academic interests of some very exceptional members of the rabbinic intellectual elite and certain pioneers of the Haskalah. Nonetheless, any suggestion of a real relationship or of genuine ideological influences, to say nothing of spiritual affinities, between the early Mithnagdim and the nascent Haskalah of Belorussia has not been fully or critically examined on the basis of the primary rabbinic (i.e., Mithnagdic) texts of this period.

That many Mithnagdim of the early enlightenment era displayed interests in a variety of non-Talmudic disciplines is in itself of little historical significance. In virtually every generation and every community of postexilic Jewish intellectual history a minority of rabbis fostered similar utilitarian interests in the value of scientific and secular studies in enhancing their understanding and appreciation of Torah.[14] For the GRA and his students, as for most of those earlier rabbis, such academic pursuits were purely utilitarian, entirely ancillary to Torah study, and therefore not at all analogous to the Haskalah's interest in secular study as both an autonomous good and a vehicle for the social transformation and economic advancement of Europe's Jews.

A more sophisticated understanding of the cardinal theological doctrines of the Mithnagdim reveals that they were for the most part as fundamentally hostile to the Haskalah as to Hasidism. Moreover, as I hope to demonstrate, many of the same basic theological convictions underlay their opposition to both movements. A different perspective on how the religious battle lines of the period might be drawn emerges from a faithful reading of the Mithnagdic theological writings. The resulting picture is a configuration of intellectual forces in which it was the Mithnagdim, and not the Hasidim, who stood in opposition to two contemporary insurgent forces in the Jewish community, namely, Hasidism and the nascent enlightenment movement. With the Mithnagdim seen in the light of their strenuous opposition to the Haskalah, the very notion of an enlightened Mithnagduth appears to be misleading and perhaps even a contradiction in terms.[15]

The Arguments for Enlightened Mithnagduth

Let us examine the nature of the argument for the existence of a class of enlightened, anti-Hasidic rabbis primarily among the followers of the GRA. The most notable early "symptoms" that historians have tended to diagnose for the germination of Haskalah tendencies in rabbinic thinkers of this century include the following:[16]

1. *Interest in medieval Jewish rationalism.* Intellectual historians have traditionally viewed an appreciation of medieval Jewish rationalism and especially a knowledge of, or interest in, Maimonides' *Guide for the Perplexed* as suggesting the presence of enlightenment proclivities in rabbinic circles. After all, the *Guide* was not published even once in eastern Europe during the course of the seventeenth and eighteenth centuries, and it was a rarely found, and even more rarely cited, source in traditional Jewish society and literature. It was the Maskilim who are credited with the "rediscovery" of the *Guide* and it was they who began to reissue the work. Throughout the history of the Jewish enlightenment and of early Wissenschaft des Judentums, an interest in Maimonidean philosophy, and in particular the rationalization of Jewish law, has been considered symptomatic of Haskalah sensitivities.

2. *Rejection of the supernatural aspects of faith.* As mentioned earlier, particularly the scientific interests of the GRA and of his disciples and admirers have been viewed by scholars as indications of nascent enlightenment interests among the Mithnagdim. In addition, the specific rejection of the Hasidic belief in miracles and Hasidism's faith in the supernatural powers of the zaddik are said to be sentiments shared by both Maskilim and Mithnagdim.[17]

3. *Advocacy of educational reform.* The critique of traditional Jewish, or rabbinic, learning and the advocacy of curricular reform were fundamental features of the Haskalah, especially in the East. The traditional method of Talmudic study in eastern Europe, most particularly the casuistic pilpul method, from the beginning had been the object of scorn and derision on the part of enlightened Jews. Jewish educational reforms were often considered by the Maskilim to be an important initial step, if not the very key, to the

realization of the Haskalah's ambitious vision of altering Jewish society in the East. Proponents of the theory of affinities between Haskalah and Mithnagduth thus point out that the GRA and a number of his disciples, such as R. Ezekiel Faivel of Dretzhyn,[18] displayed both a deep hostility to pilpul and a strong interest in curricular reform.

On the basis of these three criteria it has been compellingly argued that many of the GRA's disciples, in addition to other Mithnagdim, were harbingers of the eastern Haskalah. Yet, as a closer reading of their writings reveals, these same figures were in reality often outspoken opponents of the early Haskalah. For a classic example of this phenomenon, let us turn now to the writings of R. Phinehas b. Judah, Maggid of Polotsk.

R. Phinehas of Polotsk: Proto-Maskil?

Based on the characteristics described above, R. Phinehas of Polotsk could convincingly be portrayed as a Mithnagdic friend of the Haskalah. Indeed, he exhibited virtually all of the traits that historians considered to be the classical marks of the budding Maskil. Throughout his writings he displayed a deep interest in the rationalist philosophical tradition of the Maimonidean school. Although he relied most extensively upon more "traditional" philosophical and mystical sources than the *Guide for the Perplexed,* most notably Bahya's *Hovoth ha-Levavoth* and the biblical commentaries of R. Moses Alshikh, R. Phinehas engaged in a number of prolonged philosophical discussions, usually based upon his own interpretation of passages from the *Guide.*

R. Phinehas's commentary to Job, *Giveath Phinehas,* is largely concerned with a number of philosophical problems originally formulated by Maimonides. Already in the lengthy thematic introduction to this commentary R. Phinehas suggests that the early part of the book of Job is primarily a philosophical dialogue regarding the nature and extent of divine knowledge and is principally concerned with the issue of God's knowledge of particulars. The bulk of this introduction consists of citations, paraphrases, and explications of Maimonides' deliberations on the nature and limits of divine knowledge, found in the *Guide,* 3:16–17. In the actual text of the commentary to the book R. Phinehas contends that Job's initial protest against his bitter lot is rooted in the Aristotelian philosophical tradition, which denies God any knowledge of particulars and consequently repudiates the basic biblical doctrine of providential reward and punishment for the particular deeds of man.[19]

In the same work, R. Phinehas delved deeply into other rationalist and philosophical discussions, quoting extensively from the *Guide* and revealing a sound schooling in the medieval philosophical tradition. For example, commenting on Elihu's blunt insistence that he "will flatter no one, God or man, for I cannot use any flattering titles" (Job 33:21), R. Phinehas digresses into a discussion of the unknowability of God and the inadequacy of positive divine attributes, enthusiastically citing the Maimonidean deliberation on this issue, found in the first part of the *Guide*.[20] R. Phinehas also considered at great length the theological problem created by the apparent contradiction between the notions of human free will and divine providence, as well as the Maimonidean theory of prophecy.[21] In short, his interpretation of the book of Job is suffused with substantive philosophical discussions, including extensive citations from Maimonides' *Guide*.

R. Phinehas's rationalist deliberations are by no means restricted to this single work. Maimonides' philosophical writings are quoted and analyzed in his other books as well. One of the Maimonidean theories that R. Phinehas was most fond of citing approvingly is his naturalist theory of miracles. Maimonides, like the other medieval scholastics, had a problem harmonizing the biblical account of miracles with the prevailing Aristotelian notions of eternal existence and natural law of his time. His favored solution was that miracles were preordained, a concept that generally precluded the ongoing possibility for arbitrary divine interventions in the form of miraculous or supernatural phenomena in the postbiblical period. Throughout his writings, R. Phinehas cited and endorsed the notion that a strictly limited number of miraculous instances had been programmed by God into nature on the eve of the first Sabbath.[22] R. Phinehas also suggested that the supernatural powers attributed to the early sages and zaddikim were strictly a phenomenon of the past.[23]

Aside from an impressive knowledge of the *Guide* and unequivocal acceptance of some of its truly innovative philosophical doctrines, as well as his rejection of contemporary miracles, R. Phinehas exhibited bold critical thinking in the areas of pedagogy and rabbinic education. In his ethical will, *Rosh ha-Giveah*, he proposed a rather sophisticated and progressive regimen of study *(seder ha-limud)* to his son. In this educational proposal R. Phinehas strongly opposed precisely the types of study that the early Maskilim also found most offensive. Like the proponents of Jewish enlightenment, he insisted that the Pentateuch and Prophets be studied only in order to comprehend their plain sense *(peshat)*. He further strongly criticized excessive homiletic interpretation of sacred text *(derush)* as diverting attention from the correct understanding of the Bible. More significantly, R. Phinehas decried the prevalent ignorance of the original sociohistorical context of the words of the Prophets and argued that historical appreciation is crucial for a proper evaluation of the prophetic message. In the area of rabbinic literature, R. Phinehas discouraged abstract, theoretical study, insisting instead on a pragmatic orientation to the instruction of rabbinic texts. He also endorsed Maimonides' suggestion that for the average Jew the study of biblical texts and Mishna should be followed immediately by a simple reading ("without the commentaries") of the *Mishneh Torah* and the later codifiers. R. Phinehas discouraged any indulgence in the casuistic pilpul method of rabbinic learning, as well as the investigation of esoteric Kabbalistic sources, both of which he deemed futile. Thus, his curricular proposals were daringly critical of the prevalent, unsystematic modes of traditional Jewish study, and he suggested far-reaching educational streamlining and a variety of progressive pedagogic innovations.[24]

Finally, R. Phinehas candidly recognized the importance of mastering the physical sciences in order fully to appreciate the presence of God in the created universe. In *Kether Torah* he made this quite explicit: "In order to know and discern God's power and the wonder of His miracles in all of the universe, as well as His wisdom, providence, compassion, and energy, which infuse all, you must first study all of the wisdom of geometry, the natural sciences, and medicine."[25]

In light of the above, and employing the same yardstick by which so many Jewish historians have deemed the GRA and his disciples to be forerunners of the enlightenment in Russia, one might very easily make the argument that R. Phinehas of Polotsk too was a proto-Maskil. For one can find in his writings signs of the most significant academic tendencies and many of the intellectual inclinations of the early Maskilim. In fact, it turns out that R. Phinehas was somewhat sympathetic to all three of the cardinal concerns that historians have viewed as key symptoms of enlightenment proclivities. One might be tempted to cite the case of R. Phinehas and his "progressive" interests as yet one more illustration of the prevalence of a form of enlightened Mithnagduth among the rabbis of late-eighteenth-century Belorussia. But as we shall presently see, nothing could be further from the truth. For, his aforementioned intellectual proclivities and pedagogic progressivism notwithstanding, R. Phinehas of Polotsk was actually a consistently hostile opponent of the Haskalah. As a matter of fact, the vociferousness of his condemnation of early enlightenment tendencies among the Jews of eastern Europe was every bit as intense as the hostility he displayed toward Hasidism. Indeed, his polemic against Hasidism is even juxtaposed in *Kether Torah* to his most explicit and extensive condemnation of the enlightenment.

R. Phinehas of Polotsk's Anti-Haskalah Polemic

R. Phinehas's anti-Hasidic polemic in *Kether Torah,* which is presented in the dramatic form of a refutation of the various attempts of the evil instinct to seduce man away from his rightful preoccupation with Torah study, is preceded by a lengthy attack on the budding Jewish interest in secular, scientific studies and philosophical learning. Published in Shklov in 1788, at the very dawn of enlightenment tendencies among Russian Jewry, this critique of modernization was in all likelihood the first of its kind in eastern European rabbinic literature.[26]

R. Phinehas begins *Kether Torah* by asserting the great urgency and particular relevance in his day of the conservative moral and religious teachings of the medieval pietist Bahya ibn Pakuda.[27] He states that *Kether Torah* will be modeled both stylistically and substantively after Bahya's highly influential classic, *Hovoth ha-Levavoth,* for the message that it imparted remains of burning contemporary importance: "On account of the fact that this contagion has spread to the members of our people, and the glory of the Torah is now dissipated—woe unto the ears that hear of this, and woe unto the eyes that witness it—therefore, I feel an obligation to expound upon this matter at length in order to raise the crown of Torah high above all other crowns."[28]

The "other crowns" R. Phinehas perceived to be threatening the glory and primacy of the Torah are those of Hasidism and the Haskalah. In fact, the very first line of attack of the *yezer ha-ra,* before it distracts man with the pursuits of *devekuth,* mystical prayer, and other forms of piety commonly associated with Hasidism, is the seduction of the faithful Jew with an interest in "external," secular studies:

> The evil instinct therefore departs from before all of the nations of the world in order exclusively to pester the people of Israel—its Torah scholars in particular— and in order to quench the flame [of Torah] that normally glows within their hearts and to extinguish the blaze burning in their bones with the bitter, cursed, filthy, salty, and contaminated waters of external wisdoms and natural sciences . . . which are banned from entering the congregation of the Lord.
>
> First the evil instinct will entice you with the beauty of the gentiles' verse and songs, and [then with] their critical investigations and learning—poetry, music, logic, architecture, biology, medicine, and geography. . . . It will then tell you, "See how these disciplines instruct of the true glory of God to all the nations . . . unlike our Torah . . . which is based upon . . . petty textual nitpicking and all sorts of silly letter games . . . all of which are completely contrary to human reason . . . and as a result of which we appear as fools and idiots before the nations and in the eyes of the aristocracy of our own people."[29]

This depiction of the seductions of man's evil instinct is no ideological abstraction. Nor should it be taken as merely a rote repetition of standard literary motifs borrowed from medieval rabbinic letters. To begin with, R. Phinehas repeatedly refers very specifically to the new advocates of educational reform as members of a well-defined sect *(kat)*. And when he begins his elaborate refutation of their criticism of the Jews and proceeds to reject the call for a greater Jewish interest in secular studies, he makes it clear that his is no mere theoretical polemic: "Lately, men have arisen among the ranks of the aristocracy of our people—a breed completely unanticipated by our ancestors—and they have begun to spread this heresy through the ranks of Israel."[30] To be sure, this kind of critique of the pursuit of secular, nonrabbinic studies was a very familiar topos in earlier rabbinic literature. One might therefore be tempted to read it as not much more than R. Phinehas's recasting of standard polemical formulations. Nevertheless, considered in its historical context, it seems highly plausible that Phinehas was responding very specifically to a new challenge. For the case made for increased secular and scientific pursuits and against the exclusive attention of the Jews to rabbinic study, which Phinehas attributes to the evil instinct, certainly sounds very much like the arguments being raised in R. Phinehas's very time and place by the earliest propagandists for the Haskalah in Russia in their calls for Jewish curricular reform. R. Phinehas's *yezer ha-ra* admonishes the Jews that because of their narrow interest only in Torah study, they appear to the nations of the world among whom they dwell as primitive boors devoid of both culture and wisdom. The beauty and truth of the gentile scholars' arts and sciences are contrasted by the evil instinct with the unaesthetic and unrefined parochial pursuits of the rabbis.

To the student of Jewish enlightenment literature these are familiar arguments. That the pursuit of greater secular wisdom would polish the image and raise the prestige of the Jews in the eyes of the nations was a fundamental contention of the very first Maskilim, both in the West and, later, in Russia. In the West, this was a dominant theme of Naftali Hertz Weisel's *Divrei Shalom ve-Emeth* (1782). In Russia, R. Barukh Shick of Shklov argued, in the celebrated introduction to his Hebrew edition of *Euclid* (The Hague, 1780), and even more forcefully three years later in his work of trigonometry, *Kenei ha-Midah* (Prague, 1783), that the Jews' ignorance of the sciences had made them the object of international derision.[31] Shick insisted that a primary benefit of increased scientific study among the Jews would be the enhancement of Israel's social standing and national prestige in the world. Three of the approbations to Shick's Hebrew version of *Euclid*, by the rabbis of Amsterdam, the Hague, and Slonim, Belorussia, forcefully echoed these very sentiments.

The endorsement of the Lithuanian rabbi Samson ben Mordechai of Slonim captures this largely apologetic motif very well:

> May your strength increase as a reward for having broken the yoke of strangers and the belittling by the arrogant gentiles who unjustly slander our people, Israel, the children of the living God, about whom it is written: "This great nation is certainly a wise and learned people." But they say the opposite: "Your knowledge has vanished from your children, for where is your wisdom and discernment in the eyes of the nations?"
>
> But from now on the enemy will no longer scorn us, and Jacob shall no longer be humiliated, for the earth shall be filled with knowledge, just as the waters fill the sea.

In other words, aside from its intrinsic value, knowledge of the sciences will, according to the rabbi of Slonim, greatly enhance the reputation of the Jews among the nations as a uniquely sagacious nation.

Barukh Shick polemicized against those who insisted that Torah and science are antithetical or that modern study posed a threat to traditional learning. He countered that the widespread pursuit of the sciences in Israel would only serve to facilitate a fuller understanding of Jewish sources and a better mastery of Jewish law. And, as is well known, Shick claimed that the GRA himself had personally expressed to him his belief that the understanding of Torah increases in direct proportion to one's mastery of the sciences.[32]

R. Barukh Shick was engaged in an active campaign to spread his interests in science to his fellow Belorussian Jews, especially those of his own town of Shklov. Although he was a pioneer in the dissemination of new-worldly knowledge and Hebrew scientific writings among the Jews of Belorussia, Shick was not alone. The first currents of western Haskalah had already begun to reach Russia through a number of channels. Primary among them were wealthy merchants from Prussia and Galicia, who, according to a number of firsthand accounts, were admired by their Russian brethren for their scientific and philosophical knowledge, as well as their Western dress. A significant element within the Jewish community of Shklov was also deeply respectful of the writings of the greatest German Maskilim, Naftali Weisel and Moses Mendelssohn. In 1780 the Shklov kehillah even commissioned Weisel to compose a Hebrew poem in honor of Czarina Catharine's impending visit and requested that Mendelssohn render it into proper German. Finally, a number of wealthy merchants, such as Nathan Nota Notkin, contributed energetically to spreading Western culture to Russian Jewry.[33] Clearly, at the beginning of the nineteenth century a significant, if limited, Russian Jewish constituency had already been exposed, and was sympathetically disposed, to scientific learning, innovative pedagogic ideas, and Western culture and dress. Even in this very early phase of the eastward thrust of the Jewish enlightenment several dozen eastern European Jews were subscribers to the Maskilic journal *Ha-Me'assef,* which first appeared in Königsberg in 1784.[34]

All that notwithstanding, *Kether Torah,* written in 1788, remains a very early rabbinic critique of the eastern European proto-Haskalah, the first of its kind, to my knowledge. After all, the man to be heralded as the "Russian Mendelssohn" and the "father of the Haskalah in the East," Isaac Baer Levinsohn, was only just born that very year. While it is, however, true that R. Phinehas's anti-Haskalah polemic was written at a time when the penetration of Western ideas into the eastern European Jewish communities had barely begun, that *Kether Torah* was published in Shklov eight years after the appearance of R. Barukh of Shklov's Hebrew version of *Euclid,* with its provocative introduction and approbations, is clearly significant. Although he was not a full-time resident, R. Phinehas was obviously at home in Shklov and intimately familiar with its Jewish community. Aside from those in his own town of Polotsk, the single largest number of presubscribers *(prenumerantn)* for his edition of the Hebrew liturgy *Siddur Shaar ha-Rahamim,* which, like *Kether Torah,* was published in Shklov in 1788, came from Shklov.[35]

Both *Kether Torah* and *Siddur Shaar ha-Rahamim* had the approbation of Shklov's chief rabbi, Isaachar Baer Slutsker.[36] A friend of Shklov's rabbis and a well-received author in its Jewish community, R. Phinehas certainly was aware of the new, modernizing currents that had reached the city. It is also highly probable that R. Phinehas had personally encountered Shick or at least seen copies of his edition of *Euclid* and his work *Kenei ha-Mida.* Judging by the phraseology and the line of argumentation Phinehas pursues in the anti-Haskalah polemic with which *Kether Torah* begins, it is even plausible that he was reacting primarily and directly to R. Shick's bold claims regarding the religious importance of scientific and mathematical knowledge. Indeed, R. Phinehas's attack upon such academic pursuits explicitly refutes the two fundamental affirmations that had been made by Shick in support and praise of secular study.

Revelation versus Reason

Having established the existence of a serious threat to traditional Jewish society, paraphrased the basic arguments of the early Maskilim, and personified them as the will of man's evil inclination, R. Phinehas entered into a detailed polemic with these unnamed aristocratic reformers and religious heretics. His argument against secular and scientific studies is rooted in a very conservative epistemology, as well as a dim view of the resources and capacity of human understanding. He insisted that the roots of Jewish religious belief and the basic epistemic underpinnings of the Torah were without parallel in any other system of knowledge. Unlike all other academic disciplines, the wisdom of the Torah is exclusively divine in origin; its sole source is revelation. Consequently, reason cannot conceivably play any role in the discovery of religious truths. The newfangled scientific pursuits being advocated by the new class of Maskilim, on the other hand, were based entirely upon human reason. The pursuit of science thus threatened to train the Jew to rely exclusively upon his innate intellectual powers, which, unlike revelation, were essentially flawed. Ultimately the increasing reverence for, and reliance upon, human reason fostered by the enlightenment would undermine the Jews' faith in the very foundations of Torah knowledge; in particular, they would destroy the Jews' belief in revelation.

But R. Phinehas did not limit his critique to the pursuit of secular wisdom at the expense of Torah study. He also countered the contention, implicit in the Maimonidean philosophical traditions and later made popular by Weisel and subsequently reaffirmed by Shick, that Torah study and worldly education must be seen as two complementary disciplines rather than as competitors. He explicitly attacked the idea, found in Shick's introduction to *Euclid,* that one might first intensively pursue Torah study and then, upon attainment of a sophisticated level of traditional Jewish knowledge, go on to master other fields of worldly wisdom:

Why should the Torah preclude us from seizing upon both [forms of wisdom]? Why should I not first fill my stomach with the knowledge of Torah and the commandments of God and then go on to pursue the sweet study of external wisdoms?

Because it is not just that you must not cheat on the woman of your youth, namely, the Torah, and replace her with foreigners by latching onto the arms of gentile women. . . . Beyond this, even after getting your fill of the Holy Torah, you still may not pursue the various sweet delicacies of external wisdom, for they will ruin the taste of the Torah and *mitzvoth* already in your mouth. . . . Therefore, do not even approach the portals of [secular science]; rather, stay far away from them. For our holy Torah and its commandments are not built upon the foundations of human reasoning, and there should be no attempt to harmonize them with reason in any way.[37]

R. Phinehas extended his attack upon the enlightenment's educational agenda even further. Not only did he denounce the pursuit of secular wisdom and the sciences by any Jew at any time but he argued for a complete, radical separation of Torah from the tenets of deductive reason, rational speculation, and anything resembling scientific method. In what was clearly a severe reaction to the perceived threat of the importing of western European values to Belorussian Jewry,[38] R. Phinehas condemned any application of reason to matters of faith, even conjecture in the time-honored field of *ta'amei ha-mitzvoth*, the speculative rationalization of the commandments of Jewish law, a favorite pastime of the medieval Jewish philosophers and later a subject that deeply interested the earliest Maskilim, most notably Weisel:[39] "From now on, all of God's commands are to be [viewed as] nothing more than the demands of a king upon his servants. One must not even question the reason for any of His commandments. For would it be acceptable for a fully and permanently bonded servant to question his master regarding the reason for his demands of him. Clearly not, for his sole duty is to fulfill the will of his owner."[40] R. Phinehas's strictly positivist approach to Torah observance is finally summed up as follows:

> Our Torah must never be transformed into something like the ethical impera-
> tives of the gentiles. For God did not intend His Torah legislation to be a source
> of sweet gratification and intellectual stimulation; rather, the Torah is nothing
> more than the decrees of the King upon us. We are not supposed to understand,
> nor [even] to question, God's motives with regard to each *mitzvah;* rather, we
> must simply do what the King orders and fulfill the will of God.[41]

R. Israel Loebl's *Even Bohan*

The association of the early Haskalah with the medieval scholastic enterprise of harmonizing human reason with divine revelation was shared by another prominent Lithuanian Mithnagged, R. Israel Loebl. R. Loebl is best known to students of this period as one of the leading anti-Hasidic polemicists and a faithful disciple of the GRA, whose explicit support in the battle against the Hasidim he regularly invoked.[42] His *Sefer ha-Vikuah* is arguably the fullest and most important source for the intellectual history of the early rabbinic battle against Hasidism. What is less known about R. Israel Loebl is that this fiery Mithnagged was also a vociferous opponent of the Haskalah who in 1799 published *Even Bohan,* an important though largely overlooked antienlightenment pamphlet.[43]

The central argument of this work is that since human reason is so essentially limited and flawed, the Jews' final and unique spiritual perfection is only to be attained through observance of the nonrational commandments of the Torah. Basing his argument on R. Saadyah Gaon's seminal distinction between rational and positivist religious imperatives *(mitzvoth sikhliyoth* and *mitzvoth shimiyoth)*, R. Loebl insisted that the latter possess far greater religious significance because the reasonable moral behavior prescribed by the Torah's rational commandments is common to all civilized people, whereas the observance of the nonrational commandments constitutes a manifestation of Israel's uniqueness and chosenness. While the *mishpatim* (or rational Pentateuchal commandments) belong to all of mankind, the *hukim* (or nonrational commandments) set the Jews apart and manifest the singular legacy and spiritual superiority of Israel over the nations:

> There is no greater source of blessing through which the human species can attain its final purpose than the nonrational commandments. . . . For even though the rational commandments are in themselves good, and human reason compels their fulfillment, nonetheless man observes them naturally . . . without having as his motivation the fulfillment of the will and the faith of the King.
>
> It is for this reason that there is an abundance of nonrational commandments in the Torah; that is, in order to provide man with his true perfection. . . . For as a consequence of the multitude of *mitzvoth* that he will confront and that he will observe for the simple and only reason that he is so commanded, he will acquire the perfection of his soul.[44]

R. Loebl accused the enlightenment "heretics" of downplaying the particularist, ritualistic *mitzvoth shimiyoth* and of placing undue emphasis upon the rational commandments for the sake of advancing their dangerous brand of universalism. He charged that the Maskilim (to whom he, like R. Phinehas, repeatedly referred as a sect, or *kat*) contended, in the name of "philosophical enlightenment," that the nonrational commandments had become obsolete and that the exclusive observance of the rational laws of the Torah would help mankind realize the goal of "universal equality between all peoples." R. Loebl, however, accused them of being the "great haters of all people of true faith."[45]

For both R. Phinehas of Polotsk and R. Israel Loebl, then, reliance upon the powers of human reason was completely antithetical to both the correct understanding and the faithful observance of the Torah. Moreover, Torah study could only be pursued using the traditional methods of rabbinic hermeneutics, not the critical scientific approach. The practical daily compliance with the demands of Halakhah must therefore vigilantly be protected from the intrusions of logic or reason, for any such rational inquiry into matters of faith threatened to undermine completely the law's uniquely divine foundations and the ideally pure spiritual motivations for Halakhic obedience.

Early Rabbinic Fears of Social Assimilation

The new intellectual tendencies and academic interests fostered by the early Haskalah movement by no means represented the highest aspirations or ultimate goals of the Jewish enlightenment. Rather, the calls for modernization of Jewish learning and broadening of the Jews' scholarly horizons were perceived to be the essential means for achieving the true aim of the Haskalah, namely, the successful integration of the Jews into European society. But as scholars have noted, while that final aspiration was rather quickly being realized in western Europe, in the East, largely as a consequence of the closed nature of the gentile society there, the social and cultural absorption of the Jews did not become a significant part of the program of the Jewish enlightenment until almost a half-century later.

The first manifestoes for the modernization of eastern Europe Jewry were therefore limited, for the most part, to an agenda for academic and curricular reform. Social reform and the modernization of Jewish communal life, dress, habits, and etiquette remained almost exclusively the program of the Western Haskalah in this period. In Russia, for years to come the primary thrust of the early modernizers remained intellectual and educational. Indeed, just one year after the publication of R. Phinehas of Polotsk's *Kether Torah*, the following description of Polish and Lithuanian Jewry by Barukh Landau, which appeared in Berlin, testified to the effect of this limited campaign for enlightenment:

> They are exceedingly wise men, men of learning, knowledge, and understanding. There are to be found, especially among the ranks of our people, many great Sages in Israel, *as well as a large number of people who have a fine mastery of the other wisdoms,* and still more whose souls are inclined and able to attain all of the most exalted disciplines if, in their youth, they can only find a competent mentor with whom to study these things; for their intellects are strong, and their spirit of discernment is formidable.
>
> However, they are not as clean as people from other countries, either in their homes or in their manner of dress. Furthermore, their way of eating and drinking and their general deportment and etiquette are not quite like those of other men.[46]

Clearly, in these early years, it was only the intellectual or scholastic horizons opened to the Jews by the enlightenment, and not modern standards of personal refinement or social sophistication, that had begun to reach the Jews of Russia. To this limited form of early Haskalah important Mithnagdic disciples of the GRA, such as R. Phinehas of Polotsk and R. Israel Loebl, mounted an uncompromising opposition. Nonetheless there can also be found in the Mithnagdic literature of this period some early warnings against the threat of the social assimilation fostered by enlightenment that was yet to come.

Although, aside from a very brief and obscure reference to those "rabbis who wear gentile dress," the anti-Haskalah polemic found in *Kether Torah* is almost exclusively concerned with academic matters (the forbidden areas of study and dangerous domains of intellectual pursuit being encouraged by the proto-Maskilim), in his later writings Phinehas significantly extended the critique of the early Jewish enlightenment to include certain social concerns as well. In his commentary to Proverbs, *Shevet mi-Yehuda* (1803), Phinehas continued to develop his earlier argument against philosophy and deductive reason. He interpreted the Scripture's many cautions regarding the foreign seductress (i.e., *Isha zara*) as referring to philosophical study.[47] But beyond these familiar, repeated cautions against the threat reason poses to true piety, R. Phinehas warned the Jews about a second form of enlightenment heresy, that of the commonly accepted dictates of civil law and social behavior. The gentiles, he observed, governed themselves on the basis of two types of regulations, the universal dictates of reason and the civil laws of their society *(mitzvoth sikhliyoth* and *mitzvoth nimusiyoth)*. The fundamental contrast between both these categories of gentile legislation and the Torah is that, unlike both rational and civil laws, only the Torah is holy and divinely revealed, and therefore only it can guarantee man eternity of his soul. The gentiles' rational dictates and civil laws, on the other hand, "are only intended for the perfection of the functioning of social affairs so that the world will not deteriorate into chaos."[48]

The depiction in Proverbs of the small and feeble, yet wise, rock badgers, who "make their home among the rocks" (30:26), is taken by R. Phinehas as sound, current advise to a Jewish community surrounded, not by hostile enemies, but rather by dangerously friendly gentiles: "This applies to the people of Israel, which is likened to the 'dove in the rock's crevices.' It instructs: 'Go my people, enter into your room and lock the door behind you. Hide there until the threat subsides. *Do not mingle with the gentiles in order to imitate them and emulate their attainments.*' "[49] In his commentary to Psalms, *Derekh ha-Melekh* (1804), Phinehas openly laments the assimilationist social trends he apparently was beginning to observe among the Jews of his day:

The Lord addresses the people of Israel with the words: "Like a lily among the thorns is my beloved among the girls." The meaning of this is that today things have been reversed, that is to say, you were much better before than you are today. In those earlier days you did not mingle with the gentiles, nor did you learn from their behavior, and you did not follow in their ways or their etiquette or their manner of dress. Therefore you used to be like a lily that stands surrounded on all sides by thorns but remains distinguished from them in its appearance, smell, and image. . . . Unlike today, when you have begun to mingle with the gentiles and to imitate them in all of their wicked ways.[50]

The superiority of Jewish society and law and the chosenness of the Jews themselves are themes that reverberate throughout R. Phinehas's commentaries to both Proverbs and Psalms, in sharp contrast to the enlightenment's ultimate goal of breaking down the barriers of prejudice and exclusiveness that had prevented the Jews' admission into European society.[51]

Enlightenment Values and the Nature of Jewish Faith

Beyond the fear of reason, hostility to secular and scientific studies, and strenuous opposition to assimilation through emulating gentile culture, common law, and social behavior, another very important dimension to Mithnagdism's fundamental rejection of Haskalah values has hitherto been completely ignored by the scholars who have deliberated on this question. The fundamental assumptions upon which the rabbinic faith of this period depended, as manifested in the moral and pietistic writings of the Mithnagdim, stood in direct and immutable conflict with the new, bourgeois values of social integration and economic advancement being proposed by the leading Haskalah thinkers of the day.

In his fine analysis of the dynamics of the European Enlightenment Lucien Goldmann has observed that the conflict between Christianity and the values of the Enlightenment centered upon the latter's basic questioning of the role of divine intervention in human affairs. In the "new world" fostered by the Enlightenment, Goldmann argues,

the citizen no longer regarded his social position as the outcome of divine grace or Providence, but as the result of his own conduct; whether his actions were appropriate and successful, or misdirected and profitless, they were, at least in economic terms, morally neutral and incapable of being judged by standards of good and evil. . . .

In the thinking of people of earlier societies, this possibility of divine intervention—as providential help here below, punishment or reward in the hereafter, or merely, God's approval or wrath—was a factor in every human action and every common event. It thus constituted the psychological base of traditional belief. . . .

The economic life of the bourgeoisie was in fact—or at least in its tendency—autonomous and morally neutral, governed only by the internal criteria of success and failure, and independent of the moral criteria of "good" or "wicked," and the religious criteria of "pleasing to God" or "sinful." . . .

Thus the sociological foundation of the enlightenment is a social process which favored the growth of anti-Christian mental structures and simultaneously entailed a structural alteration of Christian belief within its old external forms.[52]

The same dynamics apply in equal measure to the confrontation between traditional rabbinic Judaism and the Haskalah. As mentioned above, it was not the academic and curricular changes advocated by the Maskilim that reflected the essence or the ultimate aspirations of the Jewish enlightenment. These were merely the instruments of the final social and economic transformation of Jewish society, which was the Haskalah's true and definitive objective. At the root of that ultimate goal lay a rejection of the very essence of established rabbinic belief and traditional Jewish behavior, the total belief in *hashgahath ha-boreh,* or divine providence, and a form of pious behavior rooted in absolute faith and trust in that providence, or *bittahon.*

Historians of the Jewish enlightenment have observed that the first to become interested in the social and intellectual improvement of the Jews were the members of the wealthy Jewish middle class, primarily businessmen and traders. And a significant motivation underlying their new interest in secular learning and gentile society was socioeconomic advancement. In his study of the socioeconomic aspects of the Haskalah, Mordechai Lewin has observed that, beyond expanding the traditional horizons of learning and promoting social progress and integration, the ideology of Jewish enlightenment also undermined three fundamental articles of classical rabbinic faith: (1) the belief in divine providence; (2) *bittahon,* or passive reliance upon divine sustenance; and (3) asceticism and pious material self-denial.[53] The Maskilim instructed that in order to improve their sad material condition and miserable social standing, the Jews must first abandon their traditionally passive reliance upon divine providence, their animosity to material fulfillment, and their indifference to economic advancement. The Maskilim proposed that the Jews shed their lethargy and take full control of their lives in order independently to support themselves and attain wealth as well as social prominence.[54]

In chapter 5 I documented the pronounced asceticism of R. Phinehas and other prominent Mithnagdic thinkers of this period. R. Phinehas's anti-materialist otherworldliness and his dualistic emphasis upon the future world that awaits man after death grew out of a deep religious pessimism about the very significance of the material life itself. Until now, however, his marked asceticism and his conviction that this life is hopelessly transitory and ultimately of no true meaning or lasting significance have been evaluated mainly in contradistinction to Hasidism's optimistic sense that so much can be accomplished spiritually in the material *olam ha-zeh*. We have observed how R. Phinehas's asceticism stands in sharp contrast to Hasidism's theory of *avodah be-gashmiyouth*, the service of God through the created physical universe.[55]

A related theme, equally central to Phinehas's ethical writings, is his specific social indictment of the materialism of contemporary Jews, his critique of the values of the wealthy classes, and his glorification of a life of poverty. R. Phinehas's condemnation of *gashmiyouth* (materialism), although often a reaction to the Hasidic sanctification of the material universe, is at times purely economic and has nothing to do with the particular spiritual pretensions of the Hasidim. In this context it is rooted not so much in the Mithnagdic pessimism about human spiritual helplessness in this life as it is in the very fundamental nature of traditional Jewish faith, namely, a pervasive confidence in and passive reliance upon divine providence, or *bittahon*. *Kether Torah*, which begins with the strenuous condemnation of secular learning, concludes with an equally strong denunciation of worldly materialism. R. Phinehas lashes out against "those wealthy members of our people who live in big, walled cities, whose arrogant hearts believe that only they are of any significance."[56] Phinehas reminds them that their wealth is illusory, their grandeur merely mundane and ephemeral, and that they will die along with the poor, arriving empty-handed before God in the future world. He angrily apprises the rich of the fact that the only true and lasting attainment of this life is the fulfillment of the will of God.

In his final work, the ethical will *Rosh ha-Giveah*, Phinehas emphasizes with great urgency the importance of passive *bittahon*, or total reliance upon divine providence. He mocks the myopic foolishness of the rich, who exhaust themselves all of their days trying to amass money and material possessions, oblivious to both the controlling hand of providence and their own inevitable demise. This critique of the rich is accompanied by repeated advise to the poor to remain content and complacent with their lot in life and not to waste any time trying to improve their economic or social standing.[57] This is a common theme in nineteenth-century Mithnagdic writings. Take, for example, the following mid-century admonition by R. Akiva of Barisov in his commentary to the Passover Haggadah:

> The Holy One wants Israel to be masters of faith and to wait for the morning when God's grace becomes manifest, that is, to those that wait for it. It turns out

that the person of faith possesses a great *bittahon* in God that is manifest day by day, much like those who ate the manna [in the desert]. . . .

So, too, in our day let all who are hungry come and eat *now*, for it is forbidden to prepare from one day to the next. Rather, one must eat day by day and have faith in Him. One should never worry about wanting tomorrow, for what good does that do. . . ?

For we are presently deep in exile, and we desire to show this our faith, by virtue of which the redemption will arrive.[58]

R. Phinehas's ethical will is literally saturated with expressions of this same sentiment. There is here an entirely different dimension to Mithnagdism's dualistic, abstemious rejection of the importance of the accomplishments of the material life and its obvious contempt for the values of the wealthy classes. As mentioned above, it was the wealthy merchants who were the very first conduits of the Haskalah into eastern Europe. And among the central motivations and chief goals of the Maskilim was the attainment of a better and more prosperous life for the Jews through their successful integration into the general society. R. Phinehas unequivocally rejected any such aspirations as both futile and symptomatic of disbelief.

This fundamental rabbinic religious opposition to the Haskalah's promotion of economic achievement and social advancement in many ways mirrors the general European experience of the confrontation between traditional Christian faith and the new bourgeois economic values of the Enlightenment. As Goldmann has noted,

The Old Christian view of society rested on the division of men into "rich" and "poor," "nobles" and "common people." . . .

The rich and mighty of the world were far more exposed to the temptations of power and pleasure than other people, and had much the harder task to resist them. . . .

As to the poor, they were required chiefly to endure their sufferings with patience as "trials," and to regard purity of heart and simplicity of faith as the sure way to heaven. . . .

In the traditional thought of the past, the search for profit and wealth was bound to be considered selfishly contrary to the general good and to concern for others. It was the un-Christian life par excellence. The beginnings of bourgeois individualist society created a new, categorically opposite mental structure—the coincidence of private interest with public advantage—which later became a basic feature of the Enlightenment.[59]

So, too, in Jewish society, at a time when the Maskilim were energetically promulgating the economic progress of the Jews, the Mithnagdim continued to preach the virtues of passive faith in divine providence and to prescribe the traditional values of the passive life of poverty and the pious lethargy of self-denial.

Conclusion

In his celebrated essay on the subject, Carl Becker summarized the "articles of faith" of the eighteenth-century Enlightenment as follows:

1. Man is not natively depraved.
2. The end of life is life itself, the good life on earth, instead of the beatific life after death.
3. Man is capable, guided solely by reason and experience, of perfecting the good life on earth.[60]

Nothing could be further from the religion of the Mithnagdim. They had precious little faith in the autonomous capabilities of man and were convinced that the perfection of humanity must indeed be deferred to the future life, *olam ha-ba*.[61] This view was also at the root of their disputation with Hasidism. The Hasidim believed that man was capable of attaining an impressive level of spiritual perfection, through mystical *devekuth,* in this earthly life and through the physical world. They were thus optimistic about man's capacities for attaining spiritual greatness in the here and now. The Mithnagdim condemned this optimism, which they viewed as a reflection of groundless religious arrogance, as dangerous. Unlike both the Hasidim and the Maskilim, then, they did indeed believe that man is essentially depraved, constantly beset by the temptations of the evil instinct from which he will be finally and completely freed only after death.

Although Hasidism's and the Haskalah's respective notions of the precise nature of human perfection in this life differed radically, and although their shared optimism did not constitute a basis for any genuine agreement between them, in the eyes of the Mithnagdim their deviances from tradition were at least phenomenologically the same. As far as the traditional rabbis were concerned, both were rooted in a shared delusion about human nature and a false optimism regarding the capacity of man to attain some form of genuine felicity, be it mystical or materialistic, while on this earth. The ideologies of both Hasidism and the Haskalah produced a self-indulgent activism that must have appeared deeply unorthodox to the conservative, religiously passive Mithnagdim. In their eyes, the sin common to both the Hasidim and the Maskilim was their celebration of *olam ha-zeh,* this terrestrial life; and their shared delinquency was the disrespect for the disciplinary restrictions and the spirit of resignation that are the hallmark of the truly pious man, and the inevitable consequence of his awareness of the fundamentally corrupt and hopelessly circumscribed human condition.

Seen from this perspective, that the polemics against Haskalah and Hasidism are juxtaposed in *Kether Torah* and form part of a continuous narrative is entirely understandable. For both these threats to the traditional status quo were perceived by the rabbis as manifestations of essentially the same *yezer ha-ra*, or evil inclination: the desire to attain too much in this life.

Although in this chapter I have focused almost exclusively on the writings of R. Phinehas, the Mithnagdic, anti-Haskalah arguments of *Kether Torah*, as well as those of his later writings, were far from unique. Although he was an early, maverick anti-Maskil Mithnagged in his day, in subsequent generations many traditional Mithnagdim were among the most vociferous opponents of the Haskalah in eastern Europe. In the course of the nineteenth century such prominent Mithnagdim as Rabbis Elijah Rogoler, Samuel of Kelm, Moses Isaac Darshan of Kelm, and the GRA's own grandnephew, Meir ben Elijah, bitterly opposed the Haskalah as the very antithesis of traditional rabbinic Judaism.[62] Samuel of Kelm saw the academic pursuits of Mendelssohn and the other early Maskilim as constituting a direct threat to the tradition of Mithnagdic Torah study and traditional intellectualism.[63] And Meir ben Elijah composed an important anti-Hasidic polemical tract, *Milhamoth Adonai*, in which the condemnations of Maskilim and Hasidim are seamlessly interwoven in much the same way as they are in *Kether Torah*.[64] In the subsequent history of Mithnagdism and the Yeshiva movement the resistance to secular studies, modernization, and social integration remains a major theme in non-Hasidic rabbinic thought. The full story of the confrontation between the Mithnagdic rabbis and the Haskalah is a chapter of modern Jewish intellectual history that has yet to be written.

The general picture that emerges from this deliberation on the anti-Haskalah polemic of an important and prototypical Mithnagged is very different from the standard one found in the intellectual historiography of our period. Scholars have argued that the intellectual sophistication and academic openness of the GRA and his disciples constitutes a bridge connecting Mithnagdism with the development of the Jewish enlightenment in eastern Europe and that the scholarship of the Mithnagdim created a fertile ground for the growth of the Haskalah. But such broad scholarly horizons were neither new nor unique to the traditional rabbis of the enlightenment era.

Moreover, scholars who argue for any such continuity between the intellectualistic religion of the Mithnagdim and the Haskalah's program for the modernization of Jewish culture and society choose to ignore the explicit opposition that the leading Mithnagdic theorists mounted against the Haskalah's promotion of reason, secular studies, and the acculturation of the Jews in European society over the course of many generations. More seriously, they disregard the axiomatic contradiction between the very essence of traditional rabbinic faith, which is rooted in the concept of *bittahon,* and the true and final goals of the Haskalah, which were predicated upon a total rejection of that very religious conviction, namely, the autonomous achievement of worldly success by the Jews and, ultimately, their absorption into the neutral, or secular, European society and economy.

When the Haskalah first emerged in Russia, the traditional rabbinic elite, the Mithnagdim, felt themselves besieged by, and accordingly waged simultaneous war against, two new perceived threats to traditional learning, traditional spiritual values, and the religious and social foundations of the traditional society, namely, the Hasidic movement and the Jewish enlightenment. Moreover, the rabbinic battles against both the Hasidim and the Maskilim often were not only historically concurrent but also in many respects ideologically congruent.

Chapter 7

THE CENTRALITY
OF TORAH STUDY IN
MITHNAGDISM

Talmud Torah: The Cornerstone of Mithnagdism

In the introduction to his monumental collection *Hasidim u-Mithnagdim* Mordechai Wilensky argued that the truly substantive catalysts for the initial rabbinic declaration of war against Hasidism were its demotion of Torah study within the hierarchy of Jewish religious values and the attending disrespect the early Hasidim displayed toward rabbinic scholars. All of the other alleged heresies and religious violations of the Hasidim cited in the Mithnagdic polemical literature were, according to Wilensky, merely tangential to this central sin against the supreme value accorded by rabbinic culture to *Talmud Torah* and the respect due its practitioners.[1] While not all scholars fully agree with Wilensky's evaluation of the root causes of the Mithnagdic antagonism toward the Hasidim,[2] the general thrust of the few critical studies of the rabbinic thinkers seems to corroborate the notion that the status of both the study and the scholars of Torah took center stage in the dramatic ideological battles between the Hasidim and the Mithnagdim.

In his monograph on the Gaon of Vilna, Hayyim Hillel ben Sasson emphasized the consummate importance of study in the religious life of the GRA and suggested that what most antagonized him and directly provoked him into open battle against Hasidism was the Hasidic inversion of the hierarchy of Jewish values to the detriment of precisely that supreme status.[3] Immanuel Etkes, Jonah ben Sasson, and Norman Lamm all make much the same claim regarding the primarily anti-Hasidic motif underlying Rabbi Hayyim of Volozhin's panegyric to Torah study found in *Nefesh ha-Hayyim*.[4] Etkes has in fact claimed that Hasidism's most significant challenge to traditional rabbinic Judaism was precisely its devaluation of Torah study as the central religious activity and highest spiritual value in Judaism. He accordingly views R. Hayyim of Volozhin's entire life's work, not only literary (the composition of *Nefesh ha-Hayyim*) but also social and educational (the founding of the

yeshiva at Volozhin), as essentially an elaborate response to the Hasidic depre-
ciation of *Talmud Torah*.[5] Some minor differences in their respective evaluations of the exact nature and intensity of R. Hayyim of Volozhin's opposition
to Hasidism notwithstanding, Lamm and Etkes agree that R. Hayyim's elevation of *Talmud Torah* to the very pinnacle of religious life and the clear
priority he assigned to study over all other forms of spiritual expression were
unique and unprecedented.[6] Moreover, his glorification of study is seen by
both Lamm and Etkes as the very nucleus of R. Hayyim of Volozhin's theology
and, by extension, as the veritable quintessence of Mithnagdic spirituality.

It is thus no accident that all of the studies of Mithnagdic thinkers to date
have focused almost exclusively on the centrality of the doctrine of *Talmud
Torah* in rabbinic thought. And it is R. Hayyim of Volozhin who is most
commonly viewed as the original author of the most brilliant and militant
expression of the supremacy of scholarship in Jewish religious life.

Jonah Ben Sasson, Etkes, and especially Lamm repeatedly claim that R.
Hayyim of Volozhin's evaluation of the status and function of Torah, particularly its study, was highly original and unparalleled in magnitude. Lamm
argues that in both Kabbalistic theory and daily application the degree of R.
Hayyim's elevation of Torah and its study was unprecedented in Jewish intellectual history.[7] According to Lamm, in Kabbalistic theory R. Hayyim was
unique in placing Torah above the universe of the sefirotic emanations, in the
realm of the *Eyn Sof*. Whereas in earlier Kabbalistic sefirotic configurations
Torah was usually identified with the first three *sefiroth*, for R. Hayyim its
place was above these emanations of the *Eyn Sof*.[8] Lamm suggests that as a
consequence of this cosmic-mystical exaltation of Torah, R. Hayyim was the
true originator of the notion, later to be accepted by all of the leading Mithnagdim, that the proper study of Torah, which itself constitutes human communion with the will of God, represents the attainment of the most lofty of
religious aspirations and ultimately results in mystical union with the highest
sector of divinity; in other words, engaging in pure *Talmud Torah* with no
ulterior motives, that is, in *Torah lishmah*, constitutes the automatic achievement of *devekuth*. In practical terms, for R. Hayyim this mystical elevation of
the Torah meant that no other religious activity could be as important as
Talmud Torah. "Thus," Lamm concludes, "there is no one who even approaches Rabbi Hayyim in terms of the priority he assigns to the study of
Torah over all other values."[9]

R. Hayyim's theory of Torah study is, however, far less original than Lamm
and others would have us believe. Their insistence on the novelty of *Nefesh
ha-Hayyim* can result in a distorted view of the intellectual history of Mithnagdism. Although he stated the case for *Talmud Torah* in unusually bold and

creative terms, R. Hayyim of Volozhin in fact innovated very little, and his championship of scholarship was simply an unusually detailed and refined articulation of ideas that had been widespread in Mithnagdic circles for several decades, as the writings of R. Phinehas of Polotsk illustrate.

The Supreme Value of Torah Study according to R. Phinehas of Polotsk

There is no question that the fourth section of *Nefesh ha-Hayyim* is a most remarkable panegyric to the supreme religious status of Torah study. Nevertheless, it was not the first such work published by the rabbinic opponents of Hasidism. Moreover, while it introduced some novel Kabbalistic delineations of the cosmic status of Torah and the powers of its study, as a rejoinder to the Hasidic demotion of intellectual study it advanced virtually nothing that was entirely original in the practical rabbinic championship of the supremacy of *Talmud Torah* over other religious acts. In fact, every one of R. Hayyim of Volozhin's practical claims for the superiority of study over other spiritual pursuits can be found in a work published thirty-six years earlier, R. Phinehas of Polotsk's *Kether Torah*.[10] Not only does Phinehas, like R. Hayyim after him, raise Torah far above all other forms of spirituality but the historical and ideological context that gave rise to *Kether Torah* was virtually identical to that which underlay R. Hayyim's panegyric to *Talmud Torah*, namely, the antischolastic challenge of Hasidic spirituality.[11]

Kether Torah is devoted almost entirely to promoting the glory and supremacy of the study of Torah and defending the honor of its scholars. In the first part of the work, stylistically modeled after "Shaar Yihud ha-Ma'aseh" of Bahya ibn Pakuda's *Hovoth ha-Levavoth,* Phinehas paraphrases, only then to demolish, a long series of challenges to the supremacy of Torah study that are advanced by the metaphoric evil inclination within man. It is clear that, aside from the very first of these challenges (the pursuit of secular sciences advanced by the Haskalah), all of these competing "temptations" were being promoted, in one form or another, by the Hasidic movement during R. Phinehas's day. R. Phinehas describes the following deviations from exclusive devotion to rabbinic study proposed by the evil inclination within man, or the *yezer ha-ra:*

1. Pursuit of the practical observance of other, more tangible *mitzvoth* (i.e., *mitzvoth ma'asiyoth*).[12]
2. Devotion to pious penitential behavior as a necessary preparation for study.[13]
3. Emphasis upon prayer as a form of divine service superior to study.[14]

4. The prior quest for piety, or the fear of God *(yirah)*.[15]
5. The ultimate quest for mystical union with God *(devekuth)*.[16]
6. Concentration upon Kabbalistic, rather than rabbinic, study.[17]
7. Insistence upon not studying Torah unless it be with the purest, unselfish, spiritual motives (i.e., *Torah lishmah,* as defined by the Hasidim).[18]

In repetitive style, R. Phinehas argues, in turn, that Torah study is far superior as a form of divine service to these other, competing religious pursuits being advanced by the *yezer ha-ra* of Hasidism and consequently must take precedence over them. He illustrates in some detail how each of these otherwise legitimate religious quests must relinquish pride of place within the total Jewish value system to rabbinic scholarship. More significantly, R. Phinehas claims that proper and diligent Torah study has the effect of rendering all of these other spiritual exercises superfluous. For through assiduous study man can achieve the final end of all his religious aspirations.

Homage to Torah Study in *Kether Torah* and *Nefesh ha-Hayyim*

The many remarkable parallels to the arguments for a scholarship-based spirituality later promulgated in *Nefesh ha-Hayyim* are to be found in virtually every paragraph of the opening section of *Kether Torah*. Since the Mithnagdic doctrine of Torah study has already been the subject of such extensive scholarly treatment, particularly by Lamm, we shall consider only some of the most conspicuous correlations between the arguments of these two works in order to illustrate the degree to which R. Phinehas of Polotsk anticipated practically all of R. Hayyim of Volozhin's major teachings.

The fourth section of *Nefesh ha-Hayyim* begins with a socioreligious critique of those who "seek the proximity of God" (R. Hayyim's appellation for the Hasidim) at the expense of the pursuit of Torah scholarship. R. Hayyim complains that these pietists seem to believe that the quest for a God-fearing heart must precede the study of Torah, lest the latter be essentially flawed. As a consequence of this reversal of religious priorities, they have replaced the study of rabbinic texts with that of pietistic works. Part of their motivation, R. Hayyim continues, lies in the misguided belief that the only worthy type of Torah study is that which is unblemished by any nonspiritual motivation, or *Torah lishmah.* Furthermore, the Hasidim mistakenly define *Torah lishmah* exclusively as study whose only final end is mystical union, or *devekuth.* They thereby not only rob the Torah of its pride of place within Judaism but also pervert the very nature of its study by turning it from an essentially academic pursuit into a mystically directed exercise. According to R. Hayyim, the Hasidim are thus guilty of a double transgression: first, they preach the notion that Torah study that is blemished by ulterior or selfish motives is an unworthy pursuit; and second, they teach that pure *Torah lishmah* remains but a means to the higher end of *devekuth*.[19]

R. Hayyim's elaborate critique of Hasidism's misplaced emphasis on piety at the expense of scholarship, as well as its mistaken evaluation of the nature and goals of *Torah lishmah*, has been the subject of extensive scholarly analysis.[20] For our present purposes his critique can be summed up as follows: A minimal level of *yirah* (fear of God) is indeed a necessary condition for the proper pursuit of Torah study. But it is only a prerequisite for study, not its final end. The ultimate goal of study is the very act of study itself, along with the acquisition of knowledge of the divine will that is the fruit of such study. Thus, one might prepare oneself spiritually for engaging in *Talmud Torah* during a very limited time devoted to the perusal of pietistic works, but intense rabbinic study must remain the priority, the major activity, and the final objective. Moreover, all study, regardless of its purity and motives, is inherently the most exalted form of religious behavior. The Hasidic contempt for unspiritual study *(Torah shelo lishmah)* is seriously misguided, for the very act of study ipso facto constitutes the connection of man with the highest spheres of divinity and thereby automatically purifies him of sin.

R. Phinehas of Polotsk fully shared R. Hayyim's consternation at the misplaced priority Hasidism assigned to acts of piety over study. Referring to the earlier rabbinic distinction between the two levels of religious fear—the lower fear of divine retribution for sin *(yirath ha-onesh)* and the higher, more spiritual fear of God's grandeur *(yirath ha-romemuth)*—R. Phinehas suggested that only a minimal level of the former, lower form of fear was required for the proper pursuit of Torah study. In a spirit similar to that of R. Hayyim's concession that some limited study of pietistic works might be engaged in before turning one's attention to the major task of rabbinic study, R. Phinehas conceded that a certain, very circumscribed degree of pious preparation, in the form of cultivating fear of God's punitive powers, might precede study. But he strictly maintained that Torah study must remain both the Jews' priority and their predominant religious activity. As for the higher goal of fear of heaven, R. Phinehas insisted that this religious attainment would be the inevitable consequence of the examination of God's will through proper, intellectual *Talmud Torah*. He therefore resolutely upheld the preeminence of Torah study over a preoccupation with pious repentance or any other spiritual exercises directed at attaining the fear of God. For, as he concluded, "There is absolutely no way in the world that anyone can attain this most important fear of heaven except through the study of the Torah."[21]

What proved most troubling to R. Hayyim of Volozhin was not the priority

assigned to various pietistic exercises but rather the Hasidic misrepresenta-
tion of the final goal of study itself. It was in his response to Hasidism's
doctrinal affirmation that the ultimate purpose of study is the attainment of
devekuth that R. Hayyim advanced his boldest and most notable claims for
the religious stature of scholarship. He instructed that true *Torah lishmah* is
the investigation of the Torah for no other reason than to comprehend it.
Moreover, R. Hayyim did not see this as the means to the more elevated
mystical goal of *devekuth;* rather, he believed that the very act of study itself
constituted the ultimate spiritual attainment. In his fundamental championship of study R. Hayyim plainly asserted that singular devotion to *Talmud
Torah* was, in fact, *devekuth.*

Daring and far-reaching as this claim for scholarship is, R. Hayyim was not
the first man to advance it. R. Phinehas of Polotsk was equally alarmed by the
Hasidic claim that the highest aspiration of the religious life is not rabbinic
study but rather the attainment of mystical union. He paraphrased the rather
famous Hasidic derision of Torah scholarship and its attendant elevation of
the mystical experience as follows:

> The evil instinct will attempt to seduce you by saying to you: "What is the point
> or the advantage of studying Torah, when you consider that it is only a means
> toward the goal of *devekuth* with God, in order to know His ways and His
> attributes? Therefore, why should you bother taxing your intellect by day and by
> night with the casuistry of the Gemara and the Codes? For you will end up
> swimming in the sea of the Talmud, in mighty waters that have no end, such that
> even if you lived a thousand years, you would never succeed in emerging from
> them. If you do so, what will be of your *devekuth* and your pursuit of God, and
> when will you find the necessary time to improve your moral traits? . . . rather, it
> is best that you minimize the time you devote to study and turn instead to
> examining the ways of God—His providence, omnipotence, wisdom, and attri-
> butes—and *cling* to them. . . . For this is the whole purpose of the Torah."[22]

R. Phinehas's double-barreled response to the Hasidic assault on rabbinic
scholarship is striking. Not only does he assert that *devekuth* is impossible
without prior Torah study but he insists that, thanks to the celestial origins of
the Torah itself, the very act of study constitutes man's attachment to the
highest heavenly spheres, or mystical union with God:

> It is certainly true that the perfection of one's ethics and the attainment of
> *devekuth* are rudimentary religious ambitions. Nonetheless, do not imagine that
> you can arrive at *devekuth* or ethical perfection except via Torah study. For it
> [i.e., study] is not merely a means toward attaining *devekuth*, as the evil instinct

suggested to you in its deceitful words; rather, *it in itself constitutes the true devekuth* (Heb., *hi hi ha-devekuth*), from which it is unworthy to separate oneself. For the entire Torah consists of the names of God, knotted and woven upon His attributes. And there is no matter, not even the lightest, among the teachings of the Sages of the Gemara that does not touch the highest conduits of divinity and does not reach the divine throne of glory, and the expanse of the Divine circumference. In the Torah are included all of the celestial luminaries to an unlimited and unending degree (Heb., *le-Eyn Sof*). . . . So that when a man clings to Your [i.e., God's] holy and glorious name, which is the Holy Torah, he will be reminded of the true quest of our souls. But without this [clinging to the Torah] he will neither remember nor recall, nor will his petty and stupid heart even think of attaining *devekuth*. But [through the Torah] he will indeed cling to God. . . . Now, if any man tells you that he has achieved *devekuth* without this [i.e., Torah study], that is most certainly a lie, for such a person is separated from truth, namely, the holy Torah, which is called truth.[23]

The pursuit of *Torah lishmah* not only offers man the opportunity for the highest mystical experience; it is the exclusive path toward such lofty spiritual achievement. And like R. Hayyim after him, R. Phinehas based his assertion that Torah study, even the study of the "lightest" texts of the rabbinic litera-ture, in itself could constitute an act of mystical union with God upon the Kabbalistic teachings regarding the supernal derivation of the word and will of God recorded in the Torah.

Another Mithnagdic thinker who anticipated many of the ideas that were later formulated by R. Hayyim, was the brother of the GRA, R. Abraham. Among many other parallels with *Nefesh ha-Hayyim*, the principal belief that Torah study in itself provides man with true *devekuth* is also to be found in R. Abraham's panegyric to Torah scholarship, *Maaloth ha-Torah:* "The general principle emanating from all of the above is that a person must always study Torah, in his peaceful moments as well as during trying times, for as a result of this he will arrive at his true tranquility. For it is as a result of Torah study that a man clings (Heb., *nidbak*) to God, and once he attains *devekuth* with God, he automatically achieves all of the above."[24]

Consistent with the long history of pietistic movements within Judaism, a central aspect of Hasidism's spiritualization of the religious life was its rejec-tion of the perfunctory observance of many of the rituals and command-ments without proper inner intent. This applied especially to the motivation for, and design underlying, the fulfillment of the *mitzvah* of Torah study. As a consequence of their emphasis upon the inner spiritual motivation underly-ing the performance of all the *mitzvoth*, including study, the early Hasidic masters not only derided the dry, purely academic rabbinic study of Torah but developed new techniques for *Talmud Torah* that transformed it from an essentially intellectual act into both a highly charged mystical exercise and a magical technique.[25] In the intermediate eight chapters between the third and fourth sections of *Nefesh ha-Hayyim* R. Hayyim engaged in a lengthy, polemical defense of the critical importance of the "technical," legal observance of all of the commandments, with or without proper intent. Clearly reacting to the general Hasidic emphasis upon *kavana,* R. Hayyim later applied the same principles to Torah study lacking the ideal motivation of *lishmah.*[26] He defended, at some length, the legitimacy and religious importance of study, even study lacking in ideal direction and inner intent.

As we had occasion to note earlier in connection with his approach to mystical prayer, R. Phinehas of Polotsk also downplayed the extent to which individual *kavana* was necessary in the proper fulfillment of the *mitzvoth.* In his commentary to the Psalms, Phinehas claimed that one of the truly meritorious attributes of the laws of the Torah is that their mere technical, legal performance, even when lacking perfect *kavana,* has the power automatically to realize their intended *tikkun* in the heavenly spheres: "How great is the performance of the commandments, for they do not require *kavana;* and as soon as a man fulfills any *mitzvah* below, he activates its supernal source above."[27]

In a similar spirit, R. Phinehas criticized the very same Hasidic delegitimation of imperfectly intended study, or *Torah shelo lishmah:*

> Now, the evil instinct will attempt a different way of trying to seduce you, by telling you: "Did our Sages not teach that he who studies Torah without proper intent [*Torah shelo lishmah*] would have been better off not being born? Now, the only condition under which you could possibly study *lishmah* is alone and in the privacy of your home, in a hidden place where you will see no one else. On the other hand, if you learn in the *Beth ha-Midrash,* especially with a group of people, your Torah study will be full of sinful, impure, and selfish motives. For your only motivation will be to show off your wisdom and the extent of your knowledge.[28]

R. Phinehas used the occasion of refuting this Hasidic argument to embark upon a very lengthy digression, a nostalgic panegyric to the glory of the *Beth ha-Midrash* in years gone by. In a style and spirit reminiscent of Nathan Hanover's classic elegy to the traditional world of learning destroyed by the massive Ukranian pogroms of 1648–49, *Yeven Mezula,* R. Phinehas contrasts the eminence of the house of study in the past with its desolation and abandonment by the Jews of his day. He blames the emptiness of the *Beth ha-Midrash* upon the Hasidim, who have convinced the Jews that organized public study of Torah is an unworthy endeavor.[29] This is, of course, a very familiar motif in rabbinic letters, especially those of the eighteenth-century Mithnagdim.[30]

Like R. Phinehas, R. Hayyim of Volozhin reflected mournfully upon the contemporary Jewish abandonment of the house of study and the decline of public Torah learning. This was, in fact, a central motivation for the establishment of the yeshiva at Volozhin, as his famous epistle calling for support of that yeshiva testifies.[31] The Mithnagdim's sense that they were members of a declined and spiritually alienated generation was in fact central to their entire religious consciousness and underlay their insistence upon the crucial role the study of Torah must play in the religious life of contemporary Jews, regardless of the integrity of their motivation to study. R. Abraham ben Solomon also declared emphatically that it was precisely because of the religious deterioration of his generation that study, to the exclusion of all other spiritual exercises, was the only effective road to repentance and, ultimately, to *devekuth*.[32]

This strong rabbinic sense of historical decline notwithstanding, the most significant part of R. Phinehas's argument against the Hasidic spiritualization of study and the resulting rejection of the worthiness of *Torah shelo lishmah* is his defense of the inherent religious validity of all study, regardless of its underlying motivation:

> In truth, I will not deny the holy statements affirming that a person must study *Torah lishmah*. Still, there is no way to attain the level of *lishmah* except via study that is *shelo lishmah*. For if they were to say to a young and tender boy at the very start of his studies, "Learn for God's sake," he would certainly escape from you like a child running away from school. Rather, at the beginning one must say to him, "Study, and I will give you so many walnuts and so many pomegranates . . ." Only later will the Lord enlighten his eyes and will the inner light of Torah restore him to virtue in order that he study *lishmah*. Thus did our Sages instruct: "Let a person study Torah even if it is *shelo lishmah*, for out of study *shelo lishmah* there will result study *lishmah*." For how is it possible that study *shelo lishmah* be forbidden? Did the Holy One Blessed Be He not proclaim: "Would that they forsake me and observe my Torah." This does not mean that they should forsake Me [i.e., God] in order to cling to other deities, God forbid. Rather its meaning is: let them study, not for My [i.e., God's] sake, but for their own and their children's benefit for all generations, and the inner light (of Torah) will of itself restore them to virtue.[33]

Like R. Hayyim, then, R. Phinehas upheld the value of all religious performance, even when it lacked proper intention. This applied equally to the more "spiritual" obligations of the Torah, such as prayer and study.[34]

The Definition of *Torah Lishma*

It has been suggested that R. Hayyim of Volozhin's most important novel contribution to Jewish thought was his strictly intellectualistic redefinition of the ideal form of study, or *Torah lishmah,* as signifying study purely for the sake of cognitive, or academic, comprehension. In his book on R. Hayyim, Norman Lamm devotes an entire chapter to the analysis of what he calls "R. Hayyim's innovation regarding the expression, *lishmah.*"[35] R. Hayyim's almost purely intellectual definition of the concept of *lishmah* is best appreciated in sharp contradistinction to Hasidism's profound spiritualization of the same notion.

R. Phinehas of Polotsk also considered, in great detail, the explication of the term *Torah lishmah.* On several occasions he contends that the purest possible motivation for Torah scholarship is a pragmatic, legal one, namely, study directed primarily, if not exclusively, at enabling man to know how properly to fulfill the commandments of the Torah. This utilitarian definition of *lishmah* is not, however, fully consistent with R. Phinehas's insistence, alluded to above, that Torah study is superior to the observance of all of the other individual commandments, including prayer. In the end, he offers three alternate definitions of *Torah lishmah,* in the order of their importance. First and foremost, he claims that *lishmah* signifies study whose sole motivation is the fulfillment of the will of God, just as in the properly intended observance of all the other commandments: "The first intention of study should be to declare that one is studying in order to fulfill the decree of the King, who has commanded: 'And you shall study them diligently day and night,' and 'this book of the Torah must never vanish from your mouth,' and 'You shall speak of them when you sit in your house,' and so on."[36]

The second, lesser definition of *lishmah* is study whose goal is the attainment of the fear of heaven. And the third, lowest form of *Torah lishmah* is study whose purpose is the acquisition of a share in the future life. But while R. Phinehas considers all three of these motivations for study worthy of the title *Torah lishmah,* it would seem that he regards none of them as representing the very highest goal of study. In a technical interpretation of the grammar of the term *lishmah,* after considering the various alternate definitions of this idiom, R. Phinehas suggests what seems to be his strongest definition of the term *Torah lishmah:*

> And now I will write for you a lovely and plausible explanation of the terminology *lishmah* [feminine], as opposed to what would be the more grammatically correct usage, *lishmo* [masculine], which implies for the sake of God's name.
> But the truth is that the real name of the Torah is truth [*emeth,* which in

Hebrew is feminine], as it is written: "Acquire truth and do not sell it." The term *Torah* may refer to the pragmatic instruction contained therein, but its authentic name is *emeth*.

This is what is then meant by the expression "one who studies *Torah lishmah*," that is, one who desires only its truth, for the truth is singular and it is the signature of the Holy One Blessed Be He. This [i.e., the attainment of the truth contained in the Torah], then, is the very purpose and foundation of everything.[37]

It is true that, unlike R. Hayyim of Volozhin, R. Phinehas did not elaborate clearly or systematically on a singular definition of *Torah lishmah*. This final interpretation of the term is only an isolated statement in his writings and is by no means as unambiguously intellectualistic as that of R. Hayyim or as central to his theology. Nonetheless, it does suggest that in the final analysis R. Phinehas viewed the true and highest goal of the study of the Torah to be the comprehension of the truths contained therein. As he ultimately affirmed, "The very root of the Torah is to cling to its true wisdom, to think about its truths and thereby to cling to God."[38]

These two works, *Kether Torah* and *Nefesh ha-Hayyim*, are, then, clearly in almost complete accord regarding the function, status, and nature of Torah study. In contradistinction to, and to a significant degree in reaction to, Hasidism's transformation of Torah study and subversion of its place in the hierarchy of Judaic values, both works strongly assert the priority of study over all other spiritual exercises. Moreover, both R. Phinehas and R. Hayyim insisted that the decisive goal of scholarship is the very acquisition of knowledge of the Torah or even simply the act of study itself. This contention, common to *Kether Torah* and *Nefesh ha-Hayyim*, is made plausible by the authors' shared conviction that it is through study alone that man can automatically attain *devekuth*, the highest form of union with the Divine. In the final analysis, however, as suggested at the beginning of this chapter, the most important affinity between *Nefesh ha-Hayyim* and *Kether Torah* is the restoration of study to the pinnacle of religious values in Judaism, which results from both the theoretical as well as the pragmatic, behavioral elevation of Torah above all other competing religious enterprises. The authors of both these works proclaimed very clearly and unambiguously not only that rabbinic study deserves priority over all other spiritual quests but also that its proper pursuit effectively renders them all unnecessary.[39] For both R. Hayyim of Volozhin and R. Phinehas of Polotsk the religious value of study far exceeds that of the performance of any of the other commandments, as well as that of prayer or any alternate spiritual exercises directed at achieving penitence or a mystical experience.

All of the central themes contained in R. Hayyim of Volozhin's famous panegyric to *Talmud Torah* had been articulated by R. Phinehas of Polotsk long before their publication in the fourth section of *Nefesh ha-Hayyim*. And they also resonate in the writings of other leading Mithnagdim, most notably Abraham ben Solomon. To be sure, certain important aspects of R. Hayyim's doctrine of the Torah are not fully articulated in *Kether Torah*. Most significant among them is *Nefesh ha-Hayyim*'s elaborate Kabbalistic exaltation of the supernal origins of the Torah and the accompanying emphasis upon the unparalleled cosmic powers R. Hayyim attributed to its study.[40] Yet, while perhaps not as bold or extensive as *Nefesh ha-Hayyim* in its panegyric to the world-sustaining potency of *Talmud Torah*, *Kether Torah*'s earlier response to the Hasidic assault upon the hallowed status of scholarship within Judaism is in actual fact more comprehensive. For R. Phinehas's polemic contains a critically important theme that is largely missing in the writings of R. Hayyim. The lavish praise of the Torah found in *Nefesh ha-Hayyim* was a response to only one component of the Hasidic challenge to the supremacy of scholarship. The other significant aspect of the Hasidic critique, namely, the question of the role and status in Jewish society of its rabbis and scholars, was responded to much more extensively by R. Phinehas, as we shall see below.

The Place of *Talmud Torah* in Mithnagdic Theology

The unparalleled enthusiasm of both R. Phinehas and R. Hayyim for the limitless scope of the religious powers of *Talmud Torah* might at first seem like a refreshing departure from the negative, pessimistic theology of Mithnagdism that I have outlined. In the lavish tributes to *Talmud Torah* found in *Nefesh ha-Hayyim*, *Kether Torah*, and other correlative Mithnagdic works, such as R. Abraham's *Maaloth ha-Torah*, there is, after all, a positively exhilarating enthusiasm about the almost boundless religious greatness available to man via the pursuit of rabbinic scholarship. The extensive citation of passages from the *Zohar* and other mystical works referring to the cosmic and supernatural powers of *Talmud Torah* adds to the positive sense of spiritual optimism and excitement that pervades all of these panegyrics to Torah study. Furthermore, this enthusiasm about the greatness of scholarship did result directly in the development of one of the most exciting social and educational phenomena in rabbinic culture, the great network of Lithuanian yeshivot spawned by Volozhin.

However, regardless of its rhapsodic appearance and obviously sincere excitement, in the final analysis the Mithnagdic glorification of study to the exclusion of all other religious pursuits was primarily restrictive in nature.

The Mithnagdic rabbis' rather narrow confinement of religious achievement to the domain of the academy must be seen as yet another manifestation of their religious pessimism and deep sense of human spiritual limitations. The all-inclusive powers attributed to study were, after all, directed mainly at discouraging the Jews from attempting to engage in any alternate, less mediated spiritual endeavors. While it is true that the Mithnagdim claimed that Torah study in itself constituted *devekuth,* thereby ostensibly granting the possibility of this sublime spiritual attainment to their followers, this was clearly intended primarily to deter Jews from the pursuit of more direct mystical undertakings. By emphasizing that the Torah, being the sole accessible expression of the divine will, was the exclusive route toward realizing the proximity of God, the Mithnagdim were in fact deliberately distancing man from any genuine mystical experiences by means of an intermediary—the text of the Torah—between man and his creator. The insistence that study alone would provide for all of man's religious needs in the most effective and inspiring manner was really a practical way of effectively frustrating any more immediate encounter with God in this earthly life.

While the Hasidim were instructing their followers to strive for direct, unmediated encounters with God in this world through a variety of mystical techniques and spiritual exercises, the Mithnagdim pointed to the Torah as the sole pathway to such lofty objectives. This difference in approaches to the path of spiritual fulfillment is one that has traditionally divided mystics from more rational and conservative religious thinkers. Evelyn Underhill, in her classic study of Christian mysticisms, vividly captures the essence of this general distinction between mystics and more conservative, traditional theologians:

> Mere knowledge, taken alone, is a matter of receiving, not of acting; of eyes, not wings: a dead alive business at the best. There is thus a sharp distinction to be drawn between these two great expressions of life: the energetic love, the passive knowledge. One is related to the eager ongoing activity, the dynamic impulse to *do* somewhat, physical, mental or spiritual which is inherent in all living things and which psychologists call *conation;* the other to the indwelling consciousness, the passive knowing somewhat, which they call *cognition.*[41]

The preoccupation of contemporary scholars of nineteenth-century rabbinic literature with the centrality of the doctrine of *Talmud Torah* in Mithnagdic thought is understandable. Torah study undoubtedly stood at the center of the religious universe of the Mithnagdim. Moreover, they attributed to it an astonishing wealth of spiritual powers, from penitence to mystical union with God right through to the maintenance of the peace of the world and the very salvation of the entire cosmos. Nonetheless, all of their enthusiasm about *Talmud Torah* ultimately amounts to an antidote to, or perhaps a mere distraction from, Hasidism's religious optimism. The truly authentic foundations of Mithnagdic theology are not to be discerned in any detailed explication of their confidence about the far-reaching religious potentialities of scholarship. For the net effect of all the enthusiasm they generated for Torah study was essentially to dissuade the Jews from striving too brazenly in other, more sublime or directly mystical religious arenas. Therefore, the glorification of scholarship in Mithnagdic thought must ultimately be understood in the broader context of the Mithnagdim's pessimistic rejection of virtually all other spiritual avenues.

To be sure, the elevation of *Talmud Torah* and the attribution of extensive spiritual powers to its practitioners resulted in a distinctive effeteness and an intellectual snobbery in the Mithnagdic culture of the late nineteenth and twentieth centuries. A palpable sense of superiority permeates the Mithnagdic scholarly elite to this day and has been particularly pronounced in the Mithnagdic yeshivot, beginning with the yeshiva of Volozhin. Both the rabbis and the students of the great Mithnagdic yeshivot shared a strong sense of being trailblazers of a new and superior Talmudic scholarship, which they traced to the GRA and R. Hayyim of Volozhin. Their pride often manifested itself as the very kind of religious hubris and pious pomposity that the earlier Mithnagdim found so offensive in Hasidic culture. However, the yeshiva students constituted an elite representing a very small fraction of the Mithnagdic world. Their sense of scholarly pride and spiritual superiority therefore only served to strengthen the earlier Mithnagdic exclusion of the Jewish masses from any truly exalted religious experience.[42]

Even R. Hayyim of Volozhin, clearly the most emphatic and enthusiastic of the Mithnagdic panegyrists regarding the transcendent powers of *Talmud Torah* and the spiritual capacities of man, finally affirmed that the decisive perfection of even the most accomplished of scholars of the Torah must await his postmortem existence in the world to come: "Even though the level of those who—while still in this dark world—toil in the Torah is so exalted that they, in their holy spirit, reach and behold the supernal light, nevertheless, the righteous are infinitely greater after their death than during their life."[43]

The Polemic concerning Rabbinic Leadership

As mentioned at the outset of this chapter, Hasidism's questioning of the absolute supremacy the rabbis accorded to *Talmud Torah* in the hierarchy of Jewish values was of a dual nature. Not only did the Hasidic theoreticians demote study within the system of religious priorities but, on a more personal level, they reproached the scholars of Torah and ventured to undermine their status as leaders of the Jewish community. While R. Hayyim of Volozhin devoted most of his energies to a strong theoretical championship of *Talmud Torah,* he addressed himself only briefly and almost parenthetically to this more subversive and personal Hasidic offensive against the rabbinic authorities, the *talmidei hakhamim.*[44] R. Phinehas's *Kether Torah,* on the other hand, included an elaborate and important response to this challenge.

The Hasidic Doctrine of the Zaddik and Critique of the Rabbis

One of the earliest doctrines of Hasidic theology was that of the "fall of the zaddik." The idea that the religious leadership of every generation must, for the purpose of cosmic restoration as well as personal perfection, consciously and cautiously descend into the realm of sinfulness and impurity has been traced by scholars of Hasidism to certain pre-Beshtian mystical circles.[45] Some scholars view the doctrine of *yeridath ha-zaddik* in Hasidism as a tame reincarnation of the central doctrine of the Sabbatean heresy, the idea that holiness can be attained only through descent into sinfulness, a concept that in turn originated in earlier Lurianic Kabbalah.[46] While it is primarily a mystical teaching, probably rooted in Lurianic principles, the idea that the zaddik must lower himself spiritually in order to elevate and restore the holy, as well as to rise personally, also had important social implications.

The early Hasidic masters insisted that the descent of the zaddik was not merely a personal spiritual odyssey nor even a purely mystical act of *tikkun* but a communal mission demanding the zaddik's temporary decline to the level of the untutored and alienated masses of the Jewish people. Entirely new criteria for effective religious leadership were established as a consequence of this aspect of the doctrine. The qualities that the Hasidic masters considered to be absolutely central to the personality of the zaddik were his concern for the mundane welfare of the common folk, his willingness to reach out to these masses and communicate with them on their level, and, above all, the personal trait that would make all of these qualities possible, the zaddik's genuine humility. One thing was obvious to the Hasidic leaders who fostered this image of the ideal religious leader: these qualities were almost entirely absent from the intellectually elitist rabbinic leadership of their day.

The first significant elucidation of these requirements for spiritual leadership, along with a strident and protracted critique of the learned rabbinic elite, appeared in 1780 with the publication of Rabbi Jacob Joseph of Polnoe's classic, *Toledoth Jacob Joseph.* The harsh criticism of the elitist, ineffective, and alienating nature of the scholarly rabbinic leadership of his day remained a theme in all of R. Jacob Joseph's subsequently published writings as well.[47] R. Jacob Joseph formulated a theory of genuinely populist leadership according to which the most important personal qualities of the true zaddik and spiritual leader were authentic modesty and a willingness to forgo his pride and honor and thereby submit to the intimate service of the everyday needs of even the most common, sinful people. This, of course, involved close social association with even the lowest elements of Jewish society. R. Jacob Joseph repeatedly and harshly castigated those rabbis who remained aloof from the Jewish masses for their selfishness and false intellectual pride.

Other Hasidic theoreticians also dealt extensively with the ideal image and function of the zaddik. Most notable among them was R. Elimelekh of Lizensk, who, in his classic work, *Noam Elimelekh,* formulated an elaborate theory of the religious role of the zaddik. According to R. Elimelekh, in order to be an effective leader the zaddik must strive to achieve not only mystical *devekuth* with God but also social *devekuth,* or bonding with the masses of Israel. This connection between leadership and people could only be forged through the zaddik's social descent and personal attachment to the simple folk. Specifically, R. Elimelekh rejected the image of the religious leader as aloof scholar and teacher of Talmudic abstractions. Instead, he suggested that the leader must be a common-folk hero who could best retain the affection of the masses not by his academic brilliance but rather by his use of the folk tale, or Hasidic *sicha* (Yiddish, *shmuez*).[48]

At the very core of this radically new theory of leadership lay Hasidism's general theological monism and its mystical notions of cosmic harmony and restoration. The idea that the zaddik must become one with the masses was an extension or yet another manifestation of the general Hasidic quest for unity *(devekuth)* and for healing various rifts *(perudim)*—between God and the universe, between God and man, and between leader and common people—all of which afflict the world.

R. Phinehas of Polotsk on Ideal Rabbinic Leadership

It is against this background of Hasidism's populist theory of the zaddik and the harsh critique of the elitism and aloofness of the contemporary rabbinic establishment that R. Phinehas of Polotsk's doctrine of religious leadership can best be appreciated. Having, in the first part of *Kether Torah,* established the absolute and unchallenged religious supremacy of scholarship, he devotes a significant portion of the latter part of the work to elucidating his philosophy of the role and ideal social stature of the rabbinic scholar.

R. Phinehas begins his discussion of the scholar's role in Jewish life by strongly affirming, in tones not entirely dissimilar to those of R. Jacob Joseph, the need for selflessness and concern with the education of the common people. The scholar must not be selfish and egotistical in his quest for learning but rather must devote himself to spreading religious knowledge to the masses of Israel. Citing a wide array of Talmudic examples of precisely this kind of devoted scholarly leadership, R. Phinehas asserts that "therefore a person must be strong like a lion and quick as a deer in chasing after students, just as he would chase after life itself. He must dedicate his soul to this purpose so as to propagate the Torah throughout Israel."[49] In R. Phinehas's view, the scholar who accordingly compromised his own selfish thirst for ever greater knowledge and devoted himself to the instruction of the masses of Israel in the Torah had attained the highest level of religious refinement (23a).

Of course, the selflessness, modesty, and dedication to spreading the knowledge of Torah among the untutored of Israel that R. Phinehas advocated required a close association between the scholar, his students, and even the simple people. Aware of this fact, R. Phinehas often cautioned the teachers of Torah against the potential pitfalls of such closeness to both their students and, *a fortiori*, to the common folk. This is where the divergence between his approach and the Hasidic one becomes manifest. The ideal pedagogue, R. Phinehas argued, must be especially careful not to allow his relationship with his students to degenerate into an intimate association. Rather, he must, from a gracious distance, always command the awe, respect, and even fear of all the people (19b–20a). The rabbi must therefore be scrupulous not to confuse the requirement for modesty with a mandate for the loss of self-esteem or for relinquishing the formality and detachment that is necessary between student and mentor. Referring unmistakably to the populist type of leadership being fostered during his day by the Hasidic movement, R. Phinehas lashed out against the "evil inclination" that insisted that in order to demonstrate the authenticity of his humble spirit the rabbinic scholar must descend to the level of the common folk and mingle socially with them:

> The evil instinct will then try to seduce you by an even more subtle means; namely, it will tell you that since you have acquired religious knowledge and the crown of Torah, it is now worthwhile for you to crown yourself with humility as well, such that you will now regard every single Jew as being more worthy than yourself. You will then relinquish all of your respect before every human . . . and you will retain no outward indication of being a scholar. You will talk with any person; you will join in any person's gathering and you will eat together with anyone; you will cease to be fastidious in your dress and appearance; and you

will no longer be particular regarding the food you eat and the manner in which you consume it. By this kind of behavior you intend to demonstrate your modesty and the fact that you do not benefit from your learning.

Woe, my brother! Be careful of this cursed and deceptive snake, for its sole intention is to shame the honor of the Torah in the eyes of the masses and students. (20b)

It is clear that R. Phinehas is not merely warning theoretically against the perniciousness of this emphasis upon the need for humility on the part of the rabbinic scholar. He gives every indication that he personally has witnessed the degradation of the social and communal status of rabbinic leadership as a direct consequence of the Hasidic doctrine of the zaddik:

> Woe unto us, for this has happened in our own day. For, as a consequence of the leadership of those who were duped by the evil instinct into thinking that they had been crowned with the diadem of modesty, the Torah and its scholars have been most severely shamed in the eyes of the ignorant masses. For the ignoramus now believes that this is the authentic way of Torah: that anyone who touches the Torah must be degraded and shamed in the sight of all creatures, and he must emerge in filthy, soiled clothes, and must appear before every simpleton and receive him on the festivals; that he must respect each one of the masses and visit with him and eat abominations at his soiled table.[50]

Beyond rejecting such populist forms of leadership, R. Phinehas advocated precisely the kind of rabbinic demeanor that the Hasidic masters found so alienating and ineffective. He insisted that the rabbis must constitute and maintain themselves as a scholarly elite; that they must cultivate the respect of the people by avoiding close contact with them; and that even as they manifested the modesty and concern required for the effective education of the masses they must not allow themselves to descend to their level. In sharp contradistinction to the Hasidic doctrine of the descent of the zaddik, then, R. Phinehas forcefully asserted the need for aristocratic leadership. Illustrating, through Talmudic precedent, that personal modesty is no warrant for any loss of self-esteem, R. Phinehas's discussion concludes with an impassioned plea to his colleagues to maintain the pride and esteem of the scholars of the Torah:

> Of course it is true that a person must distance himself as far as possible from the attribute of arrogance and he should neither chase after honors nor seek self-aggrandizement. . . .
>
> Nonetheless, just because he forgoes his own pride and honor, this does not

mean that he [i.e., the rabbinic scholar] is permitted to abandon the honor of
the Torah.

> For when a person denigrates the scholars, he thereby diminishes the honor of
> the Torah. Therefore, remove the turban of modesty and disgrace from your
> head and raise up the crown with which your Creator has endowed you. Do not
> diminish it nor deride its honor. Honor it [i.e., the Torah], and it will raise you
> to your rightful place among the noblemen. (19b, 20a)

The only effective way to preserve the dignity and respect of the rabbinic
scholarly aristocracy regarding which R. Phinehas was so adamant was by
maintaining a maximum level of social distance between the scholar and the
untutored masses. R. Phinehas cited the many Talmudic accounts of the
distance and antipathy that existed between the scholars and the ignorant
masses in early times as an idyllic situation. This classic rabbinic requirement
for aloofness, which he often reiterated, he summed up as follows:

> Behold, my brother, the extent to which the Sages warned the *talmidei hakha-
> mim* in all of their dealings and ways to maintain the honor of the Torah and
> protect it from insult, God forbid. Therefore he [i.e., the scholar] should never
> join with the gatherings of the ignoramuses and must certainly avoid the scoff-
> ers who denigrate the honor of the Torah and its students.

> And so, behold the extent to which our Sages have distanced the scholars from
> the common folk so that the former preserve their distinction.[51]

R. Phinehas did not limit himself to warning the scholars of the Torah
about preserving their own distinction and distance from the common folk.
In equal measure he adjured the uneducated masses that they must, for their
part, respect the rabbis and maintain the appropriate posture of distant
deference toward them. The tendency on the part of the uneducated masses
to deny the scholars the appropriate level of reverence and deference that was
their due was portrayed by R. Phinehas as yet another consequence of the
seductions of the evil impulse. Once again, his depiction of that sinful inclination makes it perfectly clear that he was reacting to Hasidism's populist
models of leadership, specifically to its attempt at the democratization of
spiritual attainment:

> When the evil impulse sees that it is unable to overwhelm the scholar (who is
> like unto the angel of the Lord of Hosts) with his arrows, then it will turn to his
> students . . . and try to extinguish the fire of Torah which is burning in their

midst by implanting in their hearts heretical and dissenting opinions, in order that they will doubt the authority of their teachers and so that they will mock them and show them no respect and they will remove the veil of modesty from their faces. It [the evil instinct] will tell him [i.e., the student]: "Why should you diminish your self-respect before this nobleman [i.e., the scholar], and why should you wallow in the dust of his feet, . . . and why should you have to swallow the bitter waters that he aims at his students?

After all, you too have a heart just like his, and you are no less noble than he is, and (the Torah) is the equal inheritance of all Israel. For it is a spirit within all mankind, and it is not in heaven, but rather this matter [i.e., the Torah] is very nigh close unto you in your mouth and in your heart to do it. So that your crown is, after all, greater that his [i.e., the scholar's] crown. (23b)

Phinehas responded to this seditious call for the religious democratization of Jewish society and the demotion of its scholars to the level of their own students by means of an extensive series of citations from the Talmud, all of which call for greater fear and respect for, as well as distance from, their teachers on the part of the students of Torah (24a–25a).

Clearly, this requirement of formality and respect for the scholar on the part of his students, on the one hand, and the repeated insistence that the rabbis remain aloof and detached from the masses, on the other, were primarily a reaction to the Hasidic subversion of both the supremacy of scholarly attainment in the religious life and the social stature of the scholar in the Jewish community. However, in terms of Mithnagdic theology, the strident reaffirmation and strengthening of the elitist model of rabbinic leadership must also be viewed as an extension of the deep pessimism R. Phinehas and the other Mithnagdim held in their hearts regarding the average Jew. The elitist theory of leadership was a natural by-product of the pious disdain the rabbinic figures of the time felt toward the Jewish masses.

The need to maintain social separation between that untutored riffraff and the scholarly aristocracy not only exemplifies the ultimate affirmation of the transcendent supremacy of study and the religious insignificance of all other attainments; it also dramatically underscores the very limited nature of the Mithnagdim's confidence in both the religious and the intellectual potential of the vast majority of Jews of their day. Their insistence that the divergent elements of Jewish society, learned elite and untutored rabble alike, maintain the status quo of mutual alienation and distance from each other was in that sense the ultimate, societal manifestation of the Mithnagdism's very circumscribed, bleak appraisal of the spiritual capacities of the average Jew.

CONCLUSION

R. Phinehas of Polotsk's ethical will, written during the last years of his life, was the most personal and passionate summation of his religious philosophy. In it he issued a final, fervent warning against the evils of Hasidism. The opening pages of *Rosh ha-Giveah* spell out precisely what it was that disturbed R. Phinehas most about Hasidism. As we have seen, the problem was more behavioral than theological: the Hasidim were, to put it simply, pious exhibitionists. R. Phinehas seemed to be most agitated by their manifestations of spiritual pomposity and their arrogant and blatant religious self-confidence and presumptuousness. In R. Phinehas's view, they did not know the value of humility and modesty and therefore did not respect the most elementary restrictions of sobriety and self-control in public behavior. The Hasidim lacked both the basic religious trepidation before an awesomely transcendent God and the critical self-knowledge regarding inherent human limitations. These flaws were most evident in certain of their flamboyant, public demonstrations of religious piety.

R. Phinehas specified three types of excessive piety practiced by Hasidim that were the most common symptoms of their arrogance and religious impropriety: (1) they performed strangely enthusiastic movements and emitted shrill tones during their prayers; (2) they were overly punctilious in the observance of supererogatory religious and moral precepts before having mastered conventional, mandatory Jewish law; and (3) they engaged in radical behavior in order to attain to a higher state of religious consciousness.[1]

There are two general terms that R. Phinehas repeatedly invoked in his negative characterization of this excessive piety. The first is *yuhara*, the Talmudic stigma of pious pomposity and haughtiness:[2]

> Be especially wary, my son, of the attribute of *yuhara*, for it is that which obliterates the religion of Torah and the Jewish faith generally. Our Sages have taught that not every person who desires to attain spiritual excellence may freely do so....

For on account of this attribute there has been a general decline of religion, and the Torah and justice are shamed in the eyes of the masses . . . for anyone can now say to those who rebuke him: "My deeds are greater than yours," as a consequence of the added obligations with which he has decorated himself. . . .

In the end, then, the attribute of *yuhara* destroyed every good attribute in Israel, and consequently the faces of the rabbinic scholars have become black, and the entire world has become disorderly, and the way of truth has been lost, all on account of his "good deeds."[3]

The attribute of *yuhara* is particularly seditious and dangerous precisely because in his false displays of spiritual arrogance the religious showoff breaks with legal and social convention and disregards the normal limits placed on religious behavior, thus opening the door to *hefker,* or lawlessness and licentiousness.

The second general term that captures the subversive spirit against which Phinehas warns in his ethical will is, naturally enough, *hasid.* Phinehas offers a fascinating etymological analysis of this Hebrew term.[4] He demonstrates that the root *h's'd* in Hebrew can be used to depict a high level of piety, *hasiduth,* as well as its very opposite, *hesed,* which sometimes connotes an abomination or disgrace.[5] *Hasiduth,* he continues, is also closely related to the Hebrew term for chaos and lawlessness, *hefker.* For in order to attain a level of truly ecstatic piety, or *hasiduth,* one must first abandon all of the usual personal restrictions of pride and dignity. This break with religious convention may, however, only legitimately be practiced by a spiritually select, elite group. Thus, *hasiduth* is not only a linguistically ambiguous and loaded term; it connotes a form of behavior that, when perversely directed or improperly regulated, can be the source of religious disorder and lawlessness rather than piety. The immodest and undisciplined supererogatory piety of the Hasid who is neither spiritually prepared nor genuinely motivated, is really the very opposite of what it ostensibly represents. One must therefore be most wary when confronted with those who, in the service of *hasiduth,* illegitimately abandon the normative legal, social, and religious behavioral restrictions. It is necessary to ascertain whether such alleged Hasidim are legitimate members of that small religious elite who are indeed on a higher spiritual plane than the average Jew or whether they are, like the contemporary sect that adorns itself with the title of *hasiduth,* the pompous practitioners of a spurious piety.

These attributes that R. Phinehas observed to be so objectionable in the Hasidim are, of course, the external symptoms of religious rapture shared by all mystics. The *hefker* he associates with *hasiduth* sounds very much like the manifest enthusiasm common to all those men of spirit whose conquest and transcendence of the conventional, circumscribed realm of human reason and empirical experience underlies their strange, unconventional, and often disorderly behavior. Central to the Hasid's religious experience is the mystical transcendence of the normative physical and cognitive borders of human existence. For like all mystics, he craves to pierce the veils of sensation, reason, and intellection in order to attain intimate knowledge of the Absolute beyond. Evelyn Underhill has argued that the central feature of all mystical schools is the conviction that man can and should overcome the apparent limitations of his sense perceptions:

> Mysticism alone postulates, and in the persons of its great initiates proves, not only the existence of the Absolute, but also this link: this possibility first of knowing, finally of attaining it. It denies that possible knowledge is to be limited (a) to sense perceptions, (b) to any process of intellection, (c) to the unfolding of the content of normal consciousness. . . .
>
> In theological language, their theory of knowledge is that the spirit of man, itself essentially divine, is capable of immediate communion with God, the One Reality.[6]

In the process of attaining this communion with God, the Hasid inevitably departs from the traditional, restricted modes of organized religious and social behavior. He then appears to those who are faithful to the normative limits of social, legal, and religious protocol as at best eccentric or somewhat deranged and at the very worst fraudulent.

This is precisely how the Mithnagdim perceived the adherents of Hasidism. While they were neither unaware nor disrespectful of the phenomenon of authentic mystical enthusiasm, they simply could not accept that such significant numbers from among the Jewish masses had legitimately reached the level of its attainment. Consequently, they could not tolerate the concerted attempts by the early Hasidic theoreticians to spread the knowledge and practice of Jewish mysticism as widely as possible. The net consequence of this fear and suspicion of Hasidic-sponsored *hefker,* namely, its populist transcending of the normal boundaries of accepted religious conduct, was a strengthening of precisely those conventional religious limits on the part of the Mithnagdim.

In this study of Mithnagdic thought I have documented in some detail both the general religious psychology underlying this defensive theological response and the specific manifestations of the traditional rabbis' strong, conservative reaction to Hasidic piety. Let us now sum up the salient elements of Mithnagdic religion.

The Mithnagdim did not dispute the fundamental teachings of Jewish mysticism in principle. They shared, in theory at least, the religious conviction that God is immanent in the created universe and that it is possible for the *ideal* man, through a variety of mystical endeavors, to commune with the divine presence inherent in the world, that is, to attain *devekuth*. The Mithnagdim harbored, however, a very pessimistic view of the common man of their day; they believed that he was simply unable, because of the ceaseless decline of the generations as well as the limitations inherent in his own physical and mortal nature, ever to attain such a mystical state. They insisted that the masses of Jewry must respect their innate epistemological and spiritual limits and refrain from any profound contemplation of the notion of divine immanence. For although in theory they did accept the veracity of that notion, they maintained that it remained unfathomable to the average man.

More generally, although the Mithnagdim respected the wisdom and sanctity of the Kabbalah, they counseled against its popular study for precisely the same reason. In sharp contrast to the Hasidim, who popularized Kabbalistic wisdom and disseminated it widely, the Mithnagdim were convinced that its comprehension lay far beyond the capacity of the average Jew and that it must therefore remain an esoteric discipline carefully limited to a small spiritual elite. Similarly, although the Mithnagdim also recognized the innate cosmic and theurgic potentialities embedded in the text of the Hebrew prayers, they deliberately limited their own liturgical interpretations to the literal sense of the words and phrases and warned against the attempt to transcend those very mundane meanings. In the same spirit, while they accepted that God's glory fills every material thing on earth, they insisted that this innate divinity was irretrievably hidden from man and that he must therefore both abstain from physical indulgences and desist from aspiring to any lasting or meaningful successes in the material world. At the same time, while they preached the values of simplicity and abstinence, the Mithnagdim also rejected extreme, mystical asceticism as just another manifestation of excessive religious piety.

In sum, the Mithnagdim allowed man no genuine mystical experiences in this life. They were thoroughly convinced that it was only subsequent to death and the release of the soul from its material "prison" that man might finally attain the proximity to God and the heightened spiritual state he so craved.

In sharp contrast to Hasidism's quest for the unitive life, in which the artificial and illusory borders that divide world from Creator, body from spirit, and, ultimately, man from God are deliberately and progressively overcome, Mithnagdism seems to have been intent on raising and fortifying those very borders. Whereas Hasidism encouraged all Jews to aspire to both inner spiritual harmony and mystical union with the Shekhinah, the Mithnagdim tirelessly reminded man of the irreparable dualism of his personality and the shattered nature of his universe. Therefore, whereas Hasidism instructed man to raise and transform evil, Mithnagdism insisted on the resilient nature of the evil instinct and the need to wage a vigilant war against it.

Because of this very severely limited assessment of the human condition, the Mithnagdim restricted their attention almost exclusively to carefully controlled and well-defined religious disciplines. Besides advocating the essentially defensive, conventional Jewish religious life of cautious adherence to the Halakhah, to the exclusion of any supererogatory or heroic spiritual quests, they focused almost obsessively on Torah study as the single safe channel for spiritual fulfillment. In so doing, they placed the predominant emphasis of the spiritual life upon the cognition of the religious truths found in rabbinic literature, in contrast to Hasidism's thirst for the more daring and direct conation of the divine.

The Mithnagdim were obsessed with Jewish exile and the progressive, irreversible spiritual degeneration it had wrought. They were historically resigned to the inherently alienated nature of the created universe and the chronic dualism of the mortal human soul. Consequently, they offered the individual Jew no path of redemption from his estranged, shattered existence in this world and no remedy for his divided nature and afflicted spirit. In this sense, then, the spirit of Mithnagdism is almost perfectly captured by William James's famous depiction of the "religion of the sick soul," or "the divided self," according to which "there are two lives, the natural and the spiritual, and we must lose the one before we can participate in the other."[7]

The most prominent and consistent teaching of Mithnagdism was the impotence of the human spirit. Mithnagdism absolutely forbade man from attempting to overcome his inherent inadequacies or daring to transcend the material limits of ordinary human experience. In reaction to Hasidism's various attempts—through mystical prayer, study, contemplation, and the sanctification of material existence—to encourage man to transcend those very limits and transform the natural life into the spiritual one, Mithnagdism became increasingly obsessed with human ineptitude and spiritual alienation. And in response to the perceived Hasidic threat to the conservative, confining manner of traditional rabbinic religiosity, the Mithnagdim fortified to an unprecedented degree the limits of spiritual attainment and the boundaries of acceptable religious conduct.

Appendix A

THE WORKS OF PHINEHAS
OF POLOTSK

Phinehas of Polotsk died in 1822 and was buried in plot 193 of the Old Jewish Cemetery of Vilna, not far from the grave of the GRA.[1] The inscription upon the burial monument on his grave reads almost like a bibliographical note:

> Here is interred the author of books, the rabbi and preacher who fashioned a commentary to the Order of the Liturgy, and also [authored] the work *Kether Torah*, which is a symphony to the Torah; also [commentaries] to Job, Ecclesiastes, Psalms, whose acrostic is truth [the Hebrew word *emet* is formed by an acrostic of the first letters of the titles of these three books].
>
> Also, a commentary to Ecclesiastes, The Song of Songs, as well as an ethical will entitled *Rosh ha-Giveah,* whose acrostic [in Hebrew, as above] is a tie [Heb., *kesher*] that binds together the crowns that collectively adorn his teachings.
>
> This is the renowned rabbi and preacher Phinehas ben Judah, of blessed memory.
>
> His soul departed in purity on Wednesday, the third of Shevat, 5583 [1822].[2]

As his epitaph indicates, R. Phinehas was a prolific author. He seems to have gone through two productive periods in his life: (1) the Polotsk years, during which he wrote his most significant original work, *Kether Torah*, as well as his bulky commentary to the liturgy, *Maggid Zedek*, published in a prayer book bearing the title *Shaar ha-Rahamim* (both works were published in 1788); and (2) the years 1803–9, during which he published all of his biblical commentaries—to the Proverbs (*Shevet mi-Yehuda*, 1803), Ecclesiastes (*Derekh ha-Hayyim*, 1804), The Song of Songs (*Derekh ha-Melekh*, 1804), Job (*Giveath Phinehas*, 1808) and Psalms (*Midrash Hakhamim*, 1809).

In 1820, less than three years before his death, R. Phinehas published his ethical will, together with selected sermons. He was also the author of an abbreviated version of the medieval ethical tract *Even Bohan* by Kalonymous ben Kalonymous (Vilna, 1799). A descriptive catalogue of R. Phinehas's writings follows.

1. *Siddur Shaar ha-Rahamim* (Shklov, 1788)

The book is paginated in two sections: the first section, comprising 32 double-sided folios (64 pages), covers the first part of the daily morning service *(pesukei de-zimra):*

the second section, comprising 122 folios (243 pages), includes commentaries to the rest of the daily, Sabbath, and festival services. The text of the liturgy is flanked by two commentaries, a reprint of the interpretation of Jewish liturgy by R. David Abudarham in the inner column and *Maggid Zedek,* by R. Phinehas in the outer column. The *siddur* also comprises commentaries by Phinehas to the Mishnaic tractate *Avoth* as well as to the Passover Haggadah. These commentaries were subsequently published in separate volumes.

Title page. The title page proclaims that the commentary by R. Phinehas will be based primarily on classical rabbinic sources as well as on three earlier commentaries to the liturgy, namely, those of David Abudarham, Rabbi Herz, and Rabbi Jacob Emden (Yavetz).[3] In an important disclaimer the publisher advises that the commentary by R. Phinehas will be strictly limited to either literal or rabbinic interpretations of the liturgy and will avoid speculation in more esoteric (i.e., Kabbalistic) domains.

Approbations. The *siddur* contains the approbations of the following rabbis: Issachar Baer ben Leib of Shklov, Aaron Zelig ben Aryeh of Polotsk, Benyamin ben Meir Ginzburg of Vyzhun, Moses Mordechai Katzenellenbogen of Kaidan, and Yechiel Michel ben Isaac of Polotsk. Issachar Baer of Shklov was an active Mithnagged who signed the *takanoth* of Shklov against the Hasidim.[4] Benjamin Ginzburg was also a known Mithnagged and an associate of polemicist Israel Loebl. His son was a signatory to the letter of the GRA of 1797.

Subscribers. Apparently encouraged by the explicit personal approval of the GRA to publish his original commentary to the Jewish liturgy, R. Phinehas traveled to many of the towns near both Vitebsk and Vilna in order to enlist support from advance subscribers for the publication of this work. The list of subscribers—265 names in all—is quite impressive and testifies to R. Phinehas's popularity, especially in the Vitebsk region of White Russia. Among the more notable names on the list are many rabbis, including those from the cities and towns of Shklov, Vilna, Vitebsk, Polotsk, Ula, Byshinkwiecz, Seneh, Urscha, Shumyavitz, Rasna, Dakshytz, and Toltshyn.

Introduction. The paginated *siddur* itself is prefaced by an unpaginated six-page introduction. In the major part of this introduction, R. Phinehas reviews his personal motivations in composing his own commentary to the Hebrew liturgy. Primary among them was his sense that all previous commentaries had been either limited to explicating the individual words and phrases of the *siddur* or, at the other end of the exegetical spectrum, to delving deeply into the prayers' esoteric, mystical meaning. R. Phinehas claims that his commentary will fill the gap between these two approaches by commenting on the liturgy in order to explicate its primary meaning, using classical rabbinic sources as a guide. He explicitly avows that he will not enter into any Kabbalistic interpretations of the prayers. Aside from these methodological comments, the introduction explains the only partial inclusion of the Abudarham commentary in the text of the *siddur* and includes some rare personal biographical data regarding the deaths of both his wife and his younger son, Moshe, during the period of the *siddur*'s publication, the only references to members of R. Phinehas's family in his entire corpus.

Although the *Siddur Shaar ha-Rahamim* was not reprinted in full for more than two centuries, the commentary to the Haggadah contained within it was reissued many times. The most significant of these reproductions are Elijah Landau, ed., *Seder Haggadah Shel Pesah Im Shnei Perushim* (Jerusalem, 1903), which includes the commentaries of the GRA and *Maggid Zedek* by R. Phinehas (it is noteworthy that Elijah Landau was a great-grandson of the GRA); the well-known *Siddur Ishei Yisrael: Siddur ha-GRA,* ed. Elijah Landau and Isaac Maltzan (reprint, Jerusalem, 1975) which includes the commentary *Maggid Zedek;* and a two-volume, edited edition of *Siddur Shaar ha-Rahamim,* with the complete text of *Maggid Zedek* and including an introductory biography of R. Phinehas of Polotsk and an original commentary, *Sidurah de-Zalutah,* by the editor, Dov Loketch, published in Jerusalem in 1992.

2. *Kether Torah* (Shklov, 1788)

The first edition of R. Phinehas's most famous, most important, and most original work apparently was published at approximately the same time as *Siddur Shaar ha-Rahamim* (as the very proximate dates of their respective approbations suggest) and by the same printing house. Besides the unpaginated title page and approbation, it contains 56 pages.

Title page. The title page accurately describes the purpose of the book as being "to raise the crown of Torah above all other crowns, by means of a polemic based upon the words of our Sages of Blessed Memory." Testifying to its popular goal and intended audience, the statement of purpose continues, "It is a *mitzvah* for every Israelite to purchase this book for his son, so that he may carry it in his bosom." Since the book contains R. Phinehas's most sustained attack upon both Hasidism and the Haskalah, his desire to disseminate its ideas as widely as possible is readily understandable.

Approbation. There is one approbation to *Kether Torah,* by the Mithnagdic rabbi of Shklov, Issachar Baer ben Leib, former rabbi of Slutsk. It is dated 18 Nissan 5548 (spring 1788).

Kether Torah was reprinted in Königsberg in 1859, in Jerusalem in 1896 and 1965, and in Brooklyn in 1985.

3. *Kitzur Even Bohan* (Vilna, 1799)

The books contains twenty-five pages, including the title page and the introduction.

Title page. The title page opens with the following statement regarding the author: "This book, small in size but great in importance, was written by the famous Rabbi and Maggid, Phinehas b. Judah, who *was* the chief preacher in the community of Polotsk and whose fame has already spread through the world on account of his *siddur* and book *Kether Torah,* which have already been published." It goes on to explain that the book is based upon the classic *Even Bohan,* written by "Rabbi Kalonymous the Elder."

Introduction. The author states that he has abbreviated the original *Even Bohan,* by Rabbi Kalonymous, which contained "over one hundred chapters," and has reduced it to eighteen chapters by including only the most "beautiful matters scattered throughout his chapters." More importantly, R. Phinehas claims that he has added to the original text some of his own comments regarding moral and ethical matters.

Kitzur Even Bohan was the most frequently reprinted of R. Phinehas's works, being reprinted in Königsberg in 1859, in Jerusalem in 1900, in Mihalewycz in 1931, in Petah Tikva in 1953, and in Brooklyn in 1985. The 1900 and subsequent editions incorporated anonymous editorial introductions to each of the chapters of the work.

4. *Shevet mi-Yehuda,* commentary to Proverbs (Vilna, 1803)

Besides the unpaginated title page, approbations, introduction, and list of subscribers, the book contains 70 double-sided folios (140 pages).

Title page. The title page praises the exegetical ability of the author and correctly suggests that his approach to the Proverbs is primarily a homiletical one. Thus it is claimed that the commentary will "interpret every verse homiletically and more sweetly than a honeycomb. Every single verse that was hidden or written in a cryptic or poetic style, or metaphorically, will be interpreted, and its hidden treasure will be opened with the help of citations from the writings of the Sages; these scriptures will also be expounded upon in order to reveal their ethical and moral purpose and to give proper counsel in practical religious behavior." Following the description of R. Phinehas's exegetical method, there is a long caveat begging the reader's objectivity and patience in evaluating the interpretations of scripture contained in the book.

Approbations. There are two approbations, whose obvious purpose is to ensure the author's copyright and to prevent reprinting of the work before five years have elapsed. The first of the approbations was signed by the three rabbinic judges of Vilna, while the second carries the signatures of eight other Vilna rabbis.

Introduction. In the introduction, R. Phinehas laments the contemporary Jewish neglect of scriptural study. He views this as a consequence of both the inherent difficulties of interpreting scripture and the Jews' predominant interest in practical Halakhic matters. Yet he suggests that the study of biblical books such as the Proverbs is of current importance as well. This is especially true of the Proverbs, since they contain extensive warnings against religious scoffers and heretics, who Phinehas claims have proliferated in his own day. This is a thinly concealed reference to the Hasidim and the Maskilim, both of whom are roundly attacked in the commentary *Shevet mi-Yehuda.* R. Phinehas goes on to detail the many difficulties and obscurities that confront the reader of the Proverbs, and he promises to clarify these many textual problems and exegetical ambiguities by explicating the biblical verses in the light of the classical Talmudic and Midrashic sources.

Subscribers. Phinehas prefaces his list of subscribers with a special tribute to two major financial contributors, who apparently supported him extensively, as well as six subscribers who paid one hundred Polish gold pieces each for the book. There follows a list of sixty "regular" subscribers, who prepaid one ruble each for the book. Among the most notable of these subscribers are the two sons of the GRA, Abraham and Aryeh, and the renowned Halakhic author R. Abraham Danzig.

5. *Derekh ha-Melekh,* commentary to the Song of Songs (Grodno, 1804)

The book contains thirteen pages, including the title page and the introduction.

Title page. The title page introduces the author and refers to his two previously published commentaries. It accurately claims that the nature of the commentary will be straightforward and that it will focus on elucidating the simple meaning of the text or interpreting it homiletically "without any deviations . . . and without turning from side to side." The influence of the commentary of R. Moses Alshikh on Phinehas is alluded to. It would seem that this work was brought to print simultaneously with the author's commentary to Ecclesiastes, *Derekh ha-Hayyim.*

Introduction. The introduction is basically a hymn of praise to God for allowing the author the opportunity to publicize, through his published works, God's greatness and compassion for his creatures. R. Phinehas asserts that his primary reason for writing commentaries to hagiographical works is to increase the belief in, and love of, God.

6. *Derekh ha-Hayyim,* commentary to Ecclesiastes (Grodno, 1804)

The book contains 15 folios (28 pages), including the title page and the introduction.

Title page. The title page reads more like an introduction. Here again, as in the introduction to *Shevet mi-Yehuda,* the author reveals his motivation for composing an original commentary to a biblical book. R. Phinehas again laments the contemporary Jewish neglect of scriptural study, which he says has resulted in a situation in which most Jews "are unable to decipher so much as two continuous words or two verses . . . to the point that Solomon's own words, 'and he spoke to sticks and stones,' have been fulfilled in our day." R. Phinehas states that his goal is simply to make the words of King Solomon comprehensible to those Jews who search for religious knowledge. Once again he condemns the scoffers and heretics of his day and insists that this commentary is not intended for their eyes.

Introduction. The introduction deals with the problem of the suffering and death of innocent children. Apparently, R. Phinehas was witness to a plague, presumably diphtheria, in which young children were dying of a form of asphyxiation. It is possible that his own son Moshe died as a result of this illness. R. Phinehas addresses the problem in the spirit of Ecclesiastes' perplexity regarding the ways of the world. He suggests several comforting ideas, chiefly the promise of rectitude in the future world or in another reincarnation *(gilgul).*

7. *Giveath Phinehas,* commentary to Job (Vilna, 1808)

The books consists of 49 folios (97 pages) in addition to a title page.

Title page. On the title page R. Phinehas declares that the main theme of the book of Job is the suffering of the righteous. Since the book ultimately serves to explain and justify the apparently cruel ways of the world and still to affirm divine providence, R. Phinehas asserts the importance of explicating its obscure and difficult passages.

Introduction. The true purpose of the book of Job is to strengthen personal faith in a providential God despite the many daily challenges to that faith, and especially to comfort the downtrodden Jewish people in their exile and encourage them not to despair of divine salvation. Because the final message of Job is so vital to the morale of the exiled nation of Israel, Phinehas insists on the importance of its study:

> Therefore, it is essential for us to have this book before our eyes and not to let it vanish from our mouths, so that we must read it all the days of our life in order that we might know and understand from its words, in all of their complexities and connotations, that the ways of God are just and there is no inequity in Him . . . as He himself reveals in the last words addressed by them [i.e., Job's friends] to him. . . . Thus, one must not doubt God nor suspect His judgment.

True to the spirit of the thematic title page and introduction, the commentary itself is the most highly philosophical and abstract, and the least strictly exegetical, of all R. Phinehas's biblical commentaries.

At the conclusion of the introduction, R. Phinehas refers to his six earlier works and the rabbinic approbations granted to them. He pays tribute to the rabbis and noblemen of the Vilna Jewish community for their support in the publication of the commentary. Finally, he expresses the hope that this support will continue in order to allow for the publication of his eighth work, the commentary to Psalms, which was apparently ready for publication at the same time.

8. *Midrash Hakhamim,* commentary to Psalms (Minsk, 1809)

Title page. The title page reviews the previously published exegetical works of R. Phinehas, praising his achievement of "clarifying every obscurity and explicating each enigmatic passage, all based upon the words of the Sages of Blessed Memory. He shed light on every concealed verse, using the light of the words of the Sages, which are dispersed throughout the Talmud." It is announced that this latest work, *Midrash Hakhamim,* will follow the same exegetical method of clarifying the difficult verses of the Psalms in the light of the rabbinic literature.

Introduction. In this last of his exegetical works, R. Phinehas speaks at length of the motivations underlying the composition of his many biblical commentaries. Here again he feels the need to justify writing new commentaries to biblical works, and he does so largely by referring to the inadequacies of the earlier commentaries of Rashi, Rabbi David Kimhi, and Rabbi Moses Alshikh for a contemporary audience. Most of all, however, Phinehas was exercised by the neglect of biblical studies by even the most learned classes of contemporary Jewish society. This neglect was most manifest in the ignorance of the plain sense of the most oft-repeated of biblical passages, the liturgical selections from the Psalms.

The introduction contains a biting reproach of the Jews of his day for their scriptural illiteracy:

> There is no one who examines or searches out the concealed meaning of the words he chirps in prayer. Now the matter [of reciting the Psalms during prayer] has become similar to the recital of a magical incantation over a wound: whether or not one understands it, the incantation is supposed to do its work.

So, too, no one bothers to understand the meaning of the words or the order of things, about whom they are said and what is being requested, or what the author is talking about and what his intention is, and what he is praying for and to whom he is offering songs of praise and thanksgiving. Woe unto our eyes, which have beheld such a thing that has happened in our own generation! For if you were to ask any scholar, no matter how learned in the Torah and erudite in all of its intricacies, to explain a single verse from this book [of Psalms], he would only be able to offer you a homiletical interpretation. But he does not know what the verse is really saying and what he is talking about, nor does he understand the continuation in the next verses. Now, one might judge such ignorance mercifully in the case of the other Prophetic books, since the scholar does not deal with them and is occupied only in the essence of Torah, namely, with the divine law and its adjudication, and the study of the Talmud and codes. But what can we say [to justify such ignorance] in the case of a book that every scholar recites daily in the morning prayers, and on holidays in the Hallel . . . and in times of trouble? . . .

How can the scholar not be shamed and embarrassed to articulate words before God in the manner of a complete ignoramus? Woe unto us on account of this horrible shame that has seized us. . . .

Therefore my colleagues should be especially ashamed . . . for the scholars are to be blamed for having been the first to cast this book aside and to leave it to the ignorant and light-minded, who have no understanding. Now, as a result of this, I have been zealous for the honor of God, and I have now come to remove the veil of modesty from my face and have decided to cull from all of my acquired wisdom in order to interpret the words of this book according to their plain sense and to explicate the proper intention of each of its chapters—why, when, and in what context they were said by King David. Thus there will be some sense to his words, and they will be understood according to their plain sense, so that the readers who recite these words every day will comprehend the utterances that their own mouths are pronouncing, and they will understand what they are requesting and for what they are pleading and to Whom they are offering songs of praise and thanksgiving, may He be blessed.

R. Phinehas then reviews his earlier publications and reaffirms that his sole purpose was "to benefit the people of Israel by providing them with a sufficient interpretation" of the obscure, lesser-known scriptural writings. R. Phinehas insists that his biblical interpretations are better suited to the didactic needs of his generation than any of the previously existing commentaries. Finally, he invokes his close association with the GRA as evidence of his authority as an exegete and original author.

9. *Rosh Ha-Giveah*, ethical will (Vilna, 1820)

R. Phinehas's final work consists of 47 folios (94 pages), in addition to the title page and introduction. It includes a two-part ethical will and nine sermons, also divided into two sections. The first part of the will consists of direct personal religious instruction to his son, while the second part, entitled "Birurei ha-Midoth," deals more generally with basic Jewish ethical standards. The first part of the sermons includes the sermons for Shabbat Shekalim and Shabbath Zahor, while the second section includes seven sermons on various Torah readings.

Title page. On the title page R. Phinehas hints at the contemporary urgency of his message in fighting off the guile and temptations of the evil instinct. As the text reveals, a strongly defensive, anti-Hasidic motif pervades the ethical will. Phinehas asserts that he has "reached the top of the hill, and I have seen the correct path in which I can instruct my children and peers, in order . . . that they not be entrapped by the evil instinct, which blinds the eyes of men, telling them that the evil way is indeed a good one."

Introduction. In the introduction R. Phinehas offers his thanks to God for having granted him the privilege to publish all of his previous works, which he refers to specifically. He recalls the patronage and approval of the GRA for his *siddur.* R. Phinehas indicates that he was seventy-three years old when he composed this book, which he intimates is, for reasons of failing health, to be his last publication.

Rosh Ha-Giveah was reprinted in Jerusalem in 1898. The ethical will, without the appended sermons, was again reprinted in Jerusalem in 1965 and in Brooklyn in 1985.

PHINEHAS OF POLOTSK'S
DEATH POEM

The following is a translation of Kether Torah, *36a–38a.*

And now, my brother, I will transcribe for your benefit a precious jewel that I originally wrote in my youth, while contemplating the day of death in an attempt to subdue the evil instinct, as our Sages have recommended: "Let man meditate upon the day of his death."

How dare any mortal man, one who ought to rejoice upon unearthing his own burial plot, proclaim that he is the master of his own life? For, in point of fact, in this life man migrates incessantly from misfortune to even greater anguish.

Now, does this man, who is of such a lowly stature and who will never enjoy a single moment of peace—does such a person imagine that he possesses any form of control or authority? Dare a person for whom nobody could care, who left the womb entirely bare, and who will suffer all his days from hunger—does such a person dare to say that he is wise or that discernment is his birthright?

Birth

Woe unto us for the humiliation that is man—a creature borne of woman, the lowly product of a repugnant drop who twice must pass through the urinary shaft submerged in blood. How dare such a creature establish for himself a name among the wise! Why should he bother to plant fields and to sow vineyards? Does he have any idea how long the days and the years of his life will endure? Rather, man who was, after all, born without the ability to walk or speak or comprehend should simply use this life as a mere preparation. He should forever wonder whether he will live a year or two, or perhaps only another day or two more, and whether his destiny will be that of eternal life or death. For the person who does not cleanse himself of his filth and who rejoices to the sounds of tamborines and drums—such a man deserves nothing more than shame and abuse. Man is born with no knowledge, and he spends all of his pubescent years just screeching and crying; his entire life is exhausted in servile toil, until the day of his death arrives, after which he will not even remember his original departure to this lower realm of existence.

What a shame is the great confusion whereby an ugly and painful blemish, namely, this godless earth, is considered by man to be as Mount Moriah.

Man is dominated by others all of his life, and he only blasphemes bitterly both in his youth and in his old age, until he dies. How can he thus not be aware, while the breath of life is still within him, of his final destiny?

Marriage

Man is filled with indignity and shame until the day when they will match him with a wife arrives; she too is a repugnant dribble, and even if he happened to have found an unusually good woman, she is never really more than a container filled with manure. Inevitably, bad days will arrive for them both, for there does not exist even one man who enjoys so much as a single hour's respite from his wife. Rather, all of their days together are spent in feuding, in anguish and worry, pain and sadness; for she shall only add to your mourning, and throughout the days of your meaningless life she will drive you to hoard money and to plant vineyards and to attain celebrity among the intellectuals; and thus shall you do all of your days. She will cause you to forsake your father and your mother and ultimately to desert even your Lord as well, only in order to fill your storage house with silver and gold, and ultimately only in order to bequeath it to those who will survive you. She will dissipate your soul and disperse your wealth, such that day and night neither frost nor heat, neither stormy seas nor deep rivers, neither fields nor deserts, will deter you from heeding her will. And if you do hearken unto her voice, she will certainly lead you in anguish down into Sheol.

The Family

Now, if she honors you by bearing your children, she will then only proceed to shorten your days and years; she will not let you sleep nor even allow your eyelids to rest for a second; for she will increase the burden of your work both at home and in the field; she will bellow at you from all sides with her screeching voice, and your anguish and bickering will be compounded both by her and by the troubles emanating from your household. In the end, you will be oppressed and broken all of your days. Finally, you will be forced to give away, on behalf of your own engaged son, a vast dowry and great amounts of gold from your own pocket. All this only to establish yet further misery for the members of your own household.

So consider with your own good sense what is your real moment of glory? How can you possibly say, "I praise life and the living," when in fact all of the days of your life are miserable, depressed, diseased, agonizing, and hurtful? And if such is the case in the days of your youth, what will you do about your older years? Those are the days in which "the sun and the light and the moon and the stars grow dark, and the clouds return after the rain" (Ecclesiastes 12:2). How much worse will it be if you encounter evil days in which bitches, together with their young hounds, will bark at you.

Evil will beset you when you confront the very children whom you nurtured and raised. Then, when evil will come forth from your own household, your own children, the fruit of the womb, will damn and ban you. Then you will surely wonder, "Woe, what have I done?" For you will realize that you have wasted all of your days. Still, you will simply surrender to your children just as one capitulates before mighty heroes, until they ultimately will bring your hoary white head down to hell in misery. This, then, will be the recompense for all of your hard labor.

Disease

And yet, all of this [misery] must still be considered by you as the gift of God. For it could still have been much worse, as in the case of a man who does not attain old age and who dries up and loses his strength in his vital years. The day of his death comes suddenly and snatches him away without any warning. You see him one moment, and then suddenly he disappears from the presence of his wife and children and is separated from all of his wealth and property. It is then as if he had never existed at all in this gloomy world; rather, he arrived in darkness and departed in a fog. Such grief is horrible, for there is no remedy for one who dies so suddenly.

It is, however, an even greater affliction when the enlightened man devotes himself so energetically to entirely futile goals. He gives no rest to his eyes, and yet he spends all of his days groping in the dark, much as the blind man fumbles in midday, all in order to attain a negligible end. Nothing will deter a man so driven, neither destruction by day nor frost by night, until he falls into his sickbed afflicted with terrible diseases and miserable suffering all day. From head to foot no relief comes his way. He cries and groans by day, and by night he wails bitterly. The lights of his soul are dimmed, and his sun and moon are darkened. His soul completely detests the very taste or odor of any food, and he deteriorates until his head and arms feel heavy and he cannot even turn from side to side in bed.

His only child is then brought in to see him; he grasps him by the hand and calls out, "My father, my father," but he is not recognized. He gestures with his fingers and winces with his eyes, but still there is no response. Touching any of this man's limbs is akin to trying to touch the pupil of his eye.

The Final Moments

Then he comes very close to his demise, and as we know, most failing people soon die. In struts the men of the burial society [hevra kadisha], and they immediately surround his bed, just standing there, waiting for him to die. They stand and wait, and helplessly they behold his anguish and distress as the flute plays inside of his throat. One of the men holds on to his hand, taking his pulse while at the same time inquiring whether there is sufficient good wood with which to construct the coffin. Another places his hand over the heart of the dying man and declares that he no longer has any vital energy left within him. Yet another one checks his hands, and another his eyelids and pupils, and still another discerns whether his living soul still breathes within his nostrils. Finally, they proclaim: "Behold, his death has arrived! Light the candles and place them at his head!"

The Moment of Death

At this point the Angel of Death appears in the room with his sword drawn in his hand and stands next to the deceased, grabs him by his cloak, and says: "Arise, you bloody creature, and recall the days of your life, filled as they are with dirty blotches and filth; see how you now lie here like an unblemished sacrifice." Now, when he beholds the Angel of Death looming large before him from earth to heaven with his sword drawn in his hand and staring intensely at him, a great fear grasps him deep in his loins, and his legs give way, and he tightly shuts his eyes and bares his neck like a bull before the slaughterer. The Angel of Death stands over his offering, his heart burning hot like a live coal; he grabs his dagger, closes the window, and contaminates the house.

Once his soul has departed from the place where it was and his corpse remains filled only with humiliation and shame, with his face turning green and his limbs deteriorating, his mouth wide open and his stomach bloated, then do the members of the society take him and place his body upon the ground, where he will lie silently like a stone. They place a pillow or some straw under him. His wife and darling children now come and cover him with black clothes and cry very bitterly, all the while surrounding him like a drove of bees from head to toe. They call out to one another: "Look at your poor father, the apple of our eye, who has gone to his final rest; none shall arouse him now. Just yesterday we recognized him, and suddenly he is no longer. His eyes are closed tight, and his mouth is shut; behold how radically different is your father's face from what it was so recently. He has now gone far away such that you will never again see him."

His wife approaches him, clothed in her widow's vestments, and she proclaims: "My husband, oh my husband, why have you so deserted and forsaken me? To whom have you left your own children? Where is your compassion? See how your own progeny who stand before you will become scattered to the earth's four corners! And children will predecease their parents. Oh, awake you slumberer, when will you arise?" But she will hold her peace when she hears that the Lord has dispatched him to a place from which there is no return. Finally, like a woman in pain wearing the sackcloth for the darling of her youth, she will hold her peace.

Now his lovely daughter will come forth, alone and mournful, her clothing torn, her hair wild, with tears running down her cheeks, crying out loud for her dead father. Thus will she cry and shriek: "My father, my father! How has death come so suddenly upon you? I wish that I had died instead of you and that I had suffered your curse. Who will now tend for your children, and who will comfort them when they cry out like doves? Your children are now left to be orphans. As for me, the Lord has fed me the bitter wormwood; for I know for certain that all of these obligations will now be thrust upon me. Woe unto the lost days of my youth, for my song has now turned to sadness. Cursed be the day on which I was born, and let the sun no longer shine for me."

The Burial

While she is still talking, the sexton, that paragon of truth and justice, arrives on the scene. He orders, "Hurry and do the deed." He measures the body and goes off to dig the grave while the others prepare the white shrouds. They proceed to dress him like a three-year-old baby, in a blouse and trousers, and even place a belt on his waist and a hat upon his head—this, then, is the sum total of his reward for all of the energy and toil he expended all of his days upon the earth. How pathetic is his shame and disgrace! How is it that he did not consider that this would be his final end; that he would not take it all with him when he died; that nothing would remain except his carcass; that nothing he would accomplish in life would be of any lasting value; and that he would depart barren of all his acquisitions? Even his wife speaks up only to mourn the days of her youth.

His only son now appears and rends his garments and tearfully blurts out: "My father, my father! How can you go securely along your way and thus desert your children? Oh, dear father, now no one will benefit from your labor, and there are none who will take pity upon your children. I am bitter like the wormwood. To whom have you assigned the responsibility for your flock; how scattered they will now become, one here and the other there, one in the north and the other in the south. Alas, my father, where is your compassion? How can you ask me to support them in my bosom? If you do this to me, why not better take my soul? For death is better for me now than life. I can neither tolerate seeing my own suffering nor stand by to witness the downfall of my home and my family. My brothers and sisters! Let tears pour from your eyes as you behold the great calamity before you, for I cannot possibly bear the onerous burden of your support; who, then, will take pity upon you? Who will support you?

My dear father, how can you go from a new house to a primeval one, from a high mountain to a low valley, from an exalted dwelling to a most humble one, from a good habitation to a rotten one, from a fine abode to a somber warren, from a house of light to a dark domicile, from a mighty tower to the tents of nomads—but how!"

Then the entire family will raise its voice and cry out loud until their throats become scratchy: "Woe unto us on account of our great loss, and for this day of fury when the holy ark has departed from us." Then the entire community approaches and takes the body from its house as it lies there like a dried-out piece of wood. They carry the corpse to the cemetery as the family hovers around it like a gaggle of young birds until they reach the meadow of moaning. His wife is still screeching intensely: "It is so bitter for me on your account, my husband. For wherever they take you, there is certainly a great danger."

As they approach the cemetery, there appear before the deceased his relatives and friends whom he knew all of his life. They weep and declare: "Tell us, whom do you seek, and what do you hope to accomplish by letting yourself be buried in the ground? Remember who you are and whence you have come. Consider this: how can you descend from a house of kings and officers into these lowly graves; from an exalted position to the vicinity of vermin. Woe unto you, for once you sat in tranquility, but from this time forth you will dwell in fear and need, deep in the pit of destruction. Cursed be the earth that has opened its mouth and swallowed you in."

Moral

So consider, you son of man, by what right did you ever swagger upon the earth? Therefore, may you be cursed upon this earth, may thorns and thistles grow underneath you, and may they become as barbs in your eyes and prickles in your side. You thought that you were a wise man, and now look how you lie despondently, rusting and rotting away from your wounds and your pain, and from the pests and lice that tightly surround you all about. Oh, how you have become desolate, cloaked in dishonor and covered with shame. Ultimately, your flesh will succumb to vermin and insects, snakes and scorpions, which will beset you in triumphant throngs to the sounds of musical instruments and voices of song. These pests will penetrate into your guts and cultivate thorns inside your entrails.

Oh, how you—such a precious cache—have fallen into abject desolation! You, lowly man, have deluded yourself into falsely believing that you could soar above the tops of clouds, whereas in fact it was Sheol below that was awaiting you in order to bring your empty arrogance down to hell. Down below you will be enveloped by the insects, which will mass underneath you, and the vermin, which will cover you. How filled was your home with specially selected gold and silver; and now, how you have fallen from heaven, bright morning star; how you have been felled down to earth. You thought in your heart that you would rise to the heavens and establish your seat among the great Sages. But in fact you will be brought down into the inner pits of Sheol. How, then, could you ever have gloated in the material world and bragged of your wealth, wisdom, and bravery. You should have known all along that you were destined to rejoice, together with us, only after your burial.

NOTES

Preface

1. See my review of the recent popular literature on ultra-Orthodox Judaism, "Tremblers," in *Commentary*, August 1995, 56–59.

2. Literally, "tremblers," from Isaiah 66:5, "Listen to the word of God, all ye who *tremble* at his word." Throughout this book, translations from biblical and rabbinic texts are my own.

Introduction

1. Heinrich Graetz, *History of the Jews* (Philadelphia, 1941), 5:375.

2. Shimon Dubnow published many essays on the beginnings of the Hasidic movement in various Russian and Hebrew journals. He was also the first to publish primary documents regarding the rabbinic opposition to Hasidism. Finally, in 1931 he published the classic history of the Hasidic movement, *Toledoth ha-Hasiduth*. For a brief personal summary of the progression of his research on Hasidism see Dubnow's introduction to *Toledoth ha-Hasiduth*.

Gershom Scholem also published some of the earliest documents on the beginnings of Hasidism, as well as some trailblazing essays on the mystical theology of Hasidism. See *inter alia*, his essays in the journal *Tarbiz*, vols. 20–30, and the chapter on Beshtian Hasidism in his *Major Trends in Jewish Mysticism* (New York, 1961). Scholem's contemporary Isaiah Tishby, as well as his students at the Hebrew University in Jerusalem, most notably Joseph Weiss and Rivka Shatz, have also made major contributions to the in-depth analysis of various schools of Hasidic thought. See their works cited in the bibliography.

3. See esp. Shimon Dubnow, *Hasidiana (Kitvei Hithnagduth al Kath ha-Hasidim)* (St. Petersburg, 1918), which documents the earliest sources for the controversy and contains a general historical introduction and textual background.

4. Mordechai Wilensky, *Hasidim u-Mithnagdim: le-Toledoth ha-Pulmus Beynehem*, 2 vols. (Jerusalem, 1970). This anthology remains the most important work on Mithnagdism and the major source of primary material for its study. Nonetheless, it is limited in terms of the critical analysis of the sources. On the limitations of Wilen-

sky's work see the caustic and somewhat exaggerated critique by Abraham Rubinstein in *Kiryath Sefer* 47 (1971): 361–76.

5. A good, descriptive listing of the significant scholarship on Hasidism, as well as the comparably scant material available on the rabbinic thought of this period, can be found in G. Hundert and G. Bacon, eds., *The Jews of Russia and Poland: Bibliographical Essays* (Bloomington, 1984), 57–61, 135–37. In contrast, half a page (137) is devoted to the scholarship on rabbinism in this period. Of course, since this bibilography was compiled there have been many other very important studies of Hasidism. The most notable among the recent wealth of books on Hasidism are Rachel Elior, *The Paradoxical Ascent to God: The Kabbalistic Theosophy of Habad Hasidism* (New York, 1993); Morris Faierstein, *All Is in the Hands of Heaven* (New York, 1989); Roman Foxbrunner, *Habad: The Hasidism of R. Shneur Zalman of Lyady* (Tuscaloosa, Ala., 1992); Zeev Gries, *Sifruth ha-Hanhagoth: Toldoteha u-Mekomah be-Hayei Hasidei R. Yisrael Baal Shem Tov* (Jerusalem, 1989); Moshe Idel, *Hasidism: Between Ecstasy and Magic* (New York, 1995); Yoram Jacobson, *La pensée hassidique* (Paris, 1989), Naftali Loewenthal, *Communicating the Infinite: The Emergence of the Habad School* (Chicago, 1989); Mendel Piekarz, *Hasiduth Polin* (Jerusalem, 1990) and *Beyn Ideologia le-Metziyuth* (Jerusalem, 1994); and Bezalel Safran, ed., *Hasidism: Continuity or Innovation* (Cambridge, Mass, 1988). By contrast, in all this time nothing noteworthy has been published on Mithnagdism.

6. As this book was nearing completion, Elijah Judah Schochet published *The Hasidic Movement and the Gaon of Vilna,* which focuses primarily on the personal, religious, and ideological roots of the Gaon R. Elijah ben Solomon of Vilna's opposition to Hasidism. Another scholar who has recently turned his attention to the study of Mithnagdism is Jacob Hisdai. Both in his doctoral dissertation ("The Emergence of Hasidim and Mithnagdim in the light of the Homiletical Literature") and in some essays (most notably "Early Settlement of Hasidim and Mithnagdim," *Shalem* 4 [1984]: 231–69, and "The Origins of the Conflict between Hasidim and Mitnagdim," in Safran, *Hasidism,* 27–46), Hisdai is mistakenly persuaded that the social and religious differences dividing Hasidic and Mithnagdic rabbis and preachers were insignificant and that the true source of the opposition to Hasidism was the small elite circle of ascetic Mithnagdic mystics, the *perushim* (see this claim in Hisdai's article entitled "Eved ha-Shem," in *Zion* 47 [1982]: 253–92). As a result, he tends to refer to early, obscure rabbinic-mystical sources, which are not representative of any later, developed school of Mithnagdic thought and have no clear association with the school of the Gaon. Moreover, Hisdai fails entirely to grapple with the existence of the significant literature of systematic Mithnagdic religious thought, which is documented in this book.

7. See Moshe Idel, *Kabbalah: New Perspectives* (New Haven, 1988), and, most recently, *Hasidism: Between Magic and Ecstasy.* In the latter study, Idel, through painstaking comparative textual analysis, shows the ideational connections between early schools of Jewish mysticism and magic, on the one hand, and Hasidism. Idel's antihistoricist approach tends, however, to obscure the often shocking originality of

Hasidism's new interpretations and radical social applications of older Kabbalistic ideas, to which the Mithnagdim reacted so violently (see esp. Idel's assessment of "what is new in hasidism" in *Hasidism: Between Ecstasy and Magic* [New York, 1995], 209–15).

8. See Mendel Piekarz, *Biyemei Zemihath ha-Hasiduth* (Jerusalem, 1978) and *Beyn Ideologia Le-Metziyuth*.

9. Mendel Piekarz, *Beyn Ideologiya le-Mitziyuth*, 99 (quotation), 163–75.

10. See Gries, *Sifruth ha-Hanhagoth*.

11. On Hisdai's work see above, n. 6.

12. See Moshe Rosman, *Founder of Hasidism: A Quest for the Historical Baal Shem Tov* (Berkeley, 1996), 36–38.

13. Ibid., 39.

14. On R. Elijah of Vilna see H. H. Ben Sasson, "Ishiyutho Shel ha-GRA ve-Hashpa'ato ha-Hevratith," *Zion* 31 (1966): 39–86, 197–216. Schochet's new book on the Gaon of Vilna (see above, n. 6), by focusing primarily on the Gaon's negative reactions to Hasidism and ignoring the positive theology reflected in his writings as well as in those of his disciples and other Mithnagdim, suffers from the same essential limitation as the earlier scholarship.

On R. Hayyim of Volozhin see Norman Lamm, *Torah Lishmah* (Jerusalem, 1972); Immanuel Etkes, "Shitato U-Faalo Shel Rabbi Hayyim mi-Volozhin ki-Teguvath ha-Hevrah ha-Mithnagdith la-Hasiduth," *Proceedings of the American Academy for Jewish Religion* 38 (1972): 1–45; Jonah Ben Sasson, "Olamam ha-Ruhani u-Mishnatam ha-Hinukhith Shel Meyasdei ha-Yeshiva ha-Litaith," in *Hinukh ha-Adam ve-Yiudo* (Jerusalem, 1967), 155–67; and Shaul Stampfer, *Ha-Yeshiva ha-Litait be-Hithavuta* (Jerusalem, 1995), 25–31.

15. See, for example, the use of the term *hithnagduth* by Jonah Ben Sasson in his above-cited essay on R. Hayyim of Volozhin, "Olamam ha-Ruhani shel Meyasdei ha-Yeshiva ha-Litaith."

16. The tradition of publishing the thoughts and writings of the GRA has continued, to this day. Hardly a year passes in which there do not appear several volumes of material attributed to the GRA. Recently this literature has most often taken the form of anonymously edited anthologies culling from the existing printed material. Some examples of this enduring literary phenomenon are *Hidushei u-Viurei ha-GRA al Maseketh Shabbath u-Berakhoth*, ed. Abraham Drushkavitz (Kedainiai, 1940); *Sefer Likutay Ha-GRA*, ed. Samuel Kleinerman (Jerusalem, 1963); *Arbaah Sefarim Niftahim im Perushay Ha-GRA: Shir Ha-Shirm; Megillath Ruth; Megillath Esther; Pirkey Avoth* (Jerusalem, 1982); *Mi-Perushey Ha-GRA al Ha-Torah* (Jerusalem, 1986); *Oroth ha-GRA*, ed. Issachar Dov Rubin (Bnei Berak, 1986); and *Kuntres Hilkhoth Ha-Gra* (Jerusalem, 1987).

17. R. Hayyim's personal conduct also inspired later Mithnagdim to model their behavior on his. See, for example, the ritual handbook based on R. Hayyim's religious practices, *Kether Rosh: Orhoth Hayyim* (Volozhin, 1819), by his disciple R. Asher Ha-Kohen.

18. The text of the GRA's letter can be found in Wilensky, *Hasidim u-Mithnagdim,* 1:187–90.

19. For a stereotypical example of this negative image of the GRA in early Jewish historiography see the notorious essay by Shmuel Abba Horodetsky, "Ha-GRA veha-BESHT," *Ha-Shiloah* 17 (1907): 348–56. I described the controversy provoked among the leading eastern European Jewish intellectuals and historians by Horodetsky's critique of the GRA and his romanticization of the BESHT in my monograph *Rationalism, Romanticism, Rabbis, and Rebbes* (New York, 1992). For an interesting and detailed evaluation of Horodetsky's ascription of progressive, feminist tendencies to Hasidism see Ada Rapoport-Albert, "On Women in Hasidism: S. A. Horodetsky and the Maid of Ludmir Tradition," in *Jewish History: Essays in Honour of Chimen Abramsky,* ed. Ada Rapoport-Albert and Steven Zipperstein (London, 1988), 495–528.

20. See Lamm, *Torah Lishmah,* 9–25. In 1989 Lamm's book appeared in a slightly amplified English version, *Torah Lishmah: Torah for Torah's Sake,* published in New York; references in the present book are to the original Hebrew version. See also Lamm's essay "The Phase of Dialogue and Reconciliation," in *Hasidic Mithnagdic Polemics* (New York, 1975), where he makes a strong argument for his view that R. Hayyim was a moderate rather than a true Mithnagged.

21. See Immanuel Etkes, "Review of N. Lamm's Torah Lishmah" (Hebrew), *Kiryath Sefer* 50 (1975): 638–48; and Isaiah Tishby, "Kitrugo shel R. Yisrael mi-Shklov al ha-Hasidim," ibid., 51 (1976): 300–303. Using the example of R. Israel of Shklov's anti-Hasidic polemic, Tishby argues that the intensity of the hostility against Hasidism was bequeathed to the next generation of the disciples of the GRA.

22. See Piekarz, *Beyn Ideologia Le-Mitziyuth,* 101–2, where the author points to striking parallels between the thought of R. Hayyim and that of his religious nemesis, the founder of the Ḥabad school of Hasidism, R. Shneur Zalman of Lyadi.

23. Stampfer, *Ha-Yeshiva ha-Litait be Hithavuta,* 31–36.

24. R. Hayyim of Volozhin (1749–1821) was of course the most noted of the GRA's disciples and author of the classic work *Nefesh ha-Hayyim.* There are many studies of his life and thought, most notably those by Norman Lamm and Immanuel Etkes, referred to above in n. 14.

R. Abraham ben Elijah (1750–1808), the most prolific of the GRA's sons, was the author of several works, the most important being his commentary to Psalms, *Beer Avraham.* He seems to have been a close associate and friend of Phinehas, as he presubscribed to the only two of Phinehas's works for which he solicited advance support, *Siddur Shaar ha-Rahamim* and the commentary to Psalms, *Shevet mi-Yehuda.*

Abraham Danzig (1747–1820) was a close associate of both the GRA and R. Hayyim of Volozhin. Besides his many famous Halakhic codes, which include *Hayyei Adam: Nishmath Adam* (Vilna, 1810) and *Hokhmath Adam: Binath Adam* (Vilna, 1814), Danzig was also the author of an important ethical will *Beth Avraham* (Vilna, 1821), which contains a wealth of important material regarding his personal religious philosophy and will be consulted extensively in this study. On Danzig's most popular work, *Hayyei Adam*, see the fine bibliographical essay by A. Y. Goldrath, "Al ha-Sefer *Hayyei Adam* u-Mehabro," *Sefer Margaliyoth*, ed. Y. Raphael (Jerusalem, 1973), 270–93.

R. Ezekiel Faivel (1755–1833) was a maggid in Dretzhyn, Lithuania, and later in Vilna, in the first half of the nineteenth century. He is the author of two works: the biography of R. Zalman of Volozhin, *Toledoth Adam*, and a commentary to part of the first book of Maimonides' Code, *Musar Haskel*. A hitherto neglected figure, Ezekiel Faivel has recently gained the attention of Immanuel Etkes, who has described *Toledoth Adam* as a protomodern form of biographical writing (see Immanuel Etkes, "Immanent Factors and External Influences in the Development of the Haskala Movement in Russia," in *Toward Modernity: The European Jewish Model*, ed. J. Katz [New Brunswick, 1987], 17–20). On the writings of Ezekiel Faivel see the bibliographical essay by Shraga Abramson, "Defusei *Musar Haskel* ve-*Toledoth Adam* le-Rabi Yehezkel Faivel," in Raphael, *Sefer Margaliyoth*, 189–232.

Hillel of Kovno (d. 1830) was a rabbi and maggid in the Lithuanian town of Ratsci and the author of *Heilel Ben Shahar* (Warsaw, 1804), which, as its title suggests (taken as it is from *Isaiah* 14:12, on the fall of the haughty), is a compendium of deeply pessimistic sermons pervaded by a sense of national exile and decline as well as personal religious limitation and alienation. A eulogy of the GRA appears in the back of Hillel's book. Weary of the depressions of exile, R. Hillel joined with the group of prominent disciples of the GRA and emigrated to Israel in 1806. According to a document signed by him in the spring of 1810, R. Hillel had become a leading member of the Mithnagdic *kolel* of Safed in the Galilee. For more information on R. Hillel see A. Morgenstern, *Meshihiyuth ve-Yishuv Eretz Yisrael* (Jerusalem, 1985), chaps. 3–4.

Benjamin Rivlin (d. 1812) was both an important disciple of the GRA and a remarkably "modern" thinker. On his life see S. J. Fuenn, *Kiryah Ne'emana* (Vilna, 1915), 271–73; on Rivlin as both a Mithnagged and a proto-Maskil see David Fishman, *Russia's First Modern Jews: The Jews of Shklov* (New York, 1995), 102–12.

Menahem Mendel (d. 1827) was the most important Kabbalist among the disciples of the GRA. According to his own testimony, he spent twenty months studying Kabbalah closely with his master. Furthermore, he personally transcribed, from oral dictation, the GRA's most important ethical work, the commentary to Proverbs, and also edited and published the following of the GRA's posthumously published writings: *Biur ha-GRA al Shulhan Arukh*; *Biur ha-GRA al Masekheth Avoth*; *Perush ha-GRA al Haggadah Shel Pesah*; *Zurath ha-Bayith*; and *Tavnith ha-Bayith*. While in Lithuania, R. Menahem Mendel instructed others in the GRA's Kabbalistic teachings. His most notable student was R. Yitzhaq Isaac Haber. In 1808 Menahem Mendel left Lithuania for Israel, where he established the study of the Kabbalah among the Mithnagdim there. His most significant original mystical work was the commentary to *Idra Raba*, *Mayyim Adirim*. No separate study of this most important Mithnagdic Kabbalist exists. For some details on his life and works see A. L. Frumkin, *Toledoth*

Hakhmei Yerushalayim, vol. 3 (Jerusalem, 1928), passim; Yitzhaq Raphael, "Le-Toledoth ha-Kehilla ha-Ashkenazith be-Eretz Yisrael," *Sinai* 5 (1942): 73ff.; and Wilensky, *Hasidim u-Mithnagdim,* 1:314–15.

Jacob Kranz (1740–1804), known popularly as the Maggid of Dubnow, was a friend of the GRA. His famously rich moral parables have been published in many different forms, most commonly as commentaries to books of the Bible. The work most frequently cited here is Kranz's most systematic book, the ethical guide *Sefer ha-Middoth,* which was edited and published by his disciple Abraham Flahm in 1959. On R. Jacob Kranz generally see the informative but lamentably uncritical biography by Herman A. Glatt, *He Spoke in Parables: The Life and Works of the Dubno Maggid* (New York, 1957). The bibliography to Glatt's book includes a full listing of Kranz's published works.

For a full discussion of Meir ben Elijah see my article "Meir b. Elijah of Vilna's *Milhamoth Adonai:* A Late anti-Hasidic Polemic," *Journal of Jewish Thought and Philosophy* 1 (1991): 247–80.

25. On Rabbi Israel of Polotsk see Haya Stiman-Katz, *Reyshitan Shel Aliyoth Hasidim* (Jerusalem, 1987), 20–21, 97–100.

26. See David Fishman, "Dominance of Hasidism in the Polotsk Province," in his recent study, *Russia's First Modern Jews,* 15–18. See also *Sefer Vitebsk* (Tel Aviv, 1957), 206, which describes the Vitebsk area (including Polotsk) as a "center of hasidism" and a focal point of the Hasidic-Mithnagdic controversy.

27. Etkes cites *Kether Torah* extensively to underscore the extent to which Hasidism was making inroads in eastern Europe at the end of the eighteenth century in "Shitato U-Faalo Shel Rabbi Hayyim mi-Volozhin."

28. A descriptive catalogue of Phinehas's published works is provided below, in appendix A.

29. Phinehas's close relationship with the GRA is documented in detail below, in appendix A.

Chapter 1: The Immanence of God in Mithnagdic Thought

1. The full Hebrew text of the Vilna epistle of the GRA can be found in Mordechai Wilensky, *Hasidim u-Mithnagdim: le-Toledoth ha-Pulmus Beynehem,* 2 vols. (Jerusalem, 1970), 1:187–90.

2. Ibid., 187–88.

3. See Elijah Judah Schochet, *The Hasidic Movement and the Gaon of Vilna* (Northvale, 1994), 61–66; and Immanuel Etkes, "Ha-GRA ve-Reyshith ha-Hithnagduth la Hasiduth," in *Temuroth Ba-Historiya ha-Yehudith ha-Hadasha: Kovets Maamarim Shai le-Shmuel Ettinger* (Jerusalem, 1987), 439–58.

4. *Tzava'ath ha-Rivash* (reprint, Jerusalem, 1965), 23. On the theory of divine immanence in the early rabbinic tradition see Joshua Abelson, *The Immanence of God in Rabbinic Literature* (London, 1912). In the Talmud the fullest discussion of this

belief is to be found in tractate *Berakhoth*, 10a. An excellent evaluation of a contro-versy regarding suspected pantheistic heresy in Jewish thought just one generation before the rise of the Hasidic movement can be found in Jacob J. Petuchowski, *The Theology of Hakhan David Nieto: An Eighteenth Century Defense of the Jewish Tradition* (New York, 1954).

As the above-cited quotation from the traditions attributed to the BESHT makes clear, the focus upon divine immanence was an important part of Hasidic doctrine from the beginnings of the movement. But it was in the third-generation sect of Ḥabad that the belief in divine immanence found its most radical expression, at times denying the created universe any ontological reality. This mystical acosmism is a central doctrine in the writings of the founder of Ḥabad Hasidism, R. Shneur Zalman of Lyaḍi (note esp. the "Kuntres Aharon" of his *Likutei Amarim: Tanya*), and, to an even greater extent, in his disciple R. Aaron of Starosselje's *Shaarei ha-Yihud veha-Emuna*, which focuses on the doctrine of God's immanence. On Ḥabad's radical immanentism see Rivka Shatz, "Anti-spiritualism ba-Hasiduth," *Molad* 171 (1962): 513–28; idem, *Ha-Hasiduth ke-Mistika* (Jerusalem, 1968), chap. 2; and Rachel Elior, *Torath ha-Elohuth be-Dor ha-Sheyni Shel Hasiduth Habad* (Jerusalem, 1982), chaps. 2 and 3. Despite its centrality in classical Hasidic thought, to date there has been no comprehensive study of the nature and history of the doctrine of divine immanence in Hasidism.

5. R. Shneur Zalman of Lyadi, "Shaar Ha-Yihud veha-Emuna," in *Likutei Amarim: Tanya* (reprint, Brooklyn, 1964), chap. 7, 152–54. The teachings of R. Shneur Zalman are literally saturated with similar statements. See his *Torah Or* (reprint, Brooklyn, 1986), 34, 44, for particularly strong formulations of this doctrine.

6. On Ḥabad's commitment to spreading the mystical faith in God's immanence to the widest possible audience see Naftali Lowenthal, *Communicating the Infinite: The Emergence of the Habad School* (Chicago, 1989).

7. A concise review of the various interpretations of the concept of *zimzum* in the history of Kabbalistic thought can be found in G. Scholem, "Kabbalah," *Encyclopedia Judaica*, 1975, 10:588–93. On the figurative recasting of this doctrine in Hasidic thought see Shatz, *Ha-Hasiduth ke-Mystica*, 121–30, esp. 127.

8. This is the conventional understanding of the Ḥabad school's reinterpretation of *zimzum* advanced by Teitelbaum, Scholem, Shatz, and Elior. On the Ḥabad under-standing of *zimzum* see, most recently, Rachel Elior, *The Paradoxical Ascent to God: The Kabbalistic Theosophy of Habad Hasidism* (New York, 1992), 79–91. It should be noted that not all scholars agree that R. Shneur Zalman completely abandoned the literal belief in the contraction of the highest realm of the Godhead (i.e., the *Eyn Sof*) into itself. An interesting dissenting view of R. Shneur Zalman's interpretation of *zimzum* is that of Amos Funkenstein, "Imitatio Dei u-Musag ha-Zimzum be-Mish-nath Habad," in *Raphael Mahler Festschrift* (Tel Aviv, 1974), 83–88.

9. D. Z. Hilman, *Iggeroth Baal ha-Tanya u-Venei Doro* (Jerusalem, 1953), 97; the full text of the letter is on 95–98. See also A. S. Heilman, *Beth Rabi* (Berditchev, 1903), 40–44.

10. Heilman, *Beth Rabi,* 40.

11. See M. Teitelbaum, *Ha-Rav mi-Ladi u-Miflegeth Habad* (Warsaw, 1912), pt. 2, chap. 3, esp. 87–94.

12. Dresner, accepting the above-cited Ḥabad documents at face value, concludes on the basis of Rabbi Shneur Zalman's letter: "The essence of the disagreement with the Gaon was not only social or Halakhic, but theological" (see Samuel Dresner, "Hasidism and Its Opponents," in *Great Schisms in Jewish History,* ed. Raphael Jospe and Stanley Wagner [New York, 1981], 146).

13. Ibid.

14. Schochet, *The Hasidic Movement and the Gaon of Vilna,* 63–64. Schochet's understanding of the GRA's position on divine immanence is based almost entirely on the Hasidic sources. Rather than looking closely at the writings of the GRA and his disciples in order to ascertain the Mithnagdic view, he relies on R. Shneur Zalman of Lyadi as an "undeniably knowledgeable source" regarding "the GRA's vehement feelings on the subject."

15. Elijah ben Solomon, Gaon of Vilna, *Adereth Eliyahu al Neviim u-Khetuvim* (reprint, Tel Aviv, 1962), 45.

16. Elijah ben Solomon, Gaon of Vilna, *Safra de-Zeniutha im Perush ha-GRA* (Vilna and Grodno, 1820), fol. 38a.

17. *Biur ha-GRA le-Sefer ha-Zohar,* "Parshath Bo," 41b, emphasis added. "That which is beyond you" is a reference to the Talmudic discussion of restrictions of study related to esoteric mystical matters in tractate *Hagiga,* chap. 2; the citation is actually from the apocryphal *Wisdom of Ben Sirah* 3:21.

18. A very clear and concise presentation of Ḥabad's call upon man to break through the epistemological barriers of his physical sense perceptions and the limitations of the material universe via the dialectical (or perhaps better, paradoxical) denial of all physical reality *(bitul ha-yesh)* and the simultaneous service of God in and through that very physical reality *(avodah be-gashmiyouth)* can be found in Rachel Elior, "Mekomo Shel ha-Adam ba-Avodath ha-Shem ha-Habadith," *Daat,* no. 12 (1984): 47–55.

19. There is an extensive scholarly literature comparing and contrasting the respective attempts of R. Shneur Zalman and R. Hayyim of Volozhin to harmonize the dialectically opposed notions of God's transcendence and His immanence. Since this is not the final object of our own inquiry, I will simply list and briefly summarize these various scholarly treatments:

• M. Teitelbaum, in his *Ha-Rav mi-Ladi u-Miflegeth Habad,* suggests that the differences between these two men are largely semantic and terminological and that they essentially agree about concrete theological doctrine.

• W. Wurzberger, "Rabbi Hayyim of Volozhin," in *Guardians of Our Heritage,* ed. Leo Jung (New York, 1958), 202–5, argues that for R. Hayyim *zimzum* represents the actual self-limitation by a transcendent God on himself, whereas for R. Shneur Zalman it refers to the necessary self-concealment of an immanent God to allow for creation.

• Norman Lamm, *Torah Lishmah* (Jerusalem, 1972), 71–72, follows Wurzberger's line, explaining that in R. Hayyim's view it is from God's own perspective that he is transcendent, while from the perspective of man he is immanent. *Zimzum* qualifies both of these absolute perspectives.

• Tamar Ross, "Two Interpretations of the Theory of Tzimtzum: Rabbi Hayyim of Volozhin and Rabbi Shneur Zalman of Ladi," *Mehkarei Yerushalayim be-Mahsheveth Yisrael* 2 (1982): 153–69, provides an in-depth analysis of the cosmological theories of both these rabbis and indicates (very accurately in my view) that although there may be minor differences in the fine theoretical details, the primary distinctions dividing them are really of a psychological or epistemological nature. While they perceive essentially the same absolute ontological reality of divine immanence, they differ fundamentally with regard to the conception of God and the awareness of the divine presence they expect man to attain. Ross differs significantly from Lamm in his interpretation of the meanings of the key terms in this matter, *sovev kol almin* and *memaleh kol almin*. See Lamm's response to Ross's criticisms in the English version of his book, *Torah Lishmah: Torah for Torah's Sake* (New York, 1989), 99 n. 139.

• See also M. Pachter, "Sod ha-zimzum be-Shitath Ramhal uve-Ikvoth Hashapa'atho be-Mishnatha shel ha-Mithnagduth" (paper presented to the Harvard University Conference on Jewish Thought in the Eighteenth Century, Cambridge, 1978), 13–22.

• Cf. Rachel Elior's treatment of this issue in *Torath ha-Elohuth be-Dor ha-Sheyni Shel Hasiduth Habad*, 61–64.

20. See Teitelbaum, *Ha-Rav mi-Ladi u-Miflegeth Habad*. See also Lamm, *Torah Lishmah,* 60; and Mendel Piekarz, *Beyn Ideologia le-Mitziyuth* (Jerusalem, 1994), 101–2.

21. In his recent book on the Jews of Shklov, *Russia's First Modern Jews: The Jews of Shklov* (New York, 1995), David Fishman argues compellingly that the Vitebsk province *(gubernia)* was politically controlled by the Hasidim and that the official rabbinic court of this region was made up of Hasidic rabbis. Indeed, Rabbis Shneur Zalman of Lyadi, Menahem Mendel of Vitebsk, Hayyim Haikel of Amdur, and Israel of Polotsk all flourished in this region of Belorussia at the end of the eighteenth century. In the next generation, the most radical Hasidic acosmist, R. Aaron Halevi of Starosselje, flourished and published his writings in the same region. In fact, his works were published in Shklov, formerly the bastion of Mithnagdism, in 1820–21. Following his death, his doctrines continued to be popular with the Hasidic rabbis of Belorussia. For example, R. Menahem Mendel of Polotsk and R. Yitzhaq Aizik of Vitebsk wrote approbations to R. Aaron's posthumously published *Avodath ha-Levi al ha-Torah,* a work whose dominant theological theme is precisely this radical divine immanentism.

22. Phinehas b. Judah, Maggid of Polotsk, *Kether Torah* (Jerusalem, 1965), 34a.

23. Phinehas b. Judah, Maggid of Polotsk, *Siddur Shaar ha-Rahamim in Perush Maggid Zedek* (Shklov, 1788), 1:2a. Compare the use of the same analogy by R. Shneur Zalman in *Likutei Amarim: Tanya*, "Shaar ha-Yihud veha-Emuna," chap. 3.

24. Phinehas, *Kether Torah*, 35a.

25. An extensive analysis of R. Phinehas's ambivalent attitude toward the wisdom and the study of the Kabbalah is found in chapter 2, below.

26. Phinehas b. Judah, Maggid of Polotsk, *Shevet mi-Yehuda* (Vilna, 1803), 16:33.

27. Of course not all Hasidic leaders accepted the Ḥabad approach. The best-known Hasidic critic of Ḥabad's attempt to propagate mystical knowledge to the masses of Jewry was R. Abraham of Kalisk, who shared much of the apprehension of the early Mithnagdim. In R. Abraham's view, the goal of Hasidism was to promote and instill simple faith and piety *(emunah peshuta)* rather than profound mystical insight. The sources for the contention between R. Shneur Zalman and R. Abraham of Kalisk are found in Jacob Barnai, *Iggeroth Hasidim mi-Eretz Yisrael* (Jerusalem, 1980), 211–87. R. Abraham's resistance to Ḥabad's intellectualism and activist pedagogic approach to mystical faith was maintained by his disciple R. Mordechai of Lechovitch and found continuous expression in the traditions of the Lithuanian Hasidic schools of Lechovitch and Slonim. On this school of Hasidism and its affinities with many aspects of Mithnagdic thought see R. Shalom Noach Berezovsky, "Al Pi ha-Be'er," introduction to *Be'er Avraham,* by R. Abraham of Slonim (reprint, Jerusalem, 1985).

28. Phinehas, *Siddur Shaar ha-Rahamim,* 1:6a.

29. Ibid., 1:6b. The reference by Phinehas to Deuteronomy 32:47 seems to assume an awareness of the rabbinic interpretation of that verse, which instructs that all of the obscurities of the Torah are due solely to the inherent limitations of the human intellect and are not the consequence of any deficiency in the Torah itself (see Jerusalem Talmud, *Peah,* 1:1: "'For it is not a vain thing from you'—and if it is vain, it is from you," that is, it is on account of your own imperfections and limitations). Similarly, Phinehas seems to be saying that God's immanence remains concealed from human perception only because of man's innate intellectual and spiritual limitations.

30. Phinehas, *Siddur Shaar ha-Rahamim,* 1:25b. Note the statement which follows almost immediately: "This teaches that God is removed from all of the created worlds insofar as the apprehension of the truth of His essence and glory are concerned. Nonetheless, 'the earth is filled with His glory,' insofar as his actions and wondrous deeds that are evident and manifest in this world are concerned. This is precisely the line taken by the GRA—namely, that there is a crucial distinction between God in essence, Who is truly immanent but transcendent from human perception, and God in manifestation, Who can be appreciated by man insofar as his deeds and creations on earth are concerned."

31. See the sources cited in nn. 12 and 14, above.

32. Hayyim of Volozhin, *Nefesh ha-Hayyim* (Vilna and Grodno, 1824), 3:5. See the

extensive treatment of this issue by Norman Lamm in *Torah Lishmah*, esp. 69–73. R. Hayyim and R. Phinehas furnish strikingly similar interpretations of the use of the descriptive term *kadosh* in referring to the nature of God's presence on earth. Cf. Phinehas, *Siddur Shaar ha-Rahamim*, 1:4b, 25b.

33. There are two book-length studies of the theology of Rabbi Aaron of Starosselje: Louis Jacobs, *Seeker of Unity* (London, 1966) (on divine immanence versus transcendence see esp. chaps. 4 and 5); and Elior, *Torath ha-Elohuth be-Dor ha-Sheyni Shel Hasiduth Habad.*

34. Hayyim, *Nefesh ha-Hayyim*, 3:3. In striking contrast to this Mithnagdic conservatism and didactic caution, R. Shneur Zalman and his disciples affirmed that man's central religious goal was to attain precisely the kind of spiritual understanding that R. Hayyim deemed so dangerous. Louis Jacobs described the Hasidic position as follows: "The task of man in life is to pierce the veils by which the Divine light is screened. By means of profound meditation and contemplation on the truth that all is in God, man loses himself completely in the divine 'nothingness.' He becomes aware of the truth that there is, in reality, nothing but God" (*Seeker of Unity*, 67).

35. Hence the emphasis in the *herem* upon the public and popular nature of the Hasidic preaching ("working out their evil schemes with the masses," etc.) and the reference to the biblical Aaron's proclamation of the golden calf as the God of Israel to the Israelite masses in the Sinai wilderness. According to the standard rabbinic interpretation of that event, Aaron knew full well that the calf was not a deity. He perverted true belief simply for the sake of popular support and in order to appease the ignorant masses. So too, it is implied, the Hasidic leaders, while perhaps themselves in possession of ultimate religious truths, have popularized and perverted genuine belief in God in the course of trying to spread it among the untutored and ill-prepared masses of the Jewish people.

36. See esp. Louis Jacob, introduction to *On Ecstasy—A Tract by Dobh Baer of Lubavitch* (Chappaqua, 1963), 6–10. In the next generation, R. Menahem Mendel Schneerson encouraged his followers to focus constantly upon the divine presence, which suffuses all of creation (see "Mitzvath Ahduth ha-Shem," in his *Sefer Derekh Mitzvotekha* [Poltava, 1911], 118–24).

37. Asher Ha-Kohen of Tiktin, *Birkhath Rosh* (reprint, Jerusalem, 1971), 6a.

38. On R. Meir ben Elijah, see my article "Meir b. Elijah of Vilna's *Milhamoth Adonai*: A Late Anti-Hasidic Polemic," *Journal of Jewish Thought and Philosophy* 1 (1991): 247–80.

39. Meir ben Elijah, *Milhamoth Adonai*, Hebrew University and National Library, Jerusalem, MS 801067, 7a–7b. See the similar remarks, on the primarily didactic necessity of maintaining the reality of *zimzum* from the perspective of man, by R. Yitzhaq Isaac Haber in his commentary to Abraham ben Solomon of Vilna's *Maaloth ha-Torah, Amudei ha-Torah: Or Torah* (Jerusalem, 1880), 26b.

40. See Gershom Scholem, *Major Trends in Jewish Mysticism* (New York, 1961), 340–41.

41. Ibid., 341.

Chapter 2: The Mithnagdim and the Kabbalah

1. R. Solomon ben Moses of Chelm (d. 1778) was a Polish rabbinic scholar, rationalist, grammarian, and mathematician who was deeply influenced by the writings of Maimonides. In addition to his commentary to Maimonides' code, *Merkeveth Ha-Mishna*, R. Solomon composed Talmudic novellae, mathematical treatises, and geographical studies. His primary didactic goal in the very important introduction to the *Merkeveth Ha-Mishna* seems to have been the promotion of a rigidly intellectualistic approach to Judaism according to which rabbinic study was its highest ideal. This concern led him to oppose not only Hasidism and mysticism but also the "pilpulist" approach to the study of Talmudic literature. In this limited sense he can be regarded as a forerunner of the later Mithnagdim.

2. Solomon ben Moses of Chelm, introduction to *Merkeveth Ha-Mishna* (reprint, Brooklyn, 1948), 6. R. Solomon of Chelm refers to R. Jair Hayyim Baharach's lengthy responsum regarding the contemporary legitimacy of the study of the Kabbalah (see *Havoth Jair* [Frankfurt, 1699], no. 210). Many of Baharach's early fears were later echoed by the Mithnagdim. The phrase "roaring like a lion" might well be an allusion to the title of the most famous Renaissance critique of the Kabbalah, Aryeh Loeb of Modena's (1571–1648) *Ari Nohem* (Leipzig, 1840), in which the sanctity and authenticity of the *Zohar* are critically scrutinized.

3. See however, the lengthy discussion of the introduction to *Merkeveth ha-Mishna* by Mendel Piekarz, in *Biyemei Zemihath ha-Hasiduth* (Jerusalem, 1978), chap. 8, esp. pp. 320–38, on the study of the Kabbalah). In keeping with his general tendency to minimize the originality and radicalism of early Hasidism, Piekarz insists that R. Slomon of Chelm's polemic should not necessarily be understood as being directed at the Hasidim. Nonetheless, a careful look at R. Solomon's rhetoric compels me to believe that he was responding directly and unequivocally to the deviations of the Hasidic movement.

4. Piekarz, *Biyemei Zemihath ha-Hasiduth*, 6–7.

5. Mordechai Wilensky, *Hasidim u-Mithnagdim: le-Toledoth ha-Pulmus Beynehem*, 2 vols. (Jerusalem, 1970), 1:51. Earlier in the very same epistle the Hasidim are described as being interested exclusively in mystical matters, at the expense not only of conventional rabbinic learning and Halakhic practice but also of Jewish communal unity: "They separate themselves from the community, refusing to take hold of either the oral or the revealed Torah . . . for they are only concerned with the hidden Torah" (1:50).

6. See ibid., 2:141–43.

7. David of Makow, *Shever Poshim,* in ibid., 2:164.

8. See the similar critique in David of Makow's ethical will, where he repeats the accusation that despite their concerted efforts to attain high levels of Lurianic scholarship and mystical practice, the Hasidim remained ignorant of its basic texts and fundamental teachings (see Wilensky, *Hasidim u-Mithnagdim*, 2:244–45).

9. Ibid., 2:84–85.

10. This is an unusual and important listing that reflects an awareness on the part of its author that his own contention with the Hasidic interest in mysticism is just the latest recurrence of the oft-repeated struggle in Jewish intellectual history against the popularization of religious esoterica. The list includes the conservative rabbinic reactions to many different historical manifestations of mystical interests on the part of a wide array of Jewish thinkers. It therefore includes references to those authorities who were against the popularization of Kabbalistic study, those who specifically objected to the employment of Kabbalistic sources in Halakhic adjudication, and those who feared "applied Kabbala" *(kabbala ma'asith)* or the widespread aspiration to ecstatic mystical experiences.

On the controversy concerning the use of Kabbalistic sources in Halakhah see Jacob Katz, "Yahasei Halakha ve-Kabala," *Daat,* no. 4 (1976): 57–74. Regarding the earlier rabbinic opposition to the popular study of the Kabbalah see Rachel Elior, "Ha-Maavak al Maamada Shel ha-Kabala ba-Meah ha–16," *Mehkarei Yerushalayim Be-Mahsheveth Yisrael* 1 (1981): 177–90. For a survey of critical rabbinic and Hasidic views on the state of Kabbalistic knowledge in the eighteenth century see part 1 of Moshe Idel, "Perceptions of Kabbalah in the Second Half of the Eighteenth Century," *Journal of Jewish Thought and Philosophy* 1, no. 1 (1991): 55–61. On the suppression and decline of Lurianic Kabbalah in particular see idem, *Hasidism: Between Ecstasy and Magic* (New York, 1995), 33–43.

11. See Eliezer Fishel of Stychov, *Olam Gadol: Midrash la-Perushim* (Zolkiewka, 1800), introduction. An excerpt from this text can be found in Eliezer Zweiffel, *Shalom Al Yisrael,* 2 vols. (Zhitomir, 1868), 1:84–85.

12. See Gershom Scholem, *Major Trends in Jewish Mysticism* (New York, 1961), chap. 8; and idem, "The Neutralization of the Messianic Element in Early Hasidism," in *The Messianic Idea in Judaism* (New York, 1995), 176–202.

13. This generalization is based on comments made by Professor Moshe Idel in 1986. On these two general trends in medieval Jewish mysticism see Moshe Idel, *Kabbalah: New Perspectives* (New Haven, 1988), xi–xx. See also Idel's more recent and more detailed work on the mystical and magical components of classical Hasidism in *Hasidism: Between Ecstasy and Magic.*

14. A recent study of the first generations of the Ḥabad movement, Naftali Loewenthal's *Communicating the Infinite: The Emergence of the Habad School* (Chicago, 1989), is almost entirely devoted to tracing the expansive course of this Hasidic group's communication and "translation" (i.e., popularization) of Kabbalistic theurgy to ever-widening sectors of Jewish society.

15. The writings of R. Barukh of Kossov are *Yesod ha-Emunah* (Tchernowitz, 1863) and *Amud ha-Avodah* (Tchernowitz, 1863). There is great irony in the fact that although his explicit objective was to spread the wisdom of the Kabbalah to the masses of Israel, the works of R. Barukh of Kossov were not published until more than a half-century after his death. On the writings of R. Barukh of Kossov and their

significance see Piekarz, *Biyemei Zemihath ha-Hasiduth,* 55–57; and A. J. Heschel, *The Circle of the Baal Shem Tov: Studies in Hasidism* (Hebrew), ed. S. Dresner (Chicago, 1985), 114 n. 6.

16. R. Barukh of Kossov, *Amud ha-Avodah,* 1a.

17. Ibid., 1c.

18. Ibid., 1b–1c.

19. On the Sabbatean abuse of Lurianic *kavanoth* (mystical-theurgic techniques) in advancing its heresies see Y. Liebes, "Yahaso shel Shabtai Zevi le-Hamarath Datho," *Sefunoth,* n.s., 2 (1983); cf. idem, "Shabbetai Zevi's Religious Faith," in *Studies in Jewish Myth and Jewish Messianism* (Albany, 1993), 107–14.

20. The full text of the first *herem* of Brody, from which this citation is excerpted, can be found in Y. Heilprin, ed., *Pinkas Va'ad Arba Aratzoth* (Jerusalem, 1945), 418. For a helpful review of the rabbinic attempts to limit Kabbalistic study see Moshe Idel, "On the History of the Interdiction against the Study of Kabbalah before the Age of Forty" (Hebrew) *Association for Jewish Studies Review* 5 (1980): 1–9.

21. See N. M. Gelber, *Toledoth Yehudai Brodie,* vol. 6 of *Arim ve-Imahoth be-Yisrael,* ed. Y. L. Maimon (Jerusalem, 1955), 112.

22. R. Joseph Steinhartz in fact draws no distinction between the antinomian behavior of the Sabbateans and later Hasidic religious deviations. Although both Gershom Scholem and Isaiah Tishby have pointed to extensive historical and ideological connections between the early Hasidim and the Sabbateans, current scholarship is divided on the nature of the relationship between the two movements. For a recent evaluation of this complex issue see Y. Liebes, "Hadashoth le-Inyan ha-Besht ve-Shabbetai Zevi," in *Mehkarei Yerushalayim Be-Mahsheveth Yisrael* 2, no. 4 (1982): 564–69. See also idem, "Ha-Tikun ha-Kelali shel Rabi Nahman mi-Brazlav," *Zion* 45 (1980): 201–45.

23. On the impact of the Sabbatean fiasco on the attitude of eighteenth-century rabbis towards Kabbalah in general see Piekarz, *Biyemei Zemihath ha-Hasiduth,* 336–38.

24. An examination of the writings of the mid-nineteenth-century dean of the Volozhin yeshiva, Naftali Zevi Yehudah Berlin (NeTZIV), particularly his commentary to the Torah, *Ha'amek Davar,* provides a good illustration of the declining interest in and inquiry into Kabbalistic texts. Berlin's expansive commentary on the entire Pentateuch includes almost no references to any Kabbalistic sources.

An even more dramatic example of the decline in the status of Kabbalah in Lithuanian rabbinic circles is the case of the founder of the revivalist *musar* movement, R. Israel Salanter. According to one of his biographers, R. Salanter was blissfully ignorant of all matters pertaining to the Kabbalah (see Immanuel Etkes, *Rabbi Israel Salanter ve-Reyshitah shel Tenuath ha-Mussar* [Jerusalem, 1982], 102–3). Although the other contemporary biographer of R. Salanter, Hillel Goldberg, differs with Etkes regarding the extent of the rabbi's personal knowledge of the Kabbalah, he too concedes that R. Israel was not at all interested in teaching Kabbalah to his followers and students. In fact, according to Goldberg, R. Salanter discouraged his disciples from trying their hands at mystical study, believing—like the early Mithnagdim—that its secrets were simply beyond the grasp of the contemporary human intellect (see Goldberg's *Israel Salanter: Text, Structure, Idea* [New York, 1982], 209–19). As Goldberg concludes, "The statement in the name of R. Israel, the negation of Kabbala, and the stress on reward and punishment tersely encapsulate this message—Don't overreach yourself!" (212). As we shall see throughout our study of Mithnagdic thought, the advice against trying to overreach oneself in all matters of religion is the central feature of the Mithnagdic religious mentality. Thus, R. Israel Salanter's reticence regarding the Kabbalah is the clear and consistent continuation of the traditional Mithnagdic posture.

25. There is an abundance of hagiographic praise of the Gaon's mastery of the Kabbalah. All of his students pay tribute to his legendary erudition in the *Zohar, Tikkunim,* and the writings of R. Isaac Luria. These many glowing tributes have been uncritically but very comprehensively gathered and documented by Bezalel Landau in his biography of the GRA, *Ha-Gaon ha-Hasid mi-Vilna* (Jerusalem, 1978), chap. 11, esp. pp. 133–36 and nn. 1–15; see also Landau's addenda on 361–62. A more detailed and scholarly assessment of the GRA's approach to Kabbalah is Alan Brill, "The Mystical Path of the Vilna Gaon," in *The Journal of Jewish Thought and Philosophy* (forthcoming, 1997).

26. Elijah Judah Schochet, *The Hasidic Movement and the Gaon of Vilna* (Northvale, N.J., 1994), 149.

27. See A. L. Frumkin, *Toledoth Hakhmei Yerushalayim,* 3:158. For biographical information regarding R. Menahem Mendel of Shklov see n. 24 to the introduction, above.

28. R. Yitzhaq Isaac Haber, *Magen ve-Zina* (Johannesburg, 1855), 3a. On Haber's goals in writing this work see, generally, "Hithnazluth ha-mehaber," immediately following the title page.

29. See R. Yitzhaq Isaac Haber, *Pithkhei She'arim* (Warsaw, 1888) 2b.

30. As mentioned in chapter 1, R. Shneur Zalman accused the GRA of limited knowledge of the Kabbalah as well as imperfect faith in its powers. See his letter to his Hasidim in Vilna, in Wilensky, *Hasidim u-Mithnagdim,* 2:200–201.

31. See R. Hayyim's introduction to *Safra de-Zeniutha im Perush ha-GRA* (Vilna and Grodno, 1820). See also his introduction to *Biur ha-GRA al ha-Zohar* (Vilna, 1810), regarding the place of Kabbalah in the total religious outlook of the GRA.

32. Aaron Zelig ben Eliezer Liphschitz, *Hanhagoth ve-Ezoth Shel Rabi Hayyim mi-Volozhin,* Hebrew University and National Library, Jerusalem, Microfilm 80800, pt. 2, par. 23, and pt. 1, par. 25.

33. See Hayyim Vital, *Arba Meoth Shekel Kessef* (reprint, Korets, 1804), 2: "haskamath ha-rav ha-gaon ha-gadol, Sinai ve-oker harim, harif u-baki . . . morenu harav Hayyim . . . Rosh Methivta ve-Av de-kehillah kedosha Volozhin." The approbation indicates that R. Hayyim was approached by the publisher in order to establish, on

the basis of both style and content, whether the manuscript in his possession was in fact the authentic work of R. Hayyim Vital. R. Hayyim of Volozhin confirmed the authenticity of the book and enthusiastically endorsed its publication.

For a discussion of the influence of the Kabbalistic writings of R. Moshe Hayyim Luzzato on the Mithnagdim see Isaiah Tishby, "Kithvei ha-Kabbalah le-RaMHaL be Polin uve-Lita," *Kiryath Sefer* 45 (1970).

34. The title page of manuscript 803177 of the Hebrew University and National Library, Jerusalem, reads as follows: "*Sefer ha-Bahir im Shnei Perushim: Or la-Yesharim* ('mi-talmid Ha-RaSHBA, ne'erakh al yedei Moshe Shelomo mi-Tultschyn, talmid ha-GRA') u-perush *Or la-Yehudim* ('le-rav Zadok Noah Bloh, Talmid Rabi Hayyim Volozhiner')."

35. R. Hayyim was involved in the publication of many of the GRA's works. Most notable for the present discussion are *Perush al Sefer Yezira* (Grodno, 1806), which he sponsored in collaboration with the aforementioned Kabbalist Menahem Mendel ben Barukh of Shklov. *Safra de-Zeniutha im Perush ha-GRA* (Vilna and Grodno, 1820), whose publishers, Menahem Mann ben Barukh and Simcha Zissel ben Menahem Nahum, later published R. Hayyim's *Nefesh ha-Hayyim.*

Immanuel Etkes, in his "Review of N. Lamm's Torah Lishmah" (Hebrew), *Kiryath Sefer* 50 (1975): 647, accurately characterizes R. Hayyim's attitude toward the Kabbalah as essentially positive but reticent regarding its public instruction and widespread dissemination.

36. Samuel of Dahlinov, *Minhath Shmuel* (Jerusalem, 1856), pt. 2, p. 3.

37. Samuel ben Eliezer of Kalvira, *Darkhei Noam* (Königsberg, 1764), "Haqdama Rishonah," 1–3.

38. Samuel ben Eliezer of Kalvira, *Darkhei Noam,* 98a.

39. On the spiritual profile of R. Samuel of Kalvira I must again take issue with Mendel Piekarz, who wishes to portray him as being very close to Hasidism and tends to downplay the significance of the GRA's approbation to his book. See Piekarz's profile of R. Samuel in *Biyemei Zemihath ha-Hasiduth,* 89–90, and consult the index for the extensive citations of *Darkhei Noam* as a proto-Hasidic text throughout the book. Piekarz fails, deliberately it would seem, to explain the numerous anti-Hasidic proclamations in this work.

40. See Elijah ben Solomon, *Perush al Kama Aggadoth* (Vilna, 1800), "Haqdamath Rabi Hayyim Mi-Volozhin," unpaginated.

41. Elijah ben Solomon, *Sefer Mishlei im Biur ha-GRA* (reprint, Petah Tikva, 1980), 21:17.

42. See Elijah ben Solomon, *Even Shelomo,* ed. Solomon Maltzan (Vilna, 1872; reprint, Brooklyn, 1972), chap. 8, sec. 25, for a collection of citations from the GRA's writings on the dangers of premature Kabbalistic study. Cf. Landau, *Ha-Gaon ha-Hasid mi-Vilna,* chap. 10, pp. 136–37, on the GRA's reticence regarding mystical experience and *kabbalah ma'asith.*

43. Phinehas ben Judah, Maggid of Polotsk, *Midrash Hakhamim* (Minsk, 1809), 1:2–3.

44. The vigilant maintenance of a sharp distinction between the *nigleh* and *nistar* parts of the Torah is a central theme in Mithnagdic literature and forms the very basis for the critique of the Hasidic preoccupation with Kabbalah. By rigorously maintaining this distinction the Mithnagdim established a well-defined hierarchy of learning and were thus able to argue for the priority of exoteric, or traditional Talmudic, studies. The Hasidim, as we shall see, tended to obfuscate this critical distinction.

45. Phinehas ben Judah, Maggid of Polotsk, *Kether Torah* (Jerusalem, 1965), 11a–11b. Interestingly, this paragraph implies that rabbinic study is simply a preparatory stage in the quest for the most sublime religious experience. This would seem to contradict the Mithnagdic claim, also voiced by Phinehas, that such study is the sole route in this life to *devekuth*. I would argue that Phinehas is here simply paying the requisite lip service to the sanctity and theoretical power of Kabbalistic study. In actual fact he had absolutely no practical expectation that any man could reach the highest spiritual level through mystical contemplation and study in this life.

46. *Giveath Phinehas* (Vilna, 1808), 28:25; cf. 28:23–24 for the context of this line of reasoning by Phinehas.

47. See, for example, Phinehas ben Judah, Maggid of Polotsk, *Shevet mi-Yehuda* (Vilna, 1803), 23:1.

48. Phinehas ben Judah, Maggid of Polotsk, *Rosh ha-Giveah* (Jerusalem, 1965), 4b.

49. Phinehas, *Giveath Phinehas*, 40:15. The verse "Seek not what is too difficult for you" is from Ben Sirah 3:21. This verse, originally from the pseudoepigraphy, became a central prooftext for rabbinic conservatism regarding esoteric study after its citation in the Babylonian Talmud, *Hagiga*, chap. 2. See, e.g., Maimonides' use of the phrase in *Guide for the Perplexed*, 1:32. Phinehas repeatedly quotes this verse in arguing for cautious abstention from Kabbalistic study; see, for example, *Midrash Hakhamim*, 139:14; and *Shevet mi-Yehuda*, 20:18 and 23:1.

50. Phinehas, *Shevet mi-Yehuda*, 23:2.

51. See ibid., where Phinehas suggests that "leaking" its secrets could lead to the total eradication of the Kabbalah.

52. Ezekiel Faivel of Dretzhyn, *Toledoth Adam* (Warsaw, 1856), 33b; see the lengthy and important discussion of Kabbalah on 30a–34b.

53. Ibid., 30b. It is noteworthy that Ezekiel Faivel cites the same prooftext from Ben Sirah in order to support his argument. Ezekiel Faivel was a colleague of Phinehas's and, like him, served as a maggid in several Belorussian towns and cities. In fact, Israel Klausner, in his essay "Toledoth Lita," in *Lita* (Bnai Berak, 1966), singles out Phinehas and Ezekiel Faivel as the most noteworthy populist Lithuanian preachers.

54. Abraham Danzig, *Beth Avraham* (Jerusalem, 1971), 299, par. 43.

55. Abraham Danzig, *Hayyei Adam* (reprint, Vilna, 1843), 10:12. Of course, Danzig is not here formulating anything particularly original. In style this formulation closely resembles that of Maimonides in his *Mishneh Torah*, "Hilkhoth Yesodei ha-Torah," 4:13, except that for Maimonides the forbidden subject matter was metaphysics, whereas for Danzig it was the Kabbalah.

56. Shneur Zalman of Lyadi, *Shulhan Arukh—Yoreh Deah*, "Hilkhoth Talmud

Torah," 2:2. R. Shneur Zalman seems to be following Maimonides, who in his *Mishneh Torah*, "Hilkhoth Talmud Torah," 2:12, legislates that the esoteric disciplines of the PaRDeS are included in the category of Gemara ("veha-Pardes bikhlal Gemara"). But what is missing, significantly, is the esotericism implicit in Maimonides' crucial qualificatory admonition that "not everyone is worthy to stroll in the 'PaRDeS' until he has first filled his belly with bread and meat" ("Hilkhoth Yesodei ha-Torah," 4:13). It is precisely this warning that becomes so prominent in the Mithnagdic writings and so blatantly absent from early Hasidic thought.

57. Shneur Zalman of Lyadi, *Shulhan Arukh—Yoreh Deah*, "Hilkhoth Talmud Torah," 2:3. As mentioned in chapter 1, the spread among all of the Jews of the true knowledge of God, which for R. Shneur Zalman meant the mystical, acosmic conception of a radically immanent God, was a central goal of the early Habad movement.

58. See Loewenthal, *Communicating the Infinite*, chap. 2.

59. Shneur Zalman of Lyadi, *Likutei Amarim: Tanya* (Vilna, 1930; reprint, Brooklyn, 1964), 3b.

60. For an an excellent scholarly elucidation of the theology and theosophy of R. Aaron Ha-Levi of Starosselje see Rachel Elior, *Torath ha-Elohuth be-Dor ha-Sheyni Shel Hasiduth Habad* (Jerusalem, 1982).

61. On the rabbinic notion of the spiritual and intellectual decline of the generations through history see Babylonian Talmud, *Shabbath*, 112b, and the many medieval commentaries to the epigrammatic statement that "if the early Sages were like angels we are but mortals, and if they were like mortals, we are but donkeys."

62. See Aaron of Starosselje, *Shaarei ha-Yihud veha-Emuna* (reprint, Jerusalem, 1985), "Petah u-Mavoh Shearim."

63. See Moshe Cordovero, *Or Naarav* (reprint, Vilna, 1885), chap. 1, where Cordovero refutes the arguments of those who call for abstention from Kabbalistic study. Note that the arguments raised by the Mithnagdim to counteract the Hasidic revival of interest in the Kabbalah were already familiar in Cordovero's day.

64. Aaron of Starosselje, *Shaarei ha-Yihud veha-Emuna*, "Petah u-Mavoh Shearim," 14–15.

65. Aaron of Starosselje, *Shaarei ha-Yihud veha-Emuna*, 16–19.

66. Of course, the Habad scholars were not alone among the Hasidim in their tremendous enthusiasm for spreading Kabbalistic knowledge. We have already considered the similar efforts of R. Barukh of Kossov a half-century earlier. It is worth noting that R. Barukh had the explicit support of thirteen of the leading Hasidic masters of his day, including a written approbation to his writings by the leading Hasidic master, R. Menahem Nahum of Premyszlan.

67. Loewenthal, *Communicating the Infinite*, chaps. 4–6.

68. For the text of this letter see Jacob Joseph of Polnoe, *Ben Porath Yosef* (Lemberg, 1863), 128a.

69. For a detailed account of this dispute between R. Shneur Zalman and R. Abraham of Kalisk see Loewenthal, *Communicating the Infinite*, 51–54, 77–86.

70. I am currently completing a study of the Slonim school's rejection of mystical study and insistence on "simple faith" *(emuna peshuta).*

71. See Heschel, Abraham Joshua of Apta, *Iggeroth Ohev Yisrael* (Jerusalem, 1979), letter 24 (59–64).

72. See Moshe Idel, "Perceptions of the Kabbalah in the Second Half of the Eighteenth Century," in *Kabbalah: New Perspectives,* 58–59. On the division of the Kabbalah into these two dominant schools generally, see Idel, *Kabbalah: New Perspectives,* introduction.

73. Meshulam Faivush of Zaborocz, *Yosher Divrei Emeth* (Kolomeya, 1904), 1:22 (18b). The author similarly obscures the distinction between esoteric and exoteric disciplines (see ibid., 1:7).

74. R. Shneur Zalman of Lyadi, *Shulhan Arukh—Yoreh Deah,* "Hilkhoth Talmud Torah," 2:3.

75. Phinehas, *Rosh ha-Giveah,* 11b.

76. On the Mithnagdim's deferral of direct, unmediated knowledge of God, or *devekuth,* to the posthumous life of the world to come, see below, chapter 5.

Chapter 3: Mithnagdic Prayer

1. On the Hasidic change of both the venue of prayer and the standard text of the prayer book see Louis Jacobs, *Hasidic Prayer* (New York, 1972), 36–45. Some primary sources indicating the Mithnagdic opposition to Hasidic separatism and change of the standard, "Ashkenazic" version of the liturgy can be found in M. Wilensky, *Hasidim u-Mithnagdim: le-Toledoth ha-Pulmus Beynehem,* 2 vols. (Jerusalem, 1970), 1:45–47, 62, 138, 227; 2:90, 155, 249.

The most common expression of disapproval regarding Hasidic practices in this regard is embodied in the term *bonim bama le-atzmam,* which intimates that the Hasidic separatism in prayer and the establishment of autonomous houses of worship are analogous to the ancient Israelite idolatry during prophetic times. Another central motif of the Mithnagdic polemic against Hasidic prayer is its insistence upon the importance of attending a central communal synagogue. See, on this matter, Phinehas ben Judah, Maggid of Polotsk, *Rosh ha-Giveah* (Jerusalem, 1965), 4a–4b; and idem, *Midrash Hakhamim* (Minsk, 1809), 88:3, 61:2.

2. On the importance of heeding the Halakhically mandated times for the prayer service, see Wilensky, *Hasidim u-Mithnagdim,* 1:41, 139; 2:91. Cf. Phinehas ben Judah, Maggid of Polotsk, *Shevet mi-Yehuda* (Vilna, 1803), 4:19; idem, *Rosh ha-Giveah,* 6a, 9b–10b; and Hayyim of Volozhin, *Nefesh ha-Hayyim* (Vilna and Grodno, 1824), intermediate section, chap. 8.

3. For a general discussion of the strange gesticulations and sounds of the Hasidim in prayer see Jacobs, *Hasidic Prayer,* chap. 5. The Mithnagdic critique of this phenomenon can be found in Wilensky, *Hasidim u-Mithnagdim,* 1:53–54, 66, 138–39, 227; 2:87, 90, 129, 214. According to Phinehas of Polotsk, ecstatic shouts and movements in

prayer were the signs of Hasidic arrogance and pious showiness (see, e.g., Phinehas, *Rosh ha-Giveah*, 10a).

4. Babylonian Talmud, *Shabbath*, 10a; cf. ibid., *Rosh Ha-Shanna*, 35a.

5. See, for example, Mishna, *Peah*, 1:1, and Babylonian Talmud, *Shabbath*, 127a, where the study of Torah is explicitly stated to be of greater significance than even the most intense prayer.

6. Babylonian Talmud, *Kiddushin*, 40b.

7. See, for example, Jerusalem Talmud, *Berakhoth*, 1:5, which interprets the Mishnaic view of R. Jonathan as in fact reflecting a higher evaluation of prayer over study. See also Babylonian Talmud, *Berakhoth*, 21a, and *Pesahim*, 54b.

8. Moses Ibn Makhir, *Seder ha-Yom* (Lublin, 1876), 16a.

9. Babylonian Talmud, *Berakhoth*, 6b.

10. For scholarly explications of the theurgic powers attributed by the Jewish mystics to Kabbalistic prayer and the notion of *tefilla* as an act of cosmic *tikkun* see, *inter alia*, I. Tishby, *Mishnath Ha-Zohar*, 2 vols. (Jerusalem, 1949), 2:247–306; and E. Gottleib, "Mashma'utha shel ha-Tefilla ba-Kabbala," in *Mekhkarim be-Sifruth ha-Kabbala*, ed. J. Hacker (Tel Aviv, 1976), 381ff. For a concise and helpful survey of the impact of Kabbalistic prayer upon subsequent liturgical history, see Y. Meir Elbogen, *Ha-Tefilla Be-Yisrael* (Tel Aviv, 1972), 281–91. Cf. Joseph Dan, "The Emergence of Mystical Prayer," in *Studies in Jewish Mysticism*, ed. J. Dan and F. Talmadge (Cambridge, 1982), 85–120.

11. On the transformation of mystical prayer from the Lurianic-theurgic mode to a highly subjective and enthusiastic mystical exercise see Joseph Weiss, "The Kavanoth of Prayer in Early Hasidism," *Journal of Jewish Studies* 9 (1958): 163–92; Rivka Shatz, *Ha-Hasiduth ke-Mistika* (Jerusalem, 1968), chap. 10; and Jacobs, *Hasidic Prayer*, chap. 6. Jacobs goes so far as to intimate that the practice of Lurianic *kavanoth* and the attainment of Hasidic *kavana* are in fact mutually exclusive: "In this school [of the maggid of Mezeritch], the practice of the [Lurianic] *kavvanot* was a positive hindrance to the ideal of *devekuth*" (75).

12. R. Israel ben Eliezer Baal Shem Tov, *Kether Shem Tov* (Brooklyn, 1987), 22b.

13. See the detailed analysis of the Mithnagdic elevation of *Talmud Torah* to the very summit of spiritual attainment in Judaism in chapter 7, below.

14. On the significance of prayer in the writings of the BESHT's most important disciple, R. Jacob Joseph, see G. Nigal, *Toroth Baal ha-Toledoth* (Jerusalem, 1974), introduction, 32–40.

15. See Rivka Shatz, "Contemplative Prayer in Hasidism," in *Studies in Mysticism and Religion Presented to Gershom Scholem,* ed. E. E. Urbach and R. J. Werblowsky (Jerusalem, 1967). Cf. Joseph Weiss, "The Great Maggid's Theory of Contemplative Magic," *Hebrew Union College Annual* 31 (1960): 137–47.

16. On the importance of the vocal aspect of prayer in early Hasidic thought see Moshe Idel, *Hasidism: Between Ecstasy and Magic* (New York, 1995), 152–54. Expanding on the work of earlier scholars, Idel endeavors to demonstrate that there were two distinct stages to Hasidic prayer: the mystical, in which the soul of the worshiper

cleaved to God via the conduit of the atomized letters of the liturgy, and the magical (or talismanic), in which the words and sounds of prayer caused the descent of spiritual influxes to earth. The former, mystical element of Hasidic prayer has already been amply described by Weiss, Shatz, and Jacobs. Idel's original contribution is the description of the magical role of the letters and words of prayer in Hasidic thought, which he claims followed the mystical experience in prayer. It would seem, however, that whereas in early Hasidism, at least, mystical prayer was recommended for all Hasidim, the magical/talismanic form of prayer was limited to the zaddik, a distinction Idel does not mention.

17. On the displacement of the Lurianic *kavanoth* in early Hasidic prayer with forms of mystical and talismanic worship found earlier in the teachings of R. Abraham Abulafia and R. Moshe Cordovero see Idel, *Hasidism*, 160–70. Although Idel painstakingly and eruditely traces the origins of these forms of Hasidic prayer to passages in earlier Kabbalistic texts (and even draws parallels between the lack of interest in the deep meaning of the Lurianic *kavanoth* on the part of the Great Maggid of Mezeritch and R. Hayyim of Volozhin), he seems to miss the very essence of the Hasidic revolution in prayer, namely, the simplification of the earlier esoteric techniques of a tiny number of Kabbalistic masters and their popularization among the masses of eastern European Jewry. It was that spread to the multitude of the once secretly guarded forms of mystical prayer that resulted in the Hasidic upheaval of the hierarchy of religious values that provoked the Mithnagdic response, with which we are concerned.

18. The transformed nature and status of Torah study in early Hasidic thought are analyzed by Joseph Weiss in "Torah Study in Early Hasidism" (Hebrew), *Ha-Doar* 45 (1965): 615–17.

19. A. S. Heilman, *Beth Rabi* (Berditchev, 1903), 38–40. The letter is reprinted in Wilensky, *Hasidim u-Mithnagdim*, 1:300. A good study of the contrasts between the value of prayer and the value of study in the religious systems of R. Shneur Zalman of Lyadi and R. Hayyim of Volozhin is Norman Lamm, "Prayer and Study," in *Samuel Mirsky Memorial Volume*, ed. Norman Lamm (New York, 1970), 37–52. See also idem, "Scholarship and Piety," in *Faith And Doubt* (New York, 1971), 212–47.

20. Wilensky, *Hasidim u-Mithnagdim*, 1:28.

21. Ibid., 1:227.

22. Ibid., 2:90; cf. 1:138.

23. *Sefer Mishlei im Biur ha-GRA* (reprint, Petah Tikva, 1980), 13:12, clearly based upon Babylonian Talmud, *Berakhoth*, 32b.

24. H. H. Ben Sasson, "Ishiyutho Shel ha-GRA ve-Hashpa'ato ha-Hevratith," *Zion* 31 (1966): 39–68, 197–216; note esp. Ben Sasson's concluding observations on 64–67 to the effect that the essence and main thrust of the GRA's opposition to Hasidism was directed precisely at its reversal of the traditional hierarchy of religious values.

25. This does not, of course, mean that the GRA objected to mystical prayer per se; in fact, he is the source of a vast mystical commentary to the liturgy, and many Kabbalistic traditions and *kavanoth* connected with prayer are attributed to him (see,

for example, the very important Kabbalistic commentaries to the liturgy and mystical customs in worship found in *Siddur ha-GRA be-Nigleh u-ve-Nistar*, ed. Naftali Herz Ha-Levi [Jaffa, 1867]). Rather, the GRA was distressed by the popularization and spread of esoteric doctrines meant for a small circle of Kabbalistic devotees. The affirmation of the centrality of scholarship in the religious life did not, however, necessarily involve the rejection of the great potential of mystical worship on the part of those very few who were properly initiated into its secret powers.

26. R. Hayyim of Volozhin's advocacy of mystical prayer is evident throughout the second section of *Nefesh ha-Hayyim*. For a faithful summary of the view of prayer advanced there, see Norman Lamm, *Torah Lishmah* (Jerusalem, 1972), 66–69. See also Benjamin Gross, "La priere dans le Nefesh ha-Hayyim de R. Hayyim de Volozhin," in *Priere, mystique, et judaisme*, ed. Roland Goetschel (Paris, 1987), 225–44.

27. On the absolute and uncontested supremacy of Torah study in R. Hayyim's thought see Lamm, *Torah Lishmah*, 100–173.

28. See ibid., chap. 4, regarding the elevation of study over all other religious obligations, including prayer. Note esp. 123–38, where Lamm summarizes the sharp difference between R. Hayyim and the Hasidim concerning the place of prayer in the religious hierarchy. See also idem, "Study and Prayer."

29. See Idel's analysis of R. Hayyim's dismissal of the efficacy of *kavanoth* in *Hasidism: Between Ecstasy and Magic*, 151–52.

30. Hayyim of Volozhin, *Nefesh ha-Hayyim*, intermediate section, chap. 2.

31. Ibid., chap. 8.

32. Abraham Danzig, *Beth Avraham* (reprint; Jerusalem, 1971), pars. 7, 12.

33. Meir ben Elijah of Vilna, *Milhamoth Adonai*, Hebrew University and National Library, Jerusalem, MS 801067, 63.

34. Phinehas, *Shevet mi-Yehuda*, 28:9.

35. Phinehas ben Judah, Maggid of Polotsk, *Rosh ha-Giveah* (Jerusalem, 1965), 9b–10a.

36. Phinehas ben Judah, Maggid of Polotsk, *Kether Torah* (Jerusalem, 1965), 7b.

37. Note that it is precisely this Halakhic argument used by Phinehas to affirm the supremacy of *Talmud Torah* that R. Shneur Zalman of Lyadi so emphatically rejected in his aforementioned letter to Alexander of Shklov (n. 19 above). There R. Shneur Zalman begins his argument with the words, "Those who claim that prayer is only a rabbinically binding obligation have never seen the light."

38. Compare this line of argumentation with the strikingly similar interpretation of this same text by R. Hayyim of Volozhin, published some fifty years later in *Ruah Hayyim* (Vilna, 1859), 1:2.

39. Phinehas, *Kether Torah*, 8b.

40. See Phinehas's commentary to *Avoth* in *Siddur Shaar ha-Rahamim im Perush Maggid Zedek* (Shklov, 1788), 2:94a.

41. Meir ben Elijah of Vilna, *Milhamoth Adonai*, 62.

42. On the supremacy of Torah over all other religious obligations (including prayer) see Phinehas, *Kether Torah*, 5b–6b, 9a; cf. idem, *Shevet mi-Yehuda*, 3:1, 8:11,

31:18. R. Phinehas of Polotsk and R. Hayyim of Volozhin espoused virtually identical beliefs with regard to the nature of the hierarchy of Jewish religious values and the classification of prayer together with the other commandments (see Lamm, *Torah Lishmah*, 100–131).

43. Abraham ben Solomon of Vilna, *Maaloth ha-Torah* (reprint, Jerusalem, 1975), 46a.

44. Abraham Danzig, *Hayyei Adam* (reprint, Vilna, 1843), 17:1.

45. Danzig, *Beth Abraham*, 274b.

46. See Yitzhaq Isaac Haber, *Amudei ha-Torah: Or Torah* (Jerusalem, 1880), 9b, 37a, 50b–51a.

47. For his views on prayer, see Asher Ha-Kohen of Tiktin, "Petiha Rabati be-Maaloth ha-Torah," in *Birkhath Rosh* (reprint, Jerusalem, 1971), 3b–4a.

48. Meir ben Elijah of Vilna, *Milhamoth Adonai*, 73–74. Meir devotes an entire chapter of his anti-Hasidic polemic to a critique of Hasidic prayer. He complains that the Hasidim "have been so duped by the forces of evil that they have been blinded into forsaking eternal life (i.e., *hayyei olam*) and turn all of their attention instead to temporal life *(hayyei sha'a)*, namely, the prayers and their *kavanoth*. But this (i.e., prayer) is only a rabbinic commandment that has been established by them [i.e., the rabbis] to correspond to the sacrifices" (74). For a full analysis of Meir ben Elijah's religious thought and specifically his critique of Hasidism see Allan Nadler, "Meir b. Elijah of Vilna's *Milhamoth Adonai*: A Late Anti-Hasidic Polemic," *Journal of Jewish Thought and Philosophy* 1 (1991): 247–80.

49. See chapter 7, below.

50. Mishna, *Shabbat*, 5:1.

51. Babylonian Talmud, *Berakhoth*, 31a.

52. Babylonian Talmud, *Sanhedrin*, 22b.

53. Maimonides, *Mishneh Torah*, "Hilkhoth Tefillah," 4:16. Cf. *The Guide for the Perplexed*, 3:51, where Maimonides offers a deeply spiritual definition of the very purpose of prayer.

54. Jacob ben Asher, *Tur, Orah Hayyim*, no. 98. See Moses Isserles, *Darkhei Moshe*, who bases his definition of *kavana* on the *Guide for the Perplexed*, 3:51. Cf. Bahya ibn Pakuda's almost mystical definition of the legal requirement for *kavana*, *Hovoth ha-Levavoth*, 8:3.

55. It is important to note that although he provided this dual definition of *kavana*, Jacob ben Asher later asserted that the latter type of intent in prayer, that is, the attainment of the exalted spiritual state of "hithpashtuth ha-gashmiyouth," was not Halakhically binding (see Jacob ben Asher, *Tur, Orah Hayyim*, no. 101).

56. Abraham Gumbiner, *Magen Avraham* to *Shulhan Arukh: Orah Hayyim*, no. 98, introductory paragraph. The abandonment of Lurianic *kavanoth* in this period must be seen at least partially as a consequence of Sabbateanism's messianic rejection of applied Lurianic Kabbalah. On this development see Gershom Scholem, *Sabbatai Sevi: The Mystical Messiah*, 2 vols. in 1 (Princeton, 1973), 2:412–14.

57. Alexander Zisskind of Grodno, *Yesod ve-Shoreshha-Avodah* (Grodno, 1794), 26.

See also R. Alexander Zisskind's programmatic introduction to the work, where he defines the need for *kavana* in practice and defines the nature of such *kavana* for the masses. This work is literally saturated with the theme of the powers of Lurianic prayer and its inaccessibility to the contemporary Jewish masses (see, *inter alia*, 44, 70, 78–79, 110).

58. Cf. Moshe Idel's discussion of "eighteenth-century attitudes to Lurianic kavvanot," in *Hasidism*, 149–52.

59. On Hasidic *kavana* see Y. Ysander, *Studien Zum Bestian Hasidismus* (Uppsala, 1933), 177–86. See also Jacobs, *Hasidic Prayer*, chaps. 6–8, for a detailed depiction of the various forms of contemplative and ecstatic prayer in the different schools of early Hasidism.

60. Hayyim of Tchernowitz, *Beer Mayyim Hayyim*, as cited in *Siddur Tefilla Yeshara* (Jerusalem, 1983), 47.

61. K. K. Epstein, *Ma'or va-Shemesh*, as cited *Siddur Tefilla Yeshara*, 43.

62. K. K. Epstein, "Nizavim," in *Maor va-Shemesh*, cited in Jacobs, *Hasidic Prayer*, 80–81.

63. Cited in Idel, *Hasidism*, 152.

64. Joseph Weiss has noted that whereas in classical rabbinic prayer the two different levels of *kavana* can coexist, in Hasidic prayer "the literal meaning of the sentence evaporates completely" (see Weiss, "The Kavanoth of Prayer in Early Hasidism," 96 and 104, for this contrast).

65. Hayyim of Tchernowicz, *Beer Mayyim Hayyim*, as cited in *Siddur Tefilla Yeshara*, 47. On the Hasidic spiritualization of prayer generally, see Shatz, *Ha-Hasiduth ke-Mistika*, chap. 6, esp. the sources quoted on 81–86. For the indignant Mithnagdic reaction to the Hasidic abandonment of the *kavanoth pashtiyoth,* or literal petitionary prayer, see Wilensky, *Hasidim u-Mithnagdim*, 1:39.

66. Elijah ben Solomon, Gaon of Vilna, *Hidushei u-Viurei ha-GRA al Maseketh Shabbath u-Berakhoth*, ed. Abraham Drushkovitz (Kedainiai, 1940), 43a.

67. Elijah ben Solomon, Gaon of Vilna, *Maaseh Rav: Minhagei ha-GRA ha-Shalem* (reprint, Jerusalem, 1987), no. 41.

68. Hayyim of Volozhin, *Nefesh ha-Hayyim*, 2:1.

69. Ibid., intermediate section, chap. 5.

70. Jacob Joseph of Polnoe, *Toledoth Jacob Joseph* (Lemberg, 1863), 167a–b.

71. Phinehas, *Siddur Shaar ha-Rahamim*, intro., col. 3.

72. Danzig, *Hayyei Adam*, 18:2; see also 22:12 and 24:2, where Danzig is pessimistic even about contemporary man's understanding of the true plain sense of the liturgy.

73. Phinehas, *Rosh ha-Giveah*, 2b.

74. For examples of Kabbalistic *kavanoth* prefaced by R. Phinehas to major sections of the prayer services see *Siddur Shaar ha-Rahamim*, 1:2b (talit and tefillin), 1:66b (lulav and ethrog), 1:85b *(kaparoth)*, 1:78b (shofar). See the introduction for the use of a special verse to preface the evening prayer service, the *Maariv,* based on the *Zohar* (1:42b). On the reason why the special morning prayer, the *Nishmath,* is recited only on the Sabbath morning see 1:53b–54a. For a mystical commentary to the

confessional prayers of the High Holidays adapted from the neo-Sabbatean work *Hemdath Yamim* see 1:86a–87b. A Kabbalistic interpretation of bowing the head during the *tahanun* service, including a long selection from the *Zohar,* is found on 2:38a. Phinehas also included the Lurianic *kavanoth* before the major sections of the prayers and before any ritual *mitzvoth* connected with them, despite the opposition of some Mithnagdim to their publication in any prayer book intended for mass distribution. See, for example, the famous responsum of R. Ezekiel Landau, *Noda bi-Yehuda, Yoreh Deah,* no. 93. On this controversy generally see Jacobs, *Hasidic Prayer,* 140–53.

75. See Phinehas, *Siddur Shaar ha-Rahamim,* 1:32b, for a long, mystical interpretation of the powers of the *Kaddish.* See also the lengthy general mystical introduction to the *Amidah* on 2:18a. Note the highly significant qualifier there: "Now I will write for you a few words from the holy *Zohar,* but not all of the text, for it is the honor of God to conceal these matters."

76. Ibid., 2:78b.

77. Ibid., title page.

78. Phinehas's commentary to the liturgy abounds in examples of his basically rabbinic/exegetical priorities. For clear examples of his concerns as an exegete see, *inter alia,* ibid., 1:50b–51b, where he provides different levels of *peshat;* 1:57a, for a presentation of various levels of exegesis—literal, midrashic, and mystical; 1:61a–62b, where he offers the *peshat* and then suggests a deeper, mystical level of interpretation.

79. Ibid., 1:32a.

80. Ibid., 1:26a; cf. 1:53b regarding a similar exegetical use of Exodus 17.

81. Ibid., 1:59a.

82. Ibid., 1:21a–b. Phinehas advises that given contemporary man's inability to have the proper *kavana,* he should simply attach his literal prayers to those of the earlier Sages, who had true mystical *kavana* (see Phinehas, *Midrash Hakhamim,* introductory statement to Psalms 111).

83. See Jacobs, *Hasidic Prayer,* chap. 6.

84. Jacob Kranz, "Shaar ha-tefilla," in *Sefer ha-Middoth,* ed. Abraham Flahm (Tel Aviv, 1959), 227.

85. Hillel of Kovno, *Heilel Ben Shahar* (Warsaw, 1804), 386.

86. Wilensky, *Hasidim u-Mithnagdim,* 1:248. Note the very opposite understanding of the very same biblical verse by the Hasidic master Jacob Joseph of Polnoe above, in n. 70.

Chapter 4: Mithnagdic Asceticism

1. The extent of asceticism in the classical rabbinic period has been the subject of a significant scholarly debate, most notably between Yitzhak Baer, who saw asceticism as central to early rabbinic thought, and Ephraim Urbach, who downplayed its importance in this period (see Fritz Baer, *Israel among the Nations: An Essay on the History of the Period of the Second Temple and the Mishna and the Foundations of the*

Halakha and Jewish Religion [Jerusalem, 1955]; and Ephraim Urbach, "Ascesis and Suffering in Talmudic and Midrashic Sources" [Hebrew], in *Fritz Baer Jubilee Volume* [Jerusalem, 1960], 48–68). The consensus of both earlier and later scholarly opinion seems to favor Urbach's view that the extent and influence of the ascetic ideal, even in the early rabbinic sources, were very limited.

2. See the detailed study of the transformation from biblical monism to dualistic and ascetic tendencies in classical rabbinic thought by Nissan Rubin, "From Monism to Dualism: Relationship between the Body and Soul in Talmudic Thought," *Daat,* no. 23 (1989): 31–63.

3. On the asceticism of Bahya see Allan Lazaroff, "Bahya's Asceticism against Its Rabbinic and Islamic Background," *Journal of Jewish Studies* 21 (1970): 11–38. The ascetic and penitential practices of the medieval Hasidei Ashkenaz were first identified by Fritz Baer, and attributed by him largely to Christian monastic influences (see Y. Baer, "Olama ha-Datit/Hevratit Shel Sefer Hasidim," *Zion* 3 [1938]: 1–50; see also Gershom Scholem, *Major Trends in Jewish Mysticism* [New York, 1961], chap. 3. This theme has been examined most recently by Ivan Marcus in his *Piety and Society* [Leiden, 1981] and by S. Ben Arzi in "Ha-Perishuth be-Sefer Hasidim," *Daat,* no. 11 [1983]: 39–47).

4. On the Sufi influences upon Bahya see Lazaroff, "Bahya's Asceticism." There has been a major scholarly dispute regarding the extent of Christian influences upon medieval German Hasidism. Once again it was Urbach who challenged Baer's claim that such influence was considerable (see his essay in *Zion* 12 [1947]: 149–59; and his *Baalei ha-Tosafoth* (Jerusalem, 1980), 141–94).

5. Bahya's *Hovoth ha-Levavoth* was published at least thirty-one times in eastern Europe in the course of the seventeenth and eighteenth centuries. The proliferation not only of so many editions of the work but also of new commentaries to it is testimony to its widespread influence in eastern Europe in the period being dealt with in this book. Take, for example, the following commentaries to *Hovoth ha-Levavoth:* Hayyim Hayka ben Aaron of Zamocz, *Derekh ha-Kodesh,* and Isaac ben Aaron of Zamocz, *Pahad Yitzhaq* (Frankfurt-am-Oder, 1774; Hilkenzitz, 1774; Shklov, 1783; Lemberg, 1791; Zolkiew, 1807; Sudilkov, 1819); Moses ben Reuven, *Ne'edar ba-Kodesh* (Grodno, 1790); Hayyim Avraham ben Aryeh Loeb Katz, *Path Lehem* (Shklov, 1803); and Israel of Zamocz, *Tuv ha-Levanon* (Vienna, 1809; Lemberg, 1833).

Both Phinehas and his Mithnagdic contemporaries cited *Hovoth ha-Levavoth* as a prooftext in their religious writings far more frequently than any other single work. As documented in appendix A, below, Phinehas's most important work, *Kether Torah,* was stylistically and structurally based upon the highly dualistic section of *Hovoth ha-Levavoth, Shaar Yihud ha-Ma'aseh.* Note also that the Mithnagged Moses ben Joseph of Steinhardt published his own commentary to this very section of the work in Feurth in 1765.

6. On the asceticism of the Safed mystics see R. J. Zwi Werblowsky, *Joseph Karo: Lawyer and Mystic,* (Philadelphia, 1977), chap. 4; see also Lawrence Fine, *Safed Spirituality* (New York, 1984), intro., esp. 11–18, and idem, "The Art of Metoposcopy: A

Study in Isaac Luria's Charismatic Knowledge," *Association for Jewish Studies Review* 11, no. 2 (1986): 79–82.

7. On the evolution of the realms of evil in the created physical world as a consequence of the doctrine of *zimzum* see I. Tishby, *Torath ha-Ra ve-ha-Kelippa be-Kabbalath ha-Ari* (Jerusalem, 1960), passim.

8. R. Hayyim Vital espoused ascetic spirituality most clearly and emphatically in the seventh section, "Shaar Ruah ha-Kodesh," of his colossal work *Shemona Shearim* (reprint, Jerusalem, 1963); see esp. 38–47.

9. For an English selection of Safed mystical *hanhagoth* containing much ascetic material see Fine, *Safed Spirituality,* 27–82. An excellent and thorough recent treatment of the influence and evolution of the *hanhagoth* literature in Beshtian Hasidism is Zeev Gries, *Sifruth ha-Hanhagoth: Toldoteha u-Mekomah be-Hayei Hasidei R. Yisrael Baal Shem Tov* (Jerusalem, 1989).

10. On the asceticism of the later medieval Hebrew ethical literature see Joseph Dan, *Sifruth ha-Musar veha-Derush* (Jerusalem, 1975). The attitude of an important medieval Jewish moralist to asceticism is examined by Carmi Horowitz in "The Attitude of Ibn Shouib to Asceticism" (Hebrew), *Daat,* no. 12 (1984): 29–37.

11. See esp. Hayyim Hayka of Zamocz's remarkable introduction to his *Mishneh Torah* commentary, *Zeror ha-Hayyim* (Berlin, 1770), which includes a highly dualistic and ascetic "dialogue between the matter (body) and the soul." On R. Hayyim Hayka see M. Piekarz, *Biyemei Zemihath ha-Hasiduth* (Jerusalem, 1978), 61–64.

12. See Mordechai of Vielkocz, *Shaar ha-Melekh,* esp. pt. 1, *Shaar* 5. On R. Mordechai, see Piekarz, *Biyemei Zemihath ha-Hasiduth,* 74–78.

13. Quoted in Piekarz, *Biyemei Zemihath ha-Hasiduth,* 38.

14. On the role in early Hasidic theory and worship of the "raising of holy sparks" see Joseph Weiss, "Reyshith Zemihatha Shel ha-Derekh ha-Hasidith," *Zion* 16 (1951): 89–103. On the mystical notion of *avodah be-gashmiyouth* see Rivka Schatz, *Ha-Hasiduth ke-Mistika* (Jerusalem, 1968), 14–18, 54–58. Schatz appreciates the service of God through the mundane world as a corollary of Hasidic acosmism.

15. On serving God through the evil inclination see Weiss, "Reyshith Zemihatha Shel ha-Derekh ha-Hasidith," 101–2. See also Piekarz, *Biyemei Zemihath ha-Hasiduth,* chap. 5.

16. See esp. *Zava'ath ha-Rivash,* passim. See also *Shivhei ha-BESHT,* pars. 45, 52, 62, regarding how the BESHT dissuaded both of his key pupils, Jacob Joseph of Polnoe and Dov Ber of Mezeritch, from practicing ascetic piety. For a general discussion of the BESHT's rejection of the ascetic ideal see E. Z. Zweiffel, *Shalom al Yisrael,* 2 vols. (Zhitomir, 1868), 1:141–47.

17. Zeev Wolf of Zhitomir, *Or ha-Meir* (reprint, Jerusalem, 1957), "Shemoth," 43b.

18. *Shivhei ha-BESHT,* par. 49.

19. Jacob Joseph of Polnoe, *Toledoth Jacob Joseph* (Lemberg, 1863), "Ki Tavo," 74a.

20. *Ben Porath Yosef* (Lemberg, 1863), "Bereshith," 13b. For a secondary account of R. Jacob Joseph's overcoming his asceticism" see S. Dresner, *The Zaddik* (London, 1960), 50–52.

21. On R. Abraham's self-denial and fasting see *Shivhei ha-BESHT,* par. 72.

22. On the asceticism of R. Elimelekh in general see G. Nigal, "Doctrines in the Writings of R. Elimelekh of Lizensk and His Disciples" (Hebrew) (Ph.D. diss., Hebrew University, 1972), chap. 7. See also Nigal's introduction to his critical edition of *Sefer Noam Elimelekh* (Hebrew) (Jerusalem, 1978), 69–73.

23. On the asceticism of R. Nahman of Brazlav see M. Mantel, "The Meaning of Suffering According to Rabbi Nathan of Nemirov" (Hebrew), *Daat,* no. 7 (1981): 109–18.

24. See the open letter of R. Hayyim Haikel of Amdur prefixed to the 1975 Jerusalem edition of *Hayyim va-Hesed,* 14. On R. Hayyim Haikel's mystical quietism see Shatz, *Ha-Hasiduth ke-Mistika,* chap. 2. Cf. R. Shneur Zalman of Lyadi's ambivalent attitude to the doctrine of *avodah be-gashmiyouth* as described by M. Halamish, "The Theoretical System of R. Shneur Zalman of Liady" (Hebrew) (Ph.D. diss., Hebrew University, 1976), 305–10.

25. Although the mystical doctrine of *bitul ha-yesh,* or *annihilatio,* sometimes led to an ascetic ideal, as in the case of Hayyim Haikel of Amdur, more often it resulted in the sense that since the physical world is merely an apparition that is "as nothing before Him," it need be neither feared nor avoided. Quite the contrary, one can serve God in and through it. This seemed to be the doctrine of leading disciples of the Great Maggid, such as Menahem Mendel of Vitebsk (see Shatz, *Ha-Hasiduth ke-Mistika,* 61). On the place of the technique of *avodah be-gashmiyouth* within an acosmic mystical framework see ibid., intro., esp. 14–17.

26. The "transforming all their days into festivities" is a standard critical characterization of Hasidic behavior in the anti-Hasidic polemical literature (see, *inter alia,* M. Wilensky, *Hasidim u-Mithnagdim: le Toledoth ha-Pulmus Beynehem,* 2 vols. [Jerusalem, 1970], 1:53–57, 244–45; 2:40–48, 133–35, 248–50, 301–7).

27. Jacob Joseph of Polnoe, *Toledoth Jacob Joseph,* "Mishpatim," 219. The perception of eating as an act of worship pervades the intellectual history of Hasidism, from this statement in the first printed Hasidic text up to contemporary Hasidic writings. Two important twentieth-century works contain a wealth of both primary Hasidic and original material on this theme: the enigmatic Jerusalem Hasidic master R. Aaron Roth devoted a massive volume to this theme, *Sefer Shulhan ha-Tahor* (Satmar, 1933); and the anonymous tract *Sefer Kedusath ha-Shulhan* (Jerusalem, 1985) is a compilation of primary material regarding the sanctity of food and drink from rabbinic, Kabbalistic, and Hasidic sources and particularly from the Polish Hasidic masters of the dynasty of Gur.

28. Wilensky, *Hasidim u-Mithnagdim,* 2:74. See also the similar Mithnagdic critiques of Hasidic materialism on pp. 135, 172–73.

29. *Sefer Midrash Rivash Tov,* pt. 2, p. 20.

30. Levi Isaac of Berditchev, *Kedushath Levi* (Brooklyn, 1975), "Likkutim le parshath Phinehas," 98b. For a general discussion of the religious significance of eating in Hasidism see Louis Jacobs, "Eating As an Act of Worship in Hasidic Thought," in *Studies in Jewish Religious and Intellectual History,* ed. S. Stein and R. Loewe (Tuscaloosa, 1979), 157–66.

31. See the GRA's letter written in the form of an ethical will to his family before he took leave of them to depart for Palestine, *Iggereth Ha-GRA*, printed in *Arba Iggeroth Niftahoth* (Vilna, 1882), 4–8.

32. Benjamin Rivlin of Shklov, *Geviey Gavia ha-Kessef* (Warsaw, 1897), 58. On the GRA's abstention from food and drink because of his heightened awareness of the relentless nature of the physical desires see ibid., 19.

33. Alexander Zisskind of Grodno, *The Ethical Will of the Author of Yesod ve-Shoresh ha-Avodah* (Jerusalem, 1955), 4–6.

34. Rivlin, *Geviey Gavia ha-Kessef*, 58.

35. Elijah ben Solomon, Gaon of Vilna, *Sefer Mishlei im Biur ha-GRA* (Petah Tikva, 1980), 10:16 (p. 127). In a very curious continuation of this same passage, the GRA seemed to distinguish between the masses and the zaddikim. For he allowed that the latter's eating and drinking was indeed imbued with holiness. For the vast majority of Jews, however, this was not the case. Apparently, as in his approach to the awareness of divine immanence, the GRA here too distinguished sharply between the exceptional scholars and the common folk.

36. Hayyim of Volozhin, *Ruah Hayyim* (Vilna, 1859), 6:14.

37. Hayyim of Volozhin, introduction to *Biur ha-GRA le-Seder Zeraim*, by Elijah ben Solomon, Gaon of Vilna (Vilna, 1903).

38. On the ascription to the GRA of the title "hasid," see Israel Klausner, *Vilna bi-Tekufath ha-Gaon* (Jerusalem, 1942), 18 n. 1. On the significance of the binary honorific of the GRA, specifically regarding his asceticism, see the discussion in Immanuel Etkes, *R. Yisrael Salanter ve-Reyshitah shel Tenuath ha-Mussar* (Jerusalem 1982), 27–34.

39. Abraham ben Elijah of Vilna, *Se'arath Eliyahu* (Vilna, 1877), 6a.

40. Ibid., 11a.

41. Rivlin, *Geviey Gavia ha-Kessef*, 17.

42. Legends regarding the GRA's ascetic piety abound. For a treasure of such hagiographic material see Joshua Heschel Levine, *Aliyoth Eliyahu* (Vilna, 1855) passim. See also the reverent account by B. Landau, *Ha-Gaon ha-Hasid mi-Vilna* (Jerusalem, 1978), chaps. 4 and 12. A very important primary source regarding the GRA's asceticism is Israel ben Samuel of Shklov's introduction to *Pe'ath ha-Shulhan* (Jerusalem, 1959), esp. 5b.

43. See *Iggereth ha-GRA*, 6.

44. Ibid.

45. For a full representation of the GRA's dualism and ascetic ideology, see Elijah ben Solomon, Gaon of Vilna, *Perush al Kama Aggadoth* (Vilna, 1800), passim. For the specific analogy of the human soul to a man lost at, and captive to, the sea see 3a.

46. Elijah ben Solomon, *Sefer Mishlei im Biur ha-GRA*, 7:14 (pp. 95–96); idem, *Megillath Esther im Perush ha-GRA al Derekh ha-Peshat ve-al Derekh ha-Remez* (reprint, Warsaw, 1897), 5:11.

47. Hillel of Kovno, *Heilel Ben Shahar* (Warsaw, 1804), 10b.

48. Ibid., 10b, 45b.

49. Ibid., 81b; see also 49b–50a for a similarly ascetic perspective. R. Hillel's

lengthy introduction to this work presents, in very clear terms, his asceticism, his contempt for wealth and the wealthy, and his view that spiritual and material attainments exist in an inversely proportional relationship.

50. Such an extensive critique of the materialism of the wealthy classes is, of course, by no means entirely novel in Polish Jewish intellectual history. Probably the most notable precedent for it is the sixteenth-century preacher R. Ephraim of Luntschitz's castigation of the wealthy classes. On R. Ephraim's social criticism see H. H. Ben Sasson, *Haguth ve-Hanhaga* (Jerusalem, 1959), chaps. 6–9.

51. Abraham Danzig, *Beth Avraham* (reprint, Jerusalem, 1971), pars. 15, 48.

52. Ibid., par. 2.

53. Abraham Danzig, *Toledoth Adam al ha-Hagada* (reprint, Jerusalem, 1972), 22b.

54. Ezekiel Faivel of Dretzhyn, *Toledoth Adam* (Warsaw, 1856), 11b.

55. Ezekiel Faivel of Dretzhyn, *Musar Haskel* (Lublin, 1901), 15b.

56. Phinehas ben Judah, Maggid of Polotsk, *Kether Torah* (reprint, Jerusalem, 1965), 35a.

57. See Phinehas ben Judah, Maggid of Polotsk, *Rosh ha-Giveah* (reprint, Jerusalem, 1965), 16a.

58. Phinehas, *Kether Torah,* 35a.

59. On the radically ascetic penitential techniques of Hasidei Ashkenaz, such as *teshuvath ha-mishkal* and *teshuvath ha-kathuv,* and their place in medieval Ashkenazic pietism, see Marcus, *Piety and Society,* chap. 4, esp. 36–52.

60. Phinehas, *Kether Torah,* 6b–7a.

61. Phinehas, *Rosh ha-Giveah,* 8b.

62. Phinehas, *Kether Torah,* 35a–36a.

63. Phinehas ben Judah, Maggid of Polotsk, *Kizzur Even Bohan* (reprint, Jerusalem, 1900), chap. 15.

64. Ibid., editor's introduction to chap. 16.

65. Phinehas, *Giveath Phinehas,* 6:14.

66. The novelty of R. Phinehas's exegesis of the story of Job lies in the fact that he shifts the thematic emphasis away from the traditional concern with the problem of theodicy and toward the ascetic theme of the spiritual value and rewards of poverty and material self-denial. For a good presentation of the traditional Jewish appreciation of Job see Robert Gordis, *The Book of God and Man: A Study of Job* (Chicago, 1965), esp. chap. 11, "Job and the Mystery of Suffering." Although R. Phinehas's use of Job to argue for the nobility of material denial and physical suffering does not, to my knowledge, have any major precedent in the Jewish exegetical tradition, precisely such an appreciation of Job can be found in the medieval Christian monastic tradition (see, for example, Nachum Glatzer's presentation of the monastic John Chrysostom's interpretation of Job, according to which the main lesson of this biblical book is that "'poverty is much better . . . than riches, and infirmity and sickness than health, and trial than tranquility.' Job's body became more venerable when pierced by these wounds" [N. Glatzer, *Dimensions of Job* (New York, 1969), 26]).

67. Phinehas, *Giveath Phinehas*, 1:9. On the prevalence in the Mithnagdic polemical literature of the expression "transforming all of their days into festivities" as a critique of Hasidic materialism see above, n. 26.

68. *Giveath Phinehas*, 1:9, end of chap. 42.

69. See, *inter alia*, Phinehas ben Judah, Maggid of Polotsk, *Shevet mi-Yehuda* (Vilna, 1803), 15:15, 22:3.

70. Phinehas, *Rosh ha-Giveah*, 15a; cf. *Kether Torah*, 36a.

71. Phinehas, *Shevet mi-Yehuda*, 13:18.

72. Ibid., 6:23. The quoted verse is from Psalms 118:21.

73. Phinehas ben Judah, Maggid of Polotsk, *Siddur Shaar ha-Rahamim im Perush Maggid Zedek* (Shklov, 1788), 2:99b.

74. Ibid., 2:123b, 101a.

75. Phinehas, *Shevet mi-Yehuda*, 23:13.

76. On Maimonides' rationalization of the regulations regarding the coerced divorce see *Mishneh Torah*, "Hilkhoth Gerushin," 2:20. See the excellent interpretation of this passage by David Werner Amram in *The Jewish Law of Divorce* (New York, 1975), 57–59. The Maimonidean doctrine of the complementary nature of the welfares of the body and the soul has been dealt with extensively in Maimonidean scholarship. The major primary source of this notion is, *Guide for the Perplexed*, 3:27.

77. Phinehas, *Rosh ha-Giveah*, 19a. The Hebrew root *d'm* connotes blood *(dam)* and money *(damim)*.

78. For a lengthy panegyric to physical affliction see Phinehas ben Judah, Maggid of Polotsk, *Midrash Hakhamim*, commentary to Psalms (Minsk, 1809), 94.

79. Phinehas, *Giveath Phinehas*, 2:12.

Chapter 5: The Spiritual Bliss of Death

1. Deuteronomy 30:15.

2. See Ezekiel 37.

3. Ecclesiastes 12:7.

4. E. P. Sanders, "The Covenant As a Soteriological Category and the Nature of Salvation in Palestinian and Hellenistic Judaism," in *Jews, Greeks, and Christians: Essays in Honour of William David Davies* (Leiden, 1976), 11–44.

5. Mishna, *Aboth*, 4:16.

6. See *Avoth de-Rabi Nathan*, 40a, 59b. Cf. Babylonian Talmud, *Kiddushin*, 39b, where the rabbis debate whether there is any reward or punishment at all in this life. On the theme of the deferral of salvation to the future life in classical rabbinic thought see Solomon Schechter, "The Theory of Divine Retribution in Rabbinical Literature," in *Studies in Judaism*, 2 vols. (reprint, Philadelphia, 1936), vol. 2.

7. *Bereshith Rabba*, sec. 9, par. 4.

8. Babylonian Talmud, *Shabbath*, 55a.

9. Babylonian Talmud, *Eruvin*, 13b.

10. Shimon Dubnow, *Toledoth ha-Hasiduth,* 4th ed. (Tel Aviv, 1975), intro., esp. 24–34.

11. On R. Nahman's obsession with death see M. Piekarz, *Mehkarim be-Hasiduth Brazlav* (Jerusalem, 1974), 172–81.

12. For a wealth of Hasidic material on the meaning and significance of the Yahrzeit celebration see Isaac Sperling, *Sefer Ta'amei ha-Minhagim u-Mekorei ha-Dinim* (Jerusalem, 1957), 477–87. Here and throughout the Hasidic material on death it is clear that the living could be graced by their connections with the souls of the dead. This is in sharp contrast to the dominant Mithnagdic/rabbinic attitude of the time, which discouraged the attempt to engage in any such mystical communication with the spirits of the deceased. This general reluctance is perhaps best captured by the Gaon of Vilna's rejection of the maggid who visited him periodically (see R. Hayyim of Volozhin's introduction to Elijah ben Solomon, Gaon of Vilna, *Safra de-Zeniutha im Perush ha-GRA* [Vilna and Grodno, 1820]). A remarkably critical Mithnagdic assessment of the Hasidic celebration of the Yahrzeit of the zaddik, from a later generation, is to be found in Meir ben Elijah's anti-Hasidic polemic *Milhamoth Adonai,* Hebrew University and National Library, Jerusalem, MS 801067, 56–57. Speculating on the possible basis for this custom, which Meir views as being most deplorable, he speculates:

> Perhaps they [i.e., the Hasidim] interpret literally the verse that reads: "A good name is better than fine oil, and the day of death is better than one's day of birth" [*Ecclesiastes* 7:1], meaning that it is better and more appropriate for one to celebrate with great rejoicing on the anniversary of death than on the birthday. For [when one is born] we do not know what the future will hold and what one's end will be. Thus, it is better to visit the house of mourning than to attend a celebration. For in the house of mourning the true joy and celebration are in fact greater. For the greatest of all joys is the knowledge that one is departing for the bliss of the Garden of Eden....
>
> The truth is, then, that the death of a zaddik has two aspects. On the one hand, death is a blessing, for he is leaving the travails of this world and the constant battle against the evil instinct ... for the righteous are the most afflicted by the evil instinct. ... Therefore, their [the zaddikim's] death is actually a respite ... and it is a departure for a future world of reward and rest.... Thus, from this perspective, death is a great joy for them.
>
> On the other hand, there is another perspective in which life is viewed as an opportunity to achieve the merit of Torah study and the performance of the commandments. In this sense [is it said that] a single moment of this life is more precious than the entire life of the world to come. Thus, this life is also precious and good for them....
>
> Perhaps this is precisely why the Hasidim rejoice [on the Yahrzeit]. They do not mourn the loss of Torah study and the performance of *mitzvoth,* since even in this life they eschew them.

13. Benjamin Mintz, *Sefer ha-Histalkuth* (Tel Aviv, 1930), 10. This volume contains a wealth of material on the deaths of the Hasidic masters. Martin Buber, in his *Tales of the Hasidim* (New York, 1948), relied very heavily on the material gathered by Mintz.

14. See Buber, *Tales of the Hasidim*, 1:52.

15. From the English translation of the "Letter of the Baal Shem Tov to Gershon of Kutow" by Norman Lamm in *Tradition* 14, no. 4 (1974): 116.

16. Mintz, *Sefer ha-Histalkuth*, 14.

17. Menahem Mendel of Vitebsk, *Peri ha-Aretz*, rev. ed. (Jerusalem, 1987), 66–67.

18. For a wealth of primary materials regarding the deaths of the great Hasidic masters see the massive two-volume collection edited by Moses Lipschutz, *Ashkavta de-Zadikaya* (Jerusalem, 1991). See also the earlier and slimmer volume of similar material by Isaac Alfasi, *Mi-Prozdor le-Tarkelin: Histalkutam shel Zadikim* (Tel Aviv, 1977).

19. On the concept of *retzo va-shov* in Ḥabad Hasidism see Rachel Elior, *The Paradoxical Ascent to God: The Kabbalistic Theosophy of Habad Hasidism* (New York, 1992), chap. 3, esp. 27–32. As Elior makes clear, the spiritual bliss normally associated with the future life coexists in perpetual dialectical tension with the mundane experience of the earthly here and now.

20. See Buber, *Tales of the Hasidim*, 1:57.

21. Elijah ben Solomon, Gaon of Vilna, *Megillath Esther im Perush ha-GRA al Derekh ha-Peshat ve-al Derekh ha-Remez* (reprint, Warsaw, 1897), 1:5.

22. Ibid., 1:6.

23. Shneur Zalman of Lyadi, *Torah Or* (Brooklyn, 1986), 16.

24. Ibid., 9a; cf. ibid., "Hayyei Sara," 16a–16b. The idea that it is only through its descent into the body that the soul can ascend to the highest levels is an extension of the classical Hasidic doctrine of *yeridah le-zorekh aliyah*, or the need for a prior descent in order to effect a religious ascent. This idea is also a key part of the generally paradoxical religious theory of Ḥabad mysticism. For a very elaborate account of the Ḥabad school's theory of the human soul and the methods of divine worship see Rachel Elior, *Torath ha-Elohuth be-Dor ha-Sheni Shel Hasiduth Habad* (Jerusalem, 1982), esp. chap. 5. See also idem, *The Paradoxical Ascent to God*, 103–24.

25. Elijah ben Solomon, Gaon of Vilna, *Sefer Yohah im Biur ha-Gra*, ed. Joseph Rivlin (Bnei Berak, 1986), 1:4.

26. Mishna, *Aboth*, 4:22.

27. This does not, of course, mean that the GRA rejected completely the notion that this world does present opportunities for human religious achievements that are unique and not attainable in the world to come, e.g., the study of Torah and faithful performance of the *mitzvoth*. But whereas such conventional and limited religious accomplishments are indeed the unique religious goals of worldly existence, ultimate spiritual bliss and mystical union are reserved for the future world.

28. Elijah ben Solomon, *Sefer Yonah im Biur ha-GRA*, 4:3.

29. On the compatability of dualist theologies and the belief in reincarnation and the exile of human souls see A. C. Pearson, "Transmigration," in *Encyclopedia of*

Religion and Ethics, ed. J. Hastings, vol. 12 (Edinburgh, 1921), esp. 432–33, on ancient Greek theories of transmigration.

30. Elijah ben Solomon, *Sefer Yonah im Biur ha-GRA al Yonah,* 4:7.

31. Elijah ben Solomon, Gaon of Vilna, *Devar Eliyahu: Biur Ha-GRA al Sefer Iyov* (Warsaw, 1840), 3:21–22.

32. Elijah ben Solomon, Gaon of Vilna, *Adereth Eliyahu al ha-Torah* (Warsaw, 1887), 320, commentary to Deuteronomy 1:1.

33. Ibid., commentary to Genesis 3:21. The idea that God's statement that man will die if he eats of the tree should be understood not as a threat but as a promise recurs throughout the Mithnagdic literature. Two generations later, for example, the GRA's grandnephew Meir ben Elijah of Vilna wrote in *Derekh Avoth* (Vilna, 1836), 1:12 (p. 10a):

> That which God told Adam, "that on the day you eat from it you shall surely die," was not said to him as a curse—quite the contrary, it was said for his own good. Namely, that having eaten of the tree, you will only be able to arrive at your final perfection via death. Similarly, the warning that if man ate of the tree of life he would live forever was intended for his own good. For if man were to live eternally in this physical world, he could never achieve his purpose in the future life. What possible pleasure could he have in living in this corrupt, vain, and ephemeral world? "The destiny of every animal is to be slaughtered . . . ," and that is true of all creatures in the world—their destiny is to die. It is through the death of man that he is firmly established and rises to his final purpose and original source.

34. In chapter 7, below, I offer a full presentation of the GRA's great enthusiasm about the spiritual powers with which *Talmud Torah* endows human life.

35. Elijah Landau, *Toledoth ha-GRA* (Jerusalem, 1927), 17. I am grateful to Professor Bernard Septimus for calling my attention to this important source. Besides qualifying the many sources cited in this chapter indicating an optimistic view of death, this hagiographical account can serve to remind the reader of the distinction between theoretical affirmations and the real-life passions and natural will to live that the Mithnagdim shared with all men. At least one very important latter-day exponent of Mithnagdism has greatly exaggerated the significance and implications of the GRA's moving deathbed statement. Joseph B. Soloveitchik, in his great essay *Ish ha-Halakha,* has argued that this statement of the GRA is a reflection of Halakhic Judaism's worldliness and sanctification of *olam ha-zeh* existence (see Joseph B. Soloveitchik, *Halakhic Man,* trans. Lawrence Kaplan [Philadelphia, 1983], 30; and my critique of Soloveitchik's use of Mithnagdic sources to support his own particularly this-worldly religious existentialism, "Soloveitchik's Halakhic Man: *Not* a Mithnagged," *Modern Judaism* 13 [1993]: 119–47).

36. Israel Jacob of Kremenetz, introduction to *Shevet me-Yisrael* (Zolkiew, 1772), 2. On R. Israel Jacob generally see M. Piekarz, *Biyemei Zemihath ha-Hasiduth* (Jeru-

salem, 1978), 65–71. Piekarz portrays him as a traditional, strongly anti-Sabbatean rabbi and popular preacher who, though doubtless aware of the existence of the early Hasidim, nowhere refers to them in his writings.

37. Eliezer Segal, *Siah ha-Sadeh,* Part II, 27a. On R. Eliezer Segal and his possible transformation early in life from a Hasid to a latter-day Mithnagged see M. Nadav, "Kehiloth Pinsk-Karlin beyn Hasiduth le-Hithnagduth," *Zion* 34 (1969): 98–108, esp. 101–3. That Segal relies heavily on the sixteenth-century exegesis of R. Eliezer Ha-Levi is noteworthy. As suggested in the introductory pages of this chapter, much material to be found in the earlier rabbinic literature constitutes an important precedent for the Mithnagdic view of death. New in the Mithnagdic writings, however, are the prominence and centrality these themes assume.

38. Eliezer Segal, *Siah ha-Sadeh,* 86a.

39. Zvi Hirsch Katzenellenbogen, *Giveath Shaul* (Vilna and Grodno, 1825), 6a. In his quotation of Psalms 116:15, R. Katzenellenbogen here interprets the word *yakar* literally, as "precious," as opposed to the more common rabbinic understanding of the contextual meaning "difficult" or "painful."

40. Menahem Mendel of Shklov, *Mayyim Adirim* (Jerusalem, 1987), 2a.

41. Ibid., 143–44.

42. Abraham ben Elijah of Vilna, *Be'er Avraham al Tehillim* (Warsaw, 1887), 4:9.

43. Ibid., 4:4.

44. Hillel of Kovno, *Heilel Ben Shahar* (Warsaw, 1804), 84a.

45. Phinehas ben Judah, Maggid of Polotsk, *Kether Torah* (reprint, Jerusalem, 1965), 18a.

46. Phinehas ben Judah, Maggid of Polotsk, *Midrash Hakhamim* (Minsk, 1809), 17:16.

47. On the standard rabbinic view of reward and punishment see Schechter, "The Doctrine of Divine Retribution in Rabbinical Literature," in *Studies in Judaism,* 1:259–82.

48. Phinehas ben Judah, Maggid of Polotsk, "Derush le-Parashath Shekalim," appendix to *Rosh ha-Giveah* (reprint, Jerusalem, 1965), 25a.

49. See Phinehas, *Midrash Hakhamim,* 30:5.

50. Phinehas, *Giveath Phinehas,* 7:2.

51. Phinehas, *Midrash Hakhamim,* 4:7.

52. Phinehas, *Rosh ha-Giveah,* 2a–b.

53. Phinehas ben Judah, Maggid of Polotsk, *Kizzur Even Bohan* (Jerusalem, 1900), chap. 9.

54. All the quotations below are from the full English translation of the death poem, which is found in appendix B, below.

55. On death poetry in eighteenth-century Europe see the excellent study by John McManners, *Death and the Enlightenment* (New York, 1981), chap. 10, esp. 334–53.

56. See David E. Stannard, *The Puritan Way of Death* (Oxford, 1977), 93.

57. Ibid., 150.

58. On this phenomenological classification of religious expressions with regard

to earthly existence and physical death see M. Westphal, *God, Guilt, and Death* (Bloomington, 1984), chaps. 9–10.

Chapter 6: The Mithnagdim and the Haskalah: A Reappraisal

1. J. S. Raisin, *The Haskala Movement in Russia* (Philadelphia, 1913), 74.

2. Most notable among the GRA's authentic, published "scientific" writings is *Ayil Meshulash* (Vilna and Grodno, 1834), on the principles of trigonometry, geometry, and astronomy. There are many testimonies regarding the remarkable scope of the GRA's meta-rabbinic learning, especially in the hagiographic Mithnagdic literature. The most convincing statement is found in Israel ben Samuel of Shklov, introduction to *Pe'ath ha-Shulhan* (Jerusalem, 1959), 5a–b. The most comprehensive citation of that material in the secondary literature is to be found in Bezalel Landau's *Ha-Gaon ha-Hasid mi-Vilna* (Jerusalem, 1978), chap. 17, esp. the exhaustive footnotes 1–7 (pp. 218–22). Interestingly, although Landau documents evidence for the GRA's secular knowledge in tremendous detail, he insists that for the GRA all of this wisdom was strictly ancillary to Torah learning. To that purpose he describes, in the same chapter, the GRA's strong opposition to the beginnings of Haskalah tendencies. Although much of Landau's evidence for the GRA's antienlightenment posture consists of highly unreliable tales from the hagiographies, his understanding of the very strictly limited role of secular study in the GRA's overall religious life seems to be a more accurate evaluation of the GRA than that of the Haskalah apologists and *Wissenschaft* historians. Elijah Judah Schochet, in his recent study *The Hasidic Movement and the Gaon of Vilna* (Northvale, N.J., 1994), 149–50, also views the GRA's evaluation of secular studies as purely utilitarian, of importance only in that they "lead to a better understanding of sacred texts."

3. On the GRA's pedagogic approach, see Landau, *Ha-Gaon ha-Hasid mi-Vilna*, chap. 15.

4. Shai Ish Hurwitz, "Ha-Hasiduth ve-ha-Haskala," *He-Atid* 2 (1909): 31–32. This idyllic portrayal of the Gaon of Vilna was, I believe, a direct response to the very unflattering depiction of him by the neo-Hasidic romanticist Shmuel Abba Horodetsky in an article that had appeared in the Hebrew journal *Ha-Shiloah* less than two years earlier (S. A. Horodetsky, "Ha-Gra veha-BESHT," *Ha-Shiloah* 17 [1907]: 348–56). For a fuller discussion of the dispute between Hurwitz and Horodetsky see Allan Nadler, *Rationalism, Romanticism, Rabbis, and Rebbes*, YIVO Institute for Jewish Studies Monographs (New York, 1992).

5. This claim regarding the GRA's alleged enlightenment tendencies actually was lodged as early as Isaac Baer Levinsohn's remark that "kol haburah kadisha talmidei ha-GRA" [the entire holy circle of the GRA's disciples] were sympathetic to secular studies (*Teudah be-Yisrael* [Vilna, 1828], 151–52). Subsequently, hardly a scholar wrote of the Russian Haskalah without citing the "precedent" for it in the GRA's intellectual profile. See, for example, I. H. Weiss, "Reyshith Zemihath ha-Haskala be-Russia," in

Mi-Mizrah umi-Maarav 1 (1894): 9 ("ha-Gaon Rabenu Eliyahu mi-Vilna haya ha-rishon le-haramath ha-hokhmoth bekerev amenu" [the Gaon, Rabbi Elijah, was the very first to advance the study of sciences in the midst of our people]); Raisin, *The Haskala Movement in Russia,* chap. 2, esp. 69–75; and Louis Greenberg, *The Jews in Russia; The Struggle for Emancipation* (New Haven, 1944), 22–23. See also, however, the review and critical evaluation of this literature by Immanuel Etkes in his fine essay "Ha-GRA veha-Haskala: Tadmith u-Meziuth," in *Perakim be-Toledoth ha-Hevra ha-Yehudith bi-Yemei ha-Beynaim uva-Eit Ha-Hadasha: Mukdashim le-Professor Yaakov Katz,* ed. I. Etkes (Jerusalem, 1980), 192–217. And on the beginnings of Haskalah among the rabbinic elite of eastern Europe see, *inter alia,* Israel Klausner, *Vilna bi-Tekufath ha-Gaon* (Jerusalem, 1942); and B. Z. Katz, *Rabbanuth, Hasiduth ve-Has-kala,* 2 vols. (Tel Aviv, 1956–58), 1:140–48, 2:122–39.

6. See Etkes, "Ha-GRA veha-Haskala."

7. On Barukh Shick see the fine study by David Fishman, *Russia's First Modern Jews: The Jews of Shklov* (New York, 1995), 22–45; on Shick's opposition to Hasidism, see 118–19. On Zeitlin see ibid., 56–59. On Zeitlin's opposition to Hasidism, Habad in particular, see A. S. Heilman, *Beth Rabi* (Berditchev, 1903), 75–78. On Rivlin's Haska-lah tendencies see Fishman, *Russia's First Modern Jews,* 108–12. And on Margolioth, see J. L. Margolioth, *Beth Midoth* (Dierenfürth, 1778), 20b, 22a, where the author states in strong terms the importance of the pursuit of secular knowledge. For a discussion of Margolioth's enlightened tendencies see Fishman, *Russia's First Modern Jews,* 112–15.

8. On the alleged modernity of Ezekiel Faivel see Immanuel Etkes, "Immanent Factors and External Influences in the Development of the Haskala Movement in Russia," in *Towards Modernity: The European Jewish Model,* ed. J. Katz (New Brunswick, 1987), 17–20. For a sense of Ezekiel Faivel's rather novel educational and pedagogic ideas see his *Toledoth Adam* (Warsaw, 1856), 14b, 16b, 24b, 75b, 84a.

9. Very little has been written about R. Menashe of Ilya. See, however, the essay by I. Barzilay, "The Life of Menashe of Ilya (1767–1831)," *Proceedings of the American Academy for Jewish Religion* 50 (1983): 1–35. At the time of this article, Barzilay wrote that he was working on a monograph to be entitled "Menashe of Ilya: Precursor of Modernism among the Jews of Eastern Europe."

10. On the very beginnings of organized opposition to the Hasidic movement in Shklov see M. Wilensky, *Hasidim u-Mithnagdim: le-Toledoth ha-Pulmus Beynehem,* 2 vols. (Jerusalem, 1970), 1:27–31. Cf. Immanuel Etkes, "Ha-GRA ve-Reyshith ha-Hith-nagduth la-Hasiduth," in *Temuroth Ba-Historiya ha-Yehudith ha-Hadasha: Kovets Maamarim Shai le-Shmuel Ettinger* (Jerusalem, 1987); and Fishman, *Russia's First Modern Jews,* 11–15. David Fishman's book firmly establishes Shklov as the first important center of the eastern European Haskalah.

11. See Etkes, "Immanent Factors and External Influences," 13–32, for a review of the Lithuanian and Belorussian rabbis, many of them associated with the GRA, who Etkes considers to have been precursors of the eastern European Haskalah.

12. Michael Stanislawski, *Tsar Nicholas I and the Jews: The Transformation of Jewish Society in Russia, 1825–1855* (Philadelphia, 1983), 50. On the intellectual roots of the Haskalah in traditional Russian rabbinic circles see ibid., chap. 3.

13. E. Liebes, "David of Makow," *Encyclopedia Judaica*, 1975, 5:1363.

14. A rich selection of primary rabbinic sources reflecting a wide variety of attitudes toward the use of secular studies in enhancing understanding of Torah can be found in Simha Assaf, *Mekoroth le-Toledoth ha-Hinukh be-Yisrael* (Jerusalem, 1942). For a study of the rabbinic attitude toward secular sciences in eastern European Jewish history prior to the period discussed in this book see David Fishman, "Rabbi Moses Isserles and the Study of Science among Polish Rabbis," in *Tradition and Crisis Revisited*, ed. Bernard Dov Cooperman (Cambridge, Mass., 1994).

15. Although he employs the term *Enlightened Mitnagdism* in his extensive discussion of the scientifically oriented rabbis of Shklov, David Fishman makes it clear that the nature of their "secular" interests was "essentially conservative, since it subordinated science to the purposes of Torah study" (Fishman, *Russia's First Modern Jews*, 112). Aside from the contempt for Hasidism common to the Mithnagdim and Maskillim, Fishman does not demonstrate any genuine ideological affinities or social programs shared by them and is careful to distinguish between the different uses each had for secular and scientific studies.

16. See, for example, the section of Etkes' article "Immanent Factors and External Influences" entitled "Characteristics of the Haskala," 14–15.

17. Fishman, *Russia's First Modern Jews*, 115–21, argues that a rejection of Hasidic miracles is an important component of "enlightened mitnagduth." There can be no question that the rejection of the legitimacy of Hasidic miracles is an important theme of the polemical literature, even by the non-Haskalah Mithnagdim (see esp. Israel Loebl's *Sefer ha-Vikuah* in Wilensky, *Hasidim u-Mithnagdim*, 2:321–22). R. Hayyim of Volozhin is reported to have claimed that "the source of true faith is in the hidden wonder [*nes nistar*] and not in blatant miracles [*nes nigleh*]" (see Aaron Zelig ben Eliezer Liphschitz, *Hanhagoth ve-Ezoth Shel Rabi Hayyim mi-Volozhin*, Hebrew University and National Library, Jerusalem, Microfilm 80800, pt. 2, par. 27). Yet there is a body of evidence to suggest that both the GRA and his leading disciples, most notably R. Hayyim of Volozhin, feared the Hasidim precisely because of their supernatural powers. Note esp. the remarkable statement attributed to the GRA by Aaron Zelig Liphschitz in ibid., par. 14, to the effect that the Hasidic masters possessed dangerous, supernatural powers, which they would summon for demonic purposes.

18. See Ezekiel Faivel of Dretzhyn, *Toledoth Adam*, 1:3, for an outline of his proposals regarding curricular reform. According to S. Abramson, in his article on Ezekiel Faivel's published works, "Defusei *Musar Haskel* ve *Toledoth Adam* le-Rabi Yehezkel Faivel," in *Sefer Margaliyoth* (Jerusalem, 1973), Ezekiel apparently traveled frequently to the West, most notably to Breslau, where he was exposed to the German Haskalah. Despite this exposure, he remained conservative in his religious ideology and, Abramson contends, rejected the study of philosophy and metaphysics. On Ezekiel Faivel generally, see above, introduction, n. 24.

19. See, for example, Phinehas ben Judah, Maggid of Polotsk, *Giveath Phinehas* (Vilna, 1808), introduction and commentary to chap. 3 and chap. 9, verse 23.

20. Ibid., 33:21; cf. the similar philosophical considerations of God's unknowability in 22;3, 22:22, and 24:13.

21. Ibid., 11:6, 33:15.

22. See, *inter alia*, Phinehas ben Judah, Maggid of Polotsk, *Siddur Shaar ha-Rahamim im Perush Maggid Zedek* (Shklov, 1788), pt. 1, p. 20a, and pt. 2, p. 5; and idem, *Derekh ha-Melekh* (Grodno, 1804), 1:1, 1:12. On R. Phinehas's acceptance of a vague notion of natural law see Phinehas, *Giveath Phinehas*, 35:11.

23. Phinehas, *Giveath Phinehas*, 36:28.

24. R. Phinehas's pedagogic proposals are found in *Rosh ha-Giveah* (Jerusalem, 1965), 11a–12b, as well as in *Kether Torah* (Jerusalem, 1965), 27a–29b. Consistent with this systematic, streamlined approach to Jewish education, the only approbation by R. Phinehas to a published work that I have found is his letter of support for the publication of the curious sixteenth-century Jewish catechism *Sefer Lekah Tov*, a work clearly modeled after medieval Christian catechisms. As J. J. Petuchowski has shown in his study of this subject, "Manuals and Catechisms of the Jewish Religion in the Early Period of the Emancipation," in *Studies in Nineteenth Century Jewish Intellectual History*, ed. A. Altman (Cambridge, Mass., 1964), 47–64, the educational reformers of the Haskalah were especially fond of such pedagogic manuals. R. Phinehas's unique *haskama* (approbation) to such a work can be interpreted as yet another sign of the progressive nature of his educational ideas. On the other hand, the fact that *Sefer Lekah Tov* concludes with a vehement attack upon Copernican astronomy as a form of idolatrous sun worship suggests that R. Phinehas's own scientific views were not quite up-to-date.

25. Phinehas, *Kether Torah*, 35a.

26. The following discussion of R. Phinehas's elaborate critique of the Haskalah is based entirely on ibid., 1b–5b.

27. On Bahya's critique of the modernizing, assimilationist tendencies of the "enlightened" Jews of the Spanish court in his own day see Bezalel Safran, "Bahya's Attitude to the Courtier Class," in *Studies in Medieval Jewish Intellectual History*, ed. I. Twersky (Cambridge, 1979), pp. 154–96.

28. Phinehas, *Kether Torah*, 1a.

29. Ibid., 2a.

30. Ibid., 2a, 2b.

31. A thorough evaluation of R. Shick's views as reflected in these and other texts is found in Fishman, *Russia's First Modern Jews*, 37–45. On the value of scientific study in raising the prestige of the Jews in the eyes of the world see David Fishman, "A Polish Rabbi Meets the Berlin Haskala," *Association for Jewish Studies Review* 12, no. 1 (1987): 114–19.

32. R. Barukh Shick of Shklov, introduction to *Euklidus* (The Hague, 1780), 2a (unpaginated).

33. On Notkin's career see Fishman, *Russia's First Modern Jews*, 52–56.

34. On all of these developments see ibid., esp. chaps. 3–5.

35. R. Phinehas's *Siddur Shaar ha-Rahamim,* published in Shklov in 1788, was preordered by thirty-five residents from Polotsk and thirty-two from Shklov, including the latter city's *av beth din* (rabbinic chief justice), R. Hanoch Henakh of Pruzyn.

36. Although it has its fullest expression in *Kether Torah,* the anti-Haskalah polemic, and specifically the rejection of the enlightenment's romance with secular studies, recurs in R. Phinehas's commentary to the liturgy, *Maggid Zedek,* most notably in his commentary to the tractate *Avoth* (see Phinehas, *Siddur Shaar ha-Rahamim,* 1:97b–98b; see also *Kether Torah,* 27a, 51a).

37. Phinehas, *Kether Torah,* 5a.

38. That Phinehas was reacting with a sense of great urgency to what he perceived to be a pressing problem of his day, and not merely repeating literary polemical motifs of the sort found in early antiphilosophical classics, such as Joseph Yaavetz's sixteenth-century conservative work *Or ha-Hayyim,* is evident from the personal and urgent tone of the opening, programmatic statements in *Kether Torah,* 1a–2b. It is nonetheless interesting to note that Yaavetz's *Or ha-Hayyim* was reprinted in Shklov during this period (1796), very possibly also as a reaction to the emergence of the Haskalah in Belorussia. The Shklov rabbis Hanokh Henokh and Zevi Hirsch ben Meir gave enthusiastic approbations to this edition, whose title page claims that *Or ha-Hayyim* was being reprinted "in order to bring merit to the masses so that they will not fall into these sinful traps [i.e., rationalizing the Jewish faith]." Years later the Hasidic master Zevi Elimelekh of Dinov reissued *Or ha-Hayyim,* with his own explicitly anti-Haskalah commentary to the text, "Ma'ayan Ganim" (Lublin, 1912). Zevi Elimelekh's reinterpretation of Yaavetz's antirationalist statements and their use in Yaavetz's attack on the Haskalah is a fascinating example of the polemical use of classical texts for contemporary, and entirely unanticipated, purposes. On "Ma'ayan Ganim" see the excellent article by M. Piekarz, "Al Meh Avdah Galuth Sefarad ke-Lekakh Kelapei ha-Haskalla be-Mizrakh Eiropah: ha-hasiduth be-Eynei R. Zevi Elimelekh Shapira mi-Dinov," *Daat,* no. 28 (1992): 87–115.

39. For a full discussion of the complex status of the rationalization of the commandments of the Torah in the ideology of the founders of the Haskalah see Isaac Heinemann, *Taamei ha-Mitzvoth be-Sifruth Yisrael,* 3 vols. (Jerusalem, 1956), 2:9–60.

40. Phinehas, *Kether Torah,* 2b.

41. Ibid., 4b. Later in the same work, p. 16b, in the context of a defense of Torah study that is lacking in full intent, or proper *kavana* (i.e., *Torah shelo lishmah*), R. Phinehas once again states his strong support of the rote, slavelike, positivist performance of the commandments, even the study of Torah.

42. On R. Israel Loebl's anti-Hasidic writings see the lengthy introduction to his *Sefer ha-Vikuah* in Wilensky, *Hasidim u-Mithnagdim,* 2:253–65. Note especially the close ties cited there between R. Israel and the circle of the GRA.

43. R. Michael, in "Rabi Israel Loebl ve-Kuntreso ha-Germani," *Kiryath Sefer* 51 (1976): 315–23, argues that R. Israel Loebl was personally influenced in a positive way by the Haskalah and that this is reflected in his German polemic against Hasidism,

which bears much similarity to the Haskalah's critique. Michael tries, unconvincingly in my view, to downplay the overall intention of Loebl in *Even Bohan* and to characterize it as a limited response to the reforming efforts of David Friedlander. Michael argues generally that Loebl was an exceedingly complex figure who seems to have gone through many conflicting religious and intellectual phases during the course of his life and that this renders him very difficult to classify ideologically. Be that as it may, Loebl's attack upon the Haskalah's tendency to rationalize Judaism and his own insistence on a positivist approach to Jewish legal observance are strikingly similar to the arguments advanced by R. Phinehas in *Kether Torah.*

44. Israel Loebl, *Even Bohan* (Frankfurt am Main, 1799), 10b.

45. Ibid., 17b.

46. Barukh Landau, introduction to *Reyshith Limudim* (Berlin, 1789).

47. R. Phinehas's commentary to the Proverbs, *Shevet mi-Yehuda* (Vilna, 1803), is replete with antiphilosophical and antirationalist pronouncements. See, *inter alia,* 2:16, 5:9, 5:20, 9:4, 20:17, 23:27, 24:13–14, 27:7. Except for 24:13–14, where Phinehas concedes that secular study can play a strictly limited but legitimate role as a handmaiden to Torah wisdom, these statements are all consistent with the attitude found in the anti-Haskalah polemic in *Kether Torah.*

48. Phinehas, *Shevet mi-Yehuda,* 9:4.

49. Ibid., 30:26.

50. Phinehas, *Derekh ha-Melekh,* 2:2.

51. See Jacob Katz, *Exclusiveness and Tolerance* (New York, 1961), chap. 14.

52. Lucien Goldmann, *The Philosophy of the Enlightenment: The Christian Burgess and the Enlightenment,* trans. Henry Mass (Cambridge, Mass., 1973), 54–55.

53. Mordechai Lewin, *Erkhei Hevra ve-Kalkala ba-Idiologia Shel Tekufath ha-Haskala* (Jerusalem, 1975), chap. 1, esp. 14–21.

54. In this context, R. Phinehas's extensive interpretation of the early part of the book of Job as a philosophical debate regarding divine providence and God's knowledge of particulars emerges in an entirely new light. In the commentary to Job, *Giveath Phinehas,* the Aristotelian view that severely limits divine knowledge and control of man's affairs is consistently presented as "a dangerous heresy." The final purpose of the drawn-out philosophical consideration of this issue is the strenuous affirmation of absolute divine knowledge and providence.

55. On the contrast between Mithnagdic asceticism and otherworldliness and the Hasidic doctrine of *avodah be-gashmiyouth* see chapter 4, above. The notion that man can serve God in and through indulging in the material world was central to early Hasidic thought. A most remarkable text that explicates this idea is Barukh of Mezhiboz, *Butzina di-Nehora* (Brooklyn, 1978), commentary to "Ki Teze," 59–60. R. Barukh argues that the service of God through the gratification of man's physical needs is, in fact, of an even higher spiritual order than ritual worship.

56. Phinehas, *Kether Torah,* 39a.

57. On the theme of passive faith in divine providence see Phinehas, *Rosh ha-Giveah,* 15a–17a.

58. Akivah ben Eliezer of Minsk (Chief Rabbi of Barisev), *Bizath Mitzrayim* (reprint, Jerusalem, 1960), 10a. The author was a subscriber to Phinehas's *Siddur Shaar ha-Rahamim.*

59. Goldmann, *Philosophy of the Enlightenment,* 63-64.

60. Carl Becker, *The Heavenly City of the Eighteenth Century Philosophers,* cited in Greenberg, *The Jews in Russia,* 12.

61. See, chapter 5, above.

62. On R. Elijah Rogoler see A. L. Frumkin, *Toledoth Eliyahu* (Vilna, 1900), 49-55. On R. Samuel of Kelm's vociferous opposition to the Haskalah see Immanuel Etkes, *Lita Bi-Yerushalayim* (Jerusalem, 1991), 31-38. For a discussion of R. Moses Isaac Darshan of Kelm's opposition to the Haskalah and his confrontation with such leading Russian Maskillim as Yehudah Leib Gordon see esp. the introduction to the Jerusalem, 1982, edition of his collection of sermons, *Tokhahat Hayyim.* And for a discussion of R. Meir ben Elijah's bitter opposition to both Hasidism and Haskalah see Allan Nadler, "Meir b. Elijah of Vilna's *Milhamoth Adonai:* A Late Anti-Hasidic Polemic," *Journal of Jewish Thought and Philosophy* 1 (1991): 247-80.

63. See Immanuel Etkes, "Review of N. Lamm's Torah Lishmah" (Hebrew), *Kiryath Sefer* 50 (1975): 646.

64. On Meir's critique of the Haskalah see Nadler, "Meir b. Elijah of Vilna's *Milhamoth Adonai,*" esp. 274-79.

Chapter 7: The Centrality of Torah Study in Mithnagdism

1. M. Wilensky, *Hasidim u-Mithnagdim: le-Toledoth ha-Pulmus Beynehem,* 2 vols. (Jerusalem, 1970), 1:18-19.

2. As noted in chapter 1, certain Hasidic historiographers have maintained that the Hasidic belief in divine immanence was at the root of the rabbinic opposition to the movement. The most notable and vociferous dissenter from Wilensky's position that the denigration of Torah scholarship was the true basis for the Hasidic-Mithnagdic dispute is Avraham Rubinstein in his review of Wilensky's *Hasidim u-Mithnagdim* in *Kiryath Sefer* 47 (1971): 361-76. Rubinstein's review of Wilensky is, however, generally unfair and in this instance inaccurate. Besides the ample citations in the polemical literature regarding the Hasidic affront to the honor of the Torah and its scholars, the responses of Mithnagdic thinkers in their own works to this challenge is unmistakable. As we shall see below, the structure and content of *Kether Torah* alone make clear the centrality of this issue to the Mithnagdic polemics.

M. Piekarz too has suggested that the Hasidic demotion of study as a central value and the attendant critique of the rabbinic scholars were not really the root cause of Mithnagdic anger with Hasidism. Consistent with the methodology employed throughout his study of the origins of Hasidic thought, Piekarz bases this contention on the precedents for this Hasidic critique of rabbinic intellectualism in earlier, pre-

Hasidic Jewish texts (see M. Piekarz, *Biyemei Zemihath ha-Hasiduth* [Jerusalem, 1978], 377–83). The problem with this approach is, quite simply, that the existence of precedents for Hasidic ideas in earlier, obscure and relatively uninfluential texts does not in any way detract from the unprecedented, scandalous impact the Hasidic masters' polemical and highly popular use of those same ideas later had upon the rabbinic establishment.

3. H. H. Ben Sasson, "Ishiyutho Shel ha-GRA ve-Hashpa'ato ha-Hevratith," *Zion* 31 (1966): 39–86, 197–216.

4. See Immanuel Etkes, "Shitato U-Faalo Shel Rabi Hayyim mi-Mi-Volozhin ki-Teguvath ha-Hevrah ha-Mithnagdith la-Hasiduth," *Proceedings of the American Academy for Jewish Religion* 38 (1972): 1–45; Jonah Ben Sasson, "Olamam ha-Ruhani u-Mishnatam ha-Hinukhith Shel Meyasdei ha-Yeshiva ha-Litaith," in *Hinukh ha-Adam ve-Yiudo* (Jerusalem, 1967), 155–67; and Norman Lamm, *Torah Lishmah* (Jerusalem, 1972), esp. chap. 2. The English translation of Lamm's book, *Torah For Torah's Sake in the Works of Rabbi Hayyim of Volozhin and His Contemporaries* (New York, 1989), while essentially the same as the original, does include some revised footnotes and brief responses to more recent scholarship. References in this chapter are all to the original Hebrew version of Lamm's book.

5. R. Hayyim's motivation for establishing the Volozhin yeshiva remains a matter of scholarly dispute. Shaul Stampfer, in his recent book *Ha-Yeshiva ha-Litait be-Hithavuta* (Jerusalem, 1995), 31–35, argues that the yeshiva was founded in order to raise the level and prestige of Talmudic learning, not as a response to Hasidism.

6. Although Lamm is in general agreement with Etkes' analysis of R. Hayyim's orientation, he maintains that R. Hayyim was not a truly passionate Mithnagged but rather a moderate in his attitude to Hasidism. Lamm further contends that while *Nefesh ha-Hayyim* was perhaps initially provoked in part by the Hasidic inversion of the traditional supremacy of scholarship in the value system of rabbinic Judaism, it ought to be appreciated essentially as a positive theological work intended to glorify the study of Torah and not primarily as a negative, anti-Hasidic polemical tract (see Lamm's discussion of the purpose of *Nefesh ha-Hayyim* in *Torah Lishmah*, 57–64). Dissenting from Lamm's portrait of R. Hayyim of Volozhin as a moderate who maintained a posture of forbearance toward much of Hasidic doctrine, Etkes insists that *Nefesh ha-Hayyim*'s unprecedented elevation of Torah and its radical championship of *Talmud Torah* in the hierarchy of religious values must be seen almost exclusively as a response to the Hasidic inversion of these values, which presents study as an antidote to the various forms of spiritual fulfillment that Hasidism was offering the Jews (see Etkes, "Review of N. Lamm's Torah Lishmah" [Hebrew], *Kiryath Sefer* 50 [1975]: 638–48).

7. Lamm repeatedly claims that R. Hayyim's elevation of Torah study is unique and unparalleled in the writings of his contemporaries: "The philosophy of Rabbi Hayyim regarding the exalted value of the study of Torah is imbued with a passion that has almost no precedent" (*Torah Lishmah*, 63); "The pride of place in the hier-

archy of religious values that Rabbi Hayyim assigns to *Talmud Torah* is well beyond that of any of his predecessors" (ibid., 78); "Thus, the fourth section of *Nefesh ha-Hayyim* is among the most enthusiastic panegyrics to the study of Torah in all of Hebrew literature" (93).

8. See Lamm, *Torah Lishmah*, 81.

9. Ibid., 115. Lamm states on several occasions that he is aware of only one earlier rabbinic thinker who anticipated some of R. Hayyim's doctrine of *Torah lishmah*, the eighteenth-century rabbi Judah Leib Puchovitzer.

10. *Kether Torah* appeared in 1788, whereas *Nefesh ha-Hayyim*, at the author's insistence, was only published posthumously in 1824.

11. Immanuel Etkes is the only scholar who has taken any note of the importance of *Kether Torah*. Etkes briefly notes just a few of the many striking similarities between this work and *Nefesh ha-Hayyim* (see Immanuel Etkes, *Rabbi Yisrael Salanter ve-Reyshitah shel Tenuath ha-Mussar* [Jerusalem, 1982], 13–16).

12. Phinehas ben Judah, Maggid of Polotsk, *Kether Torah* (Jerusalem, 1965), 5b–6b.

13. Ibid., 6b–7b.

14. Ibid., 7b–8b. For a full discussion of the priority R. Phinehas assigns to study over prayer see the first part of chapter 3, above.

15. Phinehas, *Kether Torah*, 8b–9b.

16. Ibid., 9b–11a. On Phinehas's attitude to Kabbalistic study and mystical endeavors generally see chapter 2, above.

17. Phinehas, *Kether Torah*, 11a–13a. It is interesting that Phinehas's rejection of the primacy of Kabbalistic study over normative rabbinic scholarship is the one item on this list in which Phinehas is in fact simply favoring one form of study over another. The objection to devotion to the study of "nistar" is then somewhat different from his other objections to Hasidic religious priorities. Even so, as indicated above in chapter 2, R. Phinehas almost always associates study of Kabbalah with its practice. Moreover, the root of the objection to such study, that is, the insufficient religious preparedness and spiritual status of the Jewish masses, is fundamentally the same as that of the other objections.

18. Ibid., 13a.

19. On this theme see Hayyim of Volozhin, *Nefesh ha-Hayyim*, 4:1–2.

20. See the studies by Etkes, Lamm, and Jonah Ben Sasson cited in n. 4, above, and also Etkes' important review of Lamm's *Torah Lishmah*.

21. Phinehas, *Kether Torah*, 9b. The distinction between the two types of *yirah* and the insistence that the higher form of the fear of heaven can only be attained through the study of Torah is a theme that recurs throughout R. Phinehas's later writings. See, for example, his commentary to Psalms, *Midrash Hakhamim* (Minsk, 1809), 1:10:

"The Fear of the Lord is pure and abides forever." This is consistent with the statement in the holy *Zohar* that there are two types of fear. There is a fear of the evil strap, namely, the fear of punishment; and there is the fear that comes from the Torah, which instructs regarding God's majesty throughout the cosmos, namely, the fear of His majesty. Regarding this [latter form of fear], our Sages have instructed that where there is no Torah there can be no *yirah*. For it is impossible to acquire the fear of the Divine majesty without the Torah.

22. Phinehas, *Kether Torah*, 9b–10a.

23. Ibid., 10a.

24. Abraham ben Solomon of Vilna, *Maaloth ha-Torah* (reprint, Jerusalem, 1975), 209.

25. On the Hasidic transformation of Torah study from an intellectual to a mystical endeavor see Joseph Weiss, "Talmud Torah be-Reyshith ha-Hasiduth," in *Ha-Doar* 44 (1964): 33; see also idem, "Talmud Torah le-Shitath R. Israel Baal Shem Tov," in *Essays Presented to Chief Rabbi Israel Brodie* (London, 1967), 151–69. Moshe Idel, in *Hasidism: Between Ecstasy and Magic* (New York, 1995), 171–88, has demonstrated that, in early Hasidism at least, the study of Torah was also seen as a magical exercise, in which the sacred texts were endowed with talismanic powers.

26. On R. Hayyim's defense of *Tora shelo lishmah* see Lamm, *Torah Lishmah*, chap. 8, esp. 179–83.

27. Phinehas, *Midrash Hakhamim*, 1:11, introductory paragraph. Note that R. Phinehas seems here to anticipate the appeal by R. Hayyim in *Nefesh ha-Hayyim* to the "automatic" theurgic powers ascribed to the *mitzvoth* in order to obviate the absolute need for *kavana*.

28. Phinehas, *Kether Torah*, 15a.

29. This tribute to the status of the Beth ha-Midrash is found in Phinehas, *Kether Torah*, 13b–15a.

30. The theme of religious and scholarly deterioration pervades much of the rabbinic literature of this period. Hillel of Kovno's *Heilel Ben Shahar* (Warsaw, 1804), cited at length in earlier chapters, is filled with the same acute sense of spiritual and intellectual decline. In his classic homiletical work, *Ohel Rachel* (Shklov, 1790), R. David Hakaro devotes a major section ("Yeted ha-din"; see esp. 17a–19b) to describing and mourning the decline of rabbinic learning and the lowly status and diminished prestige of the rabbinate in his day.

31. See Stampfer, *Ha-Yeshiva ha-Litait be-Hithavuta*, 35–38, on R. Hayyim's perception of the decline of Torah scholarship in his generation and how it served as the main motivation to establish the Volozhin yeshiva.

32. See, for example, the introduction to Abraham ben Solomon's *Maaloth ha-Torah*.

33. Phinehas, *Kether Torah*, 15a–15b. A very similar defense of the legitimacy of *Torah shelo lishmah* is to be found in Abraham ben Solomon's *Maaloth ha-Torah*, 59–60.

34. On Phinehas's assertion that perfunctory prayer too has religious value see chapter 3, above.

35. Lamm, *Torah Lishmah*, chap. 7.

36. Phinehas, *Kether Torah*, 15b. The notion that the main purpose of Torah study is to be able properly to fulfill its imperatives recurs in Phinehas's later writings; see, for example, Phinehas, *Midrash Hakhamim*, 1:2.

37. Phinehas, *Kether Torah*, 16b.

38. Ibid., 19a.

39. The notion that through *Talmud Torah* man can realize the most sublime spiritual attainments is a central theme of Abraham ben Solomon's *Maaloth ha-Torah* as well. He insists throughout that book that only Torah study has the power to refine the human attributes, overcome the evil instinct, and bring man to true repentance and closeness with God.

40. On the power of Torah to sustain the very existence of the cosmos see esp. *Nefesh ha-Hayyim*, 4:26; on the potentially catastrophic consequences of the neglect of Torah study see ibid., 4:22–24. As noted above, R. Phinehas too affirmed the theurgic power of the study of Torah, but he did not emphasize it nearly as repeatedly or dramatically as did R. Hayyim.

41. Evelyn Underhill, *Mysticism* (New York, 1955), 46.

42. Stampfer, *Ha-Yeshiva ha-Litait be-Hithavuta*, esp. pp. 103–44.

43. Hayyim of Volozhin, *Nefesh ha-Hayyim*, 4:21.

44. It was primarily through the establishment of an elite of scholars in the yeshiva R. Hayyim founded at Volozhin that he provided an antidote to the populist nature of Hasidic leadership. R. Hayyim was intent on maintaining a certain distance between the scholars of Torah and the common folk, and this was reflected in some of the social innovations he instituted in his yeshiva (see Lamm, *Torah Lishmah*, 96–98; and Stampfer, *Ha-Yeshiva ha-Litait be-Hithavuta*, 142–45. Lamm comments that R. Hayyim sensed the need to "walk a tightrope" between the requirement of modesty on the part of the rabbinic scholar, on the one hand, and to command respect and maintain distance from the masses, on the other. On p. 108, n. 53, Lamm cites some of the most important Mithnagdic complaints regarding the alleged early Hasidic mockery and derision of rabbinic scholars yet still questions the accuracy of the claims of the Mithnagdim).

45. See, for example, the discussion of this doctrine by Joseph Weiss in "Reyshith Zemihathah Shel ha-Derekh ha-Hasidith," *Zion* 16 (1951): 89–103. For a general discussion of the nature of Hasidic leadership see the excellent essay by Arthur Green, "Typologies of Leadership and the Hasidic Zaddiq," in *Jewish Spirituality from the Sixteenth Century Revival to the Present*, ed. Arthur Green (New York, 1989), 127–56.

46. On the ideational origins of the doctrine of *yeridath ha-zaddik* in earlier Kabbalah and Sabbateanism see Piekarz, *Biyemei Zemihath ha-Hasiduth*, 280–302.

47. A very thorough and faithful, yet largely uncritical, presentation of the doctrine of the zaddik in the writings of R. Jacob Joseph of Polnoe is Samuel Dresner, *The Zaddik* (London, 1960), esp. chaps. 4 ("A Critique of Leadership"), 6 ("Humility"), and 7 ("The Descent of the Zaddik").

48. On R. Elimelekh's doctrine of the zaddik see R. Shatz, "Le-Mahuto Shel ha-Zaddik ba-Hasiduth," *Molad* 144 (1960): 18.

49. Phinehas, *Kether Torah*, 19b.

50. Ibid., 21b. This critique of Hasidic eating practices is a clear reference to the Hasidic zaddik's practice of receiving the masses of his followers at his table (i.e., the rebbe's *tish*), especially on the Sabbath and religious holidays.

51. Ibid., 21a, 21b. The respect and distance that are essential to the relationship between the scholar and the masses is a theme repeated often in R. Phinehas's writings. See, for example, his *Derekh ha-Melekh* (Grodno, 1804), 9:12–14.

Conclusion

1. Phinehas ben Judah, Maggid of Polotsk, *Rosh Ha-Giveah* (Jerusalem, 1965), 6a, 2b–4b, 5b–6a.

2. *Yuhara,* the Aramaic term for a sparkling jewel, is used in the Talmud to connote showiness and pious pomposity. See, for example, *Berakhot,* 17b; *Pesakhim,* 55a; and *Sukkah,* 26b.

3. Phinehas, *Rosh Ha-Giveah,* 3b.

4. Ibid., 7b.

5. For examples of *h's'd* connoting, in biblical Hebrew, an abomination or disgrace see Leviticus 20:17 and Proverbs 14:34.

6. Evelyn Underhill, *Mysticism* (New York, 1955), 23–24.

7. William James, *The Varieties of Religious Experience* (reprint, Cambridge, Mass., 1985), 140.

Appendix A: The Works of Phinehas of Polotsk

1. On R. Phinehas's burial place see Israel Klausner, *Koroth Beth ha-Almin be-Vilna* (Vilna, 1935), 82. Klausner identifies R. Phinehas as "the author of books and the teacher of the GRA's grandchildren." The Old Jewish Cemetery in Vilna was destroyed during the Soviet rule of Lithuania.

2. The Hebrew text of this epitaph can be found in S. J. Fuenn, *Kiryah Ne'emana* (Vilna, 1915), 237.

3. R. David ben Joseph Abudarham was a mid-fourteenth-century Spanish commentator whose work *Hibbur Perush Ha'Berakhoth Veha'Tefilloth* (subsequently known simply as the *Abudarham*) has been one of the most popular and most frequently reissued liturgical commentaries in Jewish literary history.

The reference to Rabbi Herz is to a daily prayer book printed in Berlin in 1703 with a largely Kabbalistic commentary by Rabbi Herz.

Rabbi Jacob Emden published a three-part commentary to the Hebrew prayers entitled *Siddur Amudey ha-Shamayim* (Altona, 1745–48). The *siddur* comprises a liturgical commentary *(Beth El)*, grammatical and Halakhic notations *(Shaar Hasho-*

mayim), and a collection of essays and treatises *(Migdal Oz)*. The *siddur* was roundly criticized immediately following its publication for the apparently arbitrary nature of the commentary and the occasionally irreverent attitude toward the text of the liturgy.

4. See M. Wilensky, *Hasidim u-Mithnagdim: le-Toledoth ha-Pulmus Beynehem*, 2 vols. (Jerusalem, 1970), 1:159.

SELECTED
BIBLIOGRAPHY

Many of the primary sources listed below have been reprinted and photocopied in multiple editions, especially in recent years, in Jerusalem. All references to primary sources in the notes are to the specific editions listed below, unless otherwise indicated in the notes themselves. All references to the exegetical works of the GRA and of R. Phinehas of Polotsk are to the chapter and verse of the commentary rather than to the page numbers of any specific edition. As the large majority of rabbinic and Hasidic publications were printed or reproduced privately, publishers' names are not included for the primary sources. All of the primary sources are in Hebrew.

Primary Sources

Aaron Ha-Levi of Starosselje. *Avodath ha-Levi.* Reprint. Jerusalem, 1987.
——. *Shaarei ha-Yihud veha-Emuna.* Reprint. Jerusalem, 1985.
Abraham ben Elijah of Vilna. *Be'er Avraham al Tehillim.* Warsaw, 1887.
——. *Se'arath Eliyahu.* Vilna, 1877.
——. *Tirgem Avraham.* Jerusalem, 1896.
Abraham ben Solomon of Vilna. *Maaloth ha-Torah.* Reprint. Jerusalem, 1975.
——. *Pirkei de-Avraham al Masekheth Avoth.* Jerusalem, 1982.
Abraham of Slonim. *Be'er Avraham.* Reprint. Jerusalem, 1985.
Akivah ben Eliezer of Minsk. *Bizath Mitzrayim.* Reprint. Jerusalem, 1960.
Alexander Zisskind of Grodno. *Yesod ve-Shoresh ha-Avodah.* Grodno, 1794.
——. *Zava'ath Baal Yesod ve-Shoresh ha-Avodah.* Jerusalem, 1955.
Alfasi, Isaac. *Mi-Prozdor le-Tarkelin: Histalkutam Shel Zadikim.* Tel Aviv, 1977.
Asher Ha-Kohen of Tiktin. *Birkhath Rosh.* Reprint. Jerusalem, 1971.
——. *Kether Rosh: Orhoth Hayyim.* Volozhin, 1819.
Barukh of Kossov. *Amud ha-Avodah.* Tchernowitz, 1863.
Cordovero, Moshe. *Or Naarav.* Reprint. Vilna, 1885.
Danzig, Abraham. *Beth Avraham.* Reprint. Jerusalem, 1971.
——. *Hayyei Adam.* Reprint. Vilna, 1843.
——. *Hokhmath Adam.* Reprint. Vilna, 1855.
——. *Toledoth Adam al ha-Hagada.* Reprint. Jerusalem, 1972.

——. *Zikhru Torath Moshe.* Reprint. Jerusalem, 1971.

Eliezer Fishel of Stychov. *Olam Gadol: Midrash la-Perushim.* Zolkiewka, 1800.

Eliezer Segal of Pinsk. *Reah ha-Sadeh.* Shklov, 1795.

——. *Siah ha-Sadeh.* Shklov, 1787.

Elijah ben Solomon, Gaon of Vilna. *Adereth Eliyahu al ha-Torah.* Warsaw, 1887.

——. *Adereth Eliyahu al Neviim u-Khetuvim.* Reprint. Tel Aviv, 1962.

——. *Ayil Meshulash.* Vilna and Grodno, 1834.

——. *Biur ha-GRA al ha-Zohar.* Vilna, 1810.

——. *Biur ha-GRA al Sefer Habakuk.* Reprint. Jerusalem, 1898.

——. *Devar Eliyahu.* Warsaw, 1840.

——. *Dikduk Eliyahu.* Vilna and Grodno, 1837.

——. *Even Shelema.* Edited by Samuel Maltzan. Reprint. Brooklyn, 1972.

——. *Ha-Emuna veha-Hashgaha.* Edited by Samuel Maltzan. Königsberg, 1864.

——. *Hidushei u-Viurei ha-GRA al Maseketh Shabbath u-Berakhoth.* Edited by Abraham Drushkovitz. Kedainiai, 1940.

——. "Igereth ha-GRA." In *Alim Literufah.* St. Petersburg, 1924.

——. *Kol Eliyahu.* Reprint. St. Petersburg, 1904.

——. *Maaseh Rav: Minhagei ha-GRA ha-Shalem.* Reprint. Jerusalem, 1987.

——. *Masekheth Avoth: Biur ha-GRA.* Vilna, 1836.

——. *Megillath Esther im Perush ha-GRA al Derekh ha-Peshat ve-al Derekh ha-Remez.* Reprint. Warsaw, 1897.

——. *Mikhtav Eliyahu al Shir Ha-Shirim.* Prague, 1811.

——. *Oroth ha-GRA.* Edited by Issachar Dov Rubin. Bnei Berak, 1986.

——. *Perush al Kama Aggadoth.* Vilna, 1800.

——. *Piskei ha-GRA.* Edited by Zvi Hirsch ben Solomon of Novardok. Vilna, 1903.

——. *Safra de-Zeniutha im Perush ha-GRA.* Vilna and Grodno, 1820.

——. *Sefer Likutay Ha-GRA.* Edited by Samuel Kleinerman. Jerusalem, 1963.

——. *Sefer Mishlei im Biur ha-GRA.* Reprint. Petah Tikva, 1980.

——. *Sefer Yonah im Biur ha-GRA.* Edited by Joseph Rivlin. Bnei Berak, 1986.

——. *Siddur ha-GRA be-Nigleh u-ve-Nistar.* Edited by Naftali Herz Ha-Levi. Jaffa, 1867.

——. *Siddur Ishei Yisrael: Siddur ha-GRA.* Edited by Elijah Landau and Isaac Maltzan. Reprint. Jerusalem, 1975.

Ezekiel Faivel of Dretzhyn. *Musar Haskel.* Lublin, 1901.

——. *Toledoth Adam.* Warsaw, 1856.

Haber, Yitzhaq Isaac. *Amudei ha-Torah: Or Torah.* Reprint. Jerusalem, 1971.

——. *Magen ve-Zina.* Johannesburg, 1855.

——. *Pithkhei She'arim.* Warsaw, 1888.

Hakaro, David. *Ohel Rachel.* Shklov, 1790.

Hayyim Haikel of Amdur. *Hayyim va-Hesed.* Jerusalem, 1975.

Hayyim of Volozhin. *Nefesh ha-Hayyim.* Vilna and Grodno, 1824.

——. *Ruah Hayyim.* Vilna, 1859.

Hillel of Kovno. *Heilel Ben Shahar.* Warsaw, 1804.

Israel ben Eliezer Baal Shem Tov. *Kether Shem Tov.* Brooklyn, 1987.

Israel ben Samuel of Shklov. *Pe'ath ha-Shulhan.* Jerusalem, 1959.

——. *Taklin Haddetin.* Shklov, 1784.

Israel Jacob of Kremenetz. *Shevet me-Yisrael.* Zolkiewka, 1772.

Jacob Joseph of Polnoe. *Ben Porath Yosef.* Lemberg, 1863.

——. *Toledoth Jacob Joseph.* Lemberg, 1863.

Jagel, Abraham. *Lekah Tov.* Shklov, 1796.

Joseph of Shteinhardt. *Zikhron Yoseph.* Fürth, 1773.

Katzenellenbogen, Asher Zevi Hirsch. *Shaarei Rahamim.* Vilna, 1871.

Katzenellenbogen, Zevi Hirsch. *Giveath Shaul.* Vilna and Grodno, 1825.

Kranz, Jacob, of Dubno. *Kol Yaakov.* Edited by Isaac Kranz. Warsaw, 1870.

——. *Ohel Jacob.* Edited by Isaac Kranz. Warsaw, 1884.

——. *Sefer ha-Middoth.* Edited by Abraham Flahm. Tel Aviv, 1959.

Landau, Barukh. *Reyshith Limudim.* Berlin, 1789.

Landau, E. *Minhath Eliyahu.* Reprint. Jerusalem, 1927.

Levi Isaac of Berditchev. *Kedushath Levi.* Brooklyn, 1975.

Levine, J. *Aliyoth Eliyahu.* Vilna, 1855.

Levinsohn, Isaac Baer. *Teudah be-Yisrael.* Vilna, 1828.

Liphschitz, Aaron Zelig ben Eliezer. *Hanhagoth ve-Ezoth Shel Rabi Hayyim mi-Volozhin.* Hebrew University and National Library, Jerusalem. Microfilm 80800.

Lipschutz, Moses. *Ashkavta de-Zadikaya.* Jerusalem, 1991.

Loebl, Israel. *Even Bohan.* Frankfurt am Main, 1799.

Margolioth, J. L. *Beth Middoth.* Dierenfürth, 1778.

Meir ben Elijah of Vilna. *Derekh Avoth.* Vilna, 1836.

——. *Nahlath Avoth.* Vilna, 1835.

——. *Milhamoth Adonai.* Hebrew University and National Library, Jerusalem. MS 801067.

Menahem Mendel of Shklov. *Mayyim Adirim.* Jerusalem, 1987.

——. *Menahem Zion.* Jerusalem, 1985.

Menahem Mendel of Vitebsk. *Peri ha-Aretz.* Rev. ed. Jerusalem, 1987.

Menashe of Ilya. *Alphei Menashe.* Vilna, 1905.

Moses ibn Makhir. *Seder ha-Yom.* Lublin, 1876.

Phinehas ben Judah, Maggid of Polotsk. *Derekh ha-Hayyim.* Grodno, 1804.

——. *Derekh ha-Melekh.* Grodno, 1804.

——. *Giveath Phinehas.* Vilna, 1808.

——. *Kether Torah.* Reprint. Jerusalem, 1965.

——. *Kizzur Even Bohan.* Reprint. Jerusalem, 1900.

——. *Midrash Hakhamim.* Minsk, 1809.

——. *Rosh ha-Giveah.* Reprint. Jerusalem, 1965.

——. *Shevet mi-Yehuda.* Vilna, 1803.

——. *Siddur Shaar ha-Rahamim im Perush Maggid Zedek.* Shklov, 1788.

Rivlin, Benjamin, of Shklov. *Geviey Gavia ha-Kessef.* Warsaw, 1897.

Schick, Barukh ben Jacob, of Shklov. *Keney ha-Mida.* Shklov, 1793.

——. *Uklides.* The Hague, 1780.

Schneerson, Menahem Mendel. *Derekh Mitzvotekha.* Poltava, 1911.

Shaarei Rahamim: Hanhagoth ve-etzoth shekiblu mimenu Talmidei harav Hayyim Mi-volozhin ve-Harav Abraham Danzig. Vilna, 1881.

Samuel ben Eliezer of Kalvira. *Darkhei Noam.* Königsberg, 1764.

Samuel of Dahlinov. *Minhath Shmuel.* Jerusalem, 1856.

Shneur Zalman of Lyadi. *Likutei Amarim: Tanya.* Reprint. Brooklyn, 1964.

——. *Torah Or.* Reprint. Brooklyn, 1986.

Solomon ben Moses of Chelm. *Merkeveth Ha-Mishna.* Reprint. Brooklyn, 1948.

Teyvel, David. *Beth David.* Warsaw, 1854.

Vital, Hayyim. *Arba Meoth Shekel Kessef.* Reprint. Korets, 1804.

——. "Shaar Ha-Kavanoth." In *Shemona Shearim.* Reprint. Jerusalem, 1963.

Zeev Wolf of Zhitomir. *Or ha-Meir.* Reprint. Jerusalem, 1957.

Secondary Sources

Abelson, Joshua. *The Immanence of God in Rabbinic Literature.* London: Macmillan, 1912.

Abramson, S. "Defusei *Musar Haskel ve-Toledoth Adam* le-Rabi Yehezkel Faivel." In *Sefer Margaliyoth,* edited by Y. Raphael, 189–232. Jerusalem: Mossad ha-Rav Kook, 1973.

Alfasi, Y. *Mi-Prozdor le-Tarkelin: Histalkutam Shel Zadikim.* Tel Aviv: Maor, 1977.

Aronson, G., ed. *Vitebsk Amol.* New York: privately printed, 1956.

Barnai, J. "Hamagama ha-Datit-hevratith Shel Sefer Hasidim." *Zion* 3 (1938): 1–50.

——. *Iggeroth Hasidim mi-Eretz Yisrael.* Jerusalem: Yad Yitzhaq ben Zvi, 1980.

Barzilay, I. "The Life of Menashe of Ilya (1767–1831)." *Proceedings of the American Academy for Jewish Religion* 50 (1983): 1–35.

Ben Arzi, S. "Ha-Perishuth be-Sefer Hasidim." *Daat,* no. 11 (1983): 39–47.

Ben Sasson, H. H. *Haguth ve-Hanhaga.* Jerusalem: Mossad Bialik, 1959.

——. "Ishiyutho Shel ha-GRA ve-Hashpa'ato ha-Hevratith." *Zion* 31 (1966): 39–86, 197–216.

Ben Sasson, J. "Olamam ha-Ruhani u-Mishnatam ha-Hinukhith Shel Meyasdei ha-Yeshiva ha-Litaith." In *Hinukh ha-Adam ve-Yiudo,* 155–67. Jerusalem: Misrad ha-Datot veha-Hinukh, 1967.

Buber, M. *Be-Pardes ha-Hasiduth.* Jerusalem: Mossad Bialik, 1963.

——. *Tales of the Hasidim.* 2 vols. New York: Schocken, 1948.

Dan, J. "The Emergence of Mystical Prayer." In *Studies in Jewish Mysticism,* edited by J. Dan and F. Talmage, 85–120. Cambridge: Association for Jewish Studies, 1982.

——. *Sifruth ha-Musar veha-Derush.* Jerusalem: Keter, 1975.

——. *The Teachings of Hasidism.* New York: Behrman House, 1983.

Dresner, S. "Hasidism and Its Opponents." In *Great Schisms in Jewish History.* edited by R. Jospe and S. Wagner, 119–76. New York: Ktav, 1981.

——. *The Zaddik.* London: Abelard Schuman, 1960.

Dubnow, S. *Hasidiana (Kitvei Hithnagduth al Kath ha-Hasidim).* St. Petersburg: Voschod, 1918.

——. *Toledoth ha-Hasiduth.* 4th ed. Tel Aviv: Dvir, 1975.

Elbogen, Y. M. *Ha-Tefillah Be-Yisrael.* Tel Aviv: Dvir, 1972.

Elior, R. "Ha-Maavak al Maamada Shel ha-Kabala ba-Meah ha–16." *Mehkarei Yerushalayim Be-Mahsheveth Yisrael* 1 (1981): 177–90.

——. "Mekomo Shel ha-Adam ba-Avodath ha-Shem ha-Habadith." *Daat,* no. 12 (1984): 47–55.

——. *The Paradoxical Ascent to God: The Kabbalistic Theosophy of Habad Hasidism.* New York: State University of New York Press, 1992.

——. *Torath ha-Elohuth be-Dor ha-Sheyni Shel Hasiduth Habad.* Jerusalem: Magnes, 1982.

——. "Vikuah Minsk." *Mehkarei Yerushalayim Be-Mahsheveth Yisrael* 1 (1982): 179–235.

Etkes, I. "Ha-GRA veha-Haskala: Tadmith u-Meziuth." In *Perakim be-Toledoth ha-Hevra ha-Yehudith bi-Yemei ha-Beynaim Uva-Et Ha-Hadasha: Mukdashim le-Professor Yaakov Katz,* edited by I. Etkes, 192–217. Jerusalem: Magnes, 1980.

——. "Ha-GRA ve-Reyshith ha-Hithnagduth la-Hasiduth." In *Temuroth Ba-Historiya ha-Yehudith ha-Hadasha: Kovets Maamarim Shai le-Shmuel Ettinger,* 439–58. Jerusalem: Merkaz Zalman Shazar, 1987.

——. "Immanent Factors and External Influences in the Development of the Haskala Movement in Russia." In *Toward Modernity: The European Jewish Model,* edited by J. Katz, 13–32. New Brunswick: Transaction Press, 1987.

——. *Lita Bi-Yerushalayim.* Jerusalem: Yad Yitzhaq ben Zvi, 1991.

——. *Mi-habura li-Tenuah: Tenuat ha-Hasidut be-Reyshita.* Tel Aviv: Ha-Universita ha-Petuha, 1991.

——. *Rabbi Yisrael Salanter ve-Reyshitah shel Tenuath ha-Mussar.* Jerusalem: Magnes, 1982.

——. "Review of N. Lamm's Torah Lishmah" (Hebrew). *Kiryath Sefer* 50 (1975): 638–48.

——. "Shitato U-Faalo Shel Rabi Hayyim mi-Volozhin ki-Teguvath ha-Hevrah ha-Mithnagdith la-Hasiduth." *Proceedings of the American Academy for Jewish Religion* 38 (1972): 1–45.

Ettinger, S. "The Hasidic Movement: Reality and Ideals." In *Jewish Society Throughout the Ages,* edited by H. H. Ben Sasson, 251–66. New York: Schocken, 1971.

Fine, L. "The Art of Metoposcopy; A Study in Isaac Luria's Charismatic Knowledge." *Association for Jewish Studies Review* 11, no. 2 (1986): 79–101.

——. *Safed Spirituality.* New York: Paulist Press, 1984.

Fishman, D. E. "A Polish Rabbi Meets the Berlin Haskala." *Association for Jewish Studies Review* 12, no. 1 (1987): 114–19.

——. *Russia's First Modern Jews: The Jews of Shklov.* New York: New York University Press, 1995.

Foxbrunner, R. A. *Habad: The Hasidism of R. Shneur Zalman of Lyady.* Tuscaloosa: University of Alabama Press, 1992.

Frumkin, A. L. *Toledoth Eliyahu.* Vilna: Pierashnikov, 1900.

——. *Toledoth Hakhmei Yerushalayim.* 3 vols. Jerusalem: privately printed, 1928–30.

Fuenn, S. J. *Kenesseth Yisrael.* Warsaw: Baumritter, 1886.

——. *Kiryah Ne'emana.* Vilna: I. Funk, 1915.

Funkenstein, A. "Imitatio Dei u-Musag ha-Zimzum be-Mishnath Habad." In *Raphael Mahler Festschrift,* 83–88. Tel Aviv: Sifriyat Poalim/Tel Aviv University, 1974.

Gelber, N. M. *Toledoth Yehudai Brodie.* Vol. 6 of *Arim ve-Imahoth be-Yisrael,* edited by Y. L. Maimon. Jerusalem: Mossad ha-Rav Kook, 1955.

Glatt, H. A. *He Spoke in Parables: The Life and Works of the Dubno Maggid.* New York: Jay Bithmar, 1957.

Glatzer, N. *Dimensions of Job.* New York: Schocken, 1969.

Goldberg, H. *Israel Salanter: Text, Structure, Idea.* New York: Ktav, 1982.

Goldmann, Lucien. *The Philosophy of the Enlightenment: The Christian Burgess and the Enlightenment.* Translated by Henry Mass. Cambridge: Harvard University Press, 1973.

Goldrath, A. Y. "Al ha-Sefer *Hayyei Adam* u-Mehabro." In *Sefer Margaliyoth,* edited by Y. Raphael, 270–93. Jerusalem: Mossad ha-Rav Kook, 1973.

Gordis, R. *The Book of God and Man: A Study of Job.* Chicago: University of Chicago Press, 1965.

Gottlieb, E. *Mehkarim be-Sifruth ha-Kabala.* Edited by J. Hacker. Tel Aviv: University of Tel Aviv Press, 1976.

Graetz, H. *History of the Jews.* 6 vols. 1891–98. Reprint. Philadelphia: Jewish Publication Society, 1941.

Green, A., ed. *Jewish Spirituality from the Sixteenth Century Revival to the Present.* New York: Crossroad, 1989.

Greenberg, L. *The Jews in Russia: The Struggle for Emancipation.* New Haven: Yale University Press, 1944.

Gries, Z. *Sifruth ha-Hanhagoth: Toldoteha u-Mekomah be-Hayei Hasidei R. Yisrael Baal Shem Tov.* Jerusalem: Mossad Bialik, 1989.

Gross, Benjamin. "La priere dans le Nefesh ha-Hayyim de R. Hayyim of Volozhin." In *Priere, mystique, et judaisme,* edited by Roland Goetschel, 225–44. Paris: PUF, 1987.

Halamish, M. "The Theoretical System of Rabbi Shneur Zalman of Liady" (Hebrew). Ph.D. diss., Hebrew University, 1976.

Heilman, A. S. *Beth Rabi.* Berditchev: Sheftel, 1903.

Heilprin, Y., ed. *Pinkas Va'ad Arba Aratzoth.* Jerusalem: Mossad Bialik, 1945.

Heinemann, I. *Taamei ha-Mitzvoth be-Sifruth Yisrael.* 3 vols. Jerusalem: Mossad Bialik, 1956.

Heschel, A. J. *The Circle of the Baal Shem Tov: Studies in Hasidism* (Hebrew). Edited by S. Dresner. Chicago: University of Chicago Press, 1985.

Hilman, D. Z. *Iggeroth Baal ha-Tanya u-Venei Doro.* Jerusalem: privately printed, 1953.

Hisdai, J. "Early Settlement of Hasidim and Mithnagdim" (Hebrew). *Shalem* 4 (1984): 231–69.

——. "The Emergence of Hasidim and Mithnagdim in the Light of the Homiletical Literature" (Hebrew). Ph.D. diss., Hebrew University, 1984.

——. "Eved ha-Shem." *Zion* 47 (1982): 253–92.

——. "The Origins of the Conflict between Hasidim and Mitnagdim." In *Hasidism: Continuity or Innovation?* edited by Bezalel Safran, 27–46. Cambridge: Harvard University Press, 1988.

Horowitz, C. "The Attitude of Ibn Shouib to Asceticism" (Hebrew). *Daat*, no. 12 (1984): 29–37.

Idel, M. *Hasidism: Between Ecstasy and Magic.* New York: New York University Press, 1995.

——. *Kabbalah: New Perspectives.* New Haven: Yale University Press, 1988.

——. "On the History of the Interdiction against the Study of Kabbalah before the Age of Forty" (Hebrew) *Association for Jewish Studies Review* 5 (1980): 1–9.

——. "Perceptions of Kabbalah in the Second Half of the Eighteenth Century." *Journal of Jewish Thought and Philosophy* 1, no. 1 (1991): 55–61.

Jacobs, L. "Eating As an Act of Worship in Hasidic Thought." In *Studies in Jewish Religious and Intellectual History,* edited by S. Stein and R. Loewe, 157–66. Tuscaloosa: University of Alabama Press, 1979.

——. *Hasidic Prayer.* New York: Routledge & Kegan Paul, 1972.

——. *Hasidic Thought.* New York: Behrman House, 1976.

——. *Seeker of Unity.* London: Valentine Mitchell, 1966.

——, ed. *On Ecstasy—A Tract by Dobh Baer of Lubavitch.* Chappaqua, N.Y.: Rossel Books, 1963.

Jacobson, Y. "Torath ha-Beriah shel Rabbi Shneur Zalman mi-Ladi." *Eshel Beer Sheva* 1:307–38.

James, W. *The Varieties of Religious Experience.* Reprint. Cambridge: Harvard University Press, 1985.

Katz, B. Z. *Rabbanuth, Hasiduth ve-Haskala.* 2 vols. Tel Aviv: Dvir, 1956–58.

Katz, J. *Exclusiveness and Tolerance.* New York: Oxford University Press, 1961.

——. *Tradition and Crisis.* New York: New York University Press, 1993.

——. "Yahasei Halakha ve-Kabala." *Daat*, no. 4 (1976): 57–74.

Klausner, I. *Koroth Beth ha-Almin be-Vilna.* Vilna: privately printed, 1935.

——. *Vilna bi-Tekufath ha-Gaon.* Jerusalem: Reuben Mas, 1942.

Lamm, N. *Faith and Doubt.* New York: Ktav, 1971.

——. "Prayer and Study." In *Samuel Mirsky Memorial Volume,* edited by N. Lamm, 37–52. New York: Yeshiva, 1970.

——. *Torah Lishmah.* Jerusalem: Mossad ha-Rav Kook, 1972.

Landau, B. *Ha-Gaon ha-Hasid mi-Vilna.* Jerusalem: Torah mi-Zion, 1978.

Landau, E. *Toledoth ha-GRA.* Jerusalem, 1927.

Lazaroff, A. "Bahya's Asceticism against Its Rabbinic and Islamic Background." *Journal of Jewish Studies* 21 (1970): 11–38.

Lewin, M. *Erkhei Hevra ve-Kalkala ba-Idiologia Shel Tekufath ha-Haskala.* Jerusalem: Mossad Bialik, 1975.

Lieberman, H. *Ohel Rachel.* Brooklyn: Empire, 1980.

Liebes, Y. "Hadashoth le-Inyan ha-Besht ve-Shabbetai Zevi." *Mehkarei Yerushalayim Be-Mahsheveth Yisrael* 2, no. 4 (1982): 564–69.

———. "Ha-Tikun ha-Kelali shel Rabi Nahman mi-Brazlav." *Zion* 45 (1980): 201–45.

———. *Studies in Jewish Myth and Jewish Messianism.* Albany: State University of New York Press, 1993.

Loewenthal, N. *Communicating the Infinite: The Emergence of the Habad School.* Chicago: University of Chicago Press, 1989.

Maimon, L. *Toledoth ha-GRA.* Jerusalem: Mossad ha-Rav Kook, 1970.

Mantel, M. "The Meaning of Suffering According to Rabbi Nathan of Nemirov" (Hebrew). *Daat,* no. 7 (1981): 109–18.

Marcus, I. *Piety and Society.* Leiden: E. J. Brill, 1981.

McManners, J. *Death and the Enlightenment.* New York: Oxford University Press, 1981.

Michael, R. "Rabi Israel Loebl ve-Kuntreso ha-Germani." *Kiryath Sefer* 51 (1976): 315–23.

Mintz, B. *Sefer ha-Histalkuth.* Tel Aviv: privately printed, 1930.

Morgenstern, A. *Meshihiyuth ve-Yishuv Eretz Yisrael.* Jerusalem: Yad Yitzhaq ben Zvi, 1985.

Nadav, M. "Kehilloth Pinsk-Karlin beyn Hasiduth le-Hithnagduth." *Zion* 34 (1969): 98–108.

Nadler, A. "Meir b. Elijah of Vilna's *Milhamoth Adonai:* A Late Anti-Hasidic Polemic." *Journal of Jewish Thought and Philosophy* 1 (1991): 247–80.

———. *Rationalism, Romanticism, Rabbis, and Rebbes.* YIVO Institute for Jewish Research Monograph. New York: YIVO, 1992.

———. "Soloveitchik's Halakhic Man: *Not* a Mithnagged." *Modern Judaism* 13 (1993): 119–47.

Nigal, G. "Doctrines in the Writings of R. Elimelekh of Lizensk and His Disciples" (Hebrew). Ph.D. diss., Hebrew University, 1972.

———. *Ha-Siporeth ha-Hasidith: Toledoteha ve-Noseha.* Jerusalem: Y. Markus, 1981.

———. *Toroth Baal ha-Toledoth.* Jerusalem: Mossad ha-Rav Kook, 1974.

———, ed. Introduction to *Sefer Noam Elimelekh* (Hebrew). Jerusalem: Makhon la-Hasiduth, 1978.

Petuchowski, J. J. "Manuals and Catechisms in the Jewish Religion in the Early Period of the Emancipation." In *Studies in Nineteenth Century Jewish Intellectual History,* edited by A. Altmann, 47–64. Cambridge: Harvard University Press, 1964.

———. *The Theology of Hakham David Nieto: An Eighteenth Century Defense of the Jewish Tradition.* New York: Bloch, 1954.

Piekarz, M. "Al Meh Avdah Galuth Sefarad ke-Lekakh Kelapei ha-Haskalla be-Mizrakh Eiropah: ha-hasiduth be-Eynei R. Zevi Elimelekh Shapira mi-Dinov." *Daat,* no. 28 (1992): 87–115.

——. *Beyn Ideologia le-Metziyuth*. Jerusalem: Mossad Bialik, 1994.

——. *Biyemei Zemihath ha-Hasiduth*. Jerusalem: Mossad Bialik, 1978.

——." The Devekuth as Reflecting the Socio-Religious Character of the Hasidic Movement" (Hebrew). *Daat*, no. 24 (1990): 127–44.

——. *Hasiduth Polin*. Jerusalem: Mossad Bialik, 1990.

——. *Mehkarim be-Hasiduth Brazlav*. Jerusalem: Mossad Bialik, 1974.

Raisin, J. S. *The Haskala Movement in Russia*. Philadelphia: Jewish Publication Society, 1913.

Rapoport-Albert, A. "On Women in Hasidism: S. A. Horodetsky and the Maid of Ludmir Tradition." In *Jewish History: Essays in Honour of Chimen Abramsky*, edited by Ada Rapoport-Albert & Steven Zipperstein, 495–528. London: Peter Halban, 1988.

Reimer, J. *Jewish Reflections on Death*. New York: Schocken, 1974.

Rosman, M. *Founder of Hasidism: A Quest for the Historical Baal Shem Tov*. Berkeley: University of California Press, 1996.

Ross, T. "Two Interpretations of the Theory of Tzimtzum: Rabbi Hayyim of Volozhin and Rabbi Shneur Zalman of Ladi" (Hebrew). *Mehkarei Yerushalayim Be-Mahsheveth Yisrael* 2 (1982): 153–69.

Rubinstein, A. "Review of Wilensky's *Hasidim U-Mithnagdim*" (Hebrew). *Kiryath Sefer* 47 (1971): 361–76.

——, ed. *Studies in Hasidism*. Jerusalem: Merkaz Zalman Shazar, 1977.

Sanders, E. P. "The Covenant As a Soteriological Category and the Nature of Salvation in Palestinian and Hellenistic Judaism." In *Jews, Greeks, and Christians: Essays in Honour of William David Davies*, 11–44. Leiden: E. J. Brill, 1976.

Schechter, S. *Studies in Judaism*. 2 vols. Reprint. Philadelphia: Jewish Publication Society, 1936.

Schochet, E. J. *The Hasidic Movement and the Gaon of Vilna*. Northvale, N.J.: Jason Aronson, 1994.

Scholem, G. "The Concept of Kavana in Early Kabbalah." In *Studies in Jewish Thought*, edited by A. Jospe, 228–40. Detroit: Wayne State University Press, 1981.

——. *Devarim Bego*. Tel Aviv: Am Oved, 1976.

——. "Ha-Pulmus al ha-Hasiduth u-Manhigeha be-Sefer *Nezer Ha-Dema*." *Zion* 20 (1950): 228–40.

——. "Le-Inyan R. Yisrael Loebl u-Pulmuso Neged ha-Hasiduth." *Zion* 25 (1955): 361–76.

——. *Major Trends in Jewish Mysticism*. New York: Schocken, 1961.

——. "The Neutralization of the Messianic Element in Early Hasidism." In *The Messianic Idea in Judaism*, 176–202. New York: Schocken, 1995.

——. *Sabbatai Sevi: The Mystical Messiah*. 2 vols. in 1. Princeton: Princeton University Press, 1973.

——. "Shtei ha-Eduyoth ha-Rishonoth Shel Haburath ha-Hasidim ve-ha-Besht." *Tarbiz* 20 (1950): 228–40.

Shatz, R. "Anti-spiritualism ba-Hasiduth." *Molad* 171 (1962): 513–28.

——. "Contemplative Prayer in Hasidism." In *Studies in Mysticism and Religion Presented to Gershom Scholem*, edited by E. E. Urbach and R. J. Werblowsky. Jerusalem: Magnes, 1967.

——. *Ha-Hasiduth ke-Mistika*. Jerusalem: Magnes, 1968.

——. "Le-Mahuto Shel ha-Zadik ba-Hasiduth." *Molad* 144 (1960): 11–24.

Stampfer, S. *Ha-Yeshiva ha-Litait be-Hithavuta*. Jerusalem: Merkaz Zalman Shazar, 1995.

Stanislawski, M. *Tsar Nicholas and the Jews: The Transformation of Jewish Society in Russia, 1825–1855*. Philadelphia: Jewish Publication Society, 1983.

Stannard, D. *The Puritan Way of Death*. Oxford: Oxford University Press, 1977.

Steinschneider-Maggid, H. N. *Ir Vilna*. 1900.

Stiman-Katz, H. *Reyshitan Shel Aliyoth Hasidim*. Jerusalem: Yad Yitzhaq ben Zvi, 1987.

Sudarski, M., and Katzenellenbogen, A. *Lita*. New York, 1951.

Teitelbaum, M. *Ha-Rav mi-Ladi u-Miflegeth Habad*. Warsaw: Tushiya, 1912.

Tishby, I. "Kitrugo shel R. Yisrael mi-Shklov al ha-Hasidim." *Kiryath Sefer* 51 (1976): 300–303.

——. *Mishnath Ha-Zohar*. 2 vols. Jerusalem: Mossad Bialik, 1949.

——. *Torath ha-Rah ve-ha-Kelippa be-Kabbalath ha-Ari*. Jerusalem: Akaddemon, 1960.

Twersky, I. "Rabi Eliyahu mi-Vilna." *Ha-Avar* 1 (1953): 11–20.

Underhill, E. *Mysticism*. New York: New American Library, 1955.

Urbach, E. "Ascesis and Suffering in Talmudic and Midrashic Sources" (Hebrew). *Fritz Baer Jubilee Volume*. Jerusalem: Magnes, 1960.

Weiss, I. H. "Reyshith Zemihath ha-Haskala be-Russia." *Mi-Mizrah umi-Maarav* 1 (1894): 9–16.

Weiss, J. "The Great Maggid's Theory of Contemplative Magic." *Hebrew Union College Annual* 31 (1960): 137–47.

——. "The Hasidic Way of Habad" (Hebrew). *Ha-Aretz*, 13 September 1946.

——. "The Kavanoth of Prayer in Early Hasidism." *Journal of Jewish Studies* 9 (1958): 163–92.

——. "Reyshith Zemihathah Shel ha-Derekh ha-Hasidith." *Zion* 16 (1951): 89–103.

——. "Talmud Torah le-Shitath R. Israel Baal Shem Tov." In *Essays Presented to Chief Rabbi Israel Brodie*, 151–69. London: privately printed, 1967.

——. "Torah Study in Early Hasidism" (Hebrew). *Ha-Doar* 45 (1965): 615–17.

——. "Via Passiva in Early Hasidism." *Journal of Jewish Studies* 11 (1960): 137–55.

Werblowsky, R. J. Z. *Joseph Karo: Lawyer and Mystic*. Philadelphia: Jewish Publication Society, 1977.

Wertheim, A. *Halakhoth ve-Halikhoth ba-Hasiduth*. Jerusalem: Merkaz ha-Rav Kook, 1960.

Westphal, M. *God, Guilt, and Death*. Bloomington: University of Indiana Press, 1984.

Wilensky, M. *Hasidim u-Mithnagdim: le-Toledoth ha-Pulmus Beynehem*. 2 vols. Jerusalem: Mossad Bialik, 1970.

Wurzberger, W. "Rabbi Hayyim of Volozhin." In *Guardians of Our Heritage*, edited by
L. Jung, 187–206. New York: Bloch, 1958.

Yaari, A. "Ha-Defus ha-Ivri bi-Shklov." *Kiryath Sefer* 22 (1945): 49–72, 135–60.

Ysander, Y. *Studien Zum Bestian Hasidismus*. Uppsala: privately printed, 1933.

Zweiffel, E. Z. *Shalom Al Yisrael*. 2 vols. Zhitomir, 1868.

INDEX

Library of Congress Cataloging-in-Publication Data

Nadler, Allan.
The faith of the Mithnagdim : rabbinic responses to Hasidic
rapture / Allan Nadler.
   p.   cm. — (Johns Hopkins Jewish studies)
Includes bibliographical references and index.
ISBN 0-8018-5560-8 (alk. paper)
1. Mitnaggedim. 2. Hasidism—Controversial literature—History
and criticism. 3. Orthodox Judaism—Europe, Eastern—History.
I. Title. II. Series.
BM198.N34 1997
296.8'3—dc21   96-6608
                                                        CIP